P9-AOH-627

Language and thought

Interdisciplinary themes

---

edited by

Peter Carruthers

Professor of Philosophy and Director, Hang Seng Centre for Cognitive Studies, University of Sheffield

and

Jill Boucher

Associate Professor of Human Communication Sciences, University of Sheffield

Published in association with the Hang Seng Centre for Cognitive Studies, University of Sheffield

PUBLISHED BY THE PRESS SYNDICATE OF THE UNIVERSITY OF CAMBRIDGE
The Pitt Building, Trumpington Street, Cambridge CB2 1RP, United Kingdom

CAMBRIDGE UNIVERSITY PRESS
The Edinburgh Building, Cambridge CB2 2RU, United Kingdom
40 West 20th Street, New York, NY 10011-4211, USA
10 Stamford Road, Oakleigh, Melbourne 3166, Australia

First published 1998

Printed in the United Kingdom at the University Press, Cambridge

Typeset in 10/12pt Monophoto Times NR [SE]

A catalogue record for this book is available from the British Library

ISBN 1 521 63108 4 hardback
ISBN 0 521 637589 paperback

for
Sir Q W Lee
who made it possible

Contents

Contributors

JILL BOUCHER Department of Human Communication Sciences, University of Sheffield

PETER CARRUTHERS Department of Philosophy, University of Sheffield

ANDY CLARK Cognitive Science Program, Washington University, St Louis

MARTIN DAVIES Department of Experimental Psychology, University of Oxford

DANIEL DENNETT Centre for Cognitive Science, Tufts University

KEITH FRANKISH Department of Philosophy, University of Sheffield

SUSAN GOLDIN-MEADOW Department of Psychology, University of Chicago

JUAN-CARLOS GÓMEZ Department of Experimental Psychology, University of St Andrews

STEPHEN LAURENCE Department of Philosophy, London School of Economics

JOSEF PERNER Institut für Psychologie, Universität Salzburg

GABRIEL SEGAL Department of Philosophy, King's College London

DAN SPERBER Ecole Polytechnique (CREA), Paris

ROSEMARY VARLEY Department of Human Communication Sciences, University of Sheffield

DEIRDRE WILSON Department of Phonetics and Linguistics, University College London

MING-YU ZHENG Department of Psychology, University of Chicago

Preface

This volume is the culmination of the second project undertaken by Sheffield's Hang Seng Centre for Cognitive Studies, following its founding in 1992 with an endowment generously provided by the Hang Seng Bank of Hong Kong. (The first project resulted in *Theories of theories of mind*, edited by Peter Carruthers and Peter K. Smith, published by Cambridge University Press in 1996.) Five interdisciplinary workshops were held over the period 1994–6, and the concluding conference was held in Ranmoor Hall of Residence, University of Sheffield, in June 1996.

The intention behind the project was to bring together a select group of philosophers, psychologists, anthropologists, neuro-scientists, computer scientists and linguists, to forge a genuinely interdisciplinary approach to the question of the inter-relations between language and thought. For reasons which we explain in our introductory chapter, we felt that the issue of language and thought had almost dropped from sight in the cognitive sciences in recent decades, and that the time was ripe for a more fine-grained examination of the issues from an interdisciplinary perspective.

Most of the participants in the project were able to meet and discuss on a regular basis over a two-year period, before finally presenting their papers at the concluding conference. Of the twenty papers delivered to the conference, the twelve most focused, relevant and original contributions were selected for inclusion in the volume (together with one further paper which had been delivered at an earlier workshop). Most of these papers were then extensively re-written in the light of editorial advice and comments from the Cambridge referees. The result, we believe, is a set of powerful and original interdisciplinary essays. Our hope is that this volume may prove seminal in persuading philosophers and cognitive scientists alike to look afresh at the issue of the relationships between language and thought.

We would very much like to thank all those who participated in the workshop series and concluding conference, whose comments and contributions to discussions did so much to sharpen ideas and shape the final volume. Special thanks should go to all those who contributed a talk at one or other venue, but who do not have a paper in the final volume, for one reason or another. They are: George Botterill, Zoltan Dienes, Michael Gazzaniga, Stevan Harnad, Peter Hobson, Christopher Hookway, Annette Karmiloff-Smith, Paul McKevitt, Mick Perkins, Kim Plunkett, Barry Smith, Neil Smith, Ianthi-Maria Tsimpli and Yorick Wilks. Thanks also go to Susan Granger for help with the editing, and for preparation of the index. We are grateful to the British Academy for a grant to assist in funding the final conference. And last, but of course not least, we are grateful to the Hang Seng Bank for making the whole project possible.

1 Introduction: opening up options

Peter Carruthers and Jill Boucher

1 The basic dichotomy

What is the place of natural language in human cognition and thought? People's views on this matter have differed very markedly, dividing roughly into two opposing camps, as follows. (We shall shortly muddy these waters somewhat, by suggesting the possibility of a variety of intermediate positions. But we begin with a clean dichotomy, as an aid to the reader's vision.) On the one hand, there are those who espouse what we shall call *the communicative conception* of language, who view language as a mere adjunct to belief and thought. As the name suggests, they see the exclusive function and purpose of language to be the communication of thought, where thought itself is largely independent of the means of its transmission from mind to mind. The communicative conception is now dominant in many areas of the cognitive sciences (understood broadly to include cognitive psychology, empirical-minded philosophy of mind, linguistics, artificial intelligence – AI – and cognitive neuroscience), for reasons which we shall soon begin to explore. However, equally many historically have been committed to what we shall call *the cognitive conception* of language, which sees language as crucially implicated in human thinking. Roughly speaking, on this view, we think *in* natural language, in such a way that natural language sentences are the vehicles of our thoughts. Those espousing the cognitive conception have not claimed that language is used exclusively for thought, of course; they have allowed that it is also used in communication (they could hardly do otherwise).

In discussing the cognitive conception of language, care needs to be taken to distinguish a *requirement*-thesis from a *constitution*-thesis (which its adherents rarely do, in fact). It is one thing to say that language is *required for*, or is a *necessary condition of* thought, or certain kinds of thought (which can be fully consistent with a communicative conception of language, in fact); and it is quite another thing to claim that language itself is *constitutively involved in* those thoughts, or is the medium of those thoughts. Everyone should allow that some form of requirement-thesis has at least a degree of limited applicability, since it is plain that children rely upon language to acquire many of their beliefs and concepts. It seems obvious, indeed, that a languageless person could never entertain thoughts about electrons or neutrinos, genes or cell-division, for example, since it is only through language that we can learn of these things. It is quite another, and more interesting, thing to say that language remains implicated in the beliefs so acquired – in such a way, for example, that a thought about electrons can only be actively entertained by activating a representation of the *word* 'electron' (or some equivalent). Henceforward when we speak of the cognitive conception of language we should be understood to mean the constitution-thesis rather than the requirement-thesis, unless otherwise indicated.

As we shall see shortly, in recent decades many (but by no means all) of those working in the cognitive sciences have become convinced that the mind is more-or-less *modular* in structure, being made up of a number of distinct components; which are innately configured, and specialised for particular domains. (Modules can be *peripheral*, or *input* and/or *output*, including vision, face-recognition, audition, touch, taste, and motor control; or they can be *central*, including perhaps systems specialised for the social domain – 'theory of mind' – and systems dealing with naive biology, naive physics, and others. The *locus classicus* is Fodor, 1983; more recently, see Shallice, 1988; Smith and Tsimpli, 1995; Sperber, 1996.) Anyone influenced by this modular model is likely to regard the cognitive system which underpins language as just such a module. And then it seems almost inevitable (but not quite: see section 5 below) that they should come to endorse the communicative conception of language, coming to regard language as but an input and output module for central cognition.

The modular model of the mind has been highly influential and productive. But it has tended to eclipse the cognitive conception of language, and to marginalise work which does not fit in easily with its dominant paradigm. To that extent, the relationship between language and thought has been relatively little discussed in recent decades; since many have thought the issue to be closed. More recently, however, there are signs that the modular model of the mind is loosening its hold on a number of fronts. The chapters in this book reflect ways in which the currently popular version of the communicative conception of language and its related emphasis on innateness and modularity are being questioned. Many of them explore the middle ground between the traditional extreme views of the relationship between language and thought, and some seek to rehabilitate a cognitive conception of language in modified form.

In the sections which follow, we first give a brief historical overview of the traditional polarised views on the relationship between language and thought – beginning with the currently less-popular cognitive conception of language, and culminating with a brief description of the modular model of the mind, and the way in which it has generated a distinctive version of the communicative conception of language. We then indicate ways in which this model is being questioned and modified, and its implications challenged; opening up the possibility for weak versions of the cognitive conception of language to be reinstated.

2 The cognitive conception: historical overview

In this section we survey the various forms which the cognitive conception has taken, and the manner in which it has been variously defended, from the standpoint of the disciplines of philosophy, psychology and linguistics.

2.1 Philosophy

The cognitive conception of language has been endorsed by such disparate philosophers as Leibniz (1704); Wittgenstein (1921, 1953); Davidson (1975, 1982); Dummett (1981, 1991); Dennett (1991); McDowell (1994); and Carruthers (1996a). While motivations have varied, one common line of argument in favour of the cognitive conception goes something like this: human beings are unique in the range and sophistication of the thoughts of which they are capable; human beings are also unique in possessing natural language; and the simplest explanation of the co-occurrence of these two unique characteristics is that it is natural language which makes distinctively human thought possible. This argument evidently has at least some force. Notice, however, that it does not support a version of the cognitive conception according to which *all* thought involves language; nor does it support the constitution-thesis over and above the requirement-thesis. Rather, it is only an argument for the much weaker idea that those of our thoughts which are distinctively human *require* language (which is, as we noted above, fully consistent with a communicative conception of language, in fact).

Many of the philosophers mentioned in the previous paragraph (specifically, Wittgenstein, Davidson, Dummett, and McDowell) have defended the cognitive conception of language in *universal* and *conceptual* terms. That is, they have claimed that it is conceptually necessary that *all* thought should involve language – claiming that the very idea of thought implicates language. So animals and young infants lack thoughts altogether, and it is supposed to be logically impossible for a languageless creature to have propositional attitudes at all, let alone to have sophisticated beliefs and desires like ours. The arguments for this view are basically epistemological.

One form of it goes like this (see Davidson, 1982). Propositional attitudes have finely discriminated contents; for example, the thought *that Venus has set* is distinct from the thought *that the evening star has set*, even though Venus and the evening star are one and the same. But nothing except linguistic activity (for example, *asserting*, 'Venus has set' while *denying*, 'The evening star has set') could manifest, or establish, that a creature entertains the first of the above thoughts *as opposed to* the second. So only a language-using creature can *have* such a thought.

This argument depends, however, upon an objectionable verificationism, or anti-realism, about mental states. For without assuming some such view as a suppressed premise, it simply does not follow from the fact that we cannot *know* what, precisely, a creature is thinking, that it is *not* thinking anything. And if, on the contrary, thoughts have a reality which is distinct from, and independent of, our modes for evidence of them, then it is perfectly possible that non-language-using creatures may have fully determinate thoughts, but thoughts which *we* cannot have knowledge of. And the evidence is, surely, that this is the case. The evidence from ethology strongly suggests that animals are capable of a variety of kinds of thought and reasoning, even if we cannot know precisely *which* finely discriminated thoughts they entertain on any given occasion (Walker, 1983; Griffin, 1984; Byrne and Whiten, 1988; Allen and Bekoff, 1997). The same is true for the evidence from child development (Carey, 1985; Flavell, 1985; Sperber *et al.*, 1995). So if any form of cognitive conception of language is to stand a chance of being accepted by cognitive scientists, it needs to be weaker than the sort of universal conceptual thesis defended by some philosophers.

2.2 *Psychology*

Amongst psychologists, the strongest proponents of a cognitive conception of language were a group of Russian psychologists led by Sokolov (1972), who maintained that 'inner speech' was involved in many, though not all, aspects of thinking, including solving standard tests of non-verbal ability, and reproducing pictorial material. Sokolov and others sought to demonstrate this experimentally using speech-interference techniques and electromygraphic measurements of sub-vocal speech activity, with some degree of success. Another well-known Russian psychologist, Luria (1959) described inner speech as 'the second signalling system', and demonstrated its role in the conscious control of motor action, in addition to its role in more intellectual forms of thought. For example, he showed that children with language were able to inhibit a reaching response in a situation in which not-reaching was rewarded, whereas children without language were unable to inhibit the response.

In another study, Luria and Yudovich (1956) took a pair of five-year-old twins who had, through neglect and lack of motivation resulting from the self-sufficiency of the 'twin situation', acquired barely any language. They separated the twins and placed them in environments where they would have the motivation to learn to communicate, and, in addition, subjected just one of them to a course of language-training. They reported marked improvements in cognitive ability with the beginnings of acquisition of language after just three months. When first discovered, the twins appeared incapable of even rudimentary forms of play. They would move objects about and line them up, for example, but would make no attempts at construction or planning, let alone at symbolic play. They also appeared incapable of classifying heterogeneous collections of objects into kinds. But as their language improved, so their play became more ordered, thoughtful, and creative; and similarly their classification abilities became more normal. (And these improvements were considerably more marked in the case of the language-trained twin.)

Although the methodology of these early studies can be questioned, they are extremely suggestive for the thesis that some kinds of thinking actually involve natural language. Moreover, recent work in Diaz and Berk (1992) confirms Luria's early claims concerning the role of language in the control of motor action. Apart from the Russian group, other psychologists working around the middle of the century tended to favour a related set of views, including the view that language is learned using domain-general cognitive resources, and especially associative learning (Skinner, 1957); that the brain is not innately highly specialised but has, rather, a high degree of plasticity (Lashley, 1950); and that adult language and thought share a common symbolic basis (Goldstein, 1948; see Varley, this volume chapter 6, for a fuller account of the debate in aphasiology of which Goldstein's views formed a part).

Nevertheless, even psychologists who are strongly committed to the cognitive conception of language have always stopped short of arguing that languageless thought is impossible. Visual and other forms of imagistic thinking are always excepted, even if only for certain individuals, and no psychologist would wish to deny that pre-linguistic children have concepts, memories, and expectations which constitute at least some form of primitive thought. Vygotsky (1934), for example, who argued strongly for the involvement of language in thought, argued equally strongly that language and thought have different and independent roots, and different modes of operation in the pre-linguistic child. In this more guarded commitment to a cognitive conception of language, psychologists therefore differ from philosophers such as McDowell (1994), who claim that languageless thought is impossible.

2.3 Linguistics

The most radical and best-known form of the cognitive conception of language does not, however, come either from philosophers or from psychologists, but from a linguist, Benjamin Lee Whorf (1956). According to Whorf's linguistic relativity hypothesis, human concepts and ways of thinking, and indeed much of the very structure of the human mind itself, are acquired by young children from adults when they learn their native language and become inducted into the surrounding culture; these concepts and structures differing widely, depending upon the structures and conceptual resources of the natural languages in question. This mind-structuring and social-relativist view of language is still dominant in the social sciences: indeed Pinker (1994) refers to it disparagingly as the 'Standard Social Science Model'.

The line of thinking behind the Standard Social Science Model goes something like this: we find wide variations in behaviours and social structures between different cultures, and equally wide variations amongst languages; yet these variations are not genetic – children born of one culture but brought up in another will of course develop the behaviours and practices of a native; so the natural explanation is then that the mind is initially a more or less blank slate, just as traditional empiricism supposed; and that all the structure imposed upon it comes from the particular language the person acquires, and from the particular culture they find themselves immersed in. For further development, and extended criticism, of this line of thought, see Malotki (1983); Pullum (1991); Tooby and Cosmides (1992); and Pinker (1994).

3 The communicative conception: historical overview

In this section we survey the forms taken by, and the defences offered of, the communicative conception, again in connection with the three disciplines of philosophy, psychology and linguistics.

3.1 Philosophy

The communicative conception of language has also been popular amongst philosophers, having been endorsed by such varied thinkers as Locke (1690); Russell (1921); Grice (1957, 1969); Lewis (1969); Fodor (1978); and Searle (1983). According to these philosophers, the function and purpose of language is to facilitate communication, rather than to be involved in thinking (except indirectly, of course, by enabling the acquisition of new beliefs from other people). Language thus functions wholly in the public, inter-personal, domain, rather than in the domain of individual cognition. Language will still have to be represented and processed within the cognition of each individual, of course. But such processing will exist only to support the public functions of language, rather than having any direct executive role in the thinking and practical reasoning of the individual subject.

The attractions of the communicative conception of language to philosophers have been manifold. In the first place it may be argued that language is plainly used for purposes of communication; and it is equally obvious that *some* forms of thinking, particularly where visual imagery is involved, are independent of language. So considerations of simplicity then suggest that *all* thought may be independent of language, and hence that language may be for purposes of communication only. This argument on its own is weak, of course, since it would require only minimal contrary evidence to overturn a bare appeal to simplicity of this sort.

A second argument is semantic, and comes in two different forms. In its historical, empiricist, version (e.g. Locke, 1690; Russell, 1921) it goes like this. We need to give an account of how anything (be it language, thought, or whatever) can *mean* or *represent* anything else; in the case of visual (and other) imagery, it is (supposedly) *transparent* how representation takes place – namely, via resemblance; yet it is not at all obvious how language, in itself, could represent anything (let alone via resemblance); so we get a satisfying explanation if we say that the representative powers of language are derivative from the representative powers of thought (mental images), and if we say that the function of language is merely to signal thoughts from one mind to another.

This classical argument for the communicative conception collapses, however, since the imagist theory of thought is hopelessly inadequate as an account of all forms of thinking – or, indeed, as an account of *any* of our propositional thoughts. (Try expressing such concepts as *not*, *and*, *or*, *cause*, *tomorrow*, *sixty-four*, and so on, in the form of a visual or other image; or even such a simple proposition as *grass is green*!) But descendants of the argument survive on, in the work of Grice and his followers (Grice, 1957, 1969; Lewis, 1969; Searle, 1983). The idea is still that we can explain the semantic properties of language in terms of the semantic properties of thoughts. We can say, for example, that for an utterance to mean *that P* is for the speaker to intend (a) that the utterance should cause the hearer to come to believe *that P*, through (b) the hearer's recognition of the speaker's intention to do just that. (Many variations and refinements of this proposal exist in what is now an extensive literature; for further discussion, and a critique, see Laurence, 1996, and this volume chapter 10.) And the claim can be that we *should* seek such an explanation, since thought-content is plainly more basic, and more primitive, than linguistic meaning (Searle, 1983).

3.2 Psychology

The communicative conception of language and its loosely associated themes of innate mental endowments and modularity are prefigured in the work of the 'faculty psychologists' such as Gall in the early nineteenth century. In the late nineteenth century, the claim that particular abilities, and pre-eminently language, were located in particular areas of the brain where they functioned relatively independently of other abilities received some support from the work of neuropsychologists and neurosurgeons such as Broca, who demonstrated that the ability to speak is dependent on a particular area of the brain now known as Broca's area. Once psychology proper had been established, the notion of relatively discrete 'special abilities', including the distinction between verbal and non-verbal abilities, resurfaced in the work of psychologists such as Spearman (1927), whose main aim was to develop intelligence tests. The notion of special, discrete abilities, including a distinct linguistic intelligence, is currently powerfully represented in Gardner's theory of multiple intelligences (Gardner, 1983).

Implicit in the notion of special abilities is an assumption that language develops at least partly independently of other types of cognitive ability, and is not involved in all types of thinking. However, it would seem that an extreme form of the communicative conception of language has never been accepted within scientific psychology, any more than a strong form of the cognitive conception has been argued for (see above). The involvement of language in conscious thought, or what psychologists call 'natural language mediation' (NLM), was first systematically researched and documented by Reed (1918), and has since then been extensively researched by others. There is no dispute amongst psychologists concerning the fact that NLM is used by all linguistically competent children and adults in their learning and memory, planning, and problem solving, although there is some dispute about some details of its use (Paivio, 1971, chapter 9; Atkinson *et al.*, 1990, pp. 306–11). Those psychologists who argue that language is a discrete ability predominantly subserving communication nevertheless accept, therefore, that language may be used reflexively to facilitate thought. Even Piaget (1932) who considered that language is used mainly for socialisation allowed that language also serves to assist in the formation and re-organisation of thought structures.

Here it is important to distinguish, however, between the claim that language is itself the *medium* for some thoughts and is partly constitutive of those thoughts (which is a weak form of the cognitive conception), and the claim that language *facilitates* or *augments* some forms of thought. This latter is best seen as a version of the communicative conception of language, in fact (important enough for us to label it the *supra-communicative conception* – see section 5.2 below for discussion), rather than a form of the cognitive conception at all. Once this distinction is drawn, it then becomes unclear quite which of the two doctrines the psychologists mentioned above intended themselves to be committed to.

3.3 Linguistics

The most radical and best-known argument for the communicative conception of language came, as in the case of arguments for a cognitive conception of language, not from philosophers, nor from psychologists, but from a linguist, in this case Noam Chomsky. In his early work on transformational grammar, Chomsky (1957) argued that thought had to be translated into language in the process of linguistic expression, and translated out of language into a 'language of thought' in the process of linguistic comprehension. Although Chomsky subsequently abandoned the notion of transformational grammar, his view of language as separate from thought has persisted and been highly influential (Fodor, 1975, 1983; Levelt, 1989; Pinker, 1994). In addition, and related to his argument that language is an independent system, Chomsky has from the late 1950s and 1960s argued that the best explanation of linguistic universals (abstract features of grammar found to be common to all natural languages) is that humans possess an innately structured language faculty; and that poverty of the stimulus and learnability arguments imply that children's acquisition of natural language is best thought of in maturational terms, rather than in terms of learning (see Chomsky, 1988, for a review). Chomsky's views on the relationship between language and thought are therefore consistent with, and indeed have contributed substantially to, the modularist and nativist view of the mind.

4 The modularist model

Chomsky's radical version of the communicative conception of language was first articulated at much the same time as progress in neuroscience and advances in what was then called artificial intelligence were increasingly persuading workers in various disciplines that the mind is more or less modular in structure, built up out of isolable, and partly isolated, components. Chomsky himself used the expression 'faculty' to describe the self-contained system which, he believes, subserves language. Fodor (1983) introduced, or at least popularised, the term 'module', and established criteria for what constitutes a module. He argued that peripheral input and output systems are modules, and that such modules subserve each of the various senses, motor action, and also language. He further argued that the central system where thought is processed is not a module, nor open to systematic empirical investigation, and introduced the term 'Mentalese' to identify what others have called the (non-natural-linguistic) 'language of thought'.

The Chomskian–Fodorian view of the mind, including their views on the relationship between language and thought, have constituted the dominant model in many of the cognitive sciences over the last three decades or so. Aspects of the model have continued to receive empirical support. Neuroscience and the study of disorders have, for example, produced considerable evidence for the existence of highly specialised, dissociable systems and sub-systems within the brain (Lenneburg, 1967; Shallice, 1988). Developmental psychologists have demonstrated that the new-born infant is by no means the *tabula rasa* which was once suggested, and that knowledge of the object world, of people, and of language is, if not innately present, then innately constrained in ways which makes development highly predictable and universal under normal conditions (see Karmiloff-Smith, 1992, and Sperber *et al.*, 1995, for reviews).

The modular model has also been productive at a theoretical level. It has, for example, made the Gricean arguments for the communicative conception of language attractive to many researchers, who have thus come to accept that conception through something like the philosopher's route. It has also formed the basis of the much-discussed hypothesis that social cognition is subserved by a social cognition module, or 'theory of mind (TOM) mechanism' (Leslie, 1987, 1994; Baron-Cohen, 1995; Carruthers and Smith, 1996). The hypothesis concerning the existence of a social cognition, or theory of mind, module is paralleled by Brothers' work in neuroscience (Brothers, 1990). The hypothesis also builds on findings in primatology that apes seem to have a simple, perhaps largely implicit, version of this system (Byrne, 1995; Gomez, 1996a and this volume chapter 4), and with the view that the driving force behind the evolution of human intelligence may have been the demands, and benefits, of social understanding and social manipulation (Humphrey, 1986; Byrne and Whiten, 1988). This has made it natural to think that the basis of language lay in *intentions to communicate*, just as Grice supposed; and that the primary (perhaps only) function of language is communication.

According to this strong form of the communicative conception, then, language is essentially just an input/output device for central cognition. The natural language system is held to be a mere conduit through which thoughts are transmitted into, and out from, central cognitive processes of believing, thinking and reasoning, without itself actually being implicated in the latter activities. (Of course, everyone allows that language is *important for* cognition, since a vast proportion of normal adult beliefs and concepts can only be acquired from others, through linguistic communication. This is not at issue. Recall our distinction between the claim that language is *required for* certain forms of thought – which is almost certainly true, but is consistent with the communicative conception of language – and the claim that language is *involved in* or *partly constitutive of* those forms of thinking.) So on this view, if we lacked natural language then we might end up believing, and hence thinking, a good deal less than we do. And our lives might be a great deal lonelier. But our thought processes, and our basic intellectual capacities, would otherwise remain essentially unchanged.

5 Weakening the dichotomy

In recent years, the dominance of a strong version of the communicative conception of language within the cognitive sciences, with its related emphasis on modularity and innate knowledge, has begun to weaken. One important factor, here, has been the advent of connectionism, and the ability to model human learning and behaviour using parallel distributed processing in connectionist networks. Connectionism has, over the last ten to fifteen years, brought computer simulations of behaviour and brain function closer to biological reality than was previously possible. It has also opened up the possibility that the human brain can learn more, and be innately endowed with less, than has generally seemed likely over the past few decades. This in turn may suggest that the brain may have greater plasticity than has generally been thought in recent years, and be less rigidly divided into pre-specified modules (at least in early infancy) than was previously thought to be the case (Elman *et al.*, 1996). And that then suggests a less rigid division between thought and language, and clears the way for some form of the cognitive conception of language to replace the current standard model.

Furthermore, one factor which has contributed to most cognitive scientists accepting the currently dominant version of the communicative conception of language, we believe, has been a mere failure to distinguish the cognitive conception of language from the Whorfian linguistic relativity hypothesis, or what Pinker disrespectfully refers to as the 'Standard Social Science Model' (see section 2.3 above). Most researchers have assumed that if they were to accept any form of cognitive conception of language, then that would commit them to Whorfian linguistic relativism and radical empiricism, and would hence be inconsistent with what they take to be their well-founded beliefs in modularity and nativism. But this may well be a mistake. Someone endorsing the cognitive conception of language may not *have* to regard language and the mind as cultural constructs, either socially determined or culturally relative. In fact, the cognitive conception of language can equally well be deployed along with a modularist and nativist view of language and mind – or so, at any rate, one of us will later argue (Carruthers, this volume chapter 5; *see also* Carruthers, 1996a).

Another factor which has led to the premature dismissal of the cognitive conception of language by most cognitive scientists, has been that they have had in mind the most extreme forms of such a view, of the sort espoused by Wittgenstein and Davidson, for example. As we noted above, on such accounts language is held to be necessary for any thought whatever, and most animals can therefore be characterised as thoughtless brutes. Indeed, many in the Wittgensteinian tradition (such as McDowell, 1994) maintain that possession of a language is *sufficient for* all forms of thought, claiming that training in a natural language is what confers on us our status as rational agents. Believing, rightly in our view, that these extreme positions are highly implausible, many cognitive scientists have again felt warranted in rejecting the cognitive conception of language *tout court*. For in the light of our knowledge of animal behaviour and infant development, and also given the way in which cognitive abilities can be spared in global aphasia, it seems most unlikely that language should be necessary for all forms of thought. And given the way in which language can be spared in people whose cognitive deficits are otherwise very severe (such as Williams syndrome, and various forms of dementia), it seems unlikely that language mastery *confers* a capacity for all kinds of thinking, either (see Boucher, this volume chapter 3).

Yet the cognitive conception of language need not involve any commitment to extreme claims of these sorts. First, it need only maintain that language is involved in (and is partly constitutive of) *some* kinds of thinking. It can thus allow that spatial reasoning, for example, can be conducted independently of language, while claiming that many other types of reasoning – such as reasoning about unseen causes, thinking about the thoughts of another person, or reasoning about which train to catch to be in London for a 3 pm appointment – are crucially conducted in language. Second, the cognitive conception can perfectly well maintain that language is but one component of (some of) our reasoning systems, thus allowing for cases – such as Williams syndrome – where language is spared but (some forms of) reasoning disrupted.

5.1 Weakening the cognitive conception

As has already begun to emerge, the cognitive conception of language can be weakened (and rendered more plausible) in at least two distinct directions. First, all claims to the conceptual, or logical, involvement of language in thought can be dropped. Rather, it can be claimed that language is implicated in (some or all) thought as a matter of actual fact, or as a matter of *natural* necessity (resulting, perhaps, from the structure of human cognition). Amongst recent writers, Bickerton (1990, 1995), Dennett (1991), and Carruthers (1996a) have all defended views of this general sort – though considerable differences remain between them. Roughly, Dennett espouses a form of Whorfianism, maintaining that the human mind results once the parallel architectures of the brain have been re-programmed as a result of human beings acquiring language, and as a consequence of the new ideas and ways of thinking which language brings. Carruthers, on the other hand, develops a version of cognitive conception which is broadly nativist and modularist (*see also* this volume chapter 5), while Bickerton's view is nativist but *not* modularist. According to Bickerton, the human mind resulted when the brain was radically re-structured by the evolution of grammatical competence, which is held to coincide with the powers of thought available to central cognition.

The second direction in which the cognitive conception of language can be weakened, and thereby rendered more plausible, is by dropping any claims to universality. While allowing that some thoughts (particularly visuo-spatial thoughts, and the thoughts available to animals and infants) are independent of language, it can nevertheless be claimed that other thoughts crucially implicate language. This then requires us to mark a division amongst thoughts, between those which involve language and those which do not. There are roughly two ways in which this can be done. Either one can mark the division *horizontally*, in terms of types of content; or one can mark the division *vertically*, in terms of the modes in which those contents are entertained (or both). The first of these strategies is pursued by Gomez, Carruthers, and Segal (this volume, chapters 4, 5, and 7), who explore the idea that thoughts about mental states, in particular, might crucially involve natural language. The second strategy is pursued by Carruthers, Davies, Frankish, Perner, and Dennett (this volume chapters 5, 11, 12, 13, and 14), who discuss the idea that natural language may only be implicated in certain *levels* of thought – perhaps conscious as opposed to non-conscious (Carruthers, Davies, Dennett), perhaps actively as opposed to passively formed (Frankish), or perhaps explicit as opposed to implicit (Perner).

The Whorfian hypothesis, too, admits of a weaker reading. Even if the extreme empiricism of the Standard Social Science Model is rejected, there remains the possibility that differences of a conceptual and grammatical sort between different natural languages might influence the *perceptions* of those brought up to speak those languages. Indeed, there is mounting evidence that this is in fact the case (Lucy, 1992a, 1992b; Goldstone, 1994; *see also* Goldin-Meadow and Zheng, this volume chapter 2). Such a view is relatively weak, however, since consistently with it, we can allow that the *thoughts* and *thought-processes* of all human beings remain fundamentally the same (though whether this is because of the universal structures present in all natural languages, as the cognitive conception of language would maintain, can be left open).

5.2 *Weakening the communicative conception*

It is also possible to soften the edges of the communicative conception somewhat, without altering its fundamentals. Thus Clark (this volume chapter 8) argues for a conception of language as a cognitive *tool*. The idea is that language gets used, not just for communication, but also to augment human cognitive powers. Thus by writing an idea down, for example, I can off-load the demands on memory, presenting myself with an object of further leisured reflection. We shall label this view (following Clark's suggestion) *the supra-communicative conception* of language.

The main difference between the supra-communicative and cognitive conceptions of language, should *not* be expressed by saying that for the former, sentence-tokens serve to augment but do not constitute thought, whereas for the latter the sentence-token *is* the thought. For no one should want to claim that a tokened natural language sentence *is* (or is sufficient for) a thought. (Consider a monolingual speaker of Russian uttering a sentence of English, for example.) Indeed, defenders of the cognitive conception, too, should accept that the content of an inner tokened sentence will depend upon a host of more basic connections and sub-personal processes. Rather, the claim is that the sentence is a *necessary component of* the thought, and that (certain types of) reasoning necessarily involve such sentences.

The difference between the two views can be put as follows. According to the cognitive conception, a particular tokening of an inner sentence is (sometimes) an inseparable part of the mental episode which carries the content of the token thought in question; so there is no neural or mental event at the time which can exist distinct from that sentence, and which carries the relevant content; and so language is constitutively involved in (certain types of) cognition, even when our focus is on token thinkings. For the supra-communicative account, however, the involvement of language only arises when we engage in an extended *process* of thinking or reasoning over time. So far as any given token thought goes, the supra-communicative account can (and does) buy into the communicative conception of language. It can maintain that there is a neural episode which carries the content of the thought in question, where an episode of that type can exist in the absence of any natural language sentence, but which in the case in question causes the production of a natural language representation. This can then have further benefits for the system of the sort Clark explores (for example, off-loading memory demands).

Clark's supra-communicative account can provide quite a convincing explanation for the use of language (especially written language) in soliloquy, as when one writes notes to oneself, or performs a calculation on a piece of paper. It is less obvious what account he can give of *inner* speech. Since there is here no medium of representation outside the mind, Clark certainly cannot say that the function of inner speech is to *off*-load the demands on memory. What he can perhaps say, however (and this is what Varley *does* say, this volume chapter 6), is that inner speech serves to *enhance* memory. For it is now well-established that the powers of human memory systems can be greatly extended by *association* (Baddeley, 1988). If asked to memorise a list of items, for example, it will be more efficient to associate them with something else, rather than simply repeating the names to yourself (even repeating them many times over). Thus, you might imagine walking around the rooms of your house, placing a distinct item in each room. This then gives you an independent fix on those items in memory – you can either recall them directly, or you can recall the rooms, from which you might extract the associated item.

Something similar might very well take place in the case of inner verbalisation. By translating an underlying (non-natural-language) thought into its imaged natural language equivalent, we might get an independent fix on that thought in memory, so making it more likely that it will be available to enter into our reasoning processes as and when the need arises. This might then greatly enhance the range and complexity of the thoughts and sequences of reasoning which are available to us. While this memory-enhancement proposal may not necessarily provide the *best* explanation of inner speech (see Carruthers, 1996a, chs. 6 and 8), it is certainly a possible one.

6 The time is now ripe . . .

As should already be clear from the foregoing, we believe that the time is now ripe for investigators from a variety of disciplines to return to the issue of the relations between language and thought; and we hope that this volume may prove seminal in this respect. For it is striking how little recent work bears directly on the dispute between the cognitive and communicative conceptions of language, at least in their weaker and more fragmentary guises. Where cognitive scientists have addressed the issues at all, they have tended to focus on the cognitive conception in its Whorfian and all-thought-encompassing guises, and so have produced little which is relevant to more modest proposals. (For example, most of the contributors to Weiskrantz, 1988, saw their role as opposing an extreme Wittgensteinian position on the place of language in cognition.) Moreover, where scientists have gone to potentially fertile sources of evidence – such as Genie, who was kept isolated and languageless to the age of 13 (Curtiss, 1977), or deaf children who have not had exposure to conventional sign-languages

(Goldin-Meadow and Mylander, 1990) – they have tended to concentrate on matters rendered more fashionable by the dominant modular model, such as the evidence for critical learning periods in language acquisition.

As indicated above, the modularist, strongly nativist, model is now under threat from without, in the guise of connectionism. And it is also, not under threat, but subject to various forms of modification from within. These changing paradigms and shifting emphases open up new possibilities, and may make old questions seem more pertinent. What is needed now, and what the essays in this volume begin to provide, is a re-examination of the language-and-thought issue from both theoretical and empirical perspectives – both proposing possibilities not previously considered and distinguishing cases frequently lumped together, and also bringing to bear today's more fine-grained experimental techniques (including an increasing battery of non-verbal tasks of various sorts) in testing them.

What we do want to emphasise again here, however, are two distinctions which potential experimenters should be mindful of. One is the distinction Karmiloff-Smith draws (1992) between representations which are *implicit*, perhaps being embedded in some practical procedure, and those which are *explicit*, available for general use in cognition and for interactions with centrally stored information outside of any particular domain. In investigations of the cognitive abilities of people suffering from aphasia or other language disabilities, for example, we need to be careful to ensure that what is being displayed is genuinely *thought* about the cognitive domain in question, and not merely some sort of discrimination of, or sensitivity to it.

The second important distinction is between uses of language to *enhance* cognition (of the sort outlined in section 5.2 above, in our discussion of the supra-communicative views of Clark and Varley), and uses of language which are partly *constitutive of* thought in some cognitive domain. These two possibilities may not prove easy to discriminate experimentally. Suppose, for example, that one were to investigate the cognition of pre-conventional-language deaf children (Goldin-Meadow and Mylander, 1990; Goldin-Meadow and Zheng, this volume chapter 2), studying the changes which take place when they acquire a conventional sign-language like ASL (very fast) at the age of six or seven, say. (This would, in effect, be a re-run of the Luria and Yudovich 1956 twin-experiment.) And suppose that what was found was some marked improvement in particular cognitive domains – in theory of mind, as it might be. This would not yet speak in favour of (a limited form of) the cognitive conception of language, as opposed to the supra-communicative conception of language as a tool. What would in fact be needed, are tests of the sophistication of the children's thinking in the cognitive domains in question, but ones which do *not* place significant demands on memory. These may not prove easy to devise.

7 A brief guide to the volume

This section of the chapter will be brief, since each of the three parts of the book is prefaced by a short introduction.

Before saying something about the structure of the book as a whole, we should stress that decisions on which chapters to place where were often more or less arbitrary. For example, Carruthers' paper (chapter 5), currently in Part I because of its focus on the place of language in human evolution, could just as well have gone into Part III, since it also says quite a bit about the role of language in conscious thinking. Similarly, Laurence's paper (chapter 10), currently in Part II alongside other papers on concepts and reasoning, could equally well have gone into Part I, since its focus is on the implications of Gricean approaches to semantics for evolution and for child development.

We should also stress that there are multiple cross-connections and themes running across the divides between the different parts of the book. Here we pick out just one for special mention – readers will no doubt notice many other cross-connections as well. This theme has to do with possible connections between language and social cognition (theory of mind, or TOM), which figures prominently in the chapters by Gomez (chapter 4), Carruthers (chapter 5), Varley (chapter 6), Segal (chapter 7), Laurence (chapter 10), Frankish (chapter 12), and Perner (chapter 13).

The chapters in Part I all relate to the place of language in child development and/or in human evolution. Goldin-Meadow and Zheng (chapter 2) discuss the evidence of thought, and of thought-structure, concerning motion events in a pre-conventional-signing deaf child. Boucher (chapter 3) confronts Chomsky's account of language acquisition with evidence from children with specific language impairments, suggesting that it receives ambiguous support, at best. Gomez (chapter 4) provides a sketch of the likely social and ostensive–communicative abilities of our ape ancestors, which provided the seeds for the evolution of language; and suggests that the development of explicit theory of mind abilities may then have been interwoven with the evolution of language. Carruthers (chapter 5) uses evolutionary considerations to argue that language can *both* be a peripheral module of the mind *and* be crucially implicated in central (including conscious) cognition.

The chapters in Part II focus on connections and independences between language, concepts, and reasoning abilities. Varley (chapter 6) discusses the bearing of aphasiological evidence on the dispute between communicative and cognitive conceptions of language, and presents the results of tests of theory-of-mind ability, and of other sorts of reasoning, conducted on a patient with a-grammatical aphasia. Segal (chapter 7) argues tentatively that our capacity to entertain thoughts about the thoughts of other people may have to exploit the resources of our natural language faculty. Clark (chapter 8) presents a conception of language as a cognitive *tool*, and discusses a variety of ways in which language is used to augment and extend our cognitive powers. Sperber and Wilson (chapter 9) use their (1986/1995) relevance theory of communication and cognition to argue that people will standardly have many *more* concepts than they have lexical items for in their public language. Laurence (chapter 10) confronts the Gricean approach to semantics (which has often been used, as we saw above, to argue for the communicative conception of language) with contrary evidence, and sketches a contrasting Chomskian alternative.

The chapters in Part III all focus on 'vertically divided' versions of the cognitive conception of language. Davies (chapter 11) defends an argument in support of Fodor's 'language of thought' hypothesis, and explores its relationship to Carruthers' (1996a) idea that conscious propositional thought is conducted in natural language sentences. Frankish (chapter 12) argues for a distinction between passive and active belief, and defends the view that the latter constitutively involves language. Perner (chapter 13) discusses the properties shared by various models of the central executive, discussing why the latter's processes seem to be both conscious and language-involving. Finally, Dennett (chapter 14) rounds off the volume (as he did the conference from which the chapters of this book were selected) by criticising the very idea of 'central processing', and arguing that language is crucial to conscious cognition.

8 Conclusion

The purpose of this volume is not to establish firm conclusions, but rather to re-open old questions, and to raise new possibilities. Our hope is that it will encourage and stimulate cognitive scientists to re-think the issue of the relationship between language and thought, and to return to that issue armed with today's more sophisticated experimental techniques, in order to investigate a variety of more subtle possibilities than the traditional dichotomy ever allowed.

We are grateful to all those who participated in the Hang Seng Centre conferences over the period 1994–6 for advancing our understanding of these matters, and to Andy Clark and the Cambridge referees for comments on an earlier draft.

Part I

Language, development and evolution

Introduction to part I

Peter Carruthers and Jill Boucher

The chapters in Part I of this book all focus on issues concerning the emergence of language and cognition during child development, and concerning the evolution of linguistic capacities and distinctive human intelligence in our hominid past. Following some general introductory remarks on the way in which these issues are relevant to the debate over the relationship between language and thought, we will provide some brief background discussion for each of the four chapters.

Any position one might adopt on the question of the relationship between language and thought will carry commitments, of one sort or another, concerning the structure and organisation of mature human cognition. And that, in turn, may have implications for the kind of developmental story which it is possible to tell. Moreover, whatever account is given of mature human cognition had better permit some plausible account to be provided of the evolutionary origins of the latter. For example, suppose one held that language is the vehicle for certain kinds of thought; say all propositional thought – hence being committed to the cognitive conception of language in quite a strong form. In that case one had better maintain that language-acquisition is a necessary condition for young children to engage in propositional thinking; and that those children who are deprived of, or delayed in the acquisition of, language will be incapable of entertaining just these kinds of thought. Similarly, one had better be prepared to give an account of human evolution such that no capacities for propositional thought were present prior to the evolution of linguistic ability (e.g. Bickerton, 1990, 1995).

The converse is also true, however – particular theories of child development and/or human cognitive evolution may place constraints on the range of acceptable answers to the question of the relationship between language and thought. For example, accounts of child development which conceive of the child as a 'little scientist', devising theories in various domains, and revising and rejecting them in the light of in-coming data (Gopnik, 1988, 1996; Gopnik and Wellman, 1992), are of course committed to the independence of thought from language, since much of this development takes place prior to the stage at which language is acquired, and since language is itself one of the domains to be theorised. In short, the moral is that child development and data concerning human evolutionary origins are fertile testing grounds for different conceptions of the relationship between language and thought. This is a moral accepted by all of the contributors to this volume, and especially by those whose essays figure as chapters in Part I. (Note that two of the other papers in the volume also focus on developmental issues, namely those by Segal, chapter 7, and Laurence, chapter 10.)

Chapter 2: Goldin-Meadow and Zheng

Susan Goldin-Meadow and colleagues have, for a number of years, studied the gesture-systems of deaf children who have not been exposed to any conventional sign-language (e.g. Goldin-Meadow and Mylander, 1990; Butcher *et al.*, 1991; Goldin-Meadow *et al.*, 1994). These children were profoundly deaf, born of hearing parents who took a decision that they should be educated in normal hearing schools, and not exposed to any conventional sign language. As is known to occur in other cases of this sort, the children all developed their own form of simple sign-language, or 'home-sign', using and adapting the gestures made by their parents when they spoke. In her previous publications, Goldin-Meadow has focused on the grammatical properties of home-sign, finding, surprisingly, that in terms of general syntactic and morphological features, it is extremely similar to normal two-year-old language. In the present study, Goldin-Meadow and Zheng turn their attention to the semantic properties of the home-sign of one individual child, looking at the way in which he uses gesture to express thoughts about motion events in particular.

As background to their study, Goldin-Meadow and Zheng cite the work of Slobin (1985), who had hypothesised – in line with the communicative conception of language – that children would come to the language-learning situation with a set of grammaticisable notions and thoughts, ready and waiting to find linguistic expression. But what Slobin actually found when looking at the evidence across cultures, was that from the earliest stages of language-acquisition children take on the characteristics unique to their native language, already looking much more like native speakers in the things that they say than they look like other children of similar age learning a different language (Slobin, 1987). This might seem, on the contrary, to support the cognitive conception of language – it rather looks as if children's thoughts are formed and shaped, at least, by the particular language they learn; just as Whorf (1956) would have predicted. But if a deaf child can use home-sign to express a range of notions and thoughts (about motion events, for example), then Slobin's communicative conception hypothesis would appear to be re-instated; for the sign-system is *invented* by the child without a conventional language model; in which case the child's notions and thoughts can hardly be *determined by* such a model. And this is exactly what Goldin-Meadow and Zheng seem to find. So a weak form (at least) of the communicative conception of language is supported – namely, *some* thoughts are available to be communicated independently of language.

Chapter 3: Boucher

Chomsky has famously argued that human children bring to the language-learning task an innate body of domain-specific knowledge, particularly about the grammatical structures which are universal to all natural languages (Chomsky, 1980, 1988, 1995a). Such a view has seemed, to many, to provide powerful support for the communicative conception of language (e.g. Pinker, 1994). For if language acquisition is handled by a special-purpose mental faculty, not drawing on the resources of central cognition and conceptual thought, then it may be difficult to see how the latter could nevertheless be dependent upon language, in the way that a cognitive conception of language would require.

Chomsky's own arguments for his position are highly theoretical, focusing particularly on the alleged impossibility of language being learned in the time available, given the nature of the data available to the child – the so-called 'poverty of stimulus' argument. Surprisingly, few people have thought to confront Chomsky's theory with the wide range of empirical evidence available from cases of anomalous language development. This is what Jill Boucher sets out to do in her chapter. Her finding is that the data from children with Specific Language Impairment (SLI), in particular, does not support the view that there is an innate grammar-specific mechanism involved in language acquisition (though she finds that the data are consistent with the idea that language acquisition is underpinned by a broad-based linguistic faculty dealing with phonology and the lexicon, as well as with syntax). To this extent her chapter can be seen as a round-about defence of the cognitive conception of language, in so far as it suggests that language and thought may be more intimately connected than the Chomskian position would appear to allow.

Chapter 4: Gómez

Juan-Carlos Gómez, too, takes a Chomskian thesis as his main target of attack – in this case, the idea that there is a sharp discontinuity between human beings and all other species of animal (including the great apes) in respect of language capabilities. This view results from an ill-motivated identification of *language* with *syntax*, Gómez maintains. For in reality, syntax is but one part of a larger communicative system, some other basic elements of which we may well have in common with the great apes – including a shared-attention mechanism (SAM), and some form of simple theory of mind (TOM) mechanism.

Gómez adopts a broadly Gricean approach to communication (Grice, 1957), according to which a communicator will produce a signal designed to impart information to the recipient; and where the person trying to comprehend that signal will have to figure out, from the signal together with its context, just what it is that the communicator means. On such an account, plainly, a general capacity for thought, and for inference, must be in place prior to the existence of communication. But although he endorses a fairly strong form of the communicative conception of language, Gómez concedes – indeed, he argues – that the evolution of linguistic capacities in human beings may have been crucially interwoven with the evolution of our capacity for understanding the mental states of others (TOM). According to Gómez, simple theory of mind and shared attention abilities made possible the beginnings of communicative behaviours; which in turn 'called for' the evolution both of more complex theory of mind systems on the one hand, and also of grammatical systems on the other, together with their associated language-acquisition devices (LADS).

Chapter 5: Carruthers

Peter Carruthers takes as his goal to reconcile at least a weak form of cognitive conception of language with a highly modularist picture of the mind. Many cognitive scientists now believe that the mind is organised into a variety of specialised systems, or 'modules', on the one hand, together with central cognition (thought) on the other; and most believe that language itself is one such distinct module of the mind. As a result, these cognitive scientists endorse a strong form of communicative conception of language, maintaining the independence of all thought from language (e.g. Pinker, 1994). For how could language be an isolated module of the mind, distinct from central cognition, and yet be crucially implicated in the operations of the latter? Carruthers sets out to show how. He takes as his model what is known about the way central cognition, in the guise of visual imagination, accesses and utilises the resources of the visual module – it may be that in 'inner speech', similarly, central cognition deploys the resources of the language system to underpin some of its own functions.

Carruthers sketches an account of the evolution of creative human thought, in which language occupies an indispensable place, drawing on –

and where necessary contrasting his views with – the work of Bickerton (1990, 1995) and Mithen (1996). On this account, language serves both as the vehicle of conscious propositional thought, in 'inner speech'; and also as the vehicle of explicit ('inferentially promiscuous') conceptual thought, serving as the *lingua franca* between a number of specialised, quasi-modular, central cognitive systems (including theory of mind, folk biology, and naive physics). At a minimum, his claim is that there is no entailment from a modularist conception of language and mind to a communicative conception of language, and that a weak form of cognitive conception can be made to seem quite plausible within the framework of modularism.

2 Thought before language: the expression of motion events prior to the impact of a conventional language model

Susan Goldin-Meadow and Ming-Yu Zheng

1 Language and thought over developmental time

Languages across the globe vary in how they classify experience. Do such variations in classification affect the way speakers consider their worlds, even when they are not speaking? Benjamin Lee Whorf (1956) first popularised the notion that linguistic classifications might influence, not only how one talks about the world, but also how one thinks about the world when not actually speaking. In other words, one might partition the world differently depending upon the language one speaks. This hypothesis remains intriguing, although it has proved surprisingly difficult to test (cf. Lucy, 1992a).

A particularly compelling example of the type of influence Whorf suggested was reported by Lucy (1992b), who explored the impact on thought of formal linguistic devices for marking number. Lucy began by analysing the distribution of these linguistic devices in two languages – Yucatec Mayan and American English – showing that different devices are used to mark different types of objects in both languages. For example, in both Yucatec and English, words for animals are marked by the plural (e.g., 'two pig*s*'), while words for substances are not (e.g., one doesn't say 'two muds' in English unless referring to various types of mud). The two languages differ, however, in how they treat a third type of object – implements. In English, implements are marked by the plural, as are animals (e.g., 'two rake*s*', comparable to 'two pig*s*'); in Yucatec, they are marked like substances. Thus, on linguistic grounds, implements are classified with animals in English but with substances in Yucatec.

Lucy's next step was to explore how speakers of English and Yucatec deal with these same types of objects in tasks that involve *no* language at all. When asked to participate in a picture memory task, both English and Yucatec-speakers noticed when the number of animals changed across pictures, but tended to ignore changes in the number of substances.

Importantly, however, English-speakers also noticed when the number of implements changed, whereas the Yucatec-speakers did not. In other words, English-speakers treated implements like animals (and different from substances) in the memory tasks, while Yucatec-speakers treated implements like substances (and different from animals) – as would be predicted by Lucy's linguistic formulation. Thus, the routine classifications that an adult is required to make as a speaker of a given language appear, at least in this example, to have an impact on the way that the adult partitions the world in a non-linguistic task.

The issue we explore in this chapter is the relationship between language and thought over development. Lucy's work suggests that language can influence thought, even language-less thought, at least after language has been well learned and become habitual. What happens, we might ask, when language is still a novel skill? Will language still exert an influence on thought or, alternatively, will thought affect the way that language itself is learned?

Slobin (1985) hypothesised that children begin the language-learning process with a starting set of universally shared meanings or 'grammaticisable notions'. Slobin suggested that all children come to the learning situation with a language-making capacity that constructs similar early grammars from all input languages. The surface forms generated by these grammars may vary since the materials provided by the input languages vary; however, the basic notions that first receive grammatical expression remain constant across all first grammars, and independent of the input language (Slobin, 1985). According to this hypothesis, thought directs the initial stages of language-learning rather than the other way around.

In subsequent work, Slobin (1987) came to reject his own hypothesis, having found no evidence for a stage characterised by 'universal Basic Child Grammar' (Slobin, 1985). Slobin found that, as soon as children begin to speak, they demonstrate characteristics unique to the language they are learning (1987; Berman and Slobin, 1994); that is, children look much more like native speakers than universal speakers, even at the earliest stages of acquisition (*see also* Choi and Bowerman, 1991). These recent findings suggest that the language model to which children are exposed has an immediate, and large, impact on the aspects of a situation that children include in their talk, and on the formal means they use to convey those aspects.

However, did Slobin need to discard both the baby and the bath water? Just because the language model to which a child is exposed immediately affects the way the child learns language does not mean that Slobin's original hypothesis was incorrect. Children might indeed come to the language-learning situation seeking certain notions to express and grammaticise. If their language model provides an accessible device for expressing a particular notion, they will adopt it; if not, they will not. It is not at all surprising that the language model to which a child is exposed affects that child's language development. The only surprise is how quickly the influence of the language model is felt.

It appears as if conventional language is, in some sense, too effective an influence on the thoughts children express for us to test Slobin's (1985) hypothesis. Children so readily assimilate the forms and notions of the language to which they are exposed that, even if the child were to come to the language-learning situation with a universal set of grammaticisable notions and distinctions, how would we be able to tell? One way to explore the Slobin hypothesis more fully is to examine children who are *not* exposed to any model of a conventional language. Which distinctions and classifications would such a child make, if any?

This question is, of course, difficult to answer simply because most children are exposed from birth to a model of some conventional language, be it signed or spoken. There are, however, children who, although exposed to a language model, cannot make use of that model — deaf children whose hearing losses are so severe that they cannot use the spoken language model that surrounds them, and whose hearing parents have chosen not to expose them to a model of a conventional sign language. Such children are essentially deprived of an effective model of a conventional language. Interestingly, however, children in this situation communicate nonetheless, and use gesture to do so (Feldman *et al.*, 1978; Goldin-Meadow and Mylander, 1984, 1990). The particular notions that these children convey in their gestures have, of course, *not* been influenced by a conventional language model. As a result, the notions they express come as close to reflecting the expressible and grammaticisable notions that children themselves bring to the language-learning situation as we can envision. In a sense, these children allow us to see thought that has not yet been filtered through a language model (although it is thought generated within a communicative situation and thus may have been shaped by that situation, see Goldin-Meadow *et al.*, 1996, for discussion of this issue; i.e., it is 'thinking for speaking' in Slobin's (1987) sense and is not thought in a non-language task as Whorf and Lucy sought).

In this chapter, we explore the implications for the Whorfian hypothesis of gesture development by deaf children with no exposure to conventional language. We begin by providing background on deafness and language-learning, background that is important in understanding the communicative situation in which the deaf children find themselves. We then describe general characteristics of the gesture systems that the deaf children generate to communicate with their hearing parents and other hearing adults and children. We focus this paper on the deaf children's expressions in gesture of a particular type of event – motion events. Much recent work has been done showing that, from as early as we can determine, children express motion events in ways that are compatible with the particular language they are learning (Berman and Slobin, 1994; Choi and Bowerman, 1991). In our population, the components of the motion event that the deaf child conveys in gesture can be inferred to be just those components that are 'thinkable' prior to a language model – thoughts that a child can have even without the benefit of language.

2 Background on deafness and the children in our studies

Deaf children born to deaf parents and exposed from birth to a conventional sign language such as American Sign Language (ASL) acquire that language naturally; that is, these children progress through stages in acquiring sign language similar to those of hearing children acquiring a spoken language (Newport and Meier, 1985). However, 90 per cent of deaf children are not born to deaf parents who could provide early exposure to a conventional sign language. Rather, they are born to hearing parents who, quite naturally, tend to expose their children to speech (Hoffmeister and Wilbur, 1980). Unfortunately, it is extremely uncommon for deaf children with severe to profound hearing losses to acquire the spoken language of their hearing parents naturally, that is, without intensive and specialised instruction. Even with instruction, deaf children's acquisition of speech is markedly delayed when compared either to the acquisition of speech by hearing children of hearing parents, or to the acquisition of sign by deaf children of deaf parents. By age five or six, and despite intensive early training programmes, the average profoundly deaf child has limited linguistic skills in speech (Conrad, 1979; Mayberry, 1992; Meadow, 1968). Moreover, although many hearing parents of deaf children send their children to schools in which one of the manually coded systems of English is taught, some hearing parents send their deaf children to 'oral' schools in which sign systems are neither taught nor encouraged; thus, these deaf children are not likely to receive input in a conventional sign system.

The children in our studies are severely (70–90 dB bilateral hearing loss) to profoundly (>90 dB bilateral hearing loss) deaf, and their hearing parents have chosen to educate them using an oral method. At the time of our observations, the children ranged in age from fourteen months to four years, ten months and had made little progress in oral language. They occasionally produced single spoken words but never combined those words into sentences. In addition, at the time of our observations, the children had not been exposed to ASL or to a manual code of English. As pre-schoolers in oral schools for the deaf, the children spent very little time with the older deaf children in the school who might have had some knowledge of a conventional sign system (i.e., the pre-schoolers only attended school a few hours a day and were not on the playground at the same time as the older children). In addition, the children's families knew no deaf adults socially and interacted only with other hearing families, typically those with hearing children.[1] Under such inopportune circumstances, these deaf children might be expected to fail to communicate at all, or perhaps to communicate only in non-symbolic ways. This turns out not to be the case.

Studies of deaf children of hearing parents in general have shown that these children spontaneously use gestures (referred to as 'home signs') to communicate even if they are not exposed to a conventional sign language model (Fant, 1972; Lenneberg, 1964; Moores, 1974; Tervoort, 1961). Given a home environment in which family members communicate with each other through many different channels, one might expect that the deaf child would exploit the accessible modality (the manual modality) for the purposes of communication. The question we will develop is whether the gestures the deaf child uses to communicate are structured in language-like ways. To the extent that they are, then these language-like structures appear not to require conventional language input for their expression. Rather, they reveal (or come as close as we can to revealing) the thoughts and forms of developing children untainted by exposure to external linguistic modifications.

In the next section, we describe some general properties of the deaf child's gesture system, focusing in particular on aspects of the system that might suggest how the deaf child classifies his or her world (at least for the purposes of communication). After this background, we turn to the expression of motion events.

3 An overview of the deaf child's gesture system

The self-styled gesture systems of the deaf children in our studies were comprised of indexical and iconic representations. The 'lexicon' of the gesture systems contained both pointing gestures and characterising gestures. Pointing gestures were used to index or indicate objects, people, places, and the like in the surroundings. Characterising gestures were stylised pan-

[1] One of the primary reasons we were convinced that the children in our studies had had no exposure to a conventional sign system at the time of our observations was that they did not know even the most common lexical items of ASL or Signed English. When a native deaf signer reviewed our tapes, she found no evidence of any conventional signs. Moreover, when we informally presented to the children common signs such as those for mother, father, boy, girl, dog, we found that they neither recognised nor understood any of these signs.

tomimes whose iconic forms varied with the intended meaning of each gesture (e.g., a C-hand twisted in the air to indicate that someone was twisting open a jar). Gestures of this sort, particularly pointing gestures but also some characterising gestures, are produced by hearing children (Acredolo and Goodwyn, 1988; Butcher *et al.*, 1991). However, the deaf children's use of these gestures is unique in that their gestures are used for a variety of the functions that language typically serves, and their gestures fit into a structured system; hearing children's gestures do not (Goldin-Meadow and Morford, 1985; Morford and Goldin-Meadow, 1992).

The deaf children used their gesture systems not only to communicate with others, but also to communicate with themselves. In this sense, the systems appeared to be a vehicle for thought. For example, when one of the deaf children was trying to copy a configuration of blocks off a model, the child made an 'arced' gesture in the air, indicating the block he needed next; when the experimenter offered a block that fit this description, the child ignored the offer, making it clear that his gesture was not directed at her but was for his use only. In addition, the gestures the children produced could also be the object of thought – they were, at times, themselves the focus of the deaf child's communications. For example, to request a Donald Duck toy that the experimenter held behind her back, the child pursed his lips to imitate Donald Duck's bill, then pointed at his own pursed lips and pointed toward the Donald Duck toy. When offered a Mickey Mouse toy, the child shook his head, pursed his lips and pointed at his own pursed lips (Goldin-Meadow, 1993). The point at the lips is roughly comparable to the words 'I say', as in 'I say "Donald Duck bill"'. The deaf child was able to distance himself from his own gestures and treat them as objects to be reflected on and referred to, thus exhibiting in his self-styled gesture system the very beginnings of the reflexive capacity that is found in all languages and that underlies much of the power of language (cf. Lucy, 1993).

All natural languages, be they signed or spoken, have structure at more than one linguistic level (e.g., at the level of the sentence, word and phoneme). The deaf children's gesture systems are structured as well. The gestures of the ten children whose systems were examined for sentence-level structure were found to have structure across gestures within a string (Goldin-Meadow and Feldman, 1977; Feldman *et al.*, 1978; Goldin-Meadow and Mylander, 1984), and the gestures of the four children whose systems were examined for word-level structure were found to have structure within as well as across gestures (Goldin-Meadow *et al.*, 1995). Thus, in this important respect, the deaf children's gesture systems resembled natural language.

As an example of the type of sentence-level structure the deaf children introduced into their gestures, each of the deaf children combined his or her gestures into strings to create new meanings. A deaf child might combine a point at a grape with an EAT gesture (in that order) to comment on the fact that grapes can be eaten, and then later combine the EAT gesture with a point at the experimenter (in that order) to invite the experimenter to have lunch with the family. The gesture strings that the deaf children produced functioned in a number of respects like the sentences of early child language and, on this basis, warrant the label 'sentence'. For example, one deaf child produced gestures serving noun-like functions and gestures serving verb-like functions in different positions in the gesture sentence, and with different morphological markings. Moreover, these distinctions between gestures in noun-like contexts and verb-like contexts did *not* appear to be a direct coding of object vs action categories, but rather a marking of the role the gesture played in the child's sentence and discourse structure (Goldin-Meadow *et al.*, 1994). As another example, the gesture sentences the deaf children generated could be characterised in terms of underlying predicate frame structures that determined how likely it was that a gesture for a particular semantic element would appear in a sentence of a given length (Goldin-Meadow, 1985). Even the complex sentences that the children generated could be described in terms of concatenations of underlying structures; interestingly, the children's systems allowed the concatenations of phrases in underlying structure and not just whole sentences (Goldin-Meadow, 1982). Thus, many of the patterns in the deaf children's gesture systems could be described in terms of structures that were independent of idiosyncratic pragmatic concerns of the moment and were, in this sense, 'syntactic'.

We end our overview of the deaf children's gesture system with an example of a language-like pattern that appears to reflect the child's partitioning of the world. The children produced gesture strings characterised by two types of surface regularities: (1) regularities in terms of which elements were produced and deleted in a string (production probability), and (2) regularities in terms of where in the string those elements were produced (gesture order). These regularities were formulated in terms of categories such as 'patient', 'act', 'actor', 'recipient', etc. As an example of production probability, the children were more likely to produce a gesture for the patient (e.g., the cheese, in a sentence about eating) than to produce a gesture for the actor (the mouse eating the cheese). In addition, the children produced gestures for the intransitive actor (e.g., the mouse, in a sentence describing a mouse running to his hole) as often as they produced gestures for the patient (e.g., the cheese, in a sentence describing a mouse eating cheese), and far more often than they produced gestures for the transitive actor (e.g., the mouse, in a sentence describing a mouse eating cheese; Goldin-Meadow and Mylander, 1984). In this way, the likelihood of production served to distinguish systematically among thematic roles and thus mark those roles – an important function of grammatical devices.

Interestingly, the one deaf child who produced enough gestures for transitive actors to determine consistent use for the category showed precisely this same pattern in gesture order, the second type of surface regularity. The child tended to place gestures for the patient (the eaten cheese) and gestures for the intransitive actor (the runner mouse) in first position of his two-gesture sentences, while gestures for the transitive actor (the eater mouse) tended to occupy second position (Goldin-Meadow and Mylander, 1984).

The particular pattern found in the deaf children's gestures – patients and intransitive actors marked in the same way, and both different from transitive actors – is an analogue of a structural case-marking pattern found in naturally occurring conventional languages (in particular, ergative languages, cf. Dixon, 1979; Silverstein, 1976). This pattern is one in which the 'affectee' properties of the intransitive actor, the runner, are highlighted. The runner initiates the running action and, at the same time, is affected by that action. By classifying the runner with the patient (which is, by definition, the recipient of action) and not the transitive actor (the initiator of action) in his gestures, the deaf child is, in a sense, bringing into focus the fact that the runner is an affectee and downplaying the fact that the runner is also an initiator. This ergative classification pattern is one that appears in the deaf children's communication system without the benefit of a conventional language model. It is, as a consequence, a way of viewing an action and its participants that does *not* derive from language – it reflects, at least for our deaf children, thought prior to language.

We next explore how motion events are expressed in the deaf child's gesture system. Unlike our previous work in which we focused primarily on the structural arrangements of the gestures, their 'syntax', we concentrate here on their content, their semantics. We focus on the particular semantic elements of a motion event that are explicitly expressed in the deaf child's gestures; that is, on the elements that can appear in early communication systems even without guidance from a conventional language model.

4 Expressing motion events in a self-styled gesture system: the raw materials

The expression of motion and location has played a central role in recent studies of lexical semantics (Jackendoff, 1990; Jackendoff and Landau, 1991; Levin and Rappaport Hovav, 1991; Talmy, 1985). All languages seem to analyse motion/location events into components such as Manner and Path. However, languages differ in how they combine these notions into words (Talmy, 1985), and in the particular components of a motion event that are routinely expressed (Slobin, 1987; Berman and Slobin, 1994). Thus, young children must discover how spatial information is organised in their particular language. The question we are able to address with our population is whether the child comes to this discovery process with predispositions of any sort regarding the expression of motion events.

We explore this question by describing the way one of our deaf subjects, David, expressed motion events in his gestures over a two-year period. We reviewed the videotapes of seven sessions taken at 2;10 (years;months, D1[2]), 2;11 (D2), 3;0 (D3), 3;3 (D4), 3;11 (D9), 4;6 (D11), and 4;10 (D13), and selected for further analysis all discourse situations in which a motion event was the topic of conversation. Following Choi and Bowerman (1991), we focused on events resulting in a change of location. We included changes of location that took place either when a person or object spontaneously moved across space (spontaneous motion) or when an object was moved by an agent across space (caused motion).

We coded each motion event in terms of the components that the child conveyed explicitly in gesture. According to Talmy (1985), a motion event has four basic components:

Figure	The moving object
Motion	Presence of motion
Path	The course followed by the Figure with respect to the Ground
Ground	The reference-point object with respect to which the Figure moves

These four elements are exemplified in the following sentence:

The duck	went	into	its cage
(Figure)	(Motion)	(Path)	(Ground)

A motion event can also have a Manner (e.g. The duck went *waddling* into its cage) and caused motions, by definition, involve an Agent (e.g. The *boy* moved the duck into its cage). When coding the deaf child's descriptions of motion events, we adopted Talmy's system. We were, however, able to make finer distinctions within the Ground category. The deaf child distinguished the point at which the path originated (Origin), the point at which the path ended (Endpoint), and the locale in which the path occurred (Place), all of which would be coded as Ground in Talmy's system. We list below the motion components coded in these data, along with an example of each from the deaf child's gestures. In each case, the component exemplified is in italics, with characterising gestures displayed in capital letters and pointing

[2] The sessions are labelled with the child's initial (D) and a number indicating the sequence in which the session was videotaped (1 is David's first session, 4 is David's fourth, etc.).

gestures displayed in lower case letters (-'s indicate gestures produced in sequence, +'s indicate gestures produced simultaneously; the numbers in brackets indicate the session during which the sequence was produced, e.g., David 1, and the particular discourse unit from which it came, e.g., no. 26).

(a) Figure
Point at cookie (Figure) – Point at napkin where D wants cookie put (Endpoint)[3] [D1,26]

The Figure was most frequently conveyed by a distinct lexical item, typically a point at the moving object. However, the child could also indicate the Figure in several other ways: (1) by producing his characterising gesture for the motion near or toward the moving object, that is, by incorporating a reference to the object within a gesture for the motion (for example, rather than produce the GIVE gesture in neutral space, at chest level, the child extended the gesture toward the object that he wanted moved); or (2) by incorporating a hand-shape reflecting attributes of the Figure into his characterising gesture for the motion (for example, rather than use a nondescript hand-shape to convey a ball crossing space, David used a fist handshape, thus conveying the spherical shape of the moving object). Indicating the Figure via placement of a characterising gesture or hand-shape of a characterising gesture was considered a morphological technique, rather than a lexical technique, for conveying components of a motion event (see Goldin-Meadow *et al.*, 1994, for discussion of this point). The essential distinction between these two types of techniques is the separateness of the representation. In the lexical technique, each component is conveyed via an independent and distinct gesture. In contrast, in the morphological technique, one component is incorporated into the gesture for a second component; the two components are therefore 'conflated' within a single gesture (cf. Talmy, 1985).

(b) Motion
Point at cookie (Figure) – Point at napkin (Endpoint) – *GIVE (Motion)* – Point at napkin (Endpoint) [D1, 26]

The Motion component was always conveyed via a characterising gesture. We classified a gesture as expressing generic Motion when its form portrayed neither the path nor the manner of the actual motion needed to achieve relocation. For example, the GIVE gesture, open hand held palm-

[3] Note that in order to get his hand from his first point (at the Figure) to his second point (at the Endpoint), David had to move his hand along some path. We made a distinction between a movement that appeared to function merely to get the hand from one location to the next, and a movement that appeared to be an explicit portrayal of a Figure's trajectory of motion. Although this sounds like a difficult coding decision to make, in fact, it was quite easy and was one upon which we were very reliable (see Goldin-Meadow and Mylander, 1984).

up as though receiving an object, was the Motion gesture most commonly used to convey caused motion. Although this gesture looks like it might be portraying the endpoint of the path (i.e., the open hand), in fact, the GIVE gesture was used whether or not the child wanted the object placed in his hand or even given to him at all; in other words, the gesture appeared to be used to mean 'move' in general rather than 'gimme'. As a second example, the MOVE gesture, pointing finger or open palm with fingers wiggling back and forth toward the gesturer, was the Motion gesture used most often to convey spontaneous motion but was also, at times, used to convey caused motion. Here again, neither the path, nor the manner of motion is conveyed in the gesture, and the gesture appears to mean 'move' in general.

> *(c) Path*
> *COME (Path)* – Point at toy that D wants his sister to come toward (Endpoint) [D1, 1]

The Path was always conveyed by a characterising gesture moving across space.

> *(d) Origin*
> *Point at bag out of which D wants puzzle pieces taken (Origin)* – Point at experimenter to request her to give D the pieces (Agent) – *Point at bag (Origin)* [D11,5]

> *(e) Endpoint*
> TRANSFER (Path) – *Point at closet where D wants his coat put (Endpoint)* [D4,32]

The Origin and Endpoint were often conveyed by separate lexical items (typically points but occasionally by a characterising gesture portraying the action done at the beginning or the end of the path, see the toy bag example described below). However, like the Figure, these two components could also be conveyed by incorporating the beginning or endpoint of the path into the characterising gesture for the path (i.e., by morphological incorporation). If the gestured movement for the path (e.g., the sweeping motion in the TRANSFER gesture) began at the place of origin of the actual movement, the child was given credit for having conveyed the Origin (via a morphological technique) as well as the Path. If the gestured movement finished at the endpoint of the actual movement, the child was given credit for having conveyed the Endpoint (via a morphological technique) as well as the Path.

> *(f) Place*
> *BOARD (Place where D wants toy to walk)* – MOVE FORWARD (Path) [D13, 5]

At times, the Place was conveyed by a separate lexical item, as in the BOARD characterising gesture in the above example. However, most often the Place was incorporated into a characterising gesture. Indeed, in the above example, the Path gesture was produced in the locale in which the act was to occur; thus, the Place was redundantly marked, once lexically and once morphologically.

> *(g) Manner*
> *FLUTTER (Manner in which snow falls)* – FALL (Path snow follows) [D9,9]

The Manner component could be conveyed by a separate lexical item (a characterising gesture), as in the above example. However, at times, the child conflated the Manner with the Path and produced both within a single gesture. For example, David produced a gesture which combined the FLUTTER and FALL, wiggling his fingers as his hand moved downward.

> *(h) Agent*
> *Point at mother (Agent)* – Point at cookies D wants (Figure) – GIVE (Motion) [D1,49]

The agent could be conveyed lexically, as in the above example, or morphologically, by displacing the characterising gesture for the motion toward the agent of that motion.

The point we stress here is that the deaf child, without benefit of a conventional language model, expressed each of the components considered essential to linguistic depiction of an event involving movement across space. According to Talmy (1996), language users treat certain elements and their interrelations as the central identifying core of a particular event or event type (at least for the purposes of communication). A set of elements and interrelationships that are evoked together are said to constitute an 'event-frame'. Other elements, which could in principle share an equally intimate involvement in the event, appear in most languages peripheral or incidental and thus are considered by Talmy to lie outside the event-frame. The elements Talmy (1985) takes as constituting an event-frame for motion events involving change of location are Figure, Motion, Path, Ground, Manner, and Agent – all of which are elements that a deaf child, lacking a conventional language model, also takes to be important enough to be expressed when describing this type of motion event in gesture.

5 Packaging the raw materials of the motion events

Thus far we have shown that the deaf child is capable of conveying and, at times, does convey each of the elements considered core to motion events involving crossing space. The unit of analysis that we used to code motion events in the deaf child's gestures was the discourse topic. All gestures produced by the deaf child to describe a given motion event (either to request the event, to comment on its occurrence, to question it, etc.) were considered to be part of the discourse unit conveying that event, whether or not the gestures were produced within the same gesture sentence. We found that, at times, the deaf child produced almost all of the core elements of the event-frame within a single discourse unit. For example, to request that the experimenter move the toy bag to a particular spot on the floor (something the experimenter did not particularly want to do), David produced the following sequence of gestures (the entire set of gestures comprises a single discourse unit; each gesture sentence within the discourse unit begins on a new line and is numbered, with characterising gestures in capital letters and pointing gestures in lower case):

(i) Point at toy bag (Figure).
(ii) LIFT (act at Origin) – MOVE (Motion) – Point to spot on floor (Endpoint) – MOVE (Motion).
(iii) MOVE (Motion) – Point at spot on floor (Endpoint).
(iv) CARRY+PATH (Manner+Path) – Point at toy bag (Figure) – CARRY+PATH (Manner+Path).
(v) Point at toy bag (Figure) – LIFT – LIFT (act at Origin) – PUT (act at Endpoint).

In this sequence, David indicated the object that he wanted moved, where he wanted it moved from and where he wanted it moved to, and the manner and path it should take in the relocation. The only element he omitted was a reference to the agent (a pattern that turned out to be quite common for him, as we will see below). Thus, David has all of the elements of the event-frame at his disposal.

However, languages differ, not in *whether* all motion elements can be conveyed (it is possible to express each of these elements in all languages), but in *how often* the elements are conveyed and in *what form* they are expressed. For example, Manner is a component that is routinely mentioned in English sentences, usually incorporated into the verb ('I ran to the store', 'I limped to the store', 'I hurried to the store', etc.). In contrast, Manner is frequently omitted in Spanish sentences, where Path tends to be mentioned without explicitly saying what the manner of movement is (Slobin, 1996a). We first asked whether the deaf child demonstrated any particular pattern of omission and commission of motion components within a discourse unit, or whether he produced each component equally often within a unit. Figure 2.1 presents the proportion of discourse units containing each of the eight semantic elements. As noted above, the unit of analysis is the dis-

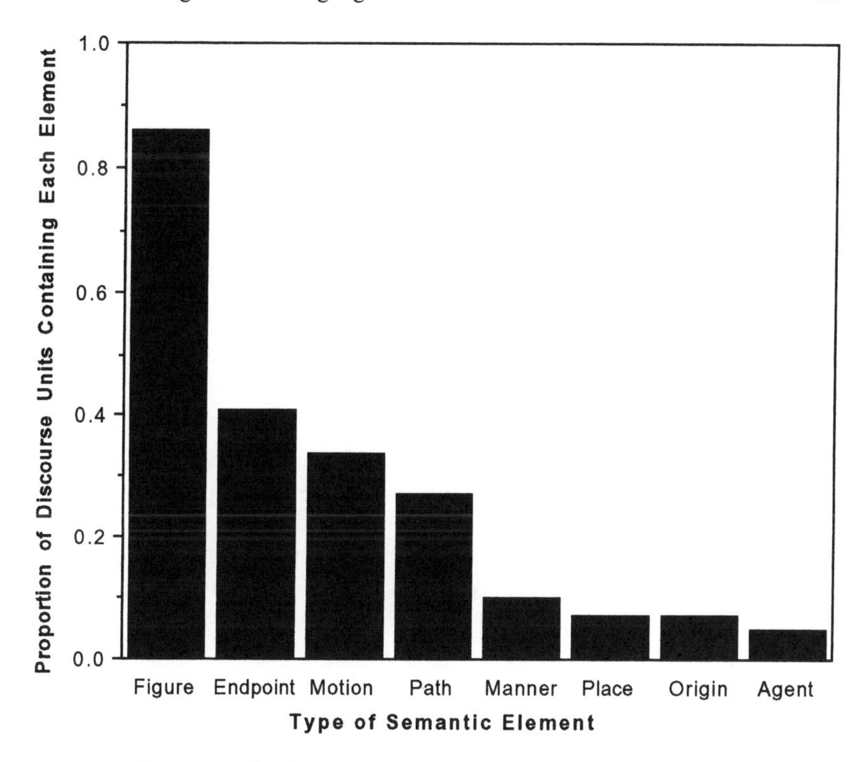

Figure 2.1. *The distribution of semantic elements in David's discourse units.*
The bars represent the proportion of discourse units in which David explicitly conveyed each of the eight semantic elements. A discourse event could, in principle, contain all eight elements; as a result, each proportion could be as high as 1.00 (the proportion for the Agent is out of the total number of caused events since, by definition, agents are not involved in spontaneous events).

course event (not the sentence); thus, each proportion represents the number of discourse events in which that particular component was expressed (either lexically or morphologically), out of the total number of relevant discourse events. David could have produced each element in 100 per cent of his discourse units; however, he did not and, in this respect, his system looked language-like. David frequently included some elements (Figure, Endpoint, Motion, Path) in his descriptions of motion events and left others (Manner, Place, Origin, Agent) to be inferred by the communication partner.

Another way in which languages differ is in whether they package elements in the same fashion in spontaneous vs caused motion events. In a spontaneous event, the object moves itself along the path. In a caused event, the object is moved along the path. English does not make a distinction between these two types of events in terms of the way manner and path are packaged. Manner is conflated into the verb in descriptions of both spontaneous motions ('I skipped across the road') and caused motions ('I skipped the rock across the road'). In contrast, Korean *does* make a distinction, bundling path information differently in sentences describing caused motion vs spontaneous motion (Choi and Bowerman, 1991). Moreover, from the earliest stages of language-learning, children appear to use the adult patterns (Choi and Bowerman, 1991). English-learners show no distinction between spontaneous and caused motions in the way manner and path are packaged, while Korean-learners do show such a distinction, a distinction they never appear to breach.

Which, then, is the natural pattern? Do children come to the language-learning situation ready to make a distinction between spontaneous and caused events in terms of manner and path, only to find that in some languages (English, for example), the distinction is not made? Or, do children come with no distinction at all, awaiting a language model such as Korean to create one? We turn to David to answer this question.

5.1 Conveying caused vs spontaneous motions

The most striking difference in the way David conveyed spontaneous vs caused motions is that caused motions were mentioned much more often than spontaneous motions (191 events vs 38 events). Choi and Bowerman (1991) found a similar focus on caused motion over spontaneous motion early in development in the Korean-learning children they observed, but not in the English-learning children. It may be that the language model to which the English-learning child is exposed serves to focus attention on spontaneous events, thereby making them more salient than they would otherwise be.

We look next at the particular elements David conveyed in descriptions of caused and spontaneous motions. Figure 2.2 represents the data found in Figure 2.1 separated into caused (the black bars) and spontaneous (the white bars) motion events. As is clear from the figure, the patterns are quite distinct for these two types of events. Almost all of the discourse events conveying spontaneous motions contained an explicit gesture for the Path, whereas very few of the events conveying caused motions did. In caused motions, David tended to convey the path indirectly by producing a gesture for the Figure, along with a gesture for the Endpoint or a generic Motion gesture. Thus, David focused attention on the initial (the Figure) and the final (the Endpoint) portions of a change of location in a caused motion

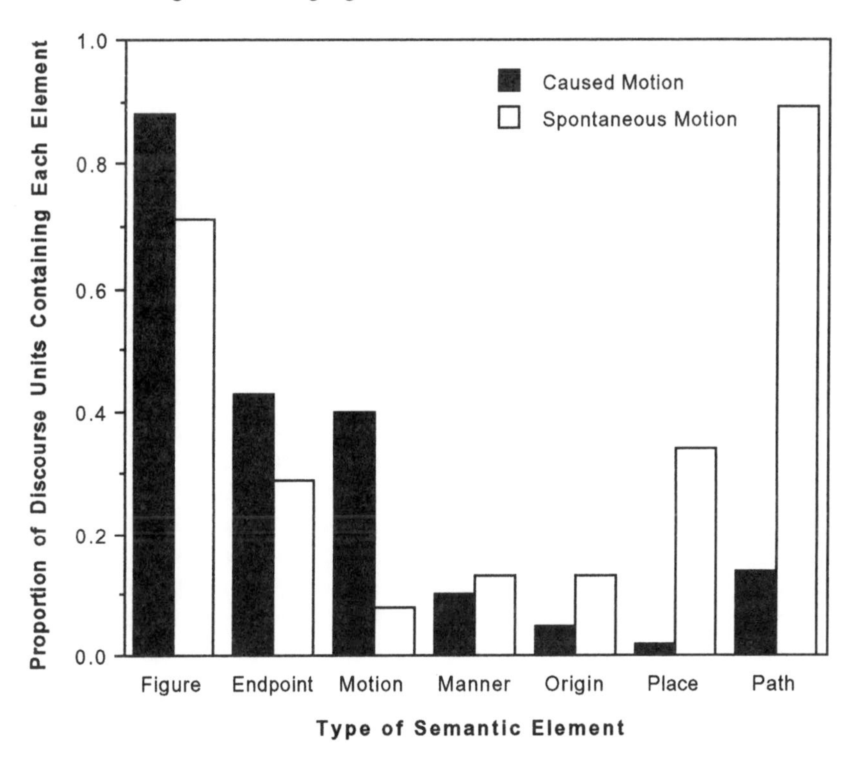

Figure 2.2. *The distribution of semantic elements in David's discourse units conveying caused motion vs spontaneous motion.*
The black bars represent the proportion of discourse units conveying caused motion in which David explicitly gestured each semantic element. The white bars represent the proportion of discourse units conveying spontaneous motion in which David explicitly gestured each semantic element (the Agent, by definition, is not part of spontaneous motion; it has therefore been omitted from both the spontaneous and caused motion graphs). A discourse unit could, in principle, contain all seven elements; as a result, each proportion could be as high as 1.00.

event, omitting any explicit mention of the medial portion (the Path itself). For example, when conveying caused motion, David frequently pointed at an object he wanted moved (the Figure), followed by a point at the location to which he wanted that object moved (the Endpoint). In contrast, in spontaneous motions, David tended to focus explicitly on the initial portion (the Figure) and the medial portion (the Path) of a change of location, omitting the final portion (the Endpoint). For example, David often pointed at a toy that moved on its own (the Figure), followed by a characterising gesture conveying the toy's trajectory (the Path). Talmy

(1996) refers to this selective attention to certain portions of a motion event as 'windowing'; the portion of an event that does not have a window upon it is backgrounded by the lack of sentence constituents referring to it, and thus is 'gapped.' In these terms, David tended to window the initial and final portions of a caused event and gap the medial portion, while windowing the initial and medial portions of a spontaneous event and gapping the final portion.[4]

According to Talmy (1996), the presence vs the absence of overt language description is only one linguistic device for packaging motion components and thereby selectively focusing attention on certain components and not on others. Another device is solo expression (akin to the lexical device David used) vs joint conflation (akin to David's morphological device). To explore how this device focused attention in David's gestures, we examined the way in which David expressed his three most frequent object elements – Figure, Endpoint, and Place. Each of these elements could, in principle, be conveyed: (1) by a separate lexical item (typically a point but, at times, a characterising gesture serving as a noun, cf. Goldin-Meadow *et al.*, 1994); (2) by altering the morphology of a characterising gesture (either by displacing the characterising gesture toward the object playing that particular role, cf. Goldin-Meadow *et al.*, 1994, or by adding to the characterising gesture a hand-shape that captures an attribute of the object playing that particular role); or (3) by both devices.

Figure 2.3 presents the proportion that each of these three elements was conveyed lexically, morphologically, or by both devices in discourse units conveying caused vs spontaneous events. Here again, we see a distinction between caused and spontaneous motions. Endpoints (Figure 2.3a) were conveyed almost exclusively in caused motions and tended to be conveyed via a separate lexical item. For example, to request that a glass be moved to the table, the child might produce a point at the glass and a MOVE gesture, followed by a separate gesture – a point at the table – to convey the

[4] 80 per cent of the caused motions David described were requests, while only 39 per cent of his spontaneous motions were requests (the rest were comments, questions, etc.). As a result, it is possible that the patterns we observe in Figure 2.2 reflect the child's attention to communicative function (in particular, the speech act) rather than the motion type. To explore this possibility, we divided the spontaneous and caused motions David described into requests and non-requests and examined the proportion of semantic elements expressed for speech acts of each motion type. We found that the patterns seen in Figure 2.2 were essentially unchanged. For example, David was as likely to produce a gesture for the Path in a spontaneous motion that was a request (0.87) as in a spontaneous motion that was a non-request (0.91). Moreover, these proportions for spontaneous motions were both higher than the comparable proportions for caused motions (0.07 and 0.42, respectively). However, the fact that David produced more Path gestures in non-request caused motions (0.42) than in request caused motions (0.07) suggests that the type of speech act also plays a role in determining which semantic elements the child explicitly encodes.

Endpoint. In contrast, the Place (Figure 2.3b) was conveyed almost exclusively in spontaneous motions and tended to be conveyed morphologically (by altering the place of articulation of the path gesture). For example, to request that a self-propelling toy be put down and allowed to move forward, the child might produce his gesture for the path over the place where he wants the toy to walk, thereby incorporating the Place into the lexical item for Path. This distinction was seen even in the Figure, an element that David produced in both caused and spontaneous motions (cf. Figure 2.2). When produced in a caused motion, the Figure tended to be conveyed lexically, as in the above example – point at the glass, the Figure, followed by a MOVE gesture and a point at the table. However, when produced in a spontaneous motion, the Figure tended to be conveyed morphologically (by altering the hand-shape of the path gesture). For example, to describe the trajectory of the bubble he was about to blow, the child might incorporate a round hand-shape, representing the bubble (the Figure), into the forward motion of his Path gesture.

As mentioned above, Choi and Bowerman (1991) have found that, from the start of language-learning, children learn to express motion events according to the pattern displayed in their target language. Although English and Korean children talk about similar motion events, they do so in different ways, even in the earliest stages of language development. English-speaking children rely on Path particles in their descriptions of motion events and use them for *both* spontaneous and caused motions from the start. In contrast, Korean children (like Korean adults) distinguish strictly between words for spontaneous and caused motions, never using the same verb in both contexts. According to Choi and Bowerman (1991, p. 106), 'a major difference between children learning English and Korean, then, is in their willingness to extend Path words across the transitivity boundary'. English-learning children, provided with a model for making this generalisation, do so – Korean-learning children, lacking such a model, do not.

Although Choi and Bowerman (1991) would like to claim, on the basis of their data, that keeping a distinct division between caused and spontaneous motions comes naturally to the child and that blurring the distinction and developing an abstract notion of Path occurs only if a model for collapsing the division is provided, in fact, their data neither confirm nor disconfirm this hypothesis. The Choi and Bowerman data show that children adhere to the language models to which they are exposed – English-speaking children are willing to blur the distinction between caused and spontaneous motions and develop a notion of Path that cuts across both types of motions because they see such blurring in their model; Korean-speaking children are not willing to blur the distinction because their model gives them no reason to do so.

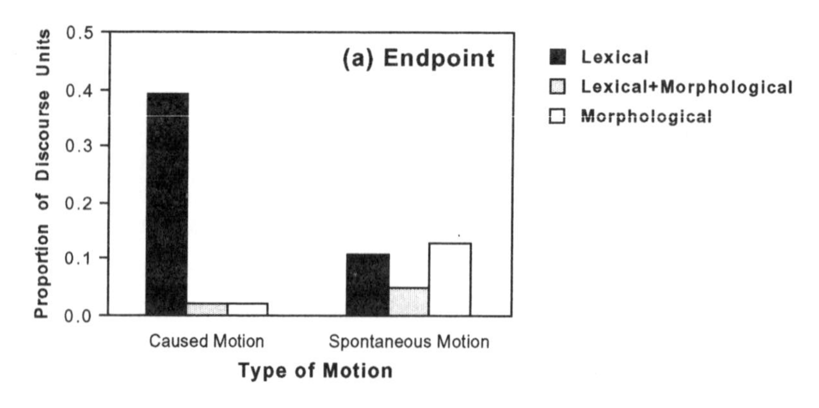

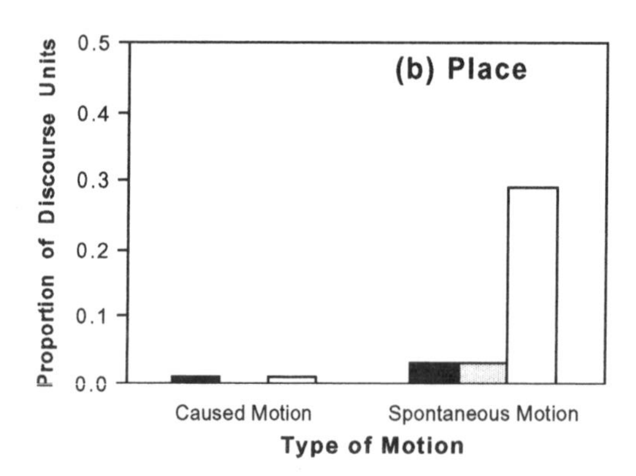

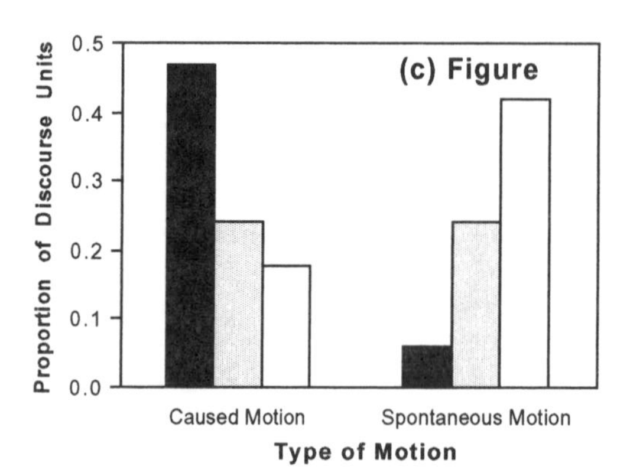

Figure 2.3. *Lexical vs morphological devices used to convey the (a) Endpoint, (b) Place, or (c) Figure in caused and spontaneous motions.* In each graph, the black bars represent the proportion of discourse units in which the semantic element was conveyed lexically (i.e., by a separate

However, strong support for at least an aspect of Choi and Bowerman's (1991) hypothesis is available and it comes from the data on the deaf child in our study. Our data show that, even without the benefit of a conventional language model, a child can distinguish between spontaneous and caused events when communicating. These findings thus support the Choi and Bowerman hypothesis that 'a full-blown sensitivity to caused versus spontaneous (or to transitive vs intransitive) may be present in children from the outset of language acquisition' (p. 116).

Moreover, by comparing the deaf child's descriptions of motion events with those of Korean and English-learners, we can begin to see the kind of impact that a language model can have on a child's language. In fact, David sits somewhere between the Korean-learners and the English-learners with respect to abstracting a Path component. David did produce gestures for the Path and, importantly, used the same types of gestures for Paths in spontaneous motions and for Paths in caused motions. For example, he moved his hand forward to convey the Path when describing a lawnmower that was pushed forward (a caused motion) and when describing a wind-up duck that moved forward on its own (a spontaneous motion). In this sense, David looks quite different from the Korean-learners who *never* use the same word in both contexts and thus do not demonstrate an abstract notion of Path in their speech (Choi and Bowerman, 1991). These findings suggest that a language model is *not* essential for the young child to develop an abstract notion of Path (since the deaf child has done so without one). The findings also suggest that having a language model such as Korean may actively get in the way of abstracting a notion of Path that cuts across spontaneous and caused motions or, at the least, may give the child no opportunity to demonstrate such an abstraction.

On the other hand, David did not use Path nearly as often for caused motions as he did for spontaneous motions and, in this sense, he looks quite different from English-learners. Having a language model such as English

Figure 2.3 (*cont.*)
gesture). The white bars represent the proportion of discourse units in which the semantic element was conveyed morphologically (i.e., by incorporating a handshape or place-of-articulation representing that element into another gesture). The gray bars represent the proportion of discourse units in which the semantic element was conveyed both lexically and morphologically. Note that when David conveyed an element in descriptions of a caused motion, he tended to convey that element lexically (i.e., Endpoints, and Figures on the left side of graph c). In contrast, when he conveyed an element in descriptions of a spontaneous motion, he tended to convey that element morphologically (i.e., Places, and Figures on the right side of graph c).

appears to encourage the child to routinely use Path in descriptions of both spontaneous and caused motions, which may, in the end, have an impact on how easily the child notes similarities between the motion of a figure when it moves on its own and when it is moved by another.

5.2 Conveying the agent in a caused motion

One glaring omission in David's motion events is the absence of gestures for the Agent in caused motions (by definition, the Agent does not play a role in spontaneous motions). David clearly *can* explicitly convey the agent in a caused motion, but he does so very rarely (see Figure 2.1).[5]

Omitting subjects (which are typically Agents) from sentences that convey caused motions is common even in young children learning English, a language that requires overt subjects (e.g., Bloom, 1970; Bloom *et al.*, 1975). Why then do English-learners omit Agents? Several researchers have argued that the young English-speaking child understands that English requires subjects, and that the child's inconsistent use of subjects reflects processing limitations, or a performance deficit (Bloom, 1970; Bloom, 1990; Gerken, 1991; Valian, 1991; Valian *et al.*, 1996). A similar argument can be made for the deaf child. Indeed, in previous work (Goldin-Meadow, 1985), we have shown that the deaf child's production of Agents is conditioned by the number of gestured elements in the surface structure of the sentence and by the number of elements in the underlying structure of the sentence. In other words, the Agent forms part of the event frame for caused motion in the deaf child's gesture system, as it does in the hearing child's spoken system. It is expressed infrequently in the surface form of the sentences of both deaf and hearing children because of a variety of performance factors (factors such as the syntactic structures of the sentences, the availability of prior discourse, and sentence length, cf. Bloom *et al.*, 1975).

Thus, with or without a conventional language model, the child appears to treat the Agent as part of the event frame for caused motion but, at the same time, treats it as a *dispensable* component within that frame. It is important to note, however, that input from a conventional language can modify this basic pattern. For example, Valian (1991) showed that,

[5] It is possible that David is conveying the agent to his communicative partner by indicating through gaze who the doer of the motion is. This same 'non-linguistic' device is, of course, also available to hearing children learning conventional languages such as English or Italian. If eye gaze were, in fact, functioning to convey the agent, making it unnecessary to produce a gesture or word for it, then we might expect first and second person agents (i.e., agents that are present in the communication situation) to be particularly likely to be omitted. However, there is no evidence for such a pattern in the deaf children's gestures – third person agents are omitted just as often as first and second person agents (Goldin-Meadow, 1985).

although all of the children in her sample omitted subjects, the children learning Italian, a language that allows subjects to be dropped, were more likely to omit subjects from their sentences than were the children learning English, a language that does not permit subject-dropping. What is not clear from the hearing child data, nor from our own data on the deaf child, is why the Agent is so dispensable – why is the Agent component most readily omitted when omission is needed?

Nevertheless, our data do provide insight into the role that a conventional language model may play with respect to the Agent. A language model does *not* appear to be necessary to understand that the Agent is an integral part of the event frame underlying descriptions of caused motion. It does, however, appear to be necessary to begin to treat the Agent as *indispensable* to those descriptions, that is, as a component that is obligatory in descriptions of caused motion.

5.3 *Conveying spontaneous motion within a causal frame*

Talmy (1996) describes another type of windowing in which a path frame event is embedded within a causal-chain event frame. One particular situation arose relatively frequently during the videotaped sessions that lent itself to this type of analysis. A number of crossing-space events involved a figure that moved on its own after being activated by an agent, for example, a toy duck which walked forward after someone twisted the key on its side. We analysed these events over developmental time, focusing particularly on which elements David chose to convey explicitly. In the first session (age 2;10), David conveyed six events of this type. In all six, David chose to produce a gesture to convey the initiating event (the twisting) rather than the resulting event (the path). In the second session (2;11), David began producing gestures conveying the resulting event as well as gestures conveying the initiating event. However, he did not convey both events within the same discourse unit; each was conveyed in its own piece of discourse – a discourse focusing on twisting or a separate discourse focusing on path. It was not until the fourth session (3;3) that David produced gestures conveying both the initiating event and the resulting path within a single discourse unit (although not yet within a single sentence); for example, David might produce a TWIST gesture in one turn and then, while still on the same topic but in another turn, produce a MOVE FORWARD gesture conveying the duck's path. Finally, in the ninth session (3;11), David produced gestures for both the initiating event and the resulting event within a single sentence, for example, TWIST – MOVE FORWARD conveyed with no break between the gestures. David continued to produce sentences of this type in his subsequent sessions (4;6 and 4;10).

Several interesting points are suggested by this developmental sequence. First, David preferred expressing the initiating aspect of the event even though, at the time, he was perfectly capable of conveying trajectories and did so for spontaneous motions that did not involve an enabling event. Second, we can see David literally building a causal-chain event frame over development. He first focused on a single segment of the causal-chain (either the initiating or the resulting event), he then produced gestures for both segments of the event and packaged them within the larger discourse unit, and finally he packaged the two segments within a single sentence. It is not clear what motivates this development, perhaps cognitive growth or a developing sense of what the listener needs for effective communication. It is clear, however, that the developmental changes the deaf child experiences are not guided by the presence of a conventional language model (see Bowerman, 1982, for evidence of a comparable developmental pattern in English-learners whose errors suggest that they begin to demonstrate productivity with cause-result constructions at about 3;6, relatively late in development).

6 Thought before language

Does the language we speak influence the thoughts we think? Lucy (1996) outlines three possible constructions of this hypothesis. First, there may be effects of language on thought which derive from having a language vs not having one – the *enabling* function of language. Second, there may be effects on thought which derive from speaking one language rather than another – the *shaping* function of language. Third, there may be effects within a given language community from using language in one way or another – the *facilitating* function of language.

The study we have described here was originally conceived as a seminal exploration of the enabling function of language. The deaf children we observed have not been exposed to a usable conventional language model and, in this sense, were language-less. Note, however, that even though these children lack a communication system that is shared by a community and passed down from generation to generation, they do have a communication system that is language-like in many respects (Goldin-Meadow and Mylander, 1990). The fact that the children in our studies developed a structured communication system without benefit of a conventional language model underscores the importance of language to the human child (particularly in light of the fact that the chimp requires massive training to develop a communication system that is far less structured and less complex than the systems the deaf children develop spontaneously, cf. Goldin-Meadow, 1997). It is, in fact, very difficult to find a child, raised in humane circumstances and suffering no cognitive deficits, who does not have a language – be it a shared system, or an idiosyncratic one such as the deaf child's. Any human who can think appears inevitably also to have language. Thus, language appears to come naturally to human children, making it extremely difficult (perhaps impossible) to explore the enabling function of language in its most stringent construction.

While not permitting us to explore the effects of having language or not, the deaf children do provide us with the opportunity to explore the effects of having *conventional* language or not – that is, the effects of a codified system shared within a cultural group and transmitted across generations. A conventional language is a cultural artefact and, as such, may have an impact on the way speakers of that language see the world (the Whorfian hypothesis). The deaf children lack this cultural artefact, although they do partake of their cultural worlds in many other ways. Thus, the deaf children allow us to observe the thoughts of a child who has not yet been socialised by language but has otherwise been socialised normally within his or her culture.

In this paper, we have explored the way the deaf child expressed motion events and found that, even without a conventional language model, the child used a basic event frame to describe motion events involving crossing space, the same frame posited by Talmy (1996) to underlie all natural languages. In addition, over time, the deaf child began to use a causal-chain event frame (also hypothesised to be universal; Talmy, 1996), at first packaging the initiating and resulting segments of the frame within the discourse unit but eventually packaging the two segments within a single sentence. Moreover, the deaf child was found to foreground or window certain components of the event frame (by producing gestures for those elements), and to background or gap other components (by omitting gestures for those elements, or by conflating gestures for the elements with gestures for other, more central elements). Talmy (1996) suggests that such devices are used in all natural languages to focus attention within the communicative act.

Interestingly, some of the particular windows and gaps found in the deaf child's gestures are commonly found in hearing children's spoken systems as well. For example, David frequently omitted the agent from his descriptions of caused motion, even though he was capable of producing gestures for this component and appeared to understand its relevance to the event frame (cf. Goldin-Meadow, 1985). The agent is frequently omitted in the talk of young hearing children, even by children learning languages that do not canonically permit agents (or subjects) to be omitted (e.g., Bloom, 1970; Valian, 1991). In addition, David distinguished spontaneous and caused motions from one another by using different windows and gaps to convey each type of motion. In describing caused motions, David tended to produce explicit lexical items for the figure and the endpoint (he rarely mentioned the path), thus focusing attention on the initial and final portions of the event. In contrast, in describing spontaneous motions, David produced an explicit lexical item for the path, incorporating gestures for any other components into the path gesture itself, thus focusing attention on the medial portion of the event. A distinction between spontaneous and caused motions is one that is easily made by young hearing children even in their earliest communications (Choi and Bowerman, 1991).

The characteristics that we have noted in David's expression of motion events, although thus far explored in only a single child and therefore admittedly tentative, have not been shaped by a conventional language model. They may thus be considered untainted manifestations of child 'thought' – for example, on cognitive grounds, the young child may see the agent as dispensable, and may appreciate the importance of the initial and final portions of an event to a caused motion and the importance of the medial portion to a spontaneous motion. However, the form that the deaf child's expressions take may well be influenced by other factors. One factor that comes to mind is the manual modality – perhaps certain distinctions are relatively easy to make in a gestural language, while others are more difficult. In other words, while the patterns we see in the deaf child have clearly not been influenced by a conventional language model, they could have been shaped, at least in part, by the modality through which they are expressed. An analysis of the particular motion event components that deaf children learning a conventional sign language from their deaf parents (e.g., ASL) spontaneously produce at the earliest stages of development would be relevant here (see Slobin and Hoiting, 1994, and Supalla, 1982, for evidence that the components posited by Talmy to comprise the event frame for motion events that involve crossing space can, not surprisingly, be encoded in a signed language).

Another obvious factor that could influence the form of the deaf child's gestures is the gestures that their hearing parents produce when communicating with their children. The hearing parents of the deaf children in our studies were attempting to teach their children to talk and, as a result, addressed their children through speech. However, they did produce gestures along with their speech, as hearing parents tend to do when they talk to their hearing children (Bekken, 1989; Shatz, 1982). The question is whether the gestures that the hearing parents used formed a model after which the deaf children could have patterned their gesture systems. In previous work, we have shown that the gestures the hearing parents produced were not sufficiently complex to serve as a model for the gesture systems their deaf children eventually developed. Indeed, even when the hearing mothers combined gestures within a string (which they did infrequently), the patterns they used were not comparable to the patterns found in their child's gesture sentences (Goldin-Meadow and Mylander, 1983, 1984).

Similarly, the gestures that the hearing mother produced were found to be inadequate models for the morphological systems that the deaf child developed (Goldin-Meadow *et al.*, 1995), for the child's use of gesture to communicate about the non-present (Butcher *et al.*, 1991), or for the distinctions between nouns, verbs, and adjectives that the child made in the gesture system (Goldin-Meadow *et al.*, 1994).

Despite the fact that the hearing mother's gestures have thus far proved to be inadequate models for her child, it is certainly possible that the gestures she used could instantiate some of the principles found to characterise the deaf child's expression of motion events. One might test this possibility by examining the way the hearing mothers use gesture along with their spoken expression of motion events, and comparing their gestures to their children's. Indeed, in an analysis of the gestures hearing adults spontaneously use when narrating a cartoon event, McNeill and Duncan (1997) found that English-speakers used gesture differently to accompany their verbal expressions of motion events than did Spanish- or Chinese-speakers. It remains to be seen whether the patterns we see in the deaf child's gestures can be traced back to patterns in the hearing mother's gestures.

Even if (as we suspect) the hearing mother's gestures do not serve as a model for the deaf child's expression of motion events, it is possible that other (non-verbal) aspects of the child's culture may have influenced the way the child conveys motion events in gesture. To explore this possibility, we have begun an analysis of the gestures produced by deaf children of hearing parents in a second culture, a Chinese culture. We have videotaped deaf children of hearing parents in Taiwan. Like the American deaf children in our studies, the Chinese deaf children had hearing losses so severe that they could not acquire spoken language naturally or with instruction, and their hearing parents had not yet exposed them to a conventional sign language. Thus far, we have found that the Chinese hearing mothers interact with their deaf children very differently than do the American hearing mothers (Wang *et al.*, 1993). To determine the extent to which the deaf children's gesture systems have (or have not) been shaped by their respective cultures, one can compare the gestures that the deaf children in these two cultures use to communicate. To the extent that there are similarities across the two gesture systems (particularly in the face of cultural differences in the way the mothers interact with the children), we will have evidence that such cultural factors play an insignificant role in shaping the deaf children's gesture systems. To the extent that there are differences across the children's gesture systems, we will have evidence for the role that cultural, albeit non-verbal, factors play in shaping the thoughts that the deaf children bring to their gesture systems.

7 Does a child's language affect that child's thought?

Our data suggest that there are indeed thoughts that children themselves bring to the language-learning situation, what Slobin (1996b), following Clark and Carpenter (1989), has called 'emergent categories'. Emergent categories are hypothesised to be the conceptual starting points for grammaticised notions. However, as Slobin (1996b) points out, we do not yet know whether these starting points are universal, or whether each child brings to the language-learning situation his or her own set of emergent categories. Further studies of the gesture systems generated by deaf children lacking exposure to conventional linguistic input, both within and across cultures, should provide useful data on this question.

Even if children come to the language-learning situation with a set of thoughts ripe for expression, it is clear that the language model to which the child is exposed quickly begins to shape the way those thoughts are expressed (cf. Berman and Slobin, 1994; Choi and Bowerman, 1991; although, as Gentner and Boroditsky, 1997, point out, the language model may influence some of those thoughts more than others). The Whorfian hypothesis suggests that having to express thoughts using the particular grammatical devices required by a language on a daily basis will, over time, begin to influence the way the speaker sees the world. There is evidence that language does indeed affect thought in non-linguistic tasks, but it does not appear to do so immediately. For example, Lucy and Gaskins (as reported in Lucy, 1996) have shown that, at the earliest stages of language-learning, English-speakers and Yucatec-speakers perform similarly on a series of non-verbal tasks, tasks that adult speakers have been shown to differ on – the language-learners both exhibit a pattern consistent with the structure of English. It is not until age eight that Yucatec speakers adopt the 'adult' Yucatec patterns on non-verbal tasks. Thus, linguistic structure does not appear to have an immediate impact on how children categorise the world in tasks that do not involve language. The linguistic structures the child has been producing with ease from the earliest stages of development do not appear to feed back and affect non-linguistic thought until later in development, after the structures have been used for a number of years (although the structures do appear to have an impact on *language* tasks from the very beginning, cf. Imai and Gentner, 1997).[6]

[6] Imai and Gentner (1997) have shown that the grammatical patterns found in Japanese (patterns which are comparable to those found in Yucatec Mayan) influence the child's performance on *word-learning* tasks very early in development; they found differences between Japanese-learners and learners of English on word-extension tasks as early as two years of age. However, consistent with Lucy's (1996) findings, Imai (1995) found that a group of Japanese four-year-olds, who showed the same patterns on the word-extension tasks as the Japanese two-year-olds, did *not* exhibit these patterns on a non-linguistic similarity task (see Gentner and Boroditsky, 1997, for further discussion of this point).

The question we end with is whether the deaf child's gesture system begins, over time, to feed back and influence the way that child thinks about the world. We have no direct evidence on this question since we have never tested thought in a non-communicative situation in the deaf children. Moreover, to even begin to address the Whorfian question with respect to the deaf children, we would have to distinguish between lexical vs grammatical devices for conveying particular notions in the deaf child's gesture system. It is, according to Whorf (1956), the obligatory grammatical devices – the distinctions that the grammar requires the speaker to make whether or not the speaker wishes to make them – that are likely to shape the way the speaker sees the world even when not talking.

Although we cannot directly consider the Whorfian question with respect to the deaf children, we do have some evidence that the deaf child's gesture system begins to function like a language in the sense that it influences the way in which the child eventually acquires a conventional language. Morford *et al.* (1995) explored David's acquisition of ASL, a process that he began in earnest after high school. They examined David's grasp of the morphological system of ASL at age twenty three. They compared the form-meaning mappings in David's childhood gesture system and in ASL, and found that David was much more successful acquiring the ASL forms for meanings that he *had* represented in his gesture system than he was acquiring the ASL forms for meanings that he had *not* represented in his gesture system. These findings suggest a transfer effect from childhood gesture to the acquisition of ASL. David did not differ from many others who have learned ASL late in life in that his ASL performance at age twenty three did not reach native levels, suggesting that a spontaneous childhood gesture system is not sufficient to offset the effects of isolation from a conventional language in childhood on subsequent language learning. Nevertheless, the gesture system that David developed during childhood appeared to be sufficiently ingrained that it shaped his acquisition of a conventional language in adulthood, facilitating the acquisition of just those meanings that had been captured in his early gestures.

In sum, we have examined the gesture systems of deaf children who developed their systems without benefit of a conventional language model. The thoughts that the deaf children were able to convey in their gestures are thoughts for which a language model is clearly not necessary. There may, of course, be many other thoughts that also do not require a conventional language model but that the deaf children did not express in their gestures – the thoughts we describe here represent a conservative set. Although it is difficult to see in the typical language-learning situation since the target language shapes the way thoughts are expressed from the start of acquisition (Berman and Slobin, 1994; Choi and Bowerman, 1991), children do appear to come to the language-learning situation with a set of notions that they are ready to express and grammaticise. Thus, Slobin (1985) was right all along – it just requires an atypical language-learning situation for us to be able to observe thought prior to the impact of a codified and culturally-shared linguistic system.

On the other hand, by comparing the deaf child's gestures to the earliest communication systems of children exposed to language models, we begin to see how the effects of a language model are overlaid upon the thoughts that children bring to the language-learning situation. Children may not need a language model to develop an abstract notion of path, for example, but they may need one to encourage them to operate routinely at this level of abstraction – and it may be the *routine* classifications that, in the end, affect thought both in and out of a linguistic context.

This work was supported by Grant No. RO1 DC00491 from NIH. We thank Melissa Bowerman, Jana Iverson, David McNeill, Dan Slobin and Len Talmy for their insightful and very helpful comments on earlier drafts of the manuscript.

3 The pre-requisites for language acquisition: evidence from cases of anomalous language development

Jill Boucher

1 Introduction: language acquisition and relationships between language and thought

The study of child language acquisition can make an important contribution to our understanding of relationships between language and thought. In fact, controversies concerning the pre-requisites for language acquisition have a long history paralleling almost exactly the history of controversies concerning relationships between language and thought (see the Introduction to this volume). In particular, theories of language acquisition which posit innate *domain-specific* knowledge and/or processes as necessary pre-requisites are committed to the notion that the development of language and the development of thought involve importantly independent processes. It follows that adult systems of language and thought are also likely to be independent, though of course interactive, a view which is associated with a communicative conception of the relationship between language and thought. This type of theory is also consistent with the notion of a language module, both in development and in adult function. Chomsky (1980; 1995a) and Pinker (1994) are well known exponents of this type of theory. Conversely, theories which posit innate *domain-general* cognitive processes as the main engines of language acquisition are committed to the notion that language and thought involve shared processes in development and in adult function, a view which is more consistent with the cognitive conception of the relationship between language and thought. This type of theory is not consistent with the notion of an innate domain-specific language module operating during development. However, it is perfectly consistent with the child's *gradual acquisition* of a body of domain-specific linguistic knowledge and skills. The best-known current theory of this type is that proposed by Bates and MacWhinney (1987). However, others developing connectionist models of language acquisition would also be identified with this type of theory (see for example Elman, 1991).

It is important to notice that innateness is not the critical variable differentiating between these two contrasting types of theory. Even Skinner's (1957) behaviourist theory of language acquisition (an extreme example of a 'domain-general' theory) assumed that innate learning mechanisms are necessary for normal language acquisition. Moreover, evidence from deaf children reared in non-signing environments (see for example Goldin-Meadow and Zheng, chapter 2, this volume) and from children's creation of Creole languages (Bickerton, 1984) shows clearly that there is an innate propensity and preparedness to develop language which will assert itself in the absence of linguistic input. Current theories therefore all agree that language acquisition is heavily dependent on innate 'givens'. The live issue concerns what these innate givens might be.

The main aim of this paper is to look at evidence from children with impaired language development, and from mentally retarded individuals with anomalously spared language development, which bears on this issue. It is increasingly recognised that the study of developmental disorders can help us to understand normal development and subsequent adult function. Autism and Williams syndrome, for example, have been widely cited over recent years as demonstrating the existence of an innately determined capacity for social cognition and an innate language acquisition mechanism, respectively. A subsidiary aim of this chapter is to demonstrate that the evidence from developmental disorders has been under-exploited, but at the same time to suggest that the evidence is more complex than it is often represented as being.

Before I consider this evidence, however, I will outline three theories of the pre-requisites for first language acquisition, namely the theories proposed by Chomsky (1980; 1995a), by Locke (1993), and by Bates and MacWhinney (1987). I will focus on a small number of contrasting claims which these theories make concerning the necessary conditions for normal language development. In making use of the theories as exemplars of particular hypotheses which I wish to examine, I understate the theories, and emphasise their differences at the expense of their similarities. I could, in fact, have stated the five hypotheses examined in isolation of any particular theories. However, that might have suggested that I plucked them out of the air, which would be untrue. In the section reviewing the evidence from impaired and anomalous language development, I will assess whether or not the evidence confirms or disconfirms predictions made on the basis of the contrasting hypotheses.

2 Theories of child language acquisition

2.1 Chomsky's theory

Chomsky (1980; 1995a) argues that normal children are born with a Language Faculty consisting of a non-modality-specific cognitive system (which I will refer to, *pace* Chomsky, as a grammar acquisition mechanism), plus input and output performance components, and close links with the non-linguistic central conceptual–intentional system. The grammar acquisition mechanism (GAM) consists of a genetically fixed, domain-specific computational procedure instantiating knowledge of the universal principles and parameters of grammar. The computational procedure within GAM computes information concerning structure dependencies in the input language, sets grammatical parameters according to the input, and deduces the phonological rules of the language. The input and output performance components of the Language Faculty subserve perception and articulation in the case of spoken language, and GAM interacts with these components via sets of instructions known as phonetic forms. The central conceptual–intentional system is not part of the Language Faculty. However, Chomsky maintains that conceptual knowledge, like linguistic knowledge, is largely innate. The conceptual–intentional system subserves the acquisition of meaning and vocabulary, as well as the acquisition of pragmatic knowledge and discourse skills. GAM interacts with the conceptual–intentional system via sets of instructions known as logical forms. Chomsky claims that language is not learned, but rather that it 'grows' or matures along a pre-determined path, given some minimum amount of normal linguistic input and an environment free of 'excessive trauma'.

In Sections 3.2 and 3.3 I will consider the evidence from cases of impaired and anomalous language development relating to Chomsky's claims: (i) that there is a *grammar-specific computational mechanism*; and (ii) that this mechanism *instantiates knowledge of universal grammar.*

2.2 Locke's theory

Locke (1993) accepts the need to postulate some kind of innately determined grammar-analysis mechanism. However, Locke's theory differs from Chomsky's in three critical ways. First, he describes the mechanism which undertakes grammar analysis as instantiating a process (or processes) that segments utterances at a variety of levels (phonological, syllabic, clausal etc.), learns the distribution of these segments in the child's own language, and abstracts rules from perceived regularities. This implies that the mechanism is not specific to the acquisition of grammar, but that it operates pre-linguistically (for example, when the infant is acquiring knowledge of the intonation patterns, phonemes, and phonological rules of the language) as well as during the acquisition of grammar. Locke's proposed mechanism is therefore a language-specific mechanism and not a grammar-specific mechanism.

The second important way in which Locke's theory differs from Chomsky's is that Locke makes no claim concerning innate knowledge as a pre-requisite for normal grammar acquisition. The poverty of the stimulus and learnability problems which motivate Chomsky's claim that innate knowledge is a pre-requisite for normal language development, are not discussed by Locke.

The third important difference between Locke's and Chomsky's theories is that Locke stresses the need for a second innately determined system which he describes as a specialisation for social cognition. This system drives the pre-linguistic development of social interaction, communication, and acquisition of early vocabulary comprehension and production. The proposed specialisation consists of innate capacities for responding preferentially to faces and to voices; genetically determined developments in the understanding of agency and causation, in shared attention and eye direction detection; and, on the output side, genetically determined vocal and gestural babbling. Locke's specialisation for social cognition resembles the social module described by Karmiloff-Smith *et al.* (1995) and the 'theory of mind module' discussed by others (Baron-Cohen, 1995; Carruthers, chapter 5, this volume). However, it goes beyond what others have proposed in that it includes the precursors of vocal and gestural language systems. Locke claims that the specialisation for social cognition ensures that the normally developing infant acquires a sufficient corpus of vocabulary to trigger the language-analysis mechanism into computing the rules of grammar (cf. Marchman and Bates, 1994).

In Sections 3.4 and 3.5, below, I will consider evidence relating to Locke's claims: (i) that a *language specific mechanism* underlies the segmenting and analysis of language in the pre-linguistic child as well as in the child who is in the process of acquiring grammar; and (ii) that a *specialisation for social cognition* is a pre-requisite for normal pre-speech development and for the acquisition of a critical corpus of vocabulary.

2.3 Bates and MacWhinney's theory

Bates and MacWhinney (1987) argue that those processes which can be built into connectionist models of language acquisition will be found to correspond to the innate but domain-general processes which are pre-requisite for language acquisition. These processes would include perceptual analysis, imitation, association, stimulus competition, and memory (Bates *et al.*, 1988, pp. 13–27; Bates *et al.*, 1991). The critical question concerning exactly how such domain-general processes deliver grammar is not answered, and, again, the poverty of the stimulus and learnability problems are not directly tackled.

Bates and MacWhinney agree with Locke that children's pre-linguistic development is innately determined in that certain attentional biases and pre-programmed behaviours come on stream and underpin conceptual development, early symbolic development, and pre-linguistic communicative behaviour. Bates and MacWhinney also agree with Locke in hypothesising that pre-grammatical and grammatical development involve the same processes, the difference between pre-grammatical and grammatical development lying in the corpus of knowledge on which the grammar-learning child operates as opposed to that on which the pre-grammatical child operates. In this, Bates and MacWhinney, and also Locke, differ from Chomsky, who considers that pre-grammatical and grammatical development depend on different and dissociable processes.

In Section 3.6. I will briefly consider how evidence already reviewed relates to Bates and MacWhinney's claim that language development is dependent on *domain-general processes.* In Section 4 of the paper, I will try to move the arguments forward in ways consistent with the evidence and arguments presented throughout Section 3.

3 Evidence from anomalous language development relating to theories of language acquisition and to relationships between language and thought

3.1 Developmental disorders as a source of evidence concerning normal development

Developmental disorders can be defined as disorders of psychological development occurring in children as a result of congenital or early acquired pathology. Disorders include impairments of sensation, perception, movement, attention, learning/cognition, social development and language. They specifically exclude psychiatric conditions (of organic or environmental origin), but may overlap with them. Most developmental disorders impair language acquisition in one way or another.

The evidence from individuals with any particular named disorder is quite heterogeneous, and it might be suggested that heterogeneity undermines the usefulness of this kind of evidence. However, given the many sources of heterogeneity which undoubtedly exist, what is remarkable is the homogeneity which makes it possible to reliably diagnose most developmental conditions using behavioural criteria. This homogeneity argues for there being some consistent causal links between certain types of aetiology, brain pathology and abnormal psychological development, and against unconstrained brain plasticity and unconstrained scope for psychological compensation. Heterogeneity introduces noise into the data, but not so much as to undermine its usefulness.

The developmental disorders which should tell us most about the prerequisites for language acquisition are (1) specific language impairments, and (2) mental retardation in forms in which language development is anomalously spared. I will briefly describe these two broad categories of developmental disorder.

(1) Specific Language Impairment (SLI) is defined by exclusion criteria: i.e. SLI is only diagnosed if a child has significant language learning difficulties but does not suffer from mental retardation, hearing loss, psychiatric disorder, clear neurological deficit, or deprivation. In theory at least, therefore, SLI is a 'pure' language learning disorder, just as developmental dyslexia is, in theory at least, a 'pure' reading/literacy disorder. Children with SLI show a variety of patterns of delay and abnormality in the comprehension and/or production of phonology, syntax, morphology, semantics and also pragmatics. There is a lack of agreement concerning a detailed taxonomy of this mixed and overlapping group of impairments. However, a taxonomy recently proposed by Rapin (1996), which would be accepted by most people working in this field, is summarised below:

Taxonomy of Specific Language Impairments (after Rapin, 1996)

(A) Mixed disorders affecting both language comprehension and expression:

- (a) *Verbal auditory agnosia*. This is characterised by profoundly impaired comprehension resulting from impaired ability to decode phonology. The severe impairment of comprehension causes profoundly impaired acquisition of linguistic knowledge and, therefore, of expressive language.
- (b) *Phonologic-syntactic disorder*. This is characterised by impaired language output consisting of short often ungrammatical utterances, impaired phonology, and limited vocabulary. Comprehension is also impaired, though usually to a lesser extent than language

expression. Phonologic-syntactic disorder is the most common form of SLI.

(B) Expressive disorders in which comprehension is normal or near normal:
   (a) *Verbal dyspraxia*. This is characterised by sparse speech output and very poor phonology. Speech is disjointed and non-fluent.
   (b) *Speech programming deficit disorder*. This is a subtype of verbal dyspraxia in which speech is fluent, but the phonology is so distorted as to produce the effect of jargon.

(C) Higher-order processing disorders:
   (a) *Lexical deficit disorder*. This is characterised by difficulties in understanding connected speech, although single words and short phrases can be understood. There is severe word-finding difficulty. This, and the problem with comprehension, disrupts conversation making it disjointed and hard to follow. Spontaneous language is superior to language on demand.
   (b) *Semantic-pragmatic deficit disorder*. This resembles lexical deficit disorder except in that the child's conversational ability is particularly impaired. Conversation is characterised by poor comprehension of connected speech, word-finding deficits, atypical and often inappropriate word choices, and verbosity. Phonology and syntax are, however, relatively unimpaired.

(2) Forms of overall mental retardation in which language learning capacities are anomalously spared include Williams syndrome and cases of hydrocephalus. In Williams syndrome, overall intelligence is low but social development and language development are much less impaired (though not entirely normal). Hydrocephalic children, like children with Williams syndrome, are sociable and chatty, with relatively good language, despite being mentally retarded overall and in need of special education and life-long care. In addition to types of mental retardation in which language acquisition and communication are typically spared, other occasional cases are reported of atypical individuals with mental retardation and spared language. Very rarely, a mentally retarded person has truly savant linguistic abilities. In the majority of cases, however, language acquisition is not normal or is in the low normal range, and is only striking by virtue of its superiority to other aspects of development.

3.2 *Evidence relating to Chomsky's claim that language acquisition involves a grammar-specific mechanism*

If a grammar-specific mechanism underpins normal grammar development, grammar development will dissociate from all or most other aspects of development in some children. Specifically, there should be (A) an identifiable group of children who have *impaired* grammar acquisition in absence of any other significant impairments (except those which result from the grammatical impairment, such as poor literacy skills and low school attainment). Conversely, there should be (B) individual children in whom *unimpaired* grammar development dissociates from other aspects of development (except those which are minimally necessary for the pre-grammatical infant to reach a stage of readiness to develop grammar).

It is important to notice that prediction A is stronger than prediction B in that it claims that a dissociation between impaired grammar acquisition and unimpaired development in all other domains will be found within individual children, whereas prediction B only claims that a dissociation between spared grammar acquisition and other individual aspects of development will be found across numbers of individual children. The difference in the predictions results from the fact that whereas it is reasonable to suppose that an innately specified GAM might be uniquely *impaired* in individual children, it is much less reasonable to suppose that such a mechanism should be uniquely *spared* in individual children.

If impairments in grammar acquisition can occur in the absence of other developmental delays and deficiencies (prediction A), then this impairment will present as a form of specific language impairment (SLI). This is because 'specific' as used here means precisely 'selective', or 'isolated', and a diagnosis of SLI is only made if various other causes of impaired language development have been excluded (see Section 3.1). However, the evidence from SLI does not appear to support prediction A.

In the first place, the taxonomy of specific language impairments reproduced in Section 3.1 does not include a group of children with unimpaired vocabulary development in whom the comprehension and production of grammatical language is uniquely impaired. It might be argued that defective grammar development would have secondary effects on the development of vocabulary, so that a 'pure' grammatical impairment was never observed. This is fair argument. However, the early stages of language development involve the acquisition of vocabulary only, and there is no research or clinical evidence to suggest that there is any group of children who develop first words at the normal age, who build up the critical corpus of approximately 400 vocabulary items at the normal age and then abruptly develop difficulties in the acquisition of grammar. In other words, there is no such thing as 'late-onset SLI' (as there is, for example, 'late-onset autism').[1]

It might be argued that GAM is unusually immune to breakdown and that the large majority of cases of SLI result from abnormalities in the performance components of the Language Faculty, or in the conceptual–intentional system. It is certainly true that some of the subtypes of SLI described by Rapin (1996) might be explained in this way. In particular, verbal auditory agnosia (Aa in the list above) by definition results from abnormalities in the spoken language input system, and it is significant that children with this form of SLI can learn sign language. Verbal dyspraxia (Ba) and speech programming deficit (Bb) might be explained in terms of abnormalities in the spoken language output system, and be described as speech problems, rather than as language problems. However, this is a controversial issue (Stackhouse, 1992). If verbal dyspraxia and speech programming deficit were speech performance deficits then children should make spontaneous use of compensatory signing, and have normal hand praxis and hand movement programming. The fact that on the whole they don't (Crary, 1993) suggests that in a majority of cases the problems are a-modal and that therefore they constitute language disorders. In Chomsky's model, non-modality-specific language impairments must derive from deficits either within GAM or at the level of phonetic – and the signing equivalent – forms, rather than in the performance components of the language faculty. Verbal dyspraxia and speech programming deficit might therefore, on Chomsky's model, be best explained as resulting from some problem at the level of phonetic forms. Less controversially, lexical deficit disorder (Ca) and semantic-pragmatic deficit disorder (Cb) would, within Chomsky's model, be explained in terms of abnormalities in the conceptual–intentional system.

It would be difficult to explain receptive-expressive phonologic-syntactic disorder (the most common form of SLI) as deriving from defects in the performance components of the Language Faculty, or in the conceptual system. On Chomsky's model, therefore, phonologic-syntactic disorder must derive from a defect in GAM. Phonologic-syntactic disorder does not, however, fit the pattern of impairments predicted by Chomsky's theory. In the first place, and most importantly, this disorder always manifests early in the form of delayed speech onset and delayed acquisition of first words and the critical corpus of vocabulary (Locke, 1994). In the second place, once language acquisition has begun, vocabulary remains impaired,

[1] There are cases in which children who have already begun to learn language sustain brain damage which impairs language. These children are described as cases of acquired child language disorder, or developmental dysphasia, and they show a quite different pattern of language difficulties from those shown by children with SLI.

although to a lesser extent than phonology and grammar. In the third place, comprehension, though impaired, is generally better than production, which is hard to explain using Chomsky's model.

No subtypes of SLI, therefore, show the pattern of impairments which would follow from a defect in GAM. But neither can all subtypes of SLI be explained in terms of defects in the performance components of the Language Faculty or in the conceptual intentional system. There is, in addition, a quite different type of evidence from SLI which is at odds with Chomsky's theory. This is the evidence indicating that the impairments of language which occur in SLI are not as selective, or isolated, as they were at one time thought to be. Nor can these additional impairments be explained as the consequences of impaired language development. For example, children with SLI have, as a group, significantly more difficulty than controls in perceiving and reproducing rhythmic sequences (Kracke, 1975). They also have impaired perception of transient or rapidly changing sensory inputs and impaired production of rapid co-ordinated motor outputs (Tallal *et al.*, 1985; Tallal *et al.*, 1991; Vargha-Khadem *et al.*, 1995). They have impaired auditory verbal memory (Gathercole and Baddeley, 1989; Shields *et al.*, 1996); impaired visual memory (Fein *et al.*, 1996), and impaired use of anticipatory visual imagery (Johnston and Ellis Weismer, 1983). It is possible, of course, that group-based research findings conceal the existence of a small minority of children with SLI who do not have any additional impairments. However, in view of the number of studies in which these additional impairments have been reliably demonstrated, such children, if they exist, must be few and far between.

Evidence in support of prediction B – that *unimpaired* grammar development will dissociate from other aspects of development (except those which are minimally necessary for the pre-linguistic infant to reach a stage of readiness to develop grammar) – should be found amongst mentally handicapped children with anomalously spared language development. What we might expect to observe, if Chomsky's claim about a grammar-specific mechanism is correct, are cases of mentally handicapped people in whom there is a history of delayed language onset and slow acquisition of early vocabulary, followed by a spurt in grammatical development, with vocabulary development significantly lagging. This is not, in fact, what is observed in most cases of anomalously spared language development. In cases of hydrocephalus or Williams syndrome, for example, although language onset is delayed (as would be predicted by Chomsky's theory), once language begins to develop, vocabulary acquisition is strikingly good (which is not predicted by Chomsky's theory). Two individual cases have been reported in which grammar is *somewhat* superior to vocabulary, and also to discourse. One of these cases is Françoise, a thirty-year-old woman described by Rondal (1994). Françoise has Down's syndrome but in an atypical form in which language development and use is relatively spared, phonology and syntax being somewhat superior to vocabulary and considerably superior to discourse. The second individual in whom grammar has been reported to be superior to vocabulary and discourse is Anthony, a retarded boy described by Curtiss and Yamada (1981). However, what is striking about both of these individuals is not how poor their vocabulary is relative to their grammar, but how good it is relative to their intelligence and most of their other abilities.

There is, therefore, little evidence to support that part of prediction B which suggests that relatively unimpaired grammar development should dissociate in at least some cases from other aspects of language development, and particularly from vocabulary. Is there any evidence to support that part of prediction B which suggests that unimpaired grammar development can also dissociate from other aspects of normal development? (excepting those which must be present for the child to reach the stage of readiness for grammar).

In children with Williams syndrome, language development (but not specifically grammar-development) dissociates from both verbal and non-verbal intelligence (as measured on IQ tests) to a striking degree. However, it does not dissociate from relatively intact social cognition and pragmatic competence, nor from at least one area of cognitive ability, namely immediate auditory–verbal memory (Karmiloff-Smith *et al.*, 1995).

In an in-depth study of a girl with hydrocephalus carried out when she was in her mid-teens (DH, reported by Cromer, 1994) relatively intact language ability (not restricted to grammar) again dissociates dramatically from both verbal and non-verbal intelligence, including auditory–verbal immediate memory and also a visual measure of the proposed general factor in intelligence, known as 'g' (Anderson, 1992). However, as in the case of children with Williams syndrome, DH's language system acquisition is not dissociated from relatively intact social cognition (including successful performance on a false belief task) and pragmatic competence. DH also performs well on a hierarchical ordering task, and, most remarkably, she performs quite well on the 'cognitive estimates' task in which the individual is asked to estimate such things as the weight of a pint of milk, or the number of slices in a loaf of bread.

The fascinating but quite brief report of Kate, a savant poet with mild cerebral palsy, overall mental retardation, and autistic traits is a striking example of the fact that a dissociation can occur between high levels of linguistic ability (not, however, confined to grammar) and low levels of social cognition as well as of intelligence (as measured on IQ tests) and other cognitive abilities (Dowker *et al.*, 1996).

In the case of Françoise (Rondal, 1994), already referred to, relatively normal grammar contrasts not only with rather poorer vocabulary, and very poor discourse skills, but also with low verbal and non-verbal intelligence (verbal IQ 67; non-verbal IQ 53). Good grammar also dissociates from immediate auditory–verbal memory, which was commensurate with other scores on intelligence tests. There is no evidence concerning Françoise's visual memory abilities. However, Rondall reports that Françoise was taught to speak and write from the age of four and a half. (Teaching some minimal language to children with Down's syndrome using the visuo-motor modalities is common, since these channels of communication are usually less impaired than the auditory–verbal modalities.) It seems likely, therefore, that Françoise suffers to at least some extent from the auditory–verbal processing problems that are typical of Down's syndrome, but that she has some anomalously spared visual processing abilities, which could include visual memory.

Extensive tests of linguistic and non-linguistic abilities showed that Anthony (Curtiss and Yamada, 1981), then aged between six and seven, had expressive language in which many aspects of grammar were at age-appropriate, or above age-appropriate, level. The only other ability at a comparable level was immediate auditory–verbal memory, which was above average for his age. These abilities contrasted with poorer semantic and pragmatic skills, poor social skills, and extremely poor or unmeasurable performance on tests of drawing, jig-saw puzzle completion, Piagetian tasks of conservation and classification, tests of hierarchical construction, and of constructional and pretend play.

In sum, therefore, there is evidence which shows that grammar and other aspects of language can develop relatively normally in individuals with poor social cognition, such as Kate or Anthony. Language also develops normally in people with Asperger's syndrome, who are not mentally retarded, but who have severely impaired social interaction and social cognition. There is also clear evidence that grammar and language in general can develop relatively normally in people who perform very poorly on standardised intelligence tests, including verbal subtests, and in individuals with a low measure of 'g'. Most strikingly, the evidence shows unambiguously that language can develop relatively normally, or in rare cases entirely normally, in people who have difficulty in acquiring day-to-day competencies in those simple, practical skills which might enable them to live independent lives, such as tying their own shoe laces or planning and preparing a simple meal. However, the evidence also suggests that people with anomalously spared language development often have spared immediate auditory–verbal memory and/or visual memory.

Does this evidence prove Chomsky's claim that grammar acquisition is subserved by a grammar-specific mechanism? The answer here is that evidence for a *grammar-specific* mechanism is almost entirely lacking. Only Françoise and Anthony show some degree of the predicted dissociation of grammar from vocabulary acquisition, and, as pointed out above, what is striking about both of these individuals is not how poor their vocabulary is relative to their grammar, but how good it is relative to their intelligence. The available evidence is, however, consistent with there being a *language-specific* mechanism, and this point will be pursued in the next section, when Locke's theory is discussed. Nor does the available evidence rule out the possibility that *domain-general* processes are both necessary and sufficient for language acquisition, and one facet of the evidence, namely the sparing of immediate memory, might be seen as giving this type of theory some encouragement. This point will be pursued in the final section of the chapter.

3.3 Evidence relating to Chomsky's claim that children have innate knowledge of universal grammar

If Chomsky's claim is correct, there should be a group of children with SLI in whom knowledge of the principles and parameters of universal grammar is wholly or partly lacking. The taxonomy of subtypes of SLI outlined in Section 3.1 suggests that these children should be found amongst those with receptive–expressive phonologic-syntactic deficit disorder, for reasons outlined in Section 3.2. Unfortunately, few research studies have focused exclusively on this subgroup of children. However, since it is the most common type of SLI it may be assumed that in studies which merely state that 'children with SLI' were tested, the majority of children will have had phonologic-syntactic disorder.

Bishop (1992) reviewed the evidence from SLI relating to the claim that children have innate knowledge of the principles and parameters of universal grammar, and concluded that it 'is both logically inadequate . . . and inconsistent from one study to another'. The evidence reviewed by Bishop is quite extensive. A typical pair of studies from amongst those reviewed examined grammatical errors in English and Italian children with SLI (Leonard *et al.*, 1987, 1988). These studies found that morphological errors did not follow the pattern predicted by Chomsky's theory, and that the patterns of errors which the children made were more easily explained in terms of perceptual limitations.

Recent work by van der Lely and her colleagues (summarised in van der Lely, 1996) claims to show that children with SLI lack knowledge of Binding Principles (one of the principles of universal grammar). However, van der Lely describes the interpretation of her findings as tentative.

Gopnik and Crago's (1991) claim to have identified an extended family in which half the members were affected with morphological 'feature blindness' looked at first to be just the kind of finding which might support Chomsky's claim concerning innate knowledge of universal grammar. However, members of this family appear to suffer from what are primarily expressive and especially articulatory language difficulties rather than the combined receptive–expressive difficulties which Chomsky's theory predicts (Fletcher, 1990). Moreover recent research shows that affected members of the family have wide-ranging intellectual and motor-output impairments, in addition to their expressive language deficits (Vargha-Khadem *et al.*, 1995). The specificity of the linguistic impairment in Family K is therefore disputed.

In sum, there is either negative, or at best tentative or disputed evidence from cases of SLI, where the evidence should be found, in support of the claim that children have innate knowledge of the principles and parameters of universal grammar. This suggests that Chomsky's claim is likely in the longer term to prove incorrect.

3.4 Evidence relating to Locke's claim that language acquisition involves a language-specific segmenting and analysis mechanism

If a language-specific mechanism underpins normal language development, language development will dissociate from all or most other aspects of development in at least some children. Specifically, there should be (A) an identifiable group of children who have *impaired* language acquisition in absence of any other significant impairments (except those which result from the language impairment). Conversely, there should be (B) individual children in whom *unimpaired* language development dissociates from other aspects of development (except those which are minimally necessary for the infant to reach a stage of readiness to develop language).

If impairments in language acquisition can occur in the absence of other developmental delays and deficiencies (prediction A), then this impairment will present as a form of SLI (see Section 3.2). The definition of SLI in terms of exclusion criteria in fact constitutes an implicit endorsement of Locke's claim that one of the critical pre-requisites for language acquisition is a language-specific processing mechanism. Moreover, the subtype of SLI described as receptive–expressive phonologic/syntactic disorder fits moderately well with the pattern of impairments which would be predicted by Locke's claim. Specifically, phonologic/syntactic disorder manifests early (as do all other forms of SLI), and is probably detectable first in terms of reduced output of babbling (Locke, 1994) although usually detected clinically by the child's late onset of language. In addition, phonologic/syntactic disorder affects language system development at all levels, namely phonological, syntactic, morphemic, and semantic; it also affects both comprehension and production. The fact that production is more affected than comprehension is not, however, so obviously consistent with Locke's theory.

Locke's theory also comes up against the same difficulty as Chomsky's, in that language acquisition impairments are not now generally considered to be as specific, or isolated, as was once thought to be the case, there being considerable evidence of abnormalities of perception, motor output, and both auditory and visual memory which cannot be seen as the secondary consequences of language impairment (see Section 3.2). As discussed in Section 3.2, it is possible that group-based studies conceal the existence of occasional children who do not have any additional, non-linguistic impairments. However, the regular occurrence of a consistent set of additional non-linguistic impairments in the majority of the children with SLI must tend to weaken Locke's claim that a language-specific mechanism, rather than domain general processes, underlies normal language development.

Evidence in support of prediction B – that *unimpaired* language development will dissociate from other aspects of development – should be found amongst mentally handicapped children with anomalously spared language development. Here the evidence reviewed in Section 3.2 is fairly consistent with Locke's theory. The fact that spared language ability is frequently (and possibly always) accompanied by spared immediate memory could be accommodated within the theory by claiming that both a language-specific acquisition mechanism and certain domain-general cognitive processes are jointly necessary and sufficient for language acquisition. Indeed, neither Locke nor Chomsky claim that a language-acquisition mechanism or Language Faculty are sufficient as well as necessary for language development. The challenge that both these theories face is the question of whether domain-general processes including spared memory are sufficient as well as necessary for language acquisition.

3.5 Evidence relating to Locke's claim that a specialisation for social cognition is a pre-requisite for the acquisition of early vocabulary

Locke's proposed specialisation covers a wide range of biologically determined attentional biases, perceptual predispositions, and motor processes which manifest during infancy (see Section 2.2). Some of these fall within what Karmiloff-Smith *et al.* (1995) have called a 'social module', and include what others have called a 'theory of mind module' (Baron-Cohen, 1995). Others appear to be more specifically related to language, and constitute a readiness for spoken language perception and production, and also, importantly, a readiness for visuo-motor language perception and production. Thus, for example, there is well-documented evidence that young infants produce 'gestural babble' and are biologically primed to develop visuo-motor language as well as being biologically primed to develop spoken language (Acredolo and Goodwyn, 1990).

The fact that children with Asperger's syndrome develop language relatively normally tends to suggest that social interaction and social cognition are not pre-requisites for the normal development of language. However, children with Asperger's syndrome usually have somewhat delayed language onset, despite their normal intelligence. Moreover, high functioning children with autism, who are more severely socially withdrawn than children with Asperger's syndrome, have more severely delayed language onset and persistently impaired language, even when their non-verbal intelligence is normal or superior. It seems likely, therefore, and also intuitively plausible, that some minimum level of social interaction and social cognition is a pre-requisite for the acquisition of first words and a critical corpus of vocabulary. Similarly, we can conclude from the fact that children with hydrocephalus or Williams syndrome have delayed language onset, that some minimum level of overall intelligence is also necessary for the acquisition of early vocabulary.

It is much less certain that language can develop normally in individuals who lack the normal non-modality-specific biological readiness for pre-linguistic language processing and production. Children who are later diagnosed as cases of SLI show very early signs of impaired ability to process and produce language (Locke, 1994). Moreover, unlike children with Asperger's syndrome or children with Williams syndrome, children with SLI do not develop normal grammar once a critical corpus of utterance material has been acquired. Nor do they develop the same pattern of *delayed and limited* grammar as children with high functioning autism. Rather, they have *deviant* development of grammar. This suggests that whatever factor, or factors, contributes to delayed acquisition of utterance material in children with SLI, subsequently causes abnormalities in the acquisition of grammar.

The evidence from Asperger's syndrome and from SLI, taken together, therefore tend to suggest that Locke's proposed specialisation for social cognition should be subdivided into those biologically determined predispositions and abilities which underlie social interaction, social cognition, and communication, as opposed to those which underlie language-system acquisition. The former may be essential at some minimum level to ensure that the child acquires first words, just as some minimum level of intelligence is required for the child to reach this stage. However, fully normal social abilities are not a necessary condition for language-system acquisition, any more than fully normal intelligence is a necessary condition. By contrast, certain language-system-related predispositions and abilities *are* a necessary condition of normal language development.

What remains to be discussed, is whether these language-related abilities are *language-specific*, or whether they are *domain-general*. This issue is considered next.

3.6 Evidence relating to Bates and MacWhinney's claim that domain-general processes underlie normal language acquisition

If Bates and MacWhinney (1987) are correct in suggesting that no grammar-specific or language-specific mechanisms are necessary for language development, then there would be no such developmental disorder, or group of related disorders, as SLI. Rather, there would be a number of sub-types of developmental language disorder resulting from deficits in whatever domain-general processes underlie normal language acquisition, and these language disorders would always be accompanied by additional behaviour impairments resulting from these same domain-general deficits. This is, in fact, consistent with the available evidence, since developmental language disorders do not appear to occur in 'pure' form (see Section 3.2; also Bishop, 1992). Equally, however, if Bates and MacWhinney are correct in suggesting that no grammar-specific or language-specific mechanisms are necessary for language development, then amongst children with anomalously spared language development those domain-general processes which underlie language development must also be consistently spared. Here the available evidence lines up against Bates and MacWhinney, with the possible exception of the existence of spared immediate memory.

4 Conclusion

4.1 An interpretation of the evidence in relation to theories of language development

It appears, therefore, that the available evidence from children with impaired language development and from children with anomalously spared language development is contradictory. On balance, the evidence from what I will continue to call SLI despite having argued against the specificity of the language impairments, tends to support the case for domain-general processes as necessary and sufficient for normal language acquisition: these children have problems from early infancy (which argues against a grammar-specific mechanism), and SLI is generally accompanied by non-linguistic developmental impairments (which argues against a language-specific mechanism). On the other hand, the evidence from children with anomalously spared language tends to support the case for a language-specific mechanism: vocabulary as well as grammar is conspicuously spared (which argues against a grammar-specific mechanism), and spared language dissociates from most if not all other aspects of development (which argues against domain-general processes).

How might these conflicting conclusions be reconciled? The most obvious and least interesting way out of the quandary is to question the adequacy of the available evidence. It is open to those who support the notion of a grammar-specific mechanism, for example, to claim that although clinicians such as Rapin (1996) do not identify any subgroup of children with grammar-specific, late-onset SLI, such children may occur, if rarely. Equally, it is open to those who support the notion of a language-specific mechanism to claim that although group studies indicate that children with SLI have a consistent set of additional impairments, group studies may mask the existence of occasional children with pure forms of SLI. Finally, those who claim that domain-general processes are sufficient for language acquisition may suggest that it is difficult to demonstrate spared abilities (even spared language ability) using formal tests with mentally handicapped people (Cromer, 1994, for example, describes how difficult it was to demonstrate DH's excellent vocabulary using formal tests), or that the critical domain-general abilities have not been looked for.

Further research is always desirable. However, questioning the adequacy of the evidence looks in this case suspiciously like clutching at straws. The available evidence may not be in quite the form we would like, or quite the evidence which supports our favoured theory, but there is plenty of evidence, and we ought to be able to make at least provisional sense of it. Having made provisional sense of what is available, then, of course, further research will be needed to test out whatever tentative conclusion is reached.

My own tentative conclusion is that the evidence from SLI and from cases of anomalous language development can be reconciled by suggesting that certain domain-general processes (other than those which can be taken as read – e.g. hearing and vision, and basic learning mechanisms such as conditioning and association) are critical pre-requisites for language acquisition, but that these processes subserve only a limited set of functions other than language development. These functions must clearly be related to the non-linguistic impairments which co-occur with SLI, and to consistently spared non-linguistic abilities in cases of anomalously spared language development. This points us towards immediate memory (whether auditory–verbal or visual), which is impaired in SLI and spared more often than would be expected to occur by chance in cases of anomalous language development. The evidence from SLI also points to the ability to perceive and to programme rapid sequential or transient inputs and outputs. These abilities have not, to the best of my knowledge, been assessed in cases of anomalous language development and clearly in cases such as that of Kate, the savant poet who is also mildly cerebral palsied, any such abilities would be masked by neuromuscular disorder. However, it may be significant that people with Williams syndrome appreciate music and are able to play musical instruments and to dance, things which they would not be able to do if they could not process transient sequential and rhythmical inputs and outputs relatively normally. Immediate memory, and the perception and production of serially ordered inputs or outputs, all involve complex temporal processing mechanisms (Treisman *et al.*, 1994; Burgess and Hitch, 1994; Brown *et al.*, in press). Immediate memory, and the perception and production of serially ordered inputs and outputs are all critically involved in acquiring language. It therefore seems plausible to hypothesise not only that impaired temporal processing causes or contributes to SLI, as Tallal and her colleagues suggest (Tallal *et al.*, 1985; Tallal *et al.*, 1991) but also that spared temporal processing relates critically to the phenomenon of anomalously spared language development.

It is beyond the scope of this paper to attempt to justify this statement or to relate impaired temporal processing to models of language acquisition in any detail. However, complex hierarchically ordered temporal processors appear to correspond well to the segmenting component of the language acquisition mechanism posited by Locke (1993). Hierarchically ordered temporal processing will also deliver information concerning the (temporal) distribution of segments (e.g. phonemes, syllables, morphemes) in the child's own language. Computation is then required to construct rules from perceived regularities in the distribution of the various segments, or elements. Might the computational mechanism be language-specific, despite the fact that the temporal processing/segmenting mechanism subserves non-linguistic as well as linguistic functions? This seems possible. And if it is language-specific, might the mechanism instantiate linguistic knowledge, as Chomsky suggested? This also seems possible, so long as the mechanism is involved in language all the way down, and not just from the onset of grammar (since we do not see cases of late-onset, grammar-specific SLI). On the other hand, it may be that a general purpose statistical computational mechanism would be capable of extracting the phonological, grammatical and semantic rules of language (Chater and Conkey, 1994), especially given the distributional information provided by the temporal processing/segmenting mechanism.

4.2 *Implications of the evidence from anomalous language development concerning relationships between language and thought*

Having, without any prior intention, followed the golden rule of the good negotiator and allowed all the contestants to win at least parts of the argument, I am left with a somewhat mixed message concerning the implications of the evidence I have reviewed for theories of the relationship between language and thought.

In the Introduction to this chapter I suggested that evidence concerning the pre-requisites for first language acquisition bears indirectly on the issue of how language and thought may be related. Specifically I suggested that theories which claim that domain-specific mechanisms are necessary for language acquisition are broadly consistent with a communicative conception of language, whereas theories which do not make such claims are more consistent with a cognitive conception of language. The evidence I have reviewed argues against strong versions of either type of language acquisition theory and indirectly against strong theories of either the independence, or the inseparability, of language and thought. If we look beyond the processes of language acquisition in children with disordered or anomalous language development we have further evidence which suggests that neither strong theory of the relationship between language and thought is correct. For example, if language were constitutive of thought, then children with Williams syndrome or hydrocephalus would be relatively normal thinkers, which they patently are not. However, if language acquisition was independent of thought, then children with Williams syndrome and hydrocephalus might be expected to use their language less appropriately than they do: their language would be markedly formulaic and unrelated to ongoing reality, which it is not. Similarly, if language were constitutive of thought, all children with abnormally poor language acquisition would be overall learning impaired, which they are not. And if language were independent of thought, then children with SLI should have normally distributed non-verbal cognitive abilities, which they don't: the distribution of non-verbal IQ in children with SLI is heavily weighted towards the lower end of the normal range i.e. between IQ 75 and 100 (SLI is defined as occurring only in children with intelligence within normal limits).

In order to make sense of observations such as these and many others within the literature on developmental disorders, we are going to have to be much more analytic than at present about what we refer to as 'thinking', 'cognition', and 'intelligence' in development. So, for example, we will need to analyse what genetically determined tendencies and processes the child with Williams syndrome brings to the acquisition of categories, concepts, semantics and then grammar which have no effective bearing on that child's ability to respond to verbal subtests of intelligence tests. We need to look at relationships between the hypothetical 'g' factor in intelligence and spared abilities in mentally retarded individuals, as well between 'g' and impaired abilities in children with SLI. This type of analysis should help to clarify relationships between subcomponents of cognition and subcomponents of language and communication during development and, in the longer term, help us to understand relationships between language and thought in normal adults.

I am grateful to Peter Carruthers and John Locke for their critical comments on early drafts of this chapter.

4 Some thoughts about the evolution of LADS, with special reference to TOM and SAM

Juan-Carlos Gómez

1 Introduction

The relationship between language and thought is a classical problem of psychology and philosophy. Can we learn anything about it from a comparative perspective? Is there such a thing as a language-and-thought issue in non-human animals? A first problem for such a comparative approach is that, although most scientists would accept that there is some degree of continuity between our closest evolutionary relatives – non-human primates – and ourselves in terms of our intellectual abilities, this is hardly considered to be the case with linguistic abilities. Although we can identify something like rudimentary 'thought' or 'intelligence' in non-human animals, it seems that there is nothing worth the name of language in them.

Our sympathy towards intellectual continuity is due, in my view, to the convincing nature of classical findings like those of Köhler (1927) and Goodall (1968), showing that one of our most cherished expressions of intelligence – tool use and problem solving – is present in both captive and wild chimpanzees. Of course there can be controversy about the extent to which there are qualitative differences between ape and human intelligence. But, even assuming that considerable differences exist, there is a relatively non-problematic acceptance of continuity in relation to the origins of thought. After all, continuity does not imply identity.

This is clearly not the case with one of the all-time favourite enigmas of science: the origins of language. An influential view in recent decades has been that language is such a radically new evolutionary product that, in contrast to intelligence, no traces of it can be found in non-human primates. Whatever the evolutionary process responsible for the appearance of human language, it occurred after our phylogenetic separation from the great ape line. This is the *discontinuity view* of language evolution. Moreover, any claims of discontinuity in intelligence are usually linked to the idea of discontinuity in language. Language is portrayed as a gift that crucially transforms the nature of human intelligence (see Dennett, 1996a; Bickerton, 1995, and chapters in this volume for recent examples of this).

In this chapter I will do two things. Firstly, I will question this discontinuity view of language evolution, suggesting that it is based upon a narrowly biased conception of human language as grammar. I will suggest that the human language faculty should rather be conceived as a more general communicative ability of which grammar is just a tool, and that, when so conceived, there is evidence of linguistic continuity between apes and humans. Secondly, once I have established the usefulness of addressing the language/thought problem in a comparative perspective, I will explore some possible evolutionary avenues in the emergence of our ability to acquire grammatical languages (the Chomskyan LAD, or Language Acquisition Device) and that special brand of thought that has come to be known as 'Theories of Mind' (TOM).

2 The 'aphasic' ape

Until recently the discontinuity view of language evolution was solidly based upon the available evidence on animal communication. The animal system that best resembled human language was not to be found in non-human primates, not even in mammals, but rather in such remote phylogenetic regions as the insect world. The dance system of bees, used to communicate the location of food resources, was deemed to be the closest animal analogy to human language, since it allows bees to communicate about displaced targets in a relatively arbitrary and productive way.

The fact that the best animal analogy to language is not found in our primate relatives was taken as a most eloquent confirmation of the discontinuity hypothesis. Continuity with our closest primate relatives could be found at the levels of facial expressions, perhaps even some vocalisations (laughter, etc.); but certainly this continuity ceased to exist as soon as we looked for a communication system endowed with semantics and syntax – a proper language. The calls of monkeys and apes were thought to transmit information only about the emotions and motivational states of the caller, much as facial expressions do, and to be mainly involuntary, reactive and automatic (Seyfarth, 1987).

3 Linguistic apes and semantic monkeys

The discontinuity view has had to meet two important challenges in recent years. One was the 'linguistic apes' phenomenon. It was claimed by some authors (e.g., Gardner and Gardner, 1969; see Sebeok and Sebeok, 1980, for an anthology of studies and interpretations) that chimpanzees, gorillas and orang-utans could be *taught* human language. The learning process was laborious and relatively slow, but the product – they claimed – was genuine language, with semantics and even rudimentary syntax. Unfortunately, this challenge lost momentum when it was shown that the would-be syntactic productions of some apes did not resist a close scrutiny; and it was even suggested that the very signs they were learning were not symbolic in nature (Terrace *et al.*, 1979; Savage-Rumbaugh *et al.*, 1980; Wallman, 1992). 'Linguistic' apes were discredited as being mere learners of conditioned responses to obtain food. At the very best, they were said to be using their 'thought' processes to engage in a problem solving activity that was tapping into abilities very different from grammar and reference. Thus, and despite recent attempts at rehabilitating the reputation of 'ape language' studies (Savage-Rumbaugh, 1991; Savage-Rumbaugh *et al.*, 1993), this challenge seems largely to have failed to convince the scientific community of the evolutionary continuity of language.

But there has been a second challenge whose reputation is still alive. This is the discovery of a 'semantic' competence in vervets and other monkey species. Dorothy Cheney and Robert Seyfarth (1990) demonstrated that the myth of non-human calls as mere emotional and automatic signals was false. They showed that vervet monkeys were capable of transmitting and understanding referential information about the environment with their repertoire of predator alarm calls. When previously recorded alarm calls were played back in the absence of real predators and potential models of escape behaviours provided by real alarm-callers, vervet monkeys would still react to them with adequate avoidance responses. Most importantly in my view, in response to the broadcast calls the monkeys would visually scan in the appropriate direction, as if they were looking for an eagle in the sky, a snake in the grass, or a leopard in the bushes. The reactions of the monkey listeners seemed to be organised in response to some kind of *representation* of the predator that was activated by the call in their minds, instead of simply responding with fear, indiscriminate evasion, or following a real caller's behaviour.

These experiments seemed to provide compelling evidence of 'semanticity' – the ability to refer to external objects by means of specialised, lexical signals – in a non-human primate species (see Macedonia and Evans, 1993; and Gozoules *et al.*, 1995 for recent reviews). Thus, the silence surrounding human language in the primate order appears to have been sharply broken, and all the more so since the newly discovered ability was not the product of artificial training, but a naturally occurring ability.

However, closer scrutiny shows that, for the problem of language continuity, this discovery is ambiguous. It is true that we now have an analogue of an important language property in primates and not in the phylogenetically remote bees. But the vervet monkey is still a relatively distant relative of man (it split from the ape/human lineage over twenty million years ago). If the semanticity of vocal alarm calls had anything to do with the evolution of language, it should be found in the great apes, whose evolutionary line separated from that of humans some five million years ago. However, so far all attempts at finding semanticity *à la* vervets in the calls of the great apes seem to have failed. Ape vocalisations do not seem to function as 'words' that refer to specific referents, such as predators, types of food, or groups of conspecifics.

Thus, the discontinuity view seems capable of surviving this challenge too. Semantic referentiality is found in the wrong species of primate. Moreover, this functional analogy of human semanticity is limited: call repertoires *à la* vervets are fixed, not productively generated by a lexical or grammatical syntax (Evans and Marler, 1995), so that the most fundamental property of language – the 'dependence of meaning upon a hierarchically rule-governed system' – continues to be an exclusive adaptation of humans. In García-Albea's (1993) words '[primate training studies and ethological observations] have shown that humans do not have the exclusive control of intelligence and other psychological functions, but at the same time they have failed to provide a single piece of evidence that the capacity for language is present in other species' (p. 179).

4 Meaning (with or without grammar)

This conclusion favourable to discontinuity is based upon the view of human language so forcefully put forward by Chomsky since 1957. According to it, language is a uniquely human faculty governed by grammar – a set of formal rules that specify the kind of operations that can be carried out with lexical items to construct valid utterances. The speaker encodes meaning into linguistic utterances by means of grammar; and by means of grammar this meaning is decoded by listeners. Nuances of meaning may be provided by context and non-verbal communication (the so called pragmatic aspects of language) but the core of language remains grammar – an exclusively human 'instinct' (Pinker, 1994).

Curiously enough, exactly the same year Chomsky started his grammatical revolution the philosopher Paul Grice (1957) put forward a none the less important proposal for the understanding of a different side of language. His proposal had to do with the complexity of the meanings we manage to convey with (or without) the grammar of language. Grice's idea (further developed in later years; see Grice, 1989 for a compendium) was essentially that meaning depends not upon grammar – the utterances we actually make – but upon what we intend to say and what other people think we intend to say. When communicating, we rely not only upon the decoding abilities of others (their knowledge of the grammar of English, for example), but also upon their ability to infer what we mean. Moreover, we can transmit meaning without having to use spoken or written language at all (e.g., by means of gestures); or, more crucially, our intended meaning may flatly contradict our encoded meaning, as in the case of metaphors and irony. From a Gricean perspective, then, grammar and the lexicon are tools in the hands of a more powerful cognitive ability that is even capable of completely overriding the meanings prescribed by the grammatical code.

To use Sperber and Wilson's (1986) terminology – in what I think is the most interesting current development of the Gricean insights – human communication involves two different kinds of processes. One is based upon the use of codes (such as natural grammar), and the other is based upon the use of our general inferential abilities. But these are not separate or alternative modes of communication: inferential communication makes use of codes as tools subordinated to the elaboration of inferential meanings. In this sense, grammar is just a component of what I think better deserves the name of the 'language faculty'. The point is that in human communication, meaning is only partially encoded (if at all); it has to be extracted – *inferred* – both from the grammatically encoded information (if there is any) and from the information provided by the context in which it occurs. Sperber and Wilson label this kind of communication 'ostensive/inferential', after the main cognitive processes which are supposed to underlie it. These cognitive processes are of two types: on the one hand, our general inferential abilities ('thought', one is tempted to say in the context of this volume), and on the other a system specialised in achieving (or avoiding) what we can call *ostension*.

Let me illustrate the nature of this process with a simple case – referring to an environmental target. Imagine that this target is a snake that I have detected in my garden: I point to it and say 'gosh!' The behaviours that I use to direct your attention in a particular direction and the processes you use to detect that particular target are the inferential component of communication. However, these inferential processes alone do not give rise to communication on their own. If I think I am alone and I just look at the snake with amazement and say 'gosh' to myself, but someone happens to be observing me, this person will still make all the necessary inferences and discover the target I am attending to. However, this would not be a proper communicative act. What is missing here is the *ostensive* component, that can be defined as 'showing that one wants to show something' (see Sperber and Wilson, 1986, for a more elaborate treatment of ostension in this sense). This is usually achieved by addressing the potentially communicative behaviours 'to the attention' of the addressee and engaging in what I have named elsewhere 'attention contact' (Gómez, 1994, 1996b).

An interesting property of ostension, in this communicative sense, is that it can turn any ordinary behaviour into a communicative signal. For example, if I happen to be looking at object X, you can follow my gaze and discover object X independently of my intending it or not. However, if I want you to follow my gaze I will direct your attention to it (for example, I will call your name, make eye contact with you, and then look at X) transforming my gaze into a communicative gesture. This is the ostensive component of communication: the ability to make clear to other people that we are displaying informative behaviours for their benefit.

Thus, ostensive/inferential communication makes use not only of the signals provided by code systems (such as grammars or facial expressions): it can use virtually any behaviour to achieve its communicative ends (a simple movement of the eyebrows, walking in a particular direction, adopting a posture, etc.); or, conversely, it can attenuate or eliminate the saliency of informative behaviours to prevent communication (e.g., by avoiding looking at a particular target, so that it is not spotted by others, etc.). Later I will discuss the behavioural and cognitive processes involved in ostension. But before that, let us reconsider the problem of language continuity from this new perspective concerning what constitutes the language faculty.

My argument is that it is in the realm of ostensive communication that we find evidence of linguistic continuity in the right primate species: I will defend the claim that apes have evolved an ostensive/referential system that enables them to refer productively to environmental targets without having a lexical-like repertoire of communicative signals, and in this they are closer to human language than vervet monkeys with their semantic alarm calls. Let me illustrate this idea with a classical experiment in primatology that, although originally designed for a different purpose, is an excellent demonstration of the virtues of ostensive communication.

5 The ostensive ape: reference without 'words' in chimpanzees and gorillas

The power of ostensive communication is dramatically demonstrated in situations where one has to produce novel communicative responses. This is what happened in a series of experiments run by Emil Menzel (1973) concerning the ability of chimpanzees to communicate or conceal information on the whereabouts of different items in a big outdoor enclosure. The procedure used in the experiment was to show an individual chimpanzee the location of an object (desirable, such as food, or dangerous, such as a snake); then this chimpanzee was returned to the rest of the group, and shortly afterwards they all were released into the enclosure. Would the knowledgeable chimpanzees alert their companions to the hidden target?

According to Menzel (1973) they managed to do so in the following way:

'The leader varied his behaviour in almost every possible fashion . . . tapping other animals on the shoulder, tugging at them, "presenting the back", or even biting a companion on the neck and dragging him along the ground by a leg in the direction of the hidden object' (p. 200). They would also 'recruit a following by means of glances, whimpering, arm signals, tapping a companion on the shoulder, presenting the back to solicit walking in tandem . . ., etc.' (p. 215). The chimpanzees, in their attempt to affect the behaviour of the other individuals, were resorting both to 'coded' signals present in their vocal and facial repertoires and to new signals created out of originally non-communicative behaviours (such as tugging, tapping, walking in a particular direction, etc.).

Furthermore, the reactions of the follower chimpanzees to their companion's efforts suggest that the result of this was the achievement of referential communication. For example, after seeing the leader's behaviour, the followers started to *look for* objects they had not actually seen. This was especially obvious in a series of experiments where the original target shown to the leader was removed from the enclosure before the whole band was let loose. The followers would start looking around as if in search of an interesting object, or, when the object was an obnoxious one (e.g., a snake), they would throw objects and make threatening displays towards the particular spot they had been oriented to by the leader; all this in the absence of any real object. All happened as if the leader's communicative behaviours were activating representations of objects or targets in the minds of the other chimpanzees and as if they were reacting to these representations, much as the played-back alarm calls seemed to activate representations in the minds of the vervet monkey listeners.

This indicates, therefore, that 'referentiality' is a property of chimpanzee communication. But this referentiality is not attached to particular signals with a specific semantic content. The referentiality of chimpanzees is not 'lexically codified', but – I suggest – the result of an ostensive system of communication that may be characteristic of all the great apes.

However, why not interpret Menzel's observations simply as an indication of the general problem solving abilities of chimpanzees, instead of an expression of their ability to engage in ostensive communication? Why not interpret the above behaviours as mere intelligent, goal-directed manipulations of the other individuals? After all Menzel's focus was upon the production (or suppression) of referential behaviours by the leaders and their perception by the followers. And, as I mentioned before, the crux of ostension lies in something else: the ability to call or deflect the attention of others upon the referential information contained in the signals. A simple referential behaviour (e.g., gazing at X) becomes intentionally referential if it is accompanied by an ostensive behaviour (e.g., eye contact). Are the great apes simply 'referential', in a loose sense of the word, or are they ostensive/referential? This question is difficult to solve on the sole basis of Menzel's observations. Let me turn to other sources of evidence.

In a study of young hand-reared gorillas interacting with human adults (Gómez 1990, 1991, 1992), I found that they were capable of using gestures to communicate with humans. For example, when they wanted people to move to a particular place, they would take their hands and gently lead them in the appropriate direction. Taking the hand of a person was also used as a way of specifying particular targets for the human (for example, taking the hand of the person to the latch of a door they wanted to open). These actions worked as gestures that had referential information for the human, and they are comparable to the actions described by Menzel in his chimpanzees. However, the gorillas would not simply perform this referential action and wait for the human to act: they systematically introduced glances at the eyes of the human as part of their requesting procedure. Moreover, they would actively call the attention of the person before executing their referential action. For example, in one subject the following procedure was regularly observed: she would approach the human, touch his knee while looking up at his face, make eye contact when the human looked at her, extend her hand towards the human's hand and then, only when the human offered her his hand, would she take it and start her request (Gómez, 1992). The gorillas developed a repertoire of gestures and body actions specialised in calling the attention of people. A common component of these attention-getting and attention-checking procedures was the establishment of eye contact with the addressee. I suggest that these procedures and their accompanying eye contact behaviours are the expression of an ostensive system operating in the gorillas. They seem to understand that for their gestures to be effective they have to make them ostensive by establishing joint attention (Gómez, 1992, 1996b).

This interpretation has been experimentally explored in a study with hand-reared captive chimpanzees (see Gómez, 1996a, for a preliminary partial report). This experiment showed that some chimpanzees (those with individual hand-rearing histories) actively looked for eye contact when a person failed to respond to a request. If, when these chimpanzees looked, the person was looking at them and eye contact occurred, they would just repeat the request. However, if the person was looking elsewhere, they would use an attention-getting behaviour (such as touching the human), and repeat the request only after making eye contact with her. This experiment shows that the chimpanzees were not merely using a system based upon the understanding of the connection between their indicative actions and the human's reactions; they were using an ostensive/referential system based upon some kind of understanding of joint attention.

We still know very little about the ostensive and joint attention behaviours of non-human primates (see Gómez, 1996b, for a review). As one would expect, there are indications that the ostensive system of apes differs from that of humans in many respects. But, all in all, the available evidence suggests that living apes possess an ostensive/referential system of communication in which these two functions can be separated and independently manipulated. Apes are capable of reading the behaviours of other apes and humans in intentional terms, i.e., ascribing to these behaviours at least physical goals and targets. They are also capable of ostensively addressing their referential behaviours to the attention of other individuals.

This changes the scenario for considering the problem of human language evolution. There is evidence of continuity between great apes and humans in relation to a fundamental property of human language – its ostensive/inferential dimension. My contention is that, although in modern human beings syntax and the lexicon may be relatively independent systems, the language faculty is best characterised as an ostensive/inferential system for meaning generation. Syntax and semantics can be considered as tools in the hands of this more powerful system. Now, from an evolutionary point of view my claim is that the evolution of syntax was not independent of the evolution of ostension. The first crucial step towards language was the evolution of a system capable of ostensive referentiality, a good model of which is provided by the ostensive abilities of currently living apes. But this was only the starting point of a long evolutionary process in which language and thought were closely intertwined. In the next section I will try to outline what could have been involved in this process.

6 Ostension and its relations to SAM and TOM

First, let us turn back to the question of the cognitive basis for ostensive communication. Since intended meaning is a mental state that has to be inferred, it would seem that for ostensive communication to occur one would need a mechanism capable of attributing mental states, i.e., what has come to be known as a Theory of Mind or TOM (see Carruthers and Smith, 1996, for a recent overview of conceptual debates around this). This impression is reinforced by the fact that people with autism, who are supposed to suffer an impairment in TOM abilities, have specific difficulties in understanding intended meanings (Happé, 1994). Thus, it seems that in ostensive/inferential communication, TOM is responsible for the inferential side, at least when what has to be inferred is a mental state. But what about the ostensive side? Is ostension also achieved by means of TOM?

In ostensive acts of communication I make the other person 'understand' that I 'want' her to 'notice' something (remember the example of gaze direction). Therefore, showing one's communicative intention seems to involve a specially convoluted exercise in theory of mind (in Gómez, 1994, I argue that it would involve at least five orders of intentionality; *see also* Sperber, 1994, for a similar argument).

My suggestion is, however, that ostension is achieved through a system different from a meta-representational TOM (Gómez, 1994). Ostension is first of all a function involving the co-ordination of attention and – as argued by Gómez (1991, 1994) and Baron-Cohen (1994, 1995) – the early understanding of attention by human infants and non-human primates may be based upon processes that do not require the meta-representations used by a TOM system. The ostensive behaviours of apes engaging in referential communication are not based upon mentalistic 'meta-representational' abilities, but upon first-order representations of attentional and expressive behaviours.

Baron-Cohen (1994, 1995) has suggested the existence of two different mechanisms in mind-reading – the Shared Attention Mechanism, or SAM, and the Theory of Mind module, or TOM. I will borrow his terms, but instead of mechanisms I will be speaking of SAM and TOM *functions*, without committment to Baron-Cohen's assumptions about the nature of the mechanisms involved in performing these functions. My claim is that ostension and reference, as demonstrated by gorillas and chimpanzees, are exclusively SAM functions subserved by mechanisms different from those operating in TOM functions.

The referential component of ape communication does not necessarily require the understanding of mental intentions or beliefs. Apes may entertain first-order representations of the intentional relations of other apes with their targets (i.e., there are physical, 'physiognomic' configurations which can express desires and that can be represented just with first-order representations). Attention-following and understanding of the seeing/not seeing relationships seem to be well within the reach of apes (but see Povinelli and Eddy, 1996, for some claims to the contrary), but this can be achieved with first-order representations (Gómez, 1991; Gómez *et al.*, 1993). However, these first-order representations can be considered to be already a mirror of the mind, in that they represent the external expression of a mental activity – attending to something. The goal of this mental activity is a concrete target in the environment and the attitude connecting the agent and its target is a physical (perhaps I should rather say *physiognomic*) state that can be directly perceived in the agent (cf. Hobson, 1993, for a similar line of argument). (Note that I am not suggesting that apes are totally devoid of TOM functions. Evidence from Gómez, 1996a, suggests that the knowing/ignorance distinction may be within the possibilities of apes. But to engage in ostensive/referential communication a TOM is not necessary. It can be achieved simply through SAM mechanisms[1]).

As to the ostensive component of communication, my argument is that it never requires TOM, not even in current adult humans. Displaying and perceiving ostension is a function carried out by specialised SAM mechanisms different from those responsible for referential gaze following. TOM mechanisms would be quite inept at performing this function, because to tackle joint attention situations they would have to engage in very unlikely and complex computations (this is the origin of the paradox of 'mutual knowledge'; see Gómez, 1994).

Therefore, current apes are capable of ostensive/referential communication, but this requires neither TOM mechanisms nor linguistic devices (LADs). My suggestion is that the common ancestors of current apes and humans were creatures armed with some kind of SAM mechanism that allowed them to engage in ostensive referential behaviours. This form of communication has the interesting property of being closely linked to general intelligence, since it crucially depends upon the inferential abilities of the creatures involved. This kind of communication is the result of a combination of general inferential abilities and specialised ostensive mechanisms. According to this scenario, communication and thought were united in those common ancestors perhaps for the first time in evolution. It was in this cognitive crucible that the evolution of TOMs and LADs was concocted; they may be later products of evolution, but products that are inconceivable outside the evolutionary pathway opened by ostension. Engaging in ostensive reference created a new psychological landscape for cognitive evolution. LADs and TOMs were two of the consequences of following this new pathway.

7 The evolutionary consequences of ostension: how SAM became a LAD

Let's start with an exploration of the linguistic consequences of ostensive communication. Essentially, what we have found is that apes possess a referential system based upon the activation of mental representations of external objects and targets. This system is not constituted as a repertoire of lexical items *à la* vervets, but is rather a *productive* system capable of generating reference to items that are not pre-specified. It is likely that the

[1] In fact, even if the apes had some kind of TOM functions (such as understanding ignorance/knowledge) these would be useful for the inferential part of the communicative process, not for the ostensive one. For example, the orang-utan in Gómez and Teixidor experiment (see Gómez, 1996a, for a brief account) could be deciding *which* objects to point to on the basis of what the human knew or ignored, but the ostensive/referential mechanisms used to produce the pointing behaviour could rely entirely on the SAM system.

human ancestors that first separated from the ape lineage were endowed with something similar to this ostensive/referential ability. But it is also very likely that they were endowed with the evolutionary potentiality for developing vocal semanticity *à la* vervets. There is evidence that different primate species (sometimes phylogenetically quite distant) are capable of developing repertoires of 'semantic' calls (see Macedonia and Evans, 1993; and Evans and Marler, 1995): the potentiality for evolving this kind of communication seems to be quite widespread among the primate order and it has been detected even in some species of birds and squirrels (Hauser, 1996). The key factor for this potentiality to be evolutionarily fulfilled in a particular species seems to be the occurrence of certain ecological factors 'calling for' it (Macedonia and Evans, 1993).

Given this, the question is what would happen if, as a consequence of ecological pressures, this ability for vocal semanticity were to reappear in a species that was already endowed with the ability for ostensive reference? I suggest that a likely product of this evolutionary meeting would be the emergence of *naming*. By 'naming' I understand the productive ability to create vocal (or other modality), labels to refer to environmental things. The re-emergence of vocal semanticity in our ancestors would have happened in a new cognitive landscape – the landscape of ostension. This would conceivably lead to a system whose semantic links were not fixed or pre-established by phylogeny, but created in the course of ontogeny.[2] Furthermore, these labels would be created in the context of an existing system of communication capable of separating reference from ostension. This would conceivably turn the vocal signals used for reference into a 'tool' (a 'symbol') separable from the act of reference itself, and therefore a new kind of object in this emerging cognitive landscape (see Noble and Davidson, 1996, for an interesting elaboration of a similar idea).

An idea of what such a system would be like can be gained from observing the development of naming in young human infants. First, children refer to objects by means of ostensive gestures (such as pointing), frequently accompanied by non-semantic vocalisations. Later, when their first semantic words are produced, it is frequently with the support of the ostensive/referential system. Of course, I am not suggesting this is the system evolved by our ancestors; I am just pointing out an existing example of an ostensive semantic system without syntax in which gestures and vocalisations play a fundamental role.

The ability of tutored captive apes to acquire manual or graphic symbols to perform at least some basic semantic functions is, I think, a good proof

[2] Observations of the ontogeny of vervet monkeys calls suggest that their system is already to some extent plastic and open to some environmental modification (Cheney and Seyfarth, 1990; Hauser, 1996).

of the likelihood of the scenario I'm suggesting. It is not clear whether the mind of an ostensive ape is capable of creating symbols for naming on its own, but it certainly seems to be capable of learning existing symbols provided by human teachers. I suggest that, when considered in the framework of their existing ostensive abilities, the great apes' capacity to learn some form of symbolic system makes very good sense. When confronted with the task of learning symbols, the apes are not using their general problem-solving abilities, but their specialised capacity for ostensive/referential communication. 'Linguistic' apes suggest that ostensive referentiality may work as a pre-adaptation for symbolic naming.

As one should expect on evolutionary grounds, the ostensive/referential system of human infants is not identical to that of apes. Although they share many essential features – such as the separation between referential and ostensive components – the system of human infants seems to be specially adapted to distal referentiality (for example, by means of pointing) and to naming (proto-declarative gestures) (Gómez *et al.*, 1993). In any case, as pointed out before, we do not yet have a precise characterisation of either of these systems.

Thus, we have important signs of evolutionary continuity in a fundamental component of language – semanticity. In other words, we have seen how SAM could easily have been evolutionarily modified into a first kind of LAD – a lexical LAD. But continuity in the realm of semanticity does not guarantee continuity in the realm of syntax – that 'jewel in the crown' of language with which the term 'LAD' is usually associated. I don't think we are going to find signs of syntax in the communicative systems of our evolutionary relatives (see Hauser, 1996, for a more optimistic approach). I feel inclined to accept that syntax and its associated LAD are a real evolutionary innovation of modern humans. (Although of course I assume the syntactic machinery did not come out of the blue; I favour the idea that the place to look for the computational forerunners of syntax is probably the realm of skilled action not related to communication – see e.g., Greenfield, 1991.)

However, there is a property of syntax – the one that has given it its role of 'jewel in the crown' of language – of which we do have evidence of evolutionary continuity: it is its generativity or creativity. The Chomskian view has always emphasised that the most distinctive feature of human language is its creativity: the possibility of generating an infinite number of utterances using a finite set of elements. It is normally assumed that this creativity of language derives from syntax. My suggestion is, however, that the creativity of language derives primarily from the ostensive/inferential mechanisms of intentional communication, and that syntax evolved as an adaptation to this already productive system. As mentioned before, a crucial advantage of having a separate system for ostension is that one can turn virtually any behaviour into a communicative behaviour, whether it is specialised for communication or not. An ostensive system allows one to generate new ways of communicating in novel situations and concerning novel targets.

I suggest that syntax emerged as an adaptation to handle the productivity generated by an ostensive communication system with lexical items. Syntax is generative and creative because it had to serve the purposes of an already generative and creative communication system. Syntax is a tool in the hands of ostension, a tool developed out of the versatility of a system capable of meaning more than it could express. However, evolutionarily the role of syntax was probably crucial in augmenting the productivity and creativity of that already productive system of communication. In the next section I explore two ways in which this could have happened: enhancing the representational and inferential abilities of the human mind, and promoting the development of a special kind of thinking: TOM.

8 Evolutionary vicissitudes of TOMs and LADs

I have argued that the ostensive system of communication developed by our ape-like ancestors paved the way for the development of creative semantic communication systems. This was not yet a language with syntax. But it was a completely new cognitive landscape that provided new adaptive challenges. What were the effects of that hypothetical ostensive semantic system upon other areas of cognition? An interesting possibility is that the new communication system that emerged out of the confluence of ostension and vocal semanticity acted back upon the system responsible for ostensive referentiality – a variety of SAM – giving rise to the conditions that made possible the emergence of TOM. One conceivable hypothesis is that this incipient language offered a means to represent the representational consequences of attention (and the representational antecedents of intentions); i.e., a means of rendering perceivable the unperceivable – the mind, or how other people see the world. The structure of a typical joint attention situation is isomorphic with a meta-representation *à la* Leslie (Leslie and Roth, 1993; cf. Baron-Cohen, 1995). The perception of X attending to O is almost the prototype or skeleton of a propositional attitude, except that there is no proposition (just a physical target) and the attitude may, literally, be a position of the body or a direction of the eyes, accompanied or not by facial and vocal expressions. Perhaps the utterances produced by our ancestors (e.g. 'there food') started to be substituted for the actual contemplation of an object by the audience in their SAM representations, i.e., the visual perception that 'X SEES FOOD THERE' could be replaced by the visual/auditory perception 'X SAYS *FOOD THERE*'. The structure is almost the same, but *FOOD THERE* is no longer a first-order, perceptual representation of food lying in a particular place, but the representation of a symbol or a string of symbols produced by another organism – a remarkable approximation to a meta-representation, but not yet the genuine thing *à la* Leslie.

I am assuming that these ancestors would have developed something similar to what Bickerton (1995) calls a 'proto-language': a repertoire of acquired lexical labels that can be put together to produce creative messages without a syntax. What I'm trying to explore now is the cognitive consequences of having such a repertoire controlled by a productive communication system based on ostension. My proposal is that the first individuals capable of storing representations of these utterances *as uttered* by particular speakers (including their gestures and physiognomic attitudes) were using cognitive abilities that were not specialised in performing this function (a combination of auditory memory plus cross-modal representations plus SAM representations, or something like that). No specialised (TOM) mechanism was available to process this kind of representation, as no specialised (syntactic) system was available to organise the vocal/gestural utterances of these hominids.

However, those individuals capable of forming these 'attributed representations' based upon the linguistic output of others or themselves may have had an advantage over other individuals not able to do so. Evolution, therefore, would favour individuals more able to perform this kind of function by means of their unspecialised – for these particular purposes – cognitive abilities. This evolutionary pressure would favour improvements in existing cognitive abilities (for example, the SAM of current apes is different from the SAM of current human babies in aspects like the latter's possession of proto-declarative pointing – an excellent pre-adaptation for naming; this may reflect the adaptive pressures of that period). But the point is that, once a need for these quasi-TOM and quasi-LAD functions was created, evolution could have favoured the emergence of individuals with more suitable *specialised* mechanisms for performing the same kinds of function in a more efficient way.[3] A corkscrew would not succeed in a world devoid of wine bottles. However, in a world where opening wine

[3] I should say 'capable of developing' instead of 'endowed with', because I want to emphasise that what we are looking for is not the evolution of ready-made 'syntaxes' or 'TOMs', but the evolution of *the ability to develop* syntaxes and TOMs. This idea is fully captured by the term LAD: language acquisition device. Actually I feel tempted to contribute to the cognitive science nomenclature with a THOMAS, or Theory of Mind Acquisition System, that better highlights the ontogenetic dimension of the ability. Adopting this developmental perspective offers a framework where the evolution of new innate abilities need not be a miracle: it can be achieved through the adjustment of a few developmental parameters. See Elman *et al.*, 1996, for a re-analysis of the notion of innate capacities from this perspective.

bottles (by means of not totally appropriate artefacts such as knives or forks) has become an important activity, if corkscrews appear, they will be selected and retained.

What I am suggesting is, therefore, that evolutionarily (some of) the functions of current LADs and TOMs were initially performed by other cognitive mechanisms (something that in current humans could still happen). This created the cognitive landscape that 'called for' specialised LADs and TOMs. Now, one possibility is that there emerged a single specialised capacity capable of transforming both domains into modern LADs and TOMs. For example, syntax could have emerged as a better solution for both TOM and LAD problems. The same cognitive step – the emergence of a syntactic LAD – would underlie the emergence of modern LADs and modern TOMs. This would mean that in modern humans language (in the traditional narrow sense) and TOM (in its meta-representational version) would be closely associated because they would both be products of the appearance of syntactic mechanisms.

However, I suggest that there is an alternative evolutionary scenario that better fits what, in my view, is compelling evidence that in modern humans the syntactic LAD and the meta-representational TOM are separate systems. According to this modular view, human ancestors confronted with TOM and LAD challenges evolved two different kinds of mechanism specialised in each kind of function. The hypothesis is the following: at some point in hominid evolution, there was an evolutionary arms-race between individuals improving their LAD-like abilities (generating and storing more complex utterances descriptive of the world) and individuals improving their TOM-like abilities, which would confer to them an advantage in interpreting the ambiguous proto-linguistic productions of their fellow hominids (see Carruthers, this volume chapter 5, for an elaboration of this idea) – LAD specialists versus TOM specialists. The latter individuals would be rather laconic, but very good at selecting what little they say and do, and at drawing conclusions from what others say and do. However, the LAD specialists would be very good at giving detailed information and at storing detailed descriptions of the world. It is difficult to imagine which of these two lines of specialisation would have been better on its own. However, if this tendency to diversification did in fact occur, it is clear and genetically plausible that a better adapted kind of individual would eventually emerge: one combining the genetic predispositions towards 'chattiness' *and* 'machiavellianism'. In such a scenario, there would still be a very close relationship between language and TOM – not because they were sharing the same cognitive machinery, but because they were competing to invade each other's adaptive domains, and this competition encouraged and shaped their parallel evolution. The engine for the development of current meta-representional TOMs and syntactic LADs may have been their mutual competition in creating 'exaptations' to domains different from their original, adaptive ones.

This evolutionary scenario is built upon the assumption that linguistic abilities (in the narrow sense of semantic-syntactic) and TOM abilities are subserved by specialised systems in modern humans. I accept the evidence from autism and other syndromes to favour a modular conception of these aspects of the mind in modern humans. However, for the evolutionary reasons discussed above, despite their specialisation, current LADs and TOMs are capable of invading each other's domains with a limited, but not negligible, degree of success. For example, individuals whose TOM is disrupted may be capable of partially compensating for this with the use of linguistic and other analogies of mental representation (e.g., high-level autistic persons, whose performance on TOM tasks highly correlates with their linguistic ability, which is not true of normal children; see Happé, 1994). Conversely, individuals with a poor syntactic/semantic language may resort to their TOM and SAM systems to generate linguistic (in the broader sense) communication; so much so that one could even be tempted to say that they are 'reinventing' language (see Goldin-Meadow and Zheng, this volume chapter 2).

LAD and TOM are also good at co-operating in normal development. LAD's outputs may be important in setting the higher versions of TOM to work. Perhaps conversations with siblings may provide early evidence on which to exercise the TOM machinery, thereby accelerating TOM development (as Harris, 1996, argues). What LAD cannot provide, unfortunately, is a TOM if this is lacking or severely damaged; only later in development can it (or other abilities) provide a prosthetic device capable of performing some of TOM's functions (cf., for example, Swettenham *et al.*, 1996, for an experimental exploration of this possibility).

But the current autonomy of LAD and TOM does not mean that a connection did not exist in evolution. I have defended the idea that this aspect of the modern human mind – its specialisation for both LAD and TOM – may partially be the result of an evolutionary arms-race in which, at least initially, LAD specialists competed with TOM specialists, with the final result that individuals capable of developing *both* specialisations were the ones that won over individuals capable of only simulating the workings of the other system with their single specialised ability.

9 Summary and conclusion

There can be discontinuity between humans and their closest evolutionary relatives at the level of syntactic and semantic machinery, but continuity exists at the level of the ostensive/inferential system to which grammars are subordinated in normal humans. I have argued that apes posses an 'ostensive/referential' system of communication that is a mixture of specialised communicative systems (e.g., ostension) and general intelligence (e.g., inferential abilities). I have also argued that ostensive communication, with its openness and creativity, may have been an important factor in 'calling for' the evolution of linguistic grammars and meta-representational theories of mind. Grammatical LADs and meta-representational TOMs appeared as an adaptation to the new cognitive landscape created by our *ostensive* ancestors. I have also proposed a hypothesis about how this evolution could have happened. A plausible first step was the combination of ostensive and semantic systems into a 'naming' system whose characteristics were probably very similar to what Bickerton has called 'proto-language'. This system was capable of performing a number of functions that today we would identify as mentalistic and linguistic. In this way, it created the cognitive conditions that made specialised devices such as grammars and meta-representations useful. I have suggested a way of explaining the evolution of separate, relatively modular, TOMs and LADs out of a situation of competition between two alternative solutions to the problem of communication and behavioural prediction (TOM specialists and LAD specialists). The combination of both solutions into the same individuals was the optimal solution that led to modern humans.

I hope to have shown that an evolutionary perspective on the thought-and-language problem has a number of relevant ideas to contribute to the debate. Perhaps the most important is that the answers to the questions outlined by Carruthers and Boucher in chapter 1 of this volume may be different depending upon whether one formulates them in relation to evolution or in relation to the current human mind. SAM, TOM, and the LADS (semantic and syntactic) may be inseparable in an evolutionary perspective, but they may be working as relatively independent systems in modern humans.

Initial drafts of this paper were written with the help of a grant of the 'Subprograma General en el Extranjero. MEC'. The final version was completed under DGICYT Grant PB95–0377. I am grateful to Peter Carruthers for very helpful comments on drafts of this paper, and to all the participants in the Hang Seng seminars.

5 Thinking in language? Evolution and a modularist possibility

Peter Carruthers

1 Introduction: the modular mind

This chapter will attempt to develop a modularist version of (a relatively weak form of) the cognitive conception of language (weak, because it only claims it to be *naturally* necessary that *some* of our thoughts should constitutively involve natural language – see chapter 1, where we point out that one obstacle to taking the cognitive conception of language seriously, amongst cognitive scientists, is an unnecessary focus on conceptual and/or universal versions of it). In my 1996a I argued at length in support of the cognitive conception of language, and responded to a variety of objections to it. I also regarded it as important to claim that the cognitive conception could be consistent with a more or less modular conception of language and mind; but the idea was not really spelled out, and the consistency not demonstrated. The purpose of this chapter is to remedy that deficiency. I should stress, however, that the main point of the chapter is to defend a *possibility* – I want to show how it is *possible* for modularism and the cognitive conception of language both to be true together, so that others may begin to investigate the possibilities. I make no attempt to present anything resembling a defence of a worked-out model of cognition. But first I need to give some background.

According to Jerry Fodor's (1983) account, the human mind is cleanly divided into two distinct aspects or parts – into a set of peripheral input (and output) modules, on the one hand, and central cognition on the other. Fodor's input modules include specialised aspects of vision, audition, taste, smell, touch, and language; output modules include a variety of systems controlling different types of motor activity, and language. Modules are held to have proprietary inputs (or outputs, for output modules) and shallow outputs; to be domain-specific; to be fast; to be hard-wired; to involve mandatory processing; and to have their processes both encapsulated from, and inaccessible to, central cognition. (The *encapsulation* of modules means that their processes are unaffected by changes in central cognition, such as alterations in background belief. The *inaccessibility* of modules means that central cognition has no awareness or knowledge of the processes which take place within them.)

In contrast with the considerable success enjoyed by cognitive science in uncovering the structure of modular cognitive processes, central cognition is thought by Fodor to remain inherently mysterious; and, indeed, we are warned off ever seeking a serious science of the central mind at all. There might seem to be something of a paradox here. For Fodor *also* claims that we *do* have a science of central cognition, embodied in the generalisations and *ceteris paribus* laws of common-sense psychology – see his 1987, chapter 1. Thus we know that, if people see something, they generally believe it; that if they want something, and believe that there is something which they can do to get it, then they generally do that thing; that if they believe that P and Q, they generally also believe that P; and so on. Such generalisations are thought by Fodor to be both true, and to have the status of counter-factual supporting *laws*, equivalent in standing to the laws of any other special science. So how can it be true that central cognition is closed to science if our folk-psychological beliefs about it *are* a science? I take it that what Fodor means is that there is no hope of making scientific progress in discovering the causal mechanisms which *instantiate* folk-psychological laws; that is, that central cognition is closed to *cognitive* science.

Now, the claim of *hard*-wiring of modules was probably always an exaggeration. For it appears that all biological systems admit of considerable degrees of neurological plasticity, especially in the early stages of development (Elman *et al.*, 1996). But it remains plausible that the development of perceptual and motor sub-systems should be largely a matter of biological *growth-in-a-normal-environment*, rather than of learning; and that to the extent to which learning *does* take place, it may involve domain-specific, rather than general, learning principles. So we can still think of the development of modular systems as being largely innately determined, in interaction with normal environments. It is also the case that modules are probably less than fully encapsulated from central cognition, as we shall see in section 2 below when we discuss the processes underpinning visual imagery. Rather, it seems likely that all input and output systems are alike in having a rich network of back-projecting neural pathways, to help to direct perceptual search and recognition, and to help to monitor and fine-tune motor output. But these points aside, Fodor's conception of the modular periphery of the mind can be embraced as broadly acceptable, I believe – that is, limited accessibility, domain-specificity, and mandatory and fast operation do characterise a range of specialised input/output systems.

Matters are otherwise, however, when it comes to the claimed mysteriousness and intractability of central cognition, where Fodor has surely been unduly pessimistic. For as the work of Baddeley and colleagues has shown, it is possible to study the structure and functioning of the central-process working-memory system, for example (Baddeley and Hitch, 1974; Baddeley, 1986; Gathercole and Baddeley, 1993); and Shallice and others have made testable proposals concerning the structure of the central executive (Norman and Shallice, 1986; Shallice, 1988, 1994; Shallice and Burgess, 1993). Moreover, a number of investigators have begun to argue that central cognition itself may be quasi-modular in structure (Baron-Cohen, 1995; Smith and Tsimpli, 1995; Sperber, 1996). Quasi-modules would differ from full modules in having conceptual (rather than perceptual or motor) inputs and outputs. And they may differ markedly in the degree to which their processes, and principles of operation, are accessible to the rest of the system. But they would still be relatively fast, special-purpose processors, resulting from substantial genetic channelling in development, and operating on principles which are largely unique to them, and at least partly impervious to changes in background belief.

A picture is thus emerging of a type of mind whose periphery is made up of a quite highly modular set of input and output modules (including language), and whose centre is structured out of a number of quasi-modular component sub-systems, in such a way that its operation is subserved by a variety of special-purpose conceptual processors. Thus it seems highly likely that there are systems designed for reasoning about the mental states of oneself and others (Baron-Cohen, 1995), and for detecting cheaters and social free-riders (Cosmides and Tooby, 1992); and there may well be systems designed to deal with causal reasoning and inferences to the best explanation (Giere, 1988), with mate-selection, with various forms of spatial reasoning, with beneficence and altruism, and with the identification, care of, and attachment to, off-spring (Barkow *et al.*, 1992).

It is likely to be important, then – if the cognitive conception of language is to be defended – to demonstrate that the latter can be rendered consistent with such a modularist picture. It needs to be shown how language can *both* be an input/output module of the mind, *and* be crucially implicated in various kinds of central cognition. This is the main task of the present chapter.

2 The use of peripheral modules in central processing

So, how is it possible for language both to be a peripheral input/output module of the mind, and to be employed in central-process cognition? To see how this can in principle be the case, compare what is known about visual imagination. Almost everyone now thinks that the visual system is a distinct input-module of the mind, containing a good deal of innate structure. But equally, most cognitive scientists now accept that visual *imagination* re-deploys the resources of the visual module for purposes of reasoning – for example, many of the same areas of the visual cortex are active when imagining as when seeing. (For a review of the evidence, see Kosslyn, 1994.) What is apparent is that central cognition can co-opt the resources of peripheral modules, activating some of their representations to subserve central cognitive functions of thinking and reasoning. The same is then possible in connection with language. It is quite consistent with language being an innately structured input and output module, that central cognition should access and deploy the resources of that module when engaging in certain kinds of reasoning and problem solving.

According to Stephen Kosslyn (1994), visual imagination exploits the top-down neural pathways (which are deployed in normal vision to direct visual search and to enhance object recognition) in order to generate visual stimuli in the occipital cortex, which are then processed by the visual system in the normal way, just as if they were visual percepts. Normal visual analysis proceeds in a number of stages, on this account. First, information from the retina is mapped into a visual buffer in the occipital lobes. From here, two separate streams of analysis then take place – encoding of spatial properties (position, movement, and so on) in the parietal lobes, and encoding of object properties (such as shape, colour, and texture) in the temporal lobes. These two streams are then pooled in an associative memory system (in the posterior superior temporal lobes), which also contains conceptual information, where they are matched to stored data.

At this stage object recognition may well take place. But if recognition is not immediately achieved, a search through stored data, guided by the partial object-information already available, then occurs. Object-representations are projected back down through the visual system to the occipital lobes, shifting visual attention, and asking relevant questions of the visual input. This last stage is subserved by a rich network of backward-projecting neural pathways from the 'higher', more abstract, visual areas of the brain to the occipital cortex. And it is this last stage which is exploited in visual imagination, on Kosslyn's account. A conceptual or other non-visual representation (of the letter 'A', as it might be) is projected back through the visual system in such a way as to generate activity in the occipital cortex (just as if a letter 'A' were being perceived). This activity is then processed by the visual system in the normal way to yield a quasi-visual percept.

Note that this account involves some weakening of the sense in which the visual system can be said to be *modular*. For it means that the processing of the system is not fully informationally encapsulated, since centrally stored information has an impact on the way in which visual data are processed; whereas a module, in Fodor's (1983) sense, is always a fully encapsulated processor. But then it is very hard to see how *else* visual images could be generated, given that imagination and perception share mechanisms (as they do) – unless, that is, there were some way for central cognition to provide inputs to the visual system from outside (perhaps generating activity in the optic nerve in such a way as to simulate appropriate retinal stimulation), which appears most unlikely. And the visual system can of course remain modular in every other respect – being fast, genetically channelled in development, having proprietary inputs and a restricted domain, involving mandatory processing which is inaccessible to central cognition, and so on.

Note, too, that hardly anyone is likely to maintain that visual imagery is a mere *epiphenomenon* of central cognitive reasoning processes, playing no real role in those processes in its own right. On the contrary, it seems likely that there are many tasks which cannot easily be solved by us without deploying a visual (or other) image. Thus, suppose you are asked (orally) to describe the shape which is enclosed within the capital letter 'A'. It seems entirely plausible that success in this task should require the generation of a visual image of that letter, from which the answer ('a triangle') can then be read off. So it certainly appears that central cognition functions, in part, by co-opting the resources of the visual system to generate visual representations, which can be of use in solving a variety of spatial-reasoning tasks. And this then opens up the very real possibility that central cognition may *also* deploy the resources of the *language* system to generate representations of natural language sentences (in 'inner speech'), which can similarly be of use in a variety of *conceptual* reasoning tasks.

An obvious problem for this suggestion, however, is as follows. If the generation of inner speech, like the generation of visual imagery, begins with some central-process *conceptual* representation, which is projected back through the system to generate a quasi-perceptual representation, then it may seem puzzling why it should occur at all. It is easy to see the potential benefits, for cognition, of using a conceptual representation to generate a visual one. But what would be the point of using a conceptual representation to generate another representation of the same general sort, namely a natural language sentence?

One kind of answer is available from the standpoint of the communicative conception of language – it is that inner verbalisation can help to extend the cognitive resources available to central (non-language-involving) cognition; perhaps serving, in particular, to enhance short-term memory. This is the *supra-communicative* account of language, defended by Rosemary Varley (this volume, chapter 6) and Andy Clark (this volume, chapter 8). On this account we use a conceptual representation to generate an item of inner speech in order to help us remember, and operate with, that very representation. One problem for this proposal is then that inner speech does not *just* occur when demands on cognition are particularly heavy. Rather, inner speech is just as likely to figure in idle day-dreaming as in complex problem-solving (Hurlburt, 1990). This is difficult to explain if inner speech is merely part of a strategy we adopt to augment our cognitive resources; but easy if it is an element of the normal functioning of the executive system, in such a way that it continues to occur even when the engine is idling, so to speak. So we already have *some* reason to prefer an account of inner speech which is consistent with the cognitive conception of language.

2.1 A language-using conscious executive

One part of an answer to the above problem (developed at length in my 1996a) which can be given by those inclined to endorse the cognitive conception of language, is that by generating items in inner speech we can gain access to our own conceptual representations, rendering them conscious, and available to critical reflection and improvement. On this account, sentences of inner speech will be constitutive of the thought-tokens they serve to express, provided that there is a special-purpose executive system which operates on just such sentences (*see also* Perner, this volume, chapter 13). So one possibility is that although *non*-conscious conceptual representations need not involve natural language (but rather some sort of Fodorian 'Mentalese', as it might be), our *conscious* conceptual (as opposed to visuo-spatial) thinking should necessarily implicate natural language sentences.

Does this appeal to a central executive require me to postulate a little homunculus sitting at the centre of the mind, taking the decisions? Is the proposal unacceptable, indeed, on the grounds that I must attribute to the central executive too many of the powers and capacities of the person as a whole? I think not. Indeed, very little, if anything, would need to be added to central cognition beyond language, imagination, and theory of mind, in order to create the sort of executive which I envisage. For with these capacities in place, people would be able to generate sentences of inner speech in imagination, which would get interpreted by the language system in the normal way, and whose contents would be available to meta-representational thought. The creation of an additional executive level of cognition can then come about quite easily in two (compatible) ways. First, as Keith Frankish suggests (this volume, chapter 12), the sentences of inner speech can be objects of further, personally motivated, *decision*. People can decide to accept or reject those sentences, and can decide to adopt policies of *premising* – acting and reasoning just as if those sentences expressed their beliefs or desires. And second, people can learn to make transitions of various sorts between sentences of inner speech, acquiring habits of inference and action which are causally dependent upon those sentences being tokened in imagination (Dennett, 1991, and this volume, chapter 14). Neither of these additional functions requires us to postulate anything like an homunculus.

But what serves to *generate* the items of inner speech? Am I required to postulate a Central Meaner, in anything like the sense which Daniel Dennett (1991) characterises as objectionable? I don't believe so. One story I could tell is the standard one in the speech-production literature (e.g. Levelt, 1989), which begins with a conceptual representation of the message to be expressed, which is then used to generate an appropriate phonological representation. This conceptual representation might be formulated in Mentalese, or perhaps in LF (and if the latter, then I can tell a story about how these LF representations might be selected; see below). But equally, I could buy into a 'pandemonium model' of speech production (Dennett, 1991), in which a variety of 'word-demons' compete with one another to see who can shout the loudest. For what matters, on my account, is what happens to an imaged natural language sentence *after* it has been generated, not how it *came to be* formulated in the first place.

2.2 *LF as the language of explicit conceptual thought*

A further possible answer to the problem above, however (also developed, but at slightly less length, in my 1996a), is that central-process conceptual representations might already consist of (*non*-imagistic, *non*-conscious) natural language symbols. For example, Noam Chomsky has maintained that there is a level of linguistic representation which he calls 'Logical Form' (LF), which is where the language faculty interfaces with central cognitive systems (Chomsky, 1995a, 1995b). It might then be claimed that some (or all) conceptual, propositional, thinking consists in the formation and manipulation of these LF representations. In particular, it could be that tokening in an LF representation is what renders a given content *explicit* (in the sense of Karmiloff-Smith, 1992) – that is, which serves make it generally inferentially available (or 'promiscuous') outside of its given cognitive domain, having the potential to interact with a wide range of central cognitive operations. On this account, it would not just be some (conscious) thought *tokens* which constitutively involve natural language representations; but certain explicit thoughts, as *types*, would involve such sentences.

The hypothesis can thus be that central-process thinking often operates by accessing and manipulating the representations of the language faculty. Where these representations are *only* in LF, the thoughts in question will be non-conscious ones. But where the LF representation is used to generate a full-blown phonological representation (a sentence in auditory imagination, or an episode of inner speech), the thought will be a conscious one. But what, now, is the basic difference between the hypothesis that (many forms of) central-process thinking and reasoning operate, in part, by deploying sentences of LF, and the hypothesis that they are conducted entirely in Mentalese? The important point, here, is that sentences of LF are *not* sentences of Mentalese – they are not pure central-process representations, but rather depend upon resources provided by the language faculty; and they are not universal to all thinkers, but are always drawn from one or another natural language.

(Philosophers and logicians should note that Chomsky's LF is very different from what *they* are apt to mean by 'Logical Form'. In particular, sentences of LF do *not* just contain logical constants and quantifiers, variables, and dummy names. Rather, they consist of lexical items drawn from the natural language in question, syntactically structured, but regimented in such a way that all scope-ambiguities and the like are resolved, and with pronouns cross-indexed to their referents and so on. And the lexical items will be semantically interpreted, linked to whatever structures in the knowledge-base secure their meanings.)

Moreover, the proposal is not that LF is the language of all central processing (as Mentalese is supposed to be). For, first, much of central cognition may in any case employ visual or other images, or cognitive models and maps (Johnson-Laird, 1983). And second, and more importantly, my proposal is that LF only serves as the intermediary between a number of quasi-modular central systems, whose internal processes will, at least partly, take place in some other medium of representation (patterns of activation in a connectionist network, perhaps). This idea will be further elaborated in section 4 below. But basically, the thought is that the various central systems may be so set up as to take natural language representations (of LF) as input, and to generate such representations as output. This makes it possible for the output of one quasi-module (theory of mind, say) to be taken as input by another (the cheater-detection system, for example), hence enabling a variety of quasi-modular systems to co-operate in the solution of a problem, and to interact in such a way as to generate trains of thought.

But how can such an hypothesis be even so much as *possible*? How can a quasi-modular central system interpret and generate natural language representations, except by first transforming an LF input into a distinct conceptual representation (of Mentalese, as it might be), then using that to generate a further conceptual representation as output, which can then be fed to the language system to build yet another LF sentence? But if *that* is the story, then the quasi-module in question does not, itself, utilise the resources of the language system. And it also becomes hard to see why quasi-modules could not communicate with one another by exchanging the sentences of Mentalese which they generate as outputs and take as immediate inputs. I shall shortly sketch one way in which (some) quasi-modules might utilise the resources of the language system for their internal operations. But first, let me briefly outline an evolutionary answer to the question how LF, rather than Mentalese, could have come to be the medium of intra-cranial communication *between* quasi-modules. (More on this in section 4 below.)

Suppose that the picture painted by Steve Mithen (1996) of the mind of *Homo erectus* and the Neanderthals is broadly correct. Suppose, that is, that their minds contained a set of more-or-less isolated central modules for dealing with their different domains of activity – a Theory of Mind (TOM) module for social relationships and behavioural explanation and prediction; a natural history module for processing information about the life-styles of plants and animals; and a physics module, crucially implicated in the manufacture of stone tools. When a language module was added to this set it would, very naturally, have evolved to take as input the outputs of the other central modules, so that hominids could talk about social relationships, the biological world, and the world of physical objects and artefacts. (It is unlikely, I think, that language would have evolved *only* for talking about social relationships, as Mithen 1996 suggests, following Dunbar 1996. For given that TOM would already have had access to non-social contents – as it would have to if it was to predict and explain non-social behaviour – there would then have been a powerful motive to communicate such contents. See Gomez, this volume, chapter 4.) It also seems plausible that each of those modules might have altered in such a way as to take linguistic as well as perceptual *in*puts, so that merely being told about some event would be sufficient to invoke the appropriate specialist processing system.

With central modules then taking linguistic inputs and generating linguistic outputs, the stage was set for language to become the intra-cranial medium of communication between modular systems, hence breaking down the barriers between specialist areas of cognition in the way Mithen characterises as distinctive of the modern human mind. All that was required, was for humans to begin exercising their imaginations on a regular basis, generating sentences internally, in 'inner speech', which could then be taken as input by the various quasi-modular systems. This process might then have become semi-automatic (either through over-learning, or through the evolution of further neural connections), so that even without conscious thought, sentences of LF were constantly generated to serve as the intermediary between central cognitive systems. (I return to this possibility in section 4 below.)

Let me turn, now, to sketch how the resources of the language system might have come to be implicated in the internal operations of the theory of mind (TOM) quasi-module, in particular. (Note that it is very unlikely that the internal structure of quasi-modules should be the same across all cases – the quasi-module dealing with causal-inference would surely not operate on principles at all similar to those employed by the cheater-detection quasi-module, or the mate-selection quasi-module, for example.)

Suppose, as I believe, that 'theory-theory' accounts of the structure of our TOM abilities are broadly correct (Lewis, 1966; Churchland, 1981; Fodor, 1987; Wellman, 1990; Carruthers, 1996b). Suppose, that is, that the mature TOM system embodies an implicit, partly non-conscious, theory of the structure and functioning of the mind. One possibility is that the system would contain a set of articulated generalisations, of the sort, 'Anyone who wants something, and believes that there is an action they can perform which will achieve it, will, other things being equal, execute that act'. Another possibility is that the system would consist of a set of inferential dispositions, which might then be said to represent the appropriate generalisation (so a disposition to infer from 'has seen that P' to 'believes that P' might be said to embody belief in the generalisation, 'Anyone who sees that P believes that P'). Either way, the various nodes in this theoretical structure might be occupied by lexical items of natural language. It may be that the normal development of a mature TOM system builds on a simpler, prelinguistic, desire-perception quasi-module, say, depending crucially on the acquisition of appropriate natural-language mentalistic vocabulary. At any rate, such an hypothesis seems consistent with everything which we know about the development of TOM (Wellman, 1990; Perner, 1991; Baron-Cohen, 1995). And the effect would be a quasi-modular system which crucially depends, for its more sophisticated operations, upon the resources of the (more fully modular) natural language faculty.

(Note that this proposal is distinct from – albeit consistent with – the one made by Gabriel Segal (this volume, chapter 7), according to which TOM operates by accessing the embedded-clause structure of natural language propositional-attitude reports. If only one, but not both, of these hypotheses is correct, then we can predict that TOM abilities will be differentially affected by a-grammatical and lexical aphasias.)

3 Comparison with the Bickerton model

The proposals being sketched here should be distinguished from the version of the cognitive conception of language put forward by Derek Bickerton

(1990, 1995), which is nativist but not (in one sense, at least) modularist. Bickerton's view is that the evolution of the brain-structures underpinning properly grammatical natural language *constituted* the evolution of human central cognition as we know it – conscious, flexible, and indefinitely creative. My view, in contrast, is that the evolution of the language system vastly extended the powers of central cognition, by providing the latter with a representational resource which could be used to increase the range and sophistication of human thinking and reasoning, as well as to render some of our thoughts conscious. I now propose to spend some time elaborating on this difference. But I also tell his story in order to use some of it, and to extract from it an additional argument in support of the cognitive conception of language.

3.1 The Bickerton model

Bickerton's account proceeds in two stages. *First*, there was a long period of hominid evolution during which what he calls *proto-language* was developed and deployed – perhaps two or more million years, through the evolution of *Homo habilis*, *Homo erectus*, and the Neanderthals. Proto-language is held to consist of essentially just a lexicon, perhaps containing broad categories of noun and verb but otherwise without any significant grammar. It is thought to be essentially similar to the language of one-year-old children, pidgin languages, and the sorts of unstructured language which can be taught to chimpanzees. Then *second*, there was the very swift evolution of properly-grammatical natural language (in Bickerton's 1990, perhaps through a single genetic mutation; somewhat more plausibly in his 1995, following a period of rapid evolutionary change) culminating in the emergence of *Homo sapiens sapiens* some 100,000 years ago.

Now, Bickerton's claim about the *swift* evolution of grammatical language seems to me very unlikely, and nothing that I shall say requires commitment to it. For, first, there is nothing in the fossil record to motivate it, since there seems in any case to have been a time-lag of some 50–60,000 years between the emergence of *Homo sapiens sapiens* and the first appearance of creative culture some 40,000 years ago (Mithen, 1996). I shall return to this point in section 4 below. And second, as a highly complex and sophisticated organ, the language faculty would almost certainly have had to evolve in stages over a considerable period of time, under a consistent selectional pressure (Pinker and Bloom, 1990). It seems to me much more likely that grammatical language might have been evolving through the 400,000–odd years between the first appearance of *Archaic Homo sapiens* some half a million years ago and the much more recent appearance of *Homo sapiens sapiens*.

A two-stage account has a number of significant advantages, Bickerton maintains. One is that it can simultaneously explain the slow emergence of the physiological adaptations (particularly of the mouth, throat, and larynx) necessary for smooth production of speech – these would have taken place during the long period when proto-language was developing – while also explaining the very late appearance in the fossil record of evidence of genuine culture and creative intelligence, which is held to coincide with the arrival of natural language proper. (Actually, given the time-lag mentioned above, some story needs to be told about what happened to trigger the onset of culture, independently in the different groups of humans dispersed around the globe at about the same time, some 50,000 years after the first emergence of *Homo sapiens sapiens*. I shall return to this point.) Bickerton can also explain some of the pressures which may have led to the dramatic increases in brain-size in early forms of *Homo*, which may have been due to the advantages, and demands, of increasingly large vocabularies, together with the processing requirements imposed by a-grammatical languages.

This latter point is worth elaborating further. For here we have a possible solution to an otherwise puzzling fact about human beings, namely that they appear to have a good deal of *excess* brain capacity. For brain tissue is, relatively, extremely costly in terms its demands on energy consumption – ten times that of other bodily tissue, in fact (Dunbar, 1993; Dunbar himself explains the growth of hominid brains in terms of the demands of social living, as group-sizes increased; but this cannot explain the *excess* brain capacity of contemporary humans relative to that required by our hunter-gatherer ancestors; see below in the text). Moreover, head size is the main cause of child-birth mortality, for both mothers and infants (in the case of mothers, even now running at about one in thirteen births in developing countries), also necessitating a uniquely long period of infant-maternal dependency. So the pressures for increases in brain size must have been considerable.

Yet in the modern world the human brain is required to retain and process amounts of information which would surely have been unthinkable in hunter-gatherer communities. (Consider that many modern children are required to learn reading, writing, and arithmetic; as well as a wealth of information about history, geography, literature, and science, up to and including sub-atomic physics.) How is this possible? The explanation may be that the brain developed as it did at a time when communication was by means of proto-language only, which would have placed very great demands on the on-line processing, interpretation, and storage of utterances. For proto-language utterances, in lacking significant structure, would have been multiply ambiguous; hence requiring a good deal of inferencing about the context and the mental states and assumptions of the speaker. The evolution of the grammar faculty would then have made interpretation semi-automatic, thus freeing cognitive space for other purposes.

3.2 Bickerton against the thesis that big brains equal intelligence

Bickerton himself sees his main opposition to be those who equate brain size with intelligence, and who think that language itself adds nothing to intelligence. His challenge to them is then to explain the evidence of the fossil record. For we know that *erectus* brains overlapped very substantially in size with the normal *sapiens* range (indeed, that Neanderthal brains were, on average, slightly larger than ours – with due adjustments made for body weight, of course). Yet there is no evidence of sophisticated *erectus* culture, or of systematic impact on, and exploitation of, the environment. Bickerton cites the limestone caverns of Zhoukoudian in northern China, for example, which were continuously inhabited by *Homo erectus* between roughly 500,000 and 200,000 years ago – that is, for 300,000 years, or roughly sixty times the length of recorded human history. Yet during that time they made no structural improvements of any kind to the caves, and the tiny handful of artefacts they produced displayed no significant change or improvement (Bickerton, 1995, p. 46; *see also* Mithen, 1996, for a good deal of data of this sort). How is this possible, if *erectus*, through having big brains (albeit lacking language, perhaps), was so intelligent?

In fact the proponents of the brain-size-equals-intelligence theory can make *some* headway in replying to this argument. For they can, of course, allow that language can be a necessary condition for humans to entertain many kinds of thought, without actually being implicated *in* those thoughts; since it is through the medium of language that children acquire most of their beliefs and many of their concepts. Thus it is obvious that no child would ever come to believe that the Earth moves round the Sun, or could ever acquire the concept of an electron or of electricity, in the absence of language. So a story can be told according to which the arrival of language, while not fundamentally altering human cognitive powers, made it possible for humans to begin to accumulate information about their environment, as well as to construct, for the first time, a transmissible culture. Such language-mediated accumulations, it may be claimed, are what underlie the dramatic success of *Homo sapiens sapiens* over earlier hominid species.

A more severe difficulty for the brain-size-equals-intelligence account might appear to be the *excess* capacity of the *sapiens* brain. For if all that changed when humans first acquired the capacity for language is that they began to acquire more and more *information*, then we might expect that they would have had substantially *less* spare capacity, and that there would have been considerable pressures for yet further increases in brain size. However, the data can be accommodated, consistent with the communicative conception of language, simply by accepting that the language-faculty is a late-evolving *module* of the mind. The story can then go like this: brain size increased steadily during the period when proto-language was being developed, due to pressures of interpreting and storing the significance of proto-language utterances, and resulting from increasing sophistication in a variety of central quasi-modules (such as for theory of mind, naive biology, naive physics, and so on). Then with the arrival of the language-module, interpretation became semi-automatic, fortuitously freeing-up cognitive space at the same time as increased powers of communication made possible a vastly expanded store of accumulated information.

In fact, however, it is not so easy for defenders of the communicative conception of language to evade Bickerton's argument. We can set them a dilemma, indeed. Suppose, on the one hand, that it is claimed that both language and human central cognitive powers evolved slowly together, appearing in modern form by about 100,000 years ago. There are three distinct problems with this account. Firstly, it is more complex than the alternative, since it postulates the evolution of two complex structures (language and the mechanisms responsible for intelligent thought) rather than just one. Second, it is hard to reconcile it with the evidence of the very late appearance of creative culture in the fossil record *circa* 40,000 years ago. And third, we have to accept that two such massive evolutionary changes took place in the *sapiens* brain without any significant increase in brain size – so much for big-brains-equal-intelligence!

The second horn of the dilemma arises if it is then claimed that human intelligence co-evolved with brain size *prior* to the arrival of language, perhaps responding to the demands of social living (Byrne and Whiten, 1988). For in that case, what would have prevented *erectus* from using its basically-human cognitive powers to make changes in its environment? In order to make a structural improvement to a cave, for example, you don't need an awful lot of accumulated beliefs (and certainly you don't need culture). You just need to be able to entertain, and reason from, explicit subjunctive or counterfactual thoughts such as, 'If there were to be a pile of rocks just *there*, then water wouldn't get in during the rainy season', or, 'If there hadn't been a second entrance to the cave over *there*, then the wind wouldn't have swept through during the storm.' Surely the most plausible story is that, prior to the evolution of natural language, proto-language using members of *Homo erectus* were not capable of such thoughts; and that it was the grammatical structures provided by our language faculty which first made it possible for us to entertain such thoughts, by being partly *constitutive of* them.

I conclude, then, that we can find in Bickerton's work a powerful new argument supporting of the cognitive conception of language, grounded in the fossil record. For if natural language and creative human intelligence are supposed to result from distinct cognitive systems, then it becomes implausible to maintain that they should each have evolved at the same time, after the brain had already reached its modern size. And yet if the core of human creative intelligence was supposed to have been in place prior to the evolution of language, then the problem is to explain the distinct *lack* of creative intelligence on the part of our immediate ancestors, *Homo erectus* and the Neanderthals.

3.3 Problems for Bickerton

Now on Bickerton's account language was, from the start, a system of representation (that is, a vehicle of thought), as well as a system of communication. What a language-vocabulary (an explicit lexicon) provided from the outset, from the very beginnings of proto-language, was a level of representation more abstract than the perceptually grounded concepts available to our ape ancestors, which could draw together under a single heading a number of different properties available through a number of different sense-modalities. (In support of this he can then cite all the evidence speaking in favour of the weak form of Whorfian conceptual relativism – see Lucy, 1992a, 1992b; Goldstone, 1994; Andrews *et al.*, submitted.) The evolution of our innate capacity for properly grammatical language then involved a major cortical re-organisation, making possible complex, indefinitely sophisticated, and conscious thinking and reasoning. So on this account, the language faculty, although innately specified, is not in any sense a *module* of the mind. Rather, it more or less coincides with central cognition itself. And with language in place, all other features of human (central) cognition are held to be products of social invention and learning, down to, and including, such matters as the incest-taboo (Bickerton, 1995).

One reason why Bickerton's model should strike us as implausible, however, is that it is quite obscure how the evolution of a grammar-faculty could, by itself, confer capacities for *non-demonstrative* social, causal, or explanatory reasoning. It is, perhaps, not wholly implausible that a grammar-faculty might involve some capacity for generating semantic entailments amongst sentences, since this might be thought to be part-and-parcel of the capacity to interpret those sentences. And language might also have conferred – crucially, in the light of the examples used above – a capacity to use and to understand conditionals, subjunctives and counterfactuals. (Or language might have given us the capacity to entertain such thoughts *explicitly*, at least, in an inferentially promiscuous way – presumably even apes entertain at least implicit, quasi-modular, conditional thoughts when they engage in deceptive strategies, say.) But why should it also involve a capacity to reason, non-demonstratively, about the mental states of other people, generating predictions and explanations of their behaviour; or a capacity to reason about the likely causes and effects of the phenomena we observe in nature? Yet it seems unquestionable that these abilities, at least in their developed forms, are distinctively human; and it seems plausible that they should have a substantial innate component (Baron-Cohen, 1995; Atran, 1990; Spelke *et al.*, 1995; Giere, 1988). Moreover, there is plenty of evidence that earlier forms of *Homo* must have been pretty good at just these forms of reasoning (Mithen, 1996).

Bickerton's account as it stands is implausible, in fact; both because it is hard to see how natural language could in any sense be *sufficient* for human reasoning, and also because it ignores the substantial evidence emerging from the evolutionary-psychology literature of the existence of a variety of innately determined – or, at any rate, innately *channelled* – aspects of central cognition (Barkow *et al.*, 1992). It is with this kind of weakly modularist picture of the mind (of the sort outlined in section 1 above) that Bickerton's version of the cognitive conception of language is surely inconsistent. So we have reason to prefer a form of cognitive conception which is more modularist than this (perhaps of the sort sketched in section 2).

Indeed, aside from his commitment to an innately determined language-faculty, Bickerton's account is otherwise highly empiricist in character. Virtually every aspect of central cognition besides language itself is put down to gradual social invention, and social transmission through teaching and learning. But the evidence for such gradualism is just not there in the fossil record, in fact (Mithen, 1996). The use of beads and necklaces as ornaments; the burying of the dead with ceremonies; the working of bone and antler into complex weapons; and the production of carved statuettes and paintings – all appear together in highly sophisticated form *circa* 40,000 years ago, in different parts of the world. So we not only need a version of cognitive conception of language which is consistent with modularism, we also need to provide for some relatively simple evolutionary change to have taken place independently in different groups of *Homo sapiens sapiens* at about the same time, irrespective of the varieties in the environmental challenges they faced. (As already noted, the evolution of the language faculty itself, as a highly complex mental organ, is likely to have required a consistent evolutionary pressure operating for a considerable period; and so it is *un*likely to have occurred independently in different parts of the globe at the same time. See Pinker and Bloom, 1990.)

4 The co-evolution of language with central cognition

According to proposals being made here, in contrast, the language faculty would have co-evolved with changes in a variety of quasi-modular central reasoning systems, each of which then came to operate, in part, by accessing and manipulating natural language representations (of LF, as it might be). What follows is a sketch of how the story might go. I should emphasise that it *is* just a sketch. There is much that needs greater elaboration than I can provide here, and the account is also presented without the benefit of any further supporting argument. But then my aim is only to convince investigators that such a modularist story is *possible*, so that they may begin to explore and develop it further, and subject it to various forms of empirical testing. (More on the latter in section 5 below.)

4.1 The evolution of language

Prior to the evolution of any form of language, I presume that our hominid ancestors would have had essentially the same sorts of perceptual and motor modules as we now enjoy (which is not to say that the visual module, for example, has undergone no further modification since the advent of language; but it is reasonable to assume that such modifications will have been relatively shallow). More important for present purposes, our ancestors might have had a number of special-purpose, quasi-modular, central computational systems for dealing with the behaviour of conspecifics (Byrne, 1995), for simple forms of cheater-detection (Cosmides and Tooby, 1992), for classifying natural kinds (Atran, 1995), and for reasoning about causes (Spelke *et al.*, 1995), say. These systems could have operated by effecting computations on the sentences of some sort of Mentalese, or they may have been associative networks of one sort or another. But the inputs to these systems would have been the *out*puts of the various perceptual (input) modules. And it seems reasonable to suppose that, in so far as the systems themselves provided our ancestors with knowledge of the relevant domains, this knowledge would have remained largely *im*plicit, as opposed to *ex*plicit, in the sense of Karmiloff-Smith (1992). That is, such systems might have provided our ancestors with sensitivity to, and hence a capacity to respond differentially to, a number of un-obvious features of their social and natural environments. But these sensitivities would have been embedded in particular procedures and contexts, and would not have been available to thought outside of those contexts. (See Mithen, 1996, for extended argument in support of the mutual isolation of the specialist cognitive systems within our remote as well as our more immediate ancestors, grounded in the archaeological record.)

Now, suppose that the story which Bickerton tells us about the next stage of hominid evolution is broadly correct. That is, suppose that our ancestors were evolving the capacity to employ 'proto-languages' – simple systems of communication and representation, with increasingly large vocabularies, but with little recognisable grammar (*see also* Gomez, this volume, chapter 4). This would have been connected with an extension in the range and abstractness of hominid thought, with proto-language lexical items forming the most abstract level of conceptual representation. Even such a simple system of communication and conceptual representation would have enabled hominids to vastly extend the store of information which each individual could accumulate during a lifetime, as well as placing very considerable demands on on-line processing. So the arrival of proto-language may very well have coincided with the step-change in brain-size which occurs with the evolution of various different species of *Homo erectus* some 1.6 to 2 million years ago.

At this stage the special-purpose reasoning systems would probably have altered, too, in such a way as to operate independently of perceptual input, now taking as input proto-language representations and generating proto-language sentences as output. This latter point is especially easy to see in connection with the theory-of-mind quasi-module. For with the appearance of proto-language, hominid speech-behaviour would then have been one of the prime objects of intentionalist (TOM) explanation and prediction. But the same is very likely true of other quasi-modules too. Thus merely being told about some recent event might have been sufficient to evoke the causal-reasoning quasi-module into activity, attempting to construct the best causal explanation of the event described.

By this stage the main building-blocks necessary for a meta-representational, reflexively-conscious, central executive, with a structure something like that depicted in section 2.1 above, may well all have been in place (*see also* my 1996a, chapter 8). We can assume that by now hominids would at least have been *capable* of imagination of various sorts, re-deploying the resources of perceptual modules in the manner outlined earlier (indeed, there is evidence from the fossil record that *Homo erectus* was capable of generating and transforming visual images, at least; see Wynn, 1993) – although I shall suggest in a moment that this capacity would rarely have been used, prior to the evolution of grammatical language. So with the arrival of proto-language, hominids may also have been capable of generating proto-language sentences in auditory or motor imagination, thus creating inner speech. Items of inner speech would then have been made available to the same set of conceptual resources as could be brought to bear on heard (overt) speech, including the resources of the theory-of-mind faculty. Whether these items could then have become objects of further, meta-representational, thought (Level 2 explicit, in the sense of Karmiloff-Smith, 1992) depends upon the question whether full TOM abilities are, or are not, dependent upon grammatical language (see Gomez, this volume chapter 4; Varley, this volume chapter 6; Segal, this volume chapter 7).

Finally, the fully grammatical natural-language faculty began to evolve, culminating with the first appearance of *Homo sapiens sapiens* in southern Africa some 100,000 years ago. This would have extended the range and sophistication of hominid thought still further – introducing explicit (as opposed to implicit/domain-specific) conditionals, subjunctives and counterfactuals, for example. And natural language representations would still have been exploited and deployed by the special-purpose reasoning systems, which would have come to operate, now, on natural-language (properly grammatical) sentences. And at this time, too, we can be confident that the materials necessary for a reflexively-conscious central executive would all have been in place. The stage was set for the explosion in creative thinking which occurred with the arrival of sophisticated culture some 50,000 years later.

But why would the evolution of grammatical language have involved anything like a natural-language *module*? After all, proto-language was (and is) not modular in any sense. So why should its successor have been modular either? The most likely answer to this question is as follows. The main problem confronting our hominid proto-language-using ancestors was, we may presume, one of speech *interpretation*. Proto-language utterances are multiply ambiguous, requiring heavy reliance upon contextual knowledge and assumptions about speaker intentions in order to be understood. There would then have been very great advantage in the evolution of a special-purpose faculty for imposing greater structure on utterances, and for deriving interpretations on the basis of such structures. With the arrival of a grammar-faculty, interpretation could become semi-automatic, in fact. (Not that it *had* to be – the same resources and cognitive effort which had previously been devoted to basic interpretation could now be applied to pragmatics, and to such matters as word-play, metaphor, and irony. For theories of the sorts of processing involved, see Sperber and Wilson, 1986/1995.)

Other answers are also possible, however, if less likely. For example, some have argued that the grammar faculty may have been the result of run-away sexual selection, like the peacock's tail (Miller, 1996). But the important point is that the main pressures leading to the evolution of the grammar faculty where those of input and output. They had to do with the need to produce, and to decode, easily interpretable utterances (or perhaps with mate-preferences for structurally elaborate speech). So, like other input and output systems, the grammar faculty would have taken on a fairly strongly modular form. But with central-process quasi-modules already geared up to operate on proto-language sentences, it would have required but small modifications for them to operate on natural-language (properly grammatical) sentences instead, paving the way for the creation of the sort of virtual executive described in section 2.1 above.

There is a problem with this story, however. For how could the pressures leading to the evolution of the grammar faculty have been basically communicative ones, if grammar was also implicated in thought, and served to extend the range of thoughts available to our ancestors? What could have led to the emergence of subjunctive and counterfactual forms of conditional, for example, if early types of *sapiens* had not already been capable of subjunctive and counterfactual *thinking*? The answer, I take it, is a kind of boot-strapping account, drawing on what I assume to be a quite general phenomenon – namely, that we can always think more than we can say, and that whenever people have a system of signs available to them, there are always more things that they can do with it, in thought, than they have explicit markers for in the public system. (See Sperber and Wilson, this volume chapter 9, for one sort of example of this phenomenon, where more-specific variants of public concepts can be introduced for use in the speaker's own thoughts.) So with each new innovation in the grammar-system, there would be, not just a new range of utterances to be *decoded*, but also a new set of communicative uses of those utterances which would need to be interpreted, laboriously, by *inference*, hence creating further selectional pressure for yet further grammatical innovations; and so on.

4.2 *The evolution of creative thinking*

We may presume, then, that the mind of early *Homo sapiens sapiens* was basically quite similar to that of some of the later species of *Homo erectus* and the Neanderthals, except that it contained a specialised grammar module (perhaps also containing a more highly developed TOM quasi-module). This would have given our species a crucial advantage, sufficient to explain its rapid colonisation of the globe (with Australia being reached by boat for the first time some 60,000 years ago), together with the extinction of competing species of *Homo*. Grammatical language – with explicit conditionals and subjunctives – would have conferred on *Homo sapiens sapiens* the capacity for more sophisticated planning of hunts, and also the ability to accumulate a much richer set of beliefs and knowledge about the world, as well as to acquire and transmit complex skills through instruction. (And indeed, the evidence is that *Homo sapiens sapiens* was more efficient at hunting than its predecessors, and soon began to carve harpoons out of bone, beginning fishing for the first time; see Mithen, 1996, pp.

178–183.) Moreover, grammatical language would have made possible whole new orders of social complexity and co-ordination, sufficient to explain the extinction of competitors (by warfare if necessary).

The evidence from the fossil record is that *Homo sapiens sapiens* of 90,000 years ago was of basically modern intelligence, accumulating knowledge about its environment and making a number of important technological innovations; but that it was crucially lacking in *imagination* (Mithen, 1996). Although the working of wooden artefacts may have undergone some change, and bone tools were introduced for the first time, essentially the same range of stone tools as had been employed by *erectus* continued to be used for tens of thousands of years. And there was no sign of the use of body-ornaments, or of the production of art (and little evidence of religion) until all these exploded onto the scene world-wide some 40,000 years ago. To explain this, we either have to suppose that the knowledge accumulated by *Homo sapiens sapiens* and transmitted via language reached some critical mass *circa* 40,000 years ago, to trigger an explosion of creative thinking; or we have to postulate some simple, multiply evolved, cognitive adaptation to underpin the change. It is hard to see how an explanation of the former sort could work, since it is difficult to understand why imaginative thinking should presuppose a large body of accumulated knowledge. So my proposal is of the latter kind, with the evolution of an innate predisposition to engage in *pretend play* marking the crucial divide. But this will require some setting up.

Why do I think that the hominid capacity for visual and other forms of imagination would not have been much used, prior to the evolution of grammatical language or for some time thereafter? Because of the evidence of the fossil record, as described by Bickerton and Mithen – if *Homo erectus* and early *Homo sapiens* had used their imaginations on a regular basis, then one would have expected them to have had a bigger impact on their environment, and to have developed a wider variety of tools and artefacts. However, I *am* assuming that grammatical language provided for the first time a capacity to entertain explicitly, and to interpret, various forms of conditional. It seems plausible that this would have been linked to a capacity to *suppose* – to entertain a supposition, and to reason hypothetically from there. This capacity lies at the very heart of *Homo sapiens sapiens*' creativity and adaptability, I believe. And it is essentially the *same* capacity as that which is exploited in pretend play (Jarrold *et al.*, 1994), which is best understood as *practice for* our adult employment of supposition in creative hypothetical reasoning (Carruthers, 1996c).

The young of all species of mammal engage in play of various distinctive sorts, the function of which seems to be to prepare them for adult activities (Smith, 1982). What is special about the play of human children, in all cultures from quite a young age, is that they engage, not just in play (e.g. rough-and-tumble fighting) but in *pretence*. They use one object to symbolise another (a pencil as an aeroplane; a banana as a telephone), they pretend to adopt social roles (cowboy; fireman; nurse), and they engage in games of pure imagination (carrying on a conversation with an imaginary friend; pretending that the woods are full of dinosaurs, or that they are on an island surrounded by alligators). So it seems reasonable to think that human children must be wired up in such a way as to detect, and to find intrinsically rewarding, their own mental state *pretending*, or *supposing*. (And it may then be the failure of this mechanism, through failure of mental-state detection – i.e. delayed or damaged TOM – which explains the marked absence of pretend play in autism; see Carruthers, 1996c.) At any rate, we can readily envisage quite a simple mechanism which would provide children with intrinsic rewards for entering into and maintaining the mental state of pretending, perhaps by boosting the level of interest which the child antecedently has in the content of the play supposition.

The evolutionary story may then go something like this. A grammar module made its first appearance with the evolution of *Homo sapiens sapiens*. This provided the representational resources to engage freely and explicitly in hypothetical and counter-factual thinking, which immediately had a considerable impact on the life of the species – in terms of planning, social co-ordination, and making possible a number of technical innovations. At this stage the use of suppositional thinking would have been entirely practical, and tied to particular domains of activity (hunting, social relations, artefacts). But it would have been important enough for there to be pressure for the evolution of a simple pretend-play mechanism, of the sort described above, designed to give children a head-start in this species-distinctive form of activity. But once *that* happened (*circa* 40–50,000 years ago) a snowball of creative thinking was set in motion which has not stopped moving yet, giving rise to the unique flexibility and recursive improvability of the distinctively modern mind.

What I am suggesting is that our disposition to make regular use of visual and other sensory forms of imagination (including inner speech) piggy-backs upon our ability to deploy and reason from language-involving suppositions, and on the fact that children are pre-disposed to find the exercise of supposition intrinsically rewarding, in pretend play. There are then two complementary ways in which a highest-level executive could thereby have been created, as we saw briefly in section 2. One picks up on the idea developed by Frankish (this volume, chapter 12), that sentences of inner speech would be available to become objects of rationally motivated *decision* – the subject might *decide* to accept the sentence in question as a premise in further practical or theoretical reasoning, for example, thus creating a new kind of *virtual belief*. The other is that subjects might be taught, or might teach themselves, to accept, and to make, certain sorts of transitions between natural-language sentences, thus engaging in new forms of inference. But since these transitions would be available to awareness and to critical reflection, they would not be fixed, but would be subject to further refinement and improvement (once again, of a rationally motivated sort).

Recall, too, that the various central quasi-modules would already have become set up so as to operate upon natural language inputs, and to produce natural language outputs. The creation of an inner-speech-using central executive would then have enabled these specialised systems to communicate with one another on a regular basis, co-operating in the solution of problems, or generating ideas which cross quasi-modular barriers, such as animals which can speak or persons who can exist without a physical body. And the regular operation of imagination, independently of any particular practical context or problem, would have paid rich dividends in the production of genuinely novel ideas and inventions.

The basic picture I want to present, then, is of an innately structured natural-language module whose resources are routinely accessed by the various reasoning and executive systems of central cognition, in such a way that the latter function, in part, by deploying and transforming natural-language representations. We can therefore predict that if this form of cognitive conception of language is correct, then an individual who had never acquired any natural language would lack any capacity for (certain forms of) explicit-conceptual (as opposed to implicit, or visuo-spatial) thought. And we can also predict that someone whose natural language system was completely destroyed, would completely lose the capacity for just those kinds of thinking. In the next section I shall develop these implications further.

5 Empirical commitments

The account sketched above is consistent, at least, with the available empirical data; and some of that data speaks tentatively in its support – see my 1996a, chs. 2 and 8 for discussion. But how might it specifically be tested? What particular empirical commitments does the theory have, which might differentiate it from other approaches, and how might they be investigated? When the theory is compared with Bickerton's account, the differences relate mostly to evidence for, or against, quasi-modularity and the existence of a central executive. Thus my account should predict that there may be cases where language is spared but various other competencies – in theory of mind, in cheater-detection, or in causal-explanatory reasoning, for example – are damaged or lost altogether; whereas Bickerton must deny this. And the autism data, at any rate, speaks strongly in favour of just such a quasi-modularist picture of central cognition (Baron-Cohen, 1995). When the theory is compared with any form of communicative conception of language, in contrast, there are roughly three sets of distinct empirical commitments which could be used to test between the two approaches. I shall discuss each of them briefly in turn.

One prediction turns specifically on the modularism of the proposal. It is that humans lacking any language would be incapable of *explicit* conceptual thought about a variety of domains, including perhaps theory of mind, social fairness, and unobservable causes. (I say *unobservable* causes to exclude Humean learning-by-association, which would not really require *reasoning*, and would almost certainly not require language. So I find the data presented by Varley – this volume, chapter 6 – of an a-grammatical aphasic who could pass a causal-reasoning task unsurprising in this regard; for the test was essentially one of causal *association*.) For the proposal is that explicit thought about such domains depends either upon the specialised quasi-modules in question being fed with language or proto-language inputs, or at least on their being capable of producing such linguistic representations as outputs, for consumption by other central systems. If reliable non-linguistic tests can then be devised for the capacity to entertain explicit thoughts about such matters, then this prediction might be tested on people with global aphasia, or on pre-conventional-language deaf children who lack any vocabulary items drawn from the test domain. (In similar spirit, such tests might be run in connection with more limited forms of aphasia, provided that the people in question lack any relevant vocabulary items; but with the added complication that the problems such people experience may simply be those of input and output, while retaining a centrally stored representation of the lexical items in question.) However, there will, of course, be the usual problems of avoiding covert training, and the Clever Hans phenomenon.

Another prediction relates to conscious (reflexively available, meta-represented) thinking. For the proposal is that the central executive runs (at least in that part of its activities which is properly conceptual) on imaged natural language representations (the other part running on visual and other images, which might underpin explicit spatial reasoning). So a test of this proposal would have to test the benefits of flexibility and revisability which attaches to conscious thinking. It is at least possible to imagine what such tests might look like, to be conducted on patients with global aphasia, for example. But unfortunately there are two distinct confounds, each arising from the involvement of theory of mind in conscious thinking. The first is that if it should turn out to be *wrong* that sophisticated TOM abilities require language, then people without language might succeed in tests of conscious thinking, but might do so, not because language is not normally implicated in such thinking, but rather because they can mimic some of the advantages of conscious thinking – thus they might be able to use their intact TOM abilities to attribute thoughts to themselves by means of a process of *self-interpretation*, for example. (I assume, here, that conscious thinking requires *non*-inferential access to our own thoughts; so thoughts self-ascribed on the basis of self-interpretation would not count as conscious ones; see my 1996a, chapter 7.) The second confound is the converse difficulty, that if it turns out to be *correct* that sophisticated TOM requires language, then those who fail tests of conscious thinking may do so, not because conscious thinking itself involves language, but rather because the TOM capacities which are necessary for occurrent thoughts to be meta-representationally available require language. It is not easy for me to see, at this stage, how tests might be devised which would control for these confounds.

The third prediction picks up on the idea that there may be some forms of explicit thinking and reasoning – such as subjunctive and counterfactual reasoning – which are specifically dependent upon the availability of the appropriate *grammatical* forms. This prediction might then be tested in two distinct ways, provided that reliable non-linguistic tests of explicit counterfactual reasoning can be devised. First, we could see whether people with global aphasia or a-grammatical aphasia can nevertheless succeed in such tasks. And second, we could see whether the performance of pre-conventional-language deaf children on such tasks improves dramatically when they are finally introduced into a Signing community. (This would, in effect, be a re-run of an aspect of the Luria and Yudovich 1956 twin-experiment, in which the pretend-play and reasoning abilities of two barely linguistic twins improved dramatically over the three-month period in which they acquired significant amounts of language.) For it would surely be implausible that any significant improvement could be due to new beliefs which the children had acquired through communication from adults, since so little time would have elapsed, and since most early uses of language involve comment upon items which are perceptually salient to both speaker and hearer. The most plausible explanation of any improvement would be that the provision of grammatical language had made it possible for the children to entertain new kinds of thought, by providing a vehicle for those thoughts.

Finally, it may be worth noting that the account of the evolution of creative thinking, sketched above, carries a commitment to a two-component theory of the mechanism responsible for pretend-play. This mechanism consists of a *pretence-detector*, which we can assume to draw on the resources of (early-developing forms of) the theory of mind quasi-module

(TOM); and a *motivator*, which gives the child some intrinsic reward whenever a mental state of pretending is detected. The prediction must then be that there could be two dissociable ways for the mechanism to break down – either the pretence-detector might fail (e.g. through delayed/damaged TOM), or the motivator might. Pleasingly, the available data support just such a dissociation. In a large screening study undertaken for childhood autism, Simon Baron-Cohen and colleagues found that in *all* cases where children lacked joint-attention and proto-declarative behaviours (thought to be early stages in the development of TOM), pretend play was also absent. But they also found children in whom pretend play was absent while joint-attention and proto-declarative behaviours were present (Baron-Cohen *et al.*, 1996). More research is needed to see if the latter group of children retain the *capacity* for pretence but lack the motivation for it (as my account predicts); and also to see if they display any marked lack of creativity in their thinking in later life.

6 Conclusion

In this chapter I have offered a limited defence of (a weak version of) the cognitive conception of language, both by offering an additional argument in its support (following Bickerton), and by showing how it can be rendered consistent with a broadly modularist conception of language and mind. I have also indicated directions in which the proposals might be tested. But, as a philosopher, I must leave the actual devising of such tests to others.

I am grateful to all those who participated in the Hang Seng Centre conferences over the period 1994–7, for providing me with much of the stimulus for my ideas; and to Derek Bickerton, Paul Bloom, George Botterill, Jill Boucher, Keith Frankish, Susan Granger, Steven Mithen, and Neil Smith for their comments on earlier drafts.

Part II

Language, reasoning and concepts

Introduction to part II

Peter Carruthers and Jill Boucher

The chapters in Part II all focus on the relationship between language, on the one hand, and concepts and reasoning abilities on the other – either in general, or within particular domains of thought, such as Theory of Mind (TOM). As previously, we first make some general introductory remarks, before saying something briefly to introduce each of the five chapters in Part II.

Anyone defending a strong form of cognitive conception of language will maintain, of course, that there is an intimate connection between language, concepts, and distinctive human reasoning abilities. At its strongest, their claim will be that the former (language) is both necessary and sufficient for the latter (McDowell, 1994). In weaker variants, the claim may only be that language is the vehicle of (and so a necessary but not a sufficient condition for) some types of concept, and/or some types of reasoning. Conversely, anyone defending a strong form of communicative conception of language will wish to maintain that our concepts and reasoning abilities are wholly independent of language. Such a person will claim that thinking is one thing, and encoding thought into language for purposes of communication is quite another. But here, too, a weaker variant of the position is possible. According to the *supra-communicative conception* of language (see chapter 1 above), thought and concepts are independent of language, and language is basically for the communication of thought; but it is also possible for language to *enhance* human cognitive powers, either via inner language, or by providing an external resource for cognition, as when one effects a complex calculation on paper, or writes out a shopping list. So on this weaker account, while individual concepts and thoughts are independent of language, it may be that some extended processes of thinking and reasoning are only possible for us when conducted in language. Weaker forms of both cognitive and communicative conceptions of language are explored and defended in Part II. (Note that many of the chapters in Part III also deal with language and reasoning, but laying greater stress on different *levels* of thinking.)

Chapter 6: Varley

Aphasia is a condition in which someone loses their capacity for language – either in whole or in part – as a result of suffering brain damage, perhaps through a stroke. This population of people is, then, of very great interest for the question of the relationship between thought and language. If an aphasic patient could retain cognitive capacities more or less intact while losing all capacity for language, then this would be powerful evidence in support of the independence of thought from language. Conversely, if aphasic patients always exhibit some or other cognitive deficit, then this would give weak support to a cognitive conception of language – *weak*, because association of deficits might always be explained, in principle, by neuro-anatomical accident, if the systems supporting the two capacities happen to be situated in similar regions of the brain.

Most linguists and aphasiologists agree that the language faculty is made up of a number of distinct systems (production, comprehension, centrally stored grammar, lexicon, and so on), which suggests that the most interesting population of aphasic people will be those with *global* aphasia, where all capacity for language is lost. For otherwise, if some preserved cognitive capacity is found in an aphasic patient, it might always be possible that this is underpinned by the remaining parts of their language faculty. And yet global aphasia brings with it its own problems for the cognitive scientist, since the brain damage involved can often be quite extensive, sometimes amounting to a whole half-hemisphere. This renders any association of deficits especially vulnerable to explanation by neuro-anatomical accident.

Rosemary Varley here reports a series of studies, including tests of theory of mind ability, undertaken with an a-grammatic aphasic whose aphasia was by no means global. But since he was very poor at processing grammatical structure (having special difficulty in accessing and comprehending verbs), the suggestion is that he ought to be poor at propositional reasoning, on the hypothesis that such reasoning is conducted in language. And since he displays almost identical deficits in both production and comprehension, it seems unlikely that he retains a centrally stored *capacity* for grammar which he is simply unable to deploy in practice. The patient in question passed tests for Theory of Mind and for causal reasoning, suggesting that these types of propositional thought, at least, may be independent of language.

Chapter 7: Segal

Gabriel Segal's paper takes its start from a theory of the semantics of propositional attitude reports which is both familiar and quite often endorsed in the philosophy of language. On this sort of account, very roughly, the content-clause in a report of the form, 'A believes that P' refers to the *sentence* used to express that content. So 'John believes that cows eat grass' has the form, 'John believes: ["Cows eat grass"]'. Such an account has many advantages, some of which are briefly sketched by Segal at the outset of his paper. He then goes on to ask what implications such a theory has for thoughts about the beliefs of others, supposing that it is correct. If *talking about* people's beliefs involves reference to natural language sentences, does *thinking about* their beliefs also involve reference to such sentences? If so, then this would mean that explicit theory of mind abilities depend crucially upon language. Segal sketches an account of how this might work, and goes on to show that the theory is consistent with, and tentatively supported by, a variety of kinds of empirical data – but not Varley's, which he now concludes by discussing. The paper is thus a (tentative) endorsement of a (weak form of) cognitive conception of language, restricted to the domain of theory of mind thinking.

Chapter 8: Clark

Andy Clark's paper is an extended and wide-ranging development of what he calls a *supra-communicative* conception of language. He argues that language should be seen as a cognitive *tool* – presupposing cognition and thought (hence this is not a form of cognitive conception of language), but nevertheless enhancing and extending cognition and thought. On this view, language re-configures the computational space of many of the problems which confront us, rendering them more tractable. How this can happen is easiest to see in connection with the Arabic – as opposed to, e.g., the Roman – number system. By virtue of utilising a decimal base, it renders routine various formal operations – addition, subtraction, multiplication – which would otherwise be difficult.

Clark, like Dennett (1991), believes that the underlying cognitive architecture of the human brain is *connectionist*, processing streams of information in parallel. But, unlike Dennett, he does not believe that the acquisition of language fundamentally re-programmes the brain into a sequential, sentence-processing, classical computer (see our introduction to Part III). Rather, language enhances and extends the computational powers of the existing system, without fundamentally altering its architecture. So we do not literally owe our minds to language, as Dennett believes (this would be quite a strong form of cognitive conception of language); but there may be a great many extended processes of thought which would not be possible for us without it.

Chapter 9: Sperber and Wilson

The background to Sperber and Wilson's chapter is their (1986/1995) relevance theory of communication and cognition. On such an account, language production and comprehension are governed by principles of relevance. Speakers will try to produce utterances which are relevant to their hearers; and hearers will try to figure out what a speaker means by assuming that what is said will be relevant. Plainly this is, then, a species of communicative conception of language. As with the Gricean account, thought and inference are presupposed by language. (But unlike the Gricean account, there is no attempt to reduce *all* semantic properties to speakers' and hearers' intentions and thoughts. So we believe that their account is consistent with Laurence's Chomskian programme in semantics – see below.)

However, it is possible to endorse the communicative conception of language and yet think that language will mirror the structure of thought quite precisely (as does Fodor, 1975) – that is, one might think that the concepts out of which a speaker's thoughts are composed will line up one-to-one with lexical items from their natural language. So although language may not be directly implicated in cognition, it does provide us with a fairly accurate *window* into cognition. This is the idea that Sperber and Wilson are aiming to undermine in their chapter. They argue that speakers will characteristically have many *more* concepts than there are items in their public lexicon. In particular, speakers will often formulate and store concepts which are more fine-grained than the distinctions which are available to them in their lexicon – for example, forming a concept for the precise degree of tiredness which is sufficient to prevent one from wanting to go to the cinema. So not only is language not constitutive of the mind, it is not a true mirror of the mind either.

Chapter 10: Laurence

As we noted in chapter 1, one powerful and common route to acceptance of a communicative conception of language runs via a Gricean approach to natural language semantics. On such an account, languages are basically conventional signalling systems, by means of which thoughts are transmitted from one mind to another. Stephen Laurence argues that such accounts are mistaken, not just in detail but fundamentally. If my utterance of 'Cows eat grass' only comes to mean [*that cows eat grass*] in virtue of my *intention* that you should come to *believe* that cows eat grass by *recognising* that I am *intending* to get you to *believe* that cows eat grass (or some other variant on the Gricean approach), then language ought only to be possible for people who have a conception of the beliefs and intentions of other persons. But in fact many autistic people, and children under the age of four, have language who appear to lack such a conception. So something may be deeply amiss with the account.

Laurence's preferred alternative is to model natural language semantics on natural language grammar, *à la* Chomsky. That is, he proposes that semantic properties of words and utterances are assigned by mechanisms at the interface between the language faculty and conceptual systems, independently of processes of thought and speaker-intention. Such an account could be made consistent with either a cognitive or a communicative conception of language, as Laurence points out. So if the negative aspect of his thesis is correct, hence undermining one of the main motivations behind a communicative conception of language, then everything may be up for grabs once again – the debate between communicative and cognitive conceptions of language will have to be resumed on the basis of other arguments, not closed off in favour of the former through semantic considerations.

6 Aphasic language, aphasic thought: an investigation of propositional thinking in an a-propositional aphasic

Rosemary Varley

1 Introduction

Aphasia is an acquired disorder of language in which, following a cortical lesion, a person who previously had normal language behaviour loses the ability to produce and understand linguistic messages. Aphasiologists generally operate with the tacit assumption that 'thinking' is unaffected by aphasia, although some might enter caveats about this assertion when referring to global aphasics and low-comprehension Wernicke's aphasics (more of them later). The source of this belief is twofold. First, information processing models of language, which provide much of the theoretical basis for contemporary aphasiology, postulate a level of knowledge which is pre-linguistic (in message production), and post-linguistic (in message comprehension) (e.g. Garrett, 1982). Aphasics generally (although not always – see Marshall *et al.*, 1993, for an example case study) are seen as having difficulties in translating language to or from an underlying intact conceptual representation. Second, this assumption is grounded in interactions with people with aphasia where the impression gained is that one is dealing with a rational individual. The aphasic person has communicative intentions which they struggle to realise through language or through other communicative means, for example, drawing, pantomime gesture, and sometimes the communicative partner's language system. Thus some aphasic individuals appear expert in tool use, augmenting their damaged language faculties with both external and internal tools. In addition to wise use of communicative resources, many people with aphasia seem to have difficulties which are confined to a modular system which is not implicated in central cognition. Some aphasic individuals still drive cars, and most show appropriate behaviour across social contexts, attempt to solve everyday problems, are curious about the world, and show predictable frustration and distress at their communicative difficulties.

Aphasiologists appear, therefore, to be supporting a 'communicative conception' of language (Carruthers, 1996a), which sees language as an input/output module to central cognition, and the use of which is largely dedicated to inter-personal communication. The opposing 'cognitive conception' accords natural language a central role in human cognition. Carruthers, in his advocacy of a cognitive conception, uncontroversially emphasises the role of language in learning (imagine a classroom or lecture theatre in which there was no language), and points to the evidence from introspection that inner speech accompanies and supports much of our cognising. This same point is made by Clark (this volume chapter 8) who advocates a supra-communicative view of language – that language has an important cognitive role as an internal scaffold of our cognisings. But Carruthers goes beyond a supra-communicative view and develops two hypotheses of varying strength. The first and weaker hypothesis suggests that conscious propositional thinking is conducted in language; whilst the second and stronger hypothesis makes the claim that some thoughts *can only* be instantiated in natural language – causal reasoning and thinking about the thoughts of another person being possible examples. Presumably, Carruthers would argue, these thoughts demand a propositional/sentential format and so cannot be realised through other modes of representation such as visual imagery. But such a thesis is in conflict with the impressionistic view of interactions with an aphasic person. If people with aphasia are indeed unable to make causal inferences, or infer to the mental states of others, how then could those interacting with them sustain the impression of rationality.

A resolution of the apparent conflict might be that the aphasic individuals who do appear rational are not globally aphasic, instead they have components of lexical or syntactic processing still available to them and so they can 'hack' propositional thought in much the same way that they 'hack' public language. This would suggest that research into the language-and-thought question in aphasia should be restricted to studies of people with global aphasia, that is individuals who experience profound impairments both in comprehension and production of language across spoken and written modalities. But there are difficulties with this proposal. First, even global aphasics may retain some implicit language knowledge. Milberg and Blumstein (1981), and Blumstein *et al.* (1982) reported that on a task which required unconscious semantic processing, global aphasics – despite apparent obliteration of performance on explicit language comprehension tasks – still showed a facilitation of speed of word recognition when the stimulus word was primed by a semantically related word. This would mean that few aphasics are 'language-less'. Second, there are difficulties for advocates of a cognitive conception of language in using association of deficits (i.e. severe language impairment *plus* failure on, for example, tests of causal reasoning) as vigorous supporting data (see the section on global aphasia for discussion of this problem). In the next section, I will consider the implications for aphasia of acceptance of a supra-communicative view of language: that is, a more limited thesis of language involvement in cognition than a full-blown cognitive conception.

2 Learning and inner speech in aphasia

Advocates of a communicative conception of language could not deny the role of language in acquiring knowledge and beliefs. The loss of language in later life is likely to have consequences for the aphasic person's acquisition of new knowledge, although not to the same degree as a similar loss experienced early in life. Without language, the aphasic is a mute apprentice, able to learn from observation, but with little access to abstract information. Language may act as a source not only of content-based learning, but also of the learning of operations such as analogy. Premack (1983, 1988) has shown some of the cognitive advantages of possession of a language system by comparisons of the abilities of language-trained and non-language-trained chimpanzees in performing tasks involving analogies, proportions and the like. Premack reports significant advantages in the favour of language-trained chimpanzees, suggesting that language may provide scaffolding for the development of certain operations within central cognition, although these processes do not themselves have to be instantiated through natural language. Because the role of language may be restricted to that of the initial configuring of systems, the cognitive disadvantages to being aphasic may not be so great as one might predict on the basis of evidence from studies of abnormal acquisition in human children or the comparative work with chimpanzees. In the aphasic adult, knowledge bases and operations for combining and transforming knowledge are in place and, once in place, the scaffolding of language can be removed without the cognitive edifice tumbling down (Pinker, 1994).

Some of Premack's findings of cognitive advantages accruing to language-trained chimpanzees may result from the fact that language provides its users with a powerful cognitive resource to support reasoning and problem solving. Inner speech is the silent speech we hear in our heads. It appears when we are talking silently to ourselves (an entirely communicative conception of the phenomenon), but it also appears at times of heavy cognitive demand when the resources of the language module are recruited to underpin the functions of central cognition – a supra-communicative view. There are many examples of demand situations. We are most aware of the phenomenon whilst trying to formulate complex arguments, or when rehearsing utterances to use in important interactions. Inner speech also occurs when we are presented with problems to solve where an immediate solution is not evident and which require attention to a number of different components. It appears in memory tasks when we are required to retain stimuli which are relatively meaningless for short periods. The potency of inner speech is also indicated by experiments which suggest that other forms of sensory data are also encoded into a phonological format to enhance their maintenance (e.g. Conrad, 1971, Baddeley, 1986).

Inner speech is clearly a powerful resource upon which central cognition can call. This view of inner speech as a support to central cognition is different from a behaviourist notion that inner speech propositions constitute thought. Inner speech represents the recruitment of language resources to add form to thoughts. This addition of form makes the thought more concrete and memorable, and once in this format it can be operated upon, transformed and developed. In this way inner speech provides an internal screen or workspace. At times it is also supplemented by external workspaces such as paper and pencil to overcome the transience of phonological codings by transfer to more permanent orthographic and pictorial representations.

Evidence from aphasic subjects suggests that inner speech is impaired (Goodglass *et al.*, 1974), although there is no evidence to indicate whether or not the nature of the inner speech impairment parallels that of public speech. Baddeley allows, in his discussion of encoding within the phonological loop, for both phonological and auditory-based coding (Gathercole and Baddeley, 1993). It is then possible for an aphasic person with a dis-association between input–output processing to be using, in the case where input processing is more intact, an auditorally-based inner speech which is distinct from the individual's output abilities. A variety of tests is used to examine inner speech in aphasic subjects, for example, effect of phonological similarity in the memorisation of to-be-remembered items, judgements of number of syllables in a word, matching a word to one that rhymes with it, and making decisions on the identity of the onset of a word. All these tasks have confounding factors: all require explicit performances, and the tests requiring phonological judgements place heavy demands on meta-phonological knowledge (e.g. sound and syllable segmentation).

Despite the methodological problems, the most likely contention is that most aphasic individuals experience inner speech difficulties which mirror their public speech impairments. This is likely to have cognitive consequences as it represents an impairment of the inner workspace, and, in the usual case, the individual with aphasia often experiences impairments in all modalities of language performance, the external orthographic workspace too. As a result, aphasic subjects may show impaired performances in tasks where central cognition would call upon the resources of the language faculty to support its operations. This disruption of inner verbal mediation may account for some reports of failures on tasks which do not obviously require language, such as the Raven's Matrices (Raven, 1965; Kelter *et al.*, 1977). At the most complex levels of this test, selection of the correct item requires a number of mental operations, for example: analogy, rotation and transformation of shapes; and verbal/mathematical reasoning (e.g. $x+y=z$), and subjects often report that they use inner speech reasoning to support problem solving on the test. Finally, some people with aphasia, given a degree of plasticity of function, may be able to engage alternative resources in order to meet the resource demands of central cognition. The enhancement of visuo-spatial scratchpad resources (Baddeley, 1986) and use of visual imagery, or, where intact, orthographic representations are possible compensatory strategies.

3 Global aphasia

Some people with aphasia give the impression of a reasoning and rational individual. But this cannot be said of all aphasics. The group of aphasics for whom there are consistent reports of cognitive impairments extending beyond language is that of global aphasics and low-comprehension Wernicke's aphasics (e.g. van Mourik *et al.*, 1992). Whereas Broca-, anomic and some Wernicke-type aphasics have remnants of a language system still intact, this is not the case in global aphasia. It may well be that the groups of aphasics who show limited involvement of cognition are able to cobble together their remaining linguistic resources in ways that still permit language to support central cognition. Thus the evidence from these aphasics may have little to tell us about the role of language in thought. Perhaps then, evidence which is pertinent to the language-and-thought debate can only be based on investigations of globally aphasic individuals. There is a difficulty, however, with such a conclusion. Experiments which show that global aphasics have non-language impairments demonstrate association of deficits, and there is considerable difficulty in interpreting such evidence (e.g. Whitehouse *et al.*, 1978; Cohen *et al.*, 1979; Semenza *et al.*, 1980; Caramazza *et al.*, 1982; Wayland and Taplin, 1982). Association of deficits may occur because one process may truly be functionally inter-related to another – although it may not always be possible to establish the direction of the association. With regard to the language-and-thought debate, a broad sweep of cognitive impairment might stem either from disruption of a conceptual language of thought with knock-on effects into public language, or the obliteration of public language as the substrate of thought. Alternatively, an association may say little about functional inter-relationships within a system, but more about anatomy. Two functionally independent processes may be mediated by geographically close brain areas. Global aphasics generally have very large lesions of the left hemisphere (e.g. Kertesz *et al.*, 1977). The co-occurrence of language and other cognitive difficulties may not be due to any functional inter-relationship between language and thinking, but to anatomical accident: that is, the cortical zones that underpin the two functions are in close proximity and are both likely to be damaged by naturally occurring brain lesions (and perhaps, given the size of the brain lesions that produce global aphasia, we do not have even to insist on 'close' proximity).

In addition to the difficulties of interpreting the co-occurrence of language and other cognitive difficulties in the global aphasic population, there is also critical evidence that not all global aphasics demonstrate the association of deficits (Zangwill, 1964; Kertesz, 1988). The obvious interpretation of dissociations is that the two functions are independent: that severe language impairment may exist in the absence of thought impairment. But there is a problem with this interpretation. The tasks used which demonstrate dissociations are usually non-linguistic tests such as the Ravens Matrices. This test requires the subject to select a design to complete a given array. As the test is predominantly visuo-spatial, supporters of a cognitive conception of language can argue that the importance of a dissociation between language and a task involving visual imagery is relatively trivial. In the modular brain such dissociations are predictable. Kertesz (1988) however argues that Raven's Matrices are heavily loaded on the g-factor of intelligence, as well as a spatial factor, which suggests that the results cannot be simply dismissed as pertaining to visuo-spatial function alone.

Much of the language-and-thought debate within aphasiology has therefore been conducted at the gross level of demonstrating intact performance on non-verbal intelligence tests; and where dissociations are found, to then refute the hypothesis of thought impairment in aphasia. The reasons for this crude level of analysis are apparent if one looks at the history of modern aphasiology.

4 Spiritualism and sensualism

Aphasiology has a relatively short history of under a century and a half, and in the first half of this life span there were many attempts to address the question of whether the aphasic, lame in speech, was also 'lame in thinking' (Hughlings Jackson, 1866). The early debate divided into dichotomous camps: those of spiritualism and sensualism. Lesser (1989) summarises the positions taken thus:

> the sensualists [took] the view that without language thought was impossible, and the spiritualists that thought could have an independent spirit-like existence (p. 10).

Prominent within the sensualist camp were Hughlings Jackson, Marie, Head and Goldstein. The sensualists were, to a degree, forced into a position of accepting that aphasia represented something more than a specific language disorder because of their opposition to the early modular accounts of language organisation (e.g. Broca, 1861, Wernicke, 1874). The first modularity theories suggested that language was organised into centres which mediated performance in individual modalities of language use, i.e. speech, auditory comprehension, reading and writing. Sensualists, unaware of the significance of dissociations, even if rare, in neuro-psychological theory, pointed out that the majority of aphasics demonstrate impairments which cross modalities. This, they argued, suggested a global, superordinate factor which mediated language performance across modalities. The superordinate factor was conceptualised in different ways: a loss of the ability to 'propositionalise' or a breakdown of propositional thought (Hughlings Jackson, 1866); a diminution of intelligence (Marie, 1906); loss of symbolic formulation and expression (Head, 1926); and loss of an abstract attitude (Goldstein, 1948).

The evidence in support of sensualist–spiritualist positions was largely 'pre-scientific', with anecdotal reports of aphasics' inability to play cards or make a good omelette. Goldstein (1948) offered better evidence in support of a sensualist position. He reported a study of an aphasic who had difficulty naming and understanding colour words. Goldstein showed that this patient also failed on colour categorisation tasks. Whereas the patient could successfully complete match-to-sample tasks where matching involved identical hues, he failed on a task which required him, for example, to put all the reds together. Goldstein suggested that the patient lacked an 'abstract attitude' and was therefore unable to transcend sensory identities. The difficulty with Goldstein's data, as with all evidence of associative relationships, is to identify the nature of the association. Does the absence of the colour word lead to the inability to complete the categorisation task (a strong statement of linguistic determinism)? or does the lack of the concept determine the naming difficulty? or are the linguistic and conceptual deficits both linked to a third factor, the option which seems to be favoured by Goldstein, the impairment of abstract attitude?

The spiritualist/sensualist debate was one which was characterised by extreme positions. For example, the sensualists in their globalist orientation did not restrict the thought impairments of aphasics to a linguistic sphere. This resulted in a simple line of research for those of a spiritualist persuasion which was to produce evidence that aphasic impairments were domain-specific and contrary to the globalistic formulations of Marie, Head and Goldstein. Evidence of intact performance on non-verbal intelligence tests was used to refute Marie's contention of a global diminution of intelligence. Evidence of double dissociations (i.e. function A impaired and function B intact in patient Y, whilst A is intact and B impaired in patient Z) between language and non-language symbolic systems, for example music, argued against Head's assertion that aphasia represents a disorder of symbolic formulation and expression (Luria *et al.*, 1965; Brust, 1980; Benton, 1977). The literature also contains reports of dissociation between language impairments and performances with other symbolic systems such as mathematical and chemical formulae, and Morse code (Lesser, 1989). Similarly, intact ability to produce narrative drawings also argued against gross a-symbolia (Hatfield and Zangwill, 1974).

The spiritualist–sensualist debate, formulated into a simple dichotomy, sits uneasily with the notion of the modular brain (Fodor, 1983). A contemporary version of the sensualist position would address more constrained issues. It would allow for intact use of representational modes such as imagery and music, and predict dissociations between performances requiring these representations and language. The constrained–sensualist view would then address more limited questions; for example: are there classes of thought which are necessarily represented in natural language? (Carruthers, 1996a), as we have already seen, might answer this question in the affirmative, giving the examples of causal reasoning and inferring another's mental state (i.e. X believes that P) as involving propositional formats which may be necessarily language-encoded. In the next section of this chapter this hypothesis is tested in an experiment with two aphasic subjects, one of whom (SA) might be described as an 'a-propositional' aphasic. If causal reasoning and inferring anther's mental state are indeed thoughts that can be instantiated only in natural language propositions, then these forms of reasoning would be unthinkable thoughts for SA. A second aphasic (BS), who is relatively well matched to SA on lexical scores, is also included. BS has minimal grammatical impairment. She has sufficient language available to her to 'hack' both the comprehension and formulation of language propositions. Her role in the study is to operate as a control subject, to assess general issues such as task difficulty.

5 An empirical test

5.1 Participants

SA is a fifty-year-old retired police sergeant. Four years prior to this investigation he developed a subdural empyema in the left sylvian fossa, with accompanying meningitis. He was left with a severe motor speech disorder (apraxia) and aphasia. He communicates via a combination of single word writing, drawing and pantomimed gesture. His aphasia can be characterised as a severe impairment of both grammatical input and output processing, crossing spoken and written modalities (see Figure 6.1 on p. 145 for a summary of test scores).

SA experienced difficulties in understanding predicates (PALPA verb semantics 14/27 – Kay *et al.*, 1992), and verbs occurred very rarely in either his written or spoken output. He had difficulties in understanding reversible sentences (40 per cent correct on reversible versus 75 per cent correct on non-reversible PALPA sentence–picture matching test), which suggests a difficulty in assigning the correct thematic role to the noun phrases of the sentence where that assignment operates on syntactic criteria alone. No clausal constructions were noted in SA's spontaneous speech or writing, whilst phrasal constructions occurred rarely, and were restricted to article-noun, adjective-noun and quantifier-noun combinations. Nominal lexical processing was more intact, which is illustrated in examples of writing (see below) and also by scores in matching spoken and written nouns to their pictured referent (PALPA word-picture matching: auditory 35/40, written: 37/40). Whereas SA's restriction of spoken output to single words (usually nouns) could possibly be accounted for through an economy of effort hypothesis because of his severe motor speech impairment, this explanation could not extend to the parallel lack of structure in his written output. Examples of SA's written output are presented below. In this task, SA was presented with a picture which depicted an agent undertaking a simple action. SA was encouraged to write a sentence to describe the event in the picture.

Example 1 (Man sitting at a table reading a book)

Man
Glasses
Book
Blue
Tie
Wood
Timex

Example 2 (Chinese man brushing his hair)
Asia (Hong Kong)
Black hair
Silver hair
Young man
Black jumper
Moustache
(Prompted to write a sentence) A brush hair

SA's output consisted largely of nominal word lists. The only spontaneous attempts at structure can be seen in noun phrases (adjective plus noun combinations). No verbs were produced spontaneously, and where they were prompted, the forms produced had dubious predicate status in that arguments were not structured around the predicate, and the predicates appeared to be adapted nominal forms. On a further sentence-writing task, SA produced either series of nouns and adjectives in a linear string e.g. 'woman red egg sekonda marriage', or pseudo-grammatical constructions such as, 'a asia as man as black a shoes', 'woman a white as glass the red', 'women a age the red a scissor'. Across twenty trials, SA did not produce a single verb. Whereas some a-grammatic aphasics may retain a impoverished grammatical system which allows them to understand and produce simple or *proto*-language propositions, SA has a grammatical impairment which includes disruption of predicates and, critically, this impairment operates across comprehension and production. Without natural language predication, SA should not be capable of understanding or forming natural language propositions (Garrett 1982; Linebarger *et al.*, 1983). He would therefore appear to be an 'a-propositional' aphasic.

A test of SA's grammatical knowledge which required him to make grammaticality judgements on written sentences which were: correct; ungrammatical in English but did not violate universal principles (e.g. prepositions following the head of the prepositional phrase, clauses with Subject-Object-Verb (SOV) order); or floridly ungrammatical (sentences with no verb, prepositions attached to subject Noun Phrase (NP) rather than Prepositional Phrase) showed SA performing at chance level (19/30, p=0.95 binomial test). SA also did not respond to the variable of the seriousness of the grammatical violation. He classified four of ten flagrantly ungrammatical sentences as correct, and three of ten SOV and post-position sentences as correct. A second set of sentences was devised for further grammaticality judgements. The set consisted of correct sentences and sentences which violated universal grammatical principles (e.g. sentences with variable position of the head of the NP, VPs with noun heads, and structure dependency violations (e.g. which does he play instrument)). SA again performed at chance level (31/60). SA was dissimilar to a-grammatic aphasics reported by Linebarger *et al.* (1983) who were a-grammatic in overt comprehension and production performances, but retained the ability to perform grammaticality judgements. Schacter *et al.*, (1988) suggest that this finding indicates a dissociation between explicit and implicit grammatical knowledge. Tyler (1992) would disagree that grammaticality judgements are a true measure of implicit grammatical knowledge, as such judgements occur off-line, permitting reflection and a high level of consciousness. At present, true measures of implicit grammatical knowledge similar to those devised by Tyler are not available for SA.

BS is a seventy-one-year-old retired book-keeper who suffered a probable embolic cerebrovascular accident two years prior to this investigation. A CT scan revealed lesions of the left occipital lobe, extending into the temporal lobe, and also a small left frontal infarct. Her stroke left BS with visual difficulties and aphasia. Her aphasia is of a very different nature to that of SA. Assessment showed that BS had fluent, well-articulated speech. Grammatical processing was largely intact in both input and output. Verb retrieval was good, but she had marked difficulties in retrieving nouns. Fluency was maintained in spontaneous speech by inserting generics and deictics (e.g. 'thing', 'it') where specific lexical retrieval had failed. In naming tasks, where specific retrieval was required, fluency broke down and her speech became full of neologisms and phonemic paraphasias. She demonstrated that she had achieved semantic access through circumlocutions and also the use of self-generated cloze sentences (e.g. for 'leaf': 'these trees have lovely . . .'). BS had a very marked breakdown in semantic to phonological mapping, and her retrieval was not assisted by initial phoneme cues or by number of syllable and tonicity cues (i.e. tapping out the number of syllables in the target and also the pattern of strong and weak stress across syllables). BS's lexical comprehension was relatively good via an auditory route. She made some errors on semantic verification tasks (110/120 on one task) and her score (44/60) on a synonym judgement test (PALPA) also indicated a degree of semantic–conceptual difficulty. She had difficulty reading because of surface dyslexia (reading via an orthographic-to-phonological conversion), which meant reading for meaning was slow and laborious. Writing was very limited and BS had difficulty accessing orthographic forms in the output lexicon.

SA and BS, whilst similar in some ways on noun lexical processing (particularly input processing), showed contrasting deficits in syntax and verb retrieval. SA's performance on a series of tasks which appear to require a propositional form of reasoning was of particular significance given his syntactic difficulties and his apparent 'a-propositionality' in all language modalities. Comparisons of subject's scores on a number of formal test measures can be found in Figure 6.1 (p. 145).

5.2 Procedure and results

SA and BS completed three tasks which have been suggested as demanding reasoning in a propositional format. The tasks were: theory of mind (first order false belief); causal reasoning; and the WAIS Picture Arrangement test (Wechsler, 1981).

Theory of mind: eight trials on a first-order false belief task were developed (Wimmer and Perner, 1983; Happé, 1991). This was an expanded version of the Smarties task. All eight trials involved familiar consumer packaging with an unexpected item contained within it (e.g. pill bottle containing buttons, cornflakes box containing clothes-pegs). It was predicted that SA would have difficulties understanding the false-belief test questions (e.g. 'What does X think is in the bottle?') because of his difficulties understanding predicates and assigning thematic roles to sentence constituents. He was therefore trained on three of the exemplars as to what the task requirements were, and then tested on all eight test items one week later, this time with no pre-training.

Results: In line with predictions, SA did have some difficulties on the training items. On the first trial, he responded promptly to false-belief questions with reality responses (i.e. what was actually in the bottle). (In the aphasia lab or clinic, there is an often used task that requires the patient to communicate new information to a naive interlocutor. SA was perhaps operating with the heuristic that the theory of mind tests were another instance of this task). But he rapidly corrected these responses on a second trial after training. The training consisted of, first, feedback that his initial responses were wrong. Second, disambiguation of the linguistic content of the question, specifically, the semantic content of the verb 'think' and that X was the subject of the sentence (versus SA's likely misinterpretation of 'tell X what is in the bottle'). He was thus exposed twice to each of the three training exemplars. In the test one week later, SA obtained correct responses on both the false belief and reality questions for six of the eight trials. On the remaining two, lexical retrieval difficulties resulted in him being unable to produce the reality response for one item (whilst the false-belief response was correct), while on the remaining trial he was unable to retrieve the false belief response, but could produce the reality one. BS required no training. She achieved perfect scores on all false-belief and reality questions (circumlocutory answers were accepted as correct e.g. 'to strike' for 'matches').

Causal reasoning: The subject was presented with a card with an 'event' depicted on the left-hand side (e.g. car crashed into a tree). On the right of the card were three pictures (alcoholic drink, helicopter, axe). The subject was asked which of the three choices was the likely cause of the event. In addition to the correct response (alcohol), at least one of the foils had strong associative links to elements of the event picture (i.e. car/helicopter; tree/axe). There were three training plates which had 'why?' printed above the pictures. The task was explained to the subject on the three training items, but no further instructions were given on the fifteen main test items.

Results: SA achieved perfect scores on both the training and main test items. Performance was rapid as well as accurate. BS completed the training items successfully, and went on to score 12/15 on the main test.

WAIS Picture Arrangement: The standard WAIS procedure (Wechsler, 1981) was used for the administration of the test. A series of line drawings is placed in front of the subject and they are asked to re-arrange the pictures so that they tell a sensible story.

Results: Scoring performance by strict WAIS criteria (acceptable sequence *plus* within the time limit) SA scored 16/20, whilst BS scored only 3/20. If responses are scored for sequence only, the scores then rose to 18/20 (SA) and 12/20 (BS). SA's performance was impressive. On the strict WAIS scoring criteria his score places him in the 91st percentile of a normal age-matched population. SA was asked to describe what was happening in one of the picture sequences. The contrast between his ability on the non-verbal ordering task and his linguistic encoding efforts was marked. He took four and a half seconds to complete the picture ordering, but three minutes to produce the written response 'house – saw – brick'. BS's performance is more difficult to interpret. On strict WAIS criteria she performs poorly (the score lies at more than 3 standard deviations from the mean of a normal age-matched population), but when the time criterion is removed, her score shows her ordering of the pictures was often logical.

5.3 *Interpretation*

Both aphasic subjects performed well (with the exception of BS's performance on the story arrangement test) on tasks which it is presumed involve propositional thought. BS had a degree of difficulty on both tasks which involved causal reasoning, but both involved pictures and often discrimination of fine visual detail. Her visual problems may be a factor here.

SA required training in order to complete the theory of mind tasks, and this creates a degree of ambiguity in the interpretation of the results. The training may result in SA successfully solving theory of mind tasks not through any inferencing about the mental states of others, but rather through some *Clever Hans* route. In order to clarify the theory of mind result, a further test of first-order false belief was performed one year and two weeks after the initial set. SA had no exposure to such tasks in the intervening period. Twenty items were presented to SA, again involving familiar packaging containing an unexpected item. All items were different from those of the first trial. On this occasion, SA received training on non-false-belief items prior to the test. SA was presented with a bag containing a variable number of balls. He was required to feel the bag and to guess how many balls there might be in the bag. Whilst he was doing this, he was presented with the verb 'think' printed on a card and was asked 'how many balls do you think are in the bag?'. After he had made a guess, SA was required to open the bag and count the balls. A card with the word 'really' was then presented, and SA was asked 'how many balls are there really?'. After disambiguation of the think/really distinction, a third person subject was introduced to 'think'. SA was handed a bag of balls and, after exploring them, the bag was passed on to a third person. The third person felt the bag, and the cue card 'X think' was introduced and SA guessed how many balls the third person would state as being in the bag. As the linguistic probes were strongly reinforced by the context, SA required few training trials. He then proceeded to first-order false-belief items, with the cue cards 'X thinks' and 'really' being used to support comprehension of the false-belief and reality questions respectively. False-belief and reality questions were presented in random order. SA scored 18/20 on the second test (i.e. items where both false-belief and reality questions were correct). This score was significantly beyond the level of chance ($p=0.0004$, binomial test).

Proponents of a cognitive conception of language might still protest that evidence that SA can complete false-belief tasks in the absence of any training beyond linguistic disambiguation, still does not suggest that he has a full-blown theory of mind, and they might demand evidence of second-order inferencing. There is an empirical problem here. Usual versions of second-order tasks place heavy demands on language processing resources – not only in the probe questions, but also understanding the premises of the task – and non-verbal second-order tasks have not been developed (moreover it is difficult to see how unambiguous non-verbal higher-order theory of mind tests can be designed). The empirical difficulty may be masking some more fundamental issue. Second-order inferencing is precisely the type of high-demand cognitive task that requires language-mediation, particularly in view of its massively serial nature (i.e. Y believes that Z believes that P).

SA's performance on the WAIS story arrangement test and the causal reasoning test cannot be dismissed as a result of *Clever Hans* phenomena. Both tasks were completed without training. The WAIS task requires complex and novel reasoning about cause and effect. The causal reasoning task, although tapping more static associations (e.g. alcohol causes accidents), still requires the participant to address causality. The design of the foils was such that if performance was mediated by simple co-ordinate type associations (e.g. car/helicopter), then the participant would make errors.

SA's performance is particularly important. SA is unable to form a clause in natural language. He has difficulty understanding and retrieving predicates. He has difficulty understanding the role that an element is playing in a sentence. The evidence of grammatical impairments which cross input–output modalities and which, in the case of the predicate impairments, are parallel deficits (i.e. the same impairment occurs in input and output performance) is critical. The results cannot be dismissed simply by suggesting that SA has an impairment of grammatical performance, but that central grammatical competence remains intact and is still able to mediate performance on the tasks used in this study. Parallel input–output impairments suggests a deficit in central competence, i.e. knowledge which mediates performance across modalities. A performance account of SA's parallel impairments is not impossible, but it is less plausible as it would demand impairments of input and output routes at identical points. SA's apparent 'a-propositionality' then begs the question of how he is completing the tasks successfully. There are a number of options to consider:

(1) SA has implicit knowledge of natural language grammar
(2) SA's thought is mediated by a non-natural language propositional code
(3) The tasks do not demand, by necessity, formation of a propositional representation

The first option is a possible explanation of the results in the absence of measures of implicit grammatical knowledge. But the argument made earlier that the evidence of SA's parallel impairments of comprehension and production suggests that he has lost central grammatical competence is relevant here. If the argument of a central competence deficit can be sustained, then there is unlikely to be any dissociation between implicit and explicit grammatical processing in SA's case. This prediction can, clearly, be put to empirical test. The results, as they currently stand, however, can argue against theories of thinking which claim that thoughts are instantiated in *explicit* natural language propositions (for example, Segal, this volume chapter 7).

The second option states that the tasks do require a propositional code, but as SA is unable to form a proposition in natural language, the propositional code he uses is not of natural language. There are two possibilities here: a deep structure of natural language might form the substrate for thought; or a code akin to Mentalese or a language of thought. The results of the grammaticality judgements – that SA failed to recognise sentences which violate universal principles as incorrect – may have a bearing here and favour the Mentalese option. There is, however, no evidence from this study to discriminate between a Mentalese explanation or the third option, that the tasks do not demand a propositional code. A non-propositional argument may be the preferred option for other reasons; for example, that of economy of computation and the elimination of duplication of propositional codes. Whilst SA might lack natural language grammar, he is not 'language-less'. He has considerable lexical resources available to him, and his semantic–conceptual knowledge is relatively intact. The conceptual network and the patterns of both relatively static and dynamic interconnectivity of the network may be the basis of first-order thoughts. Concepts can optionally be mapped onto form (phonological, orthographic, imagistic) and the dissociations that occur between form and meaning in some aphasic disorders (e.g. see BS) support such a separation. Multiply encoded information – conceptual, phonological, orthographic and imagistic is more likely to be memorable, hence the mnemonic advantages of language encoding, but occurrent first-order thoughts can be entertained independently of language.

The evidence presented here that causal and first-order false-belief reasoning is not by necessity mediated by explicit language propositions is based on evidence from a single case. A concern with single case study research is that of the generalisability of results to wider populations, and it may just be that SA is an exceptional individual with unique patterns of thought. There is, therefore, a need for replication of the findings of this study with other aphasic individuals. The number of subjects upon whom the experiments can be run is, however, likely to be small. Most a-grammatic aphasics have the remnants of a grammatical system available to them so as to be able to form simple propositions. A-propositional aphasics like SA are rare. The other aphasic group on which the experiments might be run are individuals from the globally aphasic population. These individuals are unlikely, however, to be able to complete the linguistic version of theory of mind tasks reported here. Non-verbal theory of mind tasks could be performed, for example, a typical *Sally-Ann* task scenario (Sally-Ann places an object in location A, but unknown to Sally-Ann it is moved to location B by another agent) but in which Sally Ann behaves in a way consistent with her (false) belief, or inconsistent with her belief (i.e. she immediately seeks the desired object in a place where she cannot know it to be). Measures of a participant's knowledge might include on-line ones such as, direction of gaze and signs of confusion where Sally-Ann is behaving irrationally, as well as off-line measures, for example, asking the participant to rate the video as 'sensible' or 'crazy'. A pilot version of such a task has

Task	**Chance score**	**SA**	**BS**
PALPA word-picture matching (auditory)	8	35/40	35/40
PALPA word-picture matching (written)	8	37/40	30/40
PALPA Verb semantics *	13.5	14/27	19/27
PALPA synonym judgement	30	-	44/60
PALPA sentence-picture matching (auditory)	20 (long form) 10 (short form)	23/60	20/30
PALPA sentence-picture matching (written)	10	13/30	-
PALPA picture naming (BS) writing (SA)	- -	- 24/60	26/60 7/60

Fig. 6.1. Subject scores on psycholinguistic tests.
PALPA (Psycholinguistic Assessment of Language Processing in Aphasia), Kay *et al.*, 1992.

* Verb semantics: this task involves presenting the patient with a word, followed by a possible definition of its meaning, which the patient either accepts or rejects. This is not the most direct way to study verb comprehension. An easier method is to ask the patient to respond to a command (e.g. smile) or to match a verb to a picture which depicts the corresponding action. SA's performance on such tasks produced equivocal results. This may be because many of the verbs used have a corresponding nominal form and it is not clear what is then being tested – relatively intact nominal performance or supposedly impaired predicate performance. The suggestion of specific verb comprehension problems is supported by SA's performance on a parallel PALPA adjective comprehension task, where he scored 10/14. This suggests that the complexity of the task is not an explanation of SA's verb comprehension score.

shown encouraging results, with SA and a globally aphasic individual being able to signal which clips are anomalous.

The implications of the results of the study reported here are limited only to occurrent thinking. SA had a normal language system until mid-adulthood. The results have nothing to say about the role of language in the development of thinking. It may well be that language is necessary to configure central cognition for certain types of cognitive activity (Clark 1996a; Dennett 1991). Once this configuration has taken place, the new cognitive operations may take place with continued underpinning by the language system, or, as the results of this study suggest, independently of it. The results of this study argue, however, that explicit natural language grammar and resultant natural language propositions are not a necessary component in the processes involved in solving the problems presented in this study.

I would like to thank SA (and C) and BS (and P) for their help and enthusiasm for this project; and also Peter Carruthers for encouragement to conduct some experiments in the area of aphasic thinking.

7 Representing representations

Gabriel Segal

1 Introduction

Sally believes that Anne is a doctor. Zoe believes this, and can say that it is so. She does so by uttering (1):

(1) Sally believes that Anne is a doctor.

Propositional attitude reports like (1) have received a great deal of attention in the philosophical literature over the last hundred years.

Since Zoe believes that Sally believes that Anne is a doctor, and Zoe is a common-sense psychologist, she is in a position to infer much about Sally's mind and actions. Zoe might infer that Sally has a belief about Anne. She might infer that Sally believes that at least one doctor exists. She might also infer that if Sally wants to talk to a doctor, and further believes that Anne is available for discussion, then Sally might seek Anne out. She would be likely to infer these and many other things, if she bothered to think about them.

Common-sense psychology has received considerable attention from philosophers and, more particularly from developmental and experimental psychologists, particularly since Heinz Wimmer and Josef Perner (Wimmer and Perner, 1983) began to explore children's understanding of false beliefs. Psychologists study the basis of common-sense psychology – what it consists in – which types of beings possess it, how it is acquired and so on.

There has been a certain amount of fruitful interaction between the philosophers of language and the psychologists who study theory of mind. I would like to contribute to this pooling of resources, and bring in some linguistics as well. I will adopt what might be called a 'cognitivist' approach to both language and common-sense psychology, in the sense that I will assume that both linguistic competence and common-sense psychological competence are to be explained (in part) by our possessing bodies of knowledge relevant to the areas. I'll assume further that this knowledge may be largely unconscious. And I'll assume that both bodies of knowledge have a theoretical form, in perhaps a loose sense of 'theoretical'. In each case, what is known is an interrelated set of generalisations that can be used to make inferences in the relevant domain. I will also assume that these bodies of knowledge are put to use by performance systems of some kind. In

Chomskyan spirit, I'll label these bodies of knowledge, together with the systems that use them, the 'language faculty' and the 'psychology faculty'.

This chapter will be concerned with the nature of the representations deployed by the two faculties. I will look first at how the language faculty represents propositional attitude reports and their semantic interpretations. In effect, this is the question of how we represent people's propositional attitudes in language. Then, in section 3, I will look at how the psychology faculty represents propositional attitudes; that is, in effect, how we represent the attitudes in thought when we reason about people, their psychological states and their actions. I will investigate the proposal that the psychology faculty uses representations that are made available by and only by the language faculty.

2 Semantics for propositional attitude reports

2.1 Background assumptions

I will assume that the language faculty contains a specifically semantic component. This consists in a compositional semantic theory that specifies the semantic properties of simple expressions, such as words, along with some means for deriving the semantic properties of complex expressions, such as sentences. (See Larson and Segal, 1995, for details.) The primary source of data for the study of semantic theory consists in speakers' judgements, judgements about what words and sentences do (and do not) mean, as well as certain judgements of synonymy, entailment relations and so on.

Philosophical discussions of propositional attitude reports have centred on what is called their 'referential opacity'. This opacity is marked by the apparent failures of certain normally valid inference patterns. Thus while (1a) and (1b) entail (1c), (2a) and (2b) do not entail (2c):

(1) (a) Boris Karloff acts
 (b) Boris Karloff is William Pratt
 (c) William Pratt acts

(2) (a) Zoe believes that Boris Karloff acts
 (b) Boris Karloff is William Pratt
 (c) Zoe believes that William Pratt acts

What is relevant to psycholinguistics is that people make those judgements. Most competent speakers judge that if (1a) and (1b) are both true, then (1c) must true as well. But they don't judge that if (2a) and (2b) are true, then (2c) must be also be true.

What (2) shows is that people's judgements about entailment relations among attitude reports are sensitive to more than just the referential properties of the words in the content sentences (that is, in the embedded sentences of the reports). 'Boris Karloff' and 'William Pratt' have the same reference. But even people who know this, judge that (2c) can be false, while (2a) is true. In a moment, I will try to say exactly what the relevance of this sort of data about people's judgements is. First, I want to introduce some more data of a related kind.

2.2 Hypersensitivity

Suppose that Tyler, a young boy, thinks that 'a fortnight' applies to a period of ten days. One might then have conversations with him like this: 'Tyler, how long is a fortnight?' 'Ten days' 'Are you sure? Are you sure it's not fourteen days?' 'Yes, I am sure it's not fourteen days'. Then, according to some people's judgements, (3a) could be true, while (3b) was false:

(3) (a) Tyler believes that a fortnight is ten days
(b) Tyler believes that two weeks is ten days

This is so even though 'a fortnight' and 'two weeks' are synonymous (for us, if not for the young Tyler).

Suppose that Chloe is an English woman who has spent a short time in the United States. In England she learns that the word 'nauseous' (pronounced naw-zee-ous) means sick in the stomach. In the United States she comes across the word 'nauseous' (pronounced nawshus), and, understandably in the context, comes to believe it means morally disgusted. On the ship back to England, her friend Zelda feels seasick. According to some people's judgements, (4a) could be true, while (4b) is false. (See Larson and Ludlow, 1993, for discussion of an example of this kind.)

(4) (a) Chloe believes Zelda feels nauseous (naw-zee-ous)
(b) Chloe believes Zelda feels nauseous (nawshus)

Like Chloe, Zelda has been misled by a transatlantic variation. According to some people's judgements, (5a) could be true, while (5b) was be false. (I leave it to the reader to construct a plausible scenario).

(5) (a) Zelda believes that black and white are colours
(b) Zelda believes that black and white are colors

All these stories are a little contrived. And it is only some people who make the judgements cited. Nevertheless, these facts are important. For those who make the judgements (most of them anyway) are rational and competent speakers. In each of the cases, such speakers judge that one of the sentences (3a), (4a), (5a) is true and the other (3b), (4b), (5b) is false. This means that the sentences in each a/b pair must differ in meaning. If they meant exactly the same thing, how could they differ in truth value?

2.3 *A hypersensitive semantic theory*

What (3)–(5) show is that differences in choice of words among synonyms, phonology and orthography within content sentences all induce a difference of meaning in the embedding attitude reports. I suggest that the natural way to account for this is to build these various properties into the semantic objects of the reports. What I mean is that when we say (for example) 'Zelda believes that black and white are colours' we are saying that Zelda stands in some kind of belief relation to a linguistic object, an object that has phonological, orthographic etc. properties. In effect, this object is a lot like the sentence 'Black and white are colours.' However, since the word 'sentence' has a variety of uses, I will introduce the term 'total form'. A total form is an abstract, linguistic object. It is a syntactic structure that has a variety of properties associated with it. It contains words, which are themselves spelt and pronounced in specific ways. The words have meanings, and the whole structure has a meaning (derived systematically from the words' meaning and syntactic structure). A total form is a tree structure with properties associated with the various nodes. The total form of e.g. 'Boris Karloff acts' might be partially depicted by (6):

(6) [S [NP [N Boris Karloff] [VP [V acts]]]
where: e.g. the nominal terminal node is associated with the orthographic, phonological and semantic properties of 'Boris Karloff', the S node means that *Boris Karloff* acts, and so on.

Abstracting from the details of the semantic theory, I propose that in a propositional attitude report, the content sentence refers to its own total form. So e.g. (5a) and (5b) have the meanings depicted in (7a) and (b), respectively (where 'TF(S)' is the total form of string S):

(7) (a) Zelda believes TF('black and white are colours')
(b) Zelda believes TF('black and white are colors')

Since the total forms differ, the semantics of (5) a and b differ, as desired. What Zelda is said to believe – the total form of the content sentence – differs across the two sentences. Analogously for the examples (2)–(5). In each case, the report in (a) relates the subject to a different total form from the one in (b). Hence the possibility of (a) being true and (b) false.[1]

It might seem odd that the semantic objects of attitude reports should be total forms, which are linguistic objects in the reporter's language. The fol-

[1] The total form theory is a variant of what is often called 'interpreted logical form' theory, as developed by Higginbotham (1986), Larson and Ludlow (1993) among others. The version presented here is slightly simplified. For a fuller account see Segal (forthcoming).

lowing sentence is probably true: 'Caesar believed that Rome wasn't built in a day.' On this account, this sentence means that Caesar believed TF('Rome wasn't built in a day'). But how could Caesar have stood in a believing relation to a total form of twentieth-century English? To answer this, we just need to understand the relation expressed by the verb 'believes'. Total forms have semantic properties, and are therefore representations. Since this is so, they can express cognitive states. Caesar could have expressed his belief in Latin. I can express that same belief of his in English. Thus the belief relation can be understood as follows: to believe a total form is to have a belief (or be in a belief state) that is expressed by that total form.

2.4 *A flexible pragmatic theory*

I have offered a very fine-grained semantics for attitude reports. Reports which differ in the smallest respects are not semantically equivalent. The theory was motivated by the somewhat unusual cases ((2)–(5)) which reveal that our judgements are sometimes sensitive to this fineness of grain. However, when we move away from the unusual cases and look at more everyday talk, our judgements seem to go towards the other extreme. We often regard a variety of rather different reports as equivalent, equally good ways to specify someone's attitude. (8) and (9) are examples:

(8) (a) 'Hattie will be here next Saturday', uttered by Sid on Sunday.
(b) 'Sid thinks Hattie will be here in two days', uttered by Eric the next Thursday.
(c) 'Sid thinks Hattie will be here on Saturday', uttered by Eric the next Thursday.

(9) (a) 'The match will be rained off' says Fred
(b) 'Fred thinks the match will be cancelled due to bad weather'
(c) 'Fred thinks the match will be rained off'

According to the total form theory, (8b) means something different from (8c), and (9b) means something different from (9c). Yet, in each case, we regard these reports as more or less equivalent in the context. I suggest that the way this works is as follows. When we report on someone's attitude, we have a representation in our psychology faculty. In the case of (8), for example, we have a representation of Sid thinking that Hattie will arrive on Saturday. Call this representation 'F(Sid)'. When we report on the attitude, we select a total form that suitably expresses the relevant attitude. In typical cases, there will be a fairly wide range of different total forms that are equally acceptable in the context. Often, our particular choice will have a lot to do with what know about our audience: we find some economical way of expressing the attitude that is readily understandable by the audience and that is accurate enough for our conversational purpose at the time. In other cases, the ones in which we tend towards to hypersensitivity of judgements (such as (3)–(5)), the range of appropriate total forms is severely limited. The context is set up so that we can and do use fine distinctions among total forms to represent fine distinctions among the attitudes we are talking about.

An analogy might help. Imagine a group of people who report on the colours of objects using colour samples (say, swatches of material) that they carry around. In order to say that ripe tomatoes are red, they would hold up a sample of the appropriate shade of red and say: 'Ripe tomatoes are that colour'. Propositional attitude reporting is very like that, only instead of using samples of colour to report on colours of objects, we use samples of representations – total forms – to report on representational states of people. It is plausible that speakers' judgements in the colour case would exhibit the same kind of context sensitivity as in attitude reporting. Thus, for most purposes any one of a number of different swatches, with differing shades of red, would do to report on the colour of a particular red object. But in other cases people might be interested in very specific shades, and the number of acceptable swatches that one could correctly use to report on an object's colour would be severely limited.

Further, both methods of reporting involve a third element: a representation in the reporter's mind. In the colour case, the reporter will have some internal, mental representation of the colour of the object that she is talking about, and this will be drawn upon by the cognitive systems that select a sample of the right colour. In the attitude case, there is a mental representation of the reportee's attitude: F(Sid) in the psychology faculty. But what is this F(Sid)? What is the nature of the psychology faculty's representations of people's attitudes? Section 3 addresses these questions.

3 Representation in the psychology faculty

How does the psychology faculty represent the attitudes? There are two main possibilities: either it uses language-independent representations, or it uses language-dependent ones. One can think of various possibilities under either heading. But if it uses language-dependent representations, then they are presumably the very same ones used in the language faculty itself – representing attitudes as relations to total forms. So it is either (A) or (B) in figure 7.1.

Returning to the colour reporting myth, the analogy for (B) would be

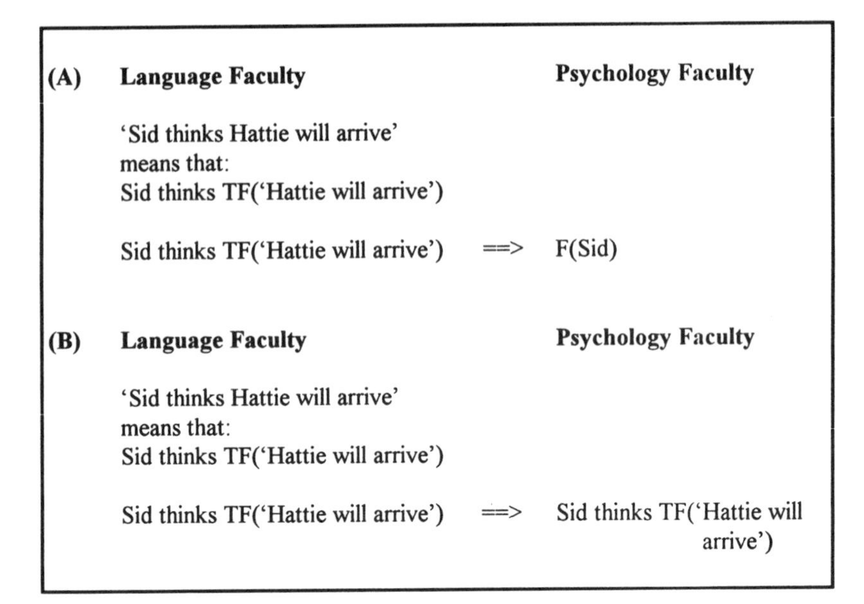

Fig. 7.1.

this: whenever one represents an object's colour in thought, one would do this by thinking about one's colour swatch. So thinking that the sky is blue would involve thinking of the sky as standing in some relation to one of one's blue swatches. In thinking about someone's belief, one thinks of that someone as standing in a relation to a total form. In one's mind one has a representation of the total form, and the total form itself is one of one's sample representations.

In (A), F(Sid) could be any language-independent representation of Sid's believing that Hattie will arrive. In fact, the two main proposals in the psychology literature both fall within category (A). Perner (1991) has suggested that the psychology faculty uses mental models. The representation in the psychology faculty is a meta-model, and what it models is Sid standing in a relation to a modelled situation – a hypothetical situation in which Hattie is due to arrive. And Alan Leslie (see e.g. Leslie, 1994) has suggested that the psychology faculty meta-represents representations in the thinker's own language of thought. So Sid would be represented as standing in a relation to a sentence of the language of thought. Neither of these proposals implicates natural language representations in any direct way.

I have no particular arguments against either of these latter proposals. And I think, at this relatively early stage in the study of representation in the psychology faculty, it is worth developing any proposal that has its own merits. However, I want to explore the credentials of (B). I will first sketch out how the theory might work. Then I will discuss some ontogenetic evidence that tends to support it. I will also discuss some evidence that appears to point the other way, and see how it might be accounted for.

3.1 The explanatory adequacy of the total form theory

Thought about attitudes, like talk about attitudes, involves referential opacity. The linguistic judgements about failures of intersubstitution of co-referring terms reflect the way we think and reason about attitudes. Thus I can believe (a) that Zoe believes that Boris Karloff acts, and (b) that Boris Karloff is William Pratt, while not believing (c) that Zoe believes that William Pratt acts. Representations in the psychology faculty, like attitude reports in language, are referentially opaque. Total form theory explains the opacity of attitude reports. And, of course, it could explain the opacity of representation in the psychology faculty. The psychology faculty's representation of Zoe's believing that Boris Karloff acts would represent Zoe as standing in a relation to one total form; the faculty's representation of Zoe's believing that William Pratt acts would represent Zoe as standing in a relation to another.

In addition to being referentially opaque, representations in the psychology faculty must of course be able to sustain the kind of explanations produced by the psychology faculty. They must represent attitudes in such a way as to allow for the theoretical reasoning that the faculty is capable of. Let us see how representing attitudes as relations to total forms would serve.

There are three basic kinds of inferences that the psychology faculty makes about propositional attitudes: influence of the world on the attitudes, intra-mental interactions, and influence of the attitudes on action. In each case, what is crucial about the attitudes is their representational properties. In representing what someone believes or desires, one needs to represent the representational properties of the attitude in question. And a natural way to do this would be to represent the individual standing in a relation to a representation of some kind – something like a proposition, or a Fregean Thought, or a total form. Total forms are representations. So representing attitudes as relations to total forms serves as way to represent the attitude's representational properties. Let us consider a couple of simplified cases.

Sid and Eric look up at the clock, which says that it's ten to six. Eric infers that Sid believes that the clock says it's ten to six. Here, Eric represents an aspect of the world that confronts Sid; the fact that there's a clock saying it's ten to six. Using some theory of mind principle along the lines of 'seeing is believing, *ceteris paribus*', Eric infers that Sid has a belief that represents this aspect of the world. To do this, he selects some total form that has an appropriate representational content, and uses this to construct a representation of Sid's belief. For example, Eric might hold: *Sid believes TF('the clock says it's ten to six')*. The processes underlying this cognitive performance of Eric's are rather mysterious. What determines which particular total form is selected to give the contents of Sid's belief? I have no good answer to this question. But it is reasonable to suppose that the processes involved here are the same as those involved in speech production. If Eric thinks the clock says it's ten to six and wishes to express this belief in language, then he – or rather, his speech production mechanisms – must select an appropriate sentence of his language. The problem here seems to be identical. Some cognitive mechanisms need to find a total form that represents the aspect of the world that confronts Sid. The only difference is that in this case, the total form is then used by the psychology faculty to reason about Sid, rather than being used by language processing mechanisms to select a string of words to utter. But that needn't make any difference to the business of finding a total form that represents a specific aspect of the world. So I hope, anyway.

Sid says 'The train is due in ten minutes.' Using some theory of mind principle like 'people come to believe obvious consequences of what they already believe, if they bother to think about it, *ceteris paribus*', Eric reasons: Sid believes it's ten to six, and he believes that the train is due in ten minutes, so he believes that the train is due at six. Maybe this works along the following lines. Eric's psychology faculty represents the contents of Sid's two beliefs by TF*('It's ten to six')* and TF*('The train is due in ten minutes')*. Some cognitive systems of Eric's then draw out a logical consequence of these two total forms. Again, I don't know how this is done. But one possibility is that, once again, the cognitive systems are ones that are already needed for language and other areas of cognition. For example, the language faculty might provide interpretations for the two total forms: TF*('It's ten to six') means that it is ten to six*, and TF*('The train is due in ten minutes') means that the train is due in ten minutes*. Ordinary reasoning about the world shows that if it's ten to six and the train is due in ten minutes, then the train is due at six. The language faculty further reveals that TF*('The train is due at six') means that the train is due at six* and these two pieces of information – the result of reasoning about the world and the language faculty's provision of a total form – can now go back to the psychology faculty, which then infers: Sid believes TF('The train is due at six'). So part of the story might be schematically depicted in Figure 7.2.

Although what I have provided is skinny even by way of a sketch, it does suggest that some theory along the recommended lines should work. The

Psychology Faculty
  Sid thinks TF('it's ten to six')
  Sid thinks TF('the train is due in ten minutes')
Language Faculty
  TF('It's ten to six') means that it's ten to six
  TF('The train is due is ten minutes') means that the train is due in ten minutes
Ordinary Reasoning
  If it's ten to six and the train is due in ten minutes, then the train is due at six.
Language Faculty
  TF('The train is due at six') means that the train is due at six
Psychology Faculty
  Sid believes TF('The train is due at six')

Fig. 7.2.

key point, as I mentioned above, is that since total forms are representational items, they have the right kind of properties to feature in the representation of attitudes. Moreover, although the theory itself is slightly complicated, involving the language faculty, the psychology faculty and other cognitive systems, it is also conservative in an important sense. It requires no more of the various faculties than we have independent reason to credit them with. So it is not implausible to conclude that the theory is a workable and simple one. Is there any more specific evidence that it is actually true? Yes, a little. But there is also some evidence that appears, at least, *prima facie* to point the other way. I will discuss each in turn.

3.2 Evidence from ontogeny

While some cases of autism may suggest that language is ontogenetically independent of theory of mind, it is notable that there is no known analogous condition providing evidence that theory of mind is ontogenetically independent of language. To be sure, there are various possible explanations for this. It is possible that there are such cases and we don't know about them. But perhaps a more plausible explanation is that language is indeed a necessary ontogenetic precursor of mature theory of mind. And, as we will see in a moment, it is also plausible that the reason for this is that the psychology faculty uses the representational resources of the language faculty. Let us look first at some aspects of the ontogeny of the psychology faculty, before turning to the specific question of the ontogenetic dependence of one faculty on another.

There is an important and in some respects clear change in the way children reason about psychology that usually takes place at around four years of age. The most discussed mark of this change concerns the children's performance on false-belief tests. Here is a classic example. The subject child is told a story, usually with the aid of pictures or models. The story goes: Sally places her chocolate in a drawer, then goes out to play. While Sally is out, and cannot see what is going on, Anne comes in and moves the chocolate to a cupboard. The subject child is then asked: 'Where does Sally think the chocolate is?' Three-year-olds typically answer: 'In the cupboard', where the chocolate actually is, not where Sally would think it is. The more mature children answer, correctly, that Sally thinks it's in the drawer. Alternatively (or additionally) the child is asked 'Where will Sally look for the chocolate?', or 'Where will Sally first look for the chocolate?' Again, most of the younger children say 'In the cupboard', the older ones say 'In the drawer'.

This is just one example of a phenomenon that seems to be quite general: three-year-olds don't behave as if they understand that beliefs can be false. It seems that in their view either one has no beliefs about a situation at all, or one has true beliefs about it. More or less analogous results hold for the other attitudes. Thus (idealising somewhat), younger children don't seem to realise that someone else could desire something that the child herself does not. And they don't manifest much grasp of the idea that things can look to be other than they are (i.e. that visual representations can misrepresent). These concepts – of perception, desire, belief – mature at different stages, desire coming first. But the kind of change involved is rather similar in nature. (For extended discussion see Perner, 1991 and Wellman, 1990; see also Leslie, 1994 and Fodor, 1992 for a different view).

The maturation of the psychology faculty, as judged by passing false-belief tests, correlates with several changes in children's understanding of the language of attitude attributions. Here follows a sample.

Jill de Villiers (1995) has found evidence that children who fail false-belief tests also fail to register the referential opacity of attitude reporting. For example, children are told a story like this: Mom puts a silver box on the top shelf. The silver box is a birthday present. The birthday present is candy. A little girl walked into the room and saw a silver box on the top shelf. She thought 'I wonder what the silver box is.' The subject children are then asked: 'Does the little girl know the silver box is on the shelf?' and 'Does the little girl know the candy is on the shelf?' The children who fail false-belief tests also fail to register the opacity of 'knows', allowing substitution of 'the candy' for 'the silver box'. Children who pass false-belief tests do register the opacity, and do not allow the substitution of 'the candy' for 'the silver box'.

Young children who fail false-belief tests also have an immature grasp of the syntactic structure of attitude reports. The most important point is that in certain types of attitude construction, these young children appear to tend to treat content sentences as if they were unembedded, appearing in isolation from their matrix clauses. E.g., they answer the question 'When did the boy say how he hurt himself?' by saying how the boy hurt himself, as if merely registering the clause 'how he hurt himself?' (de Villiers *et al.*, 1990; Roeper and de Villiers, 1994).

More evidence that children tend in certain contexts to treat content sentences as unembedded emerged serendipitously from an experiment by Helen Tager-Flusberg (Tager-Flusberg, forthcoming). Children were told a standard false-belief story, as follows. Mommy told Johnny that she would make hamburgers for dinner. Johnny goes out to play, and Mommy changes the menu and cooks some spaghetti. Among the questions the children were asked was: 'Does Johnny know what Mommy made for dinner?' Eight children who failed false-belief tests featured in this experiment. Five out of those eight, instead of answering 'yes' or 'no', answered 'spaghetti', indicating that they were answering only the embedded interrogative 'what Mommy made for dinner'.

In these latter cases there is a strong correlation between immature theory of mind, judged by failing false-belief tests, and immature grasp of the syntactic structure of attitude reporting. This correlation cannot be explained simply by the children's failure to understand the language used in the false-belief tests. For some of the tests do not require use of any attitude reports. It is true that most these tests involve slightly related constructions: 'Sally puts the chocolate in the drawer', 'where will Sally look for the chocolate?' But children do not seem to have trouble with the syntax of these constructions, which don't involve embedding of a content sentence within a propositional attitude verb phrase. It is specifically some subgroup of embeddings within propositional attitude verbs that young children have trouble parsing.

It is difficult to piece together a clear picture of the three-year-old's understanding of the syntax and semantics of attitude reports. However the various data do suggest (to me at least) that (i) they do not understand them as embedding constructions, with one sentence embedded inside another (cp. de Villiers, 1995, and Tager-Flusberg, 1995) and (ii) they do not understand them as expressing relations between subjects and representations. The data seem to be consistent with the idea that they treat the reports as fully referentially transparent (or *de re*, in the philosophical jargon). It may be that they take the reports to express relations between subjects and situations in the world. This is suggested by their failure to register opacity. And it would fit nicely with Perner's (1991) proposal that they hold a 'situation theory' of mind. However, the syntactic problems suggest an alternative. It may be that they are unable fully to parse the reports at all, and assign them no definite structure. For example, they might understand 'Johnny believes the chocolate is in the drawer' along the lines of: Johnny has a belief concerning the chocolate and the drawer (or Johnny has a belief concerning the chocolate, the relation of being in, and the drawer). (See de Villiers, 1995, for a related suggestion.)

The correlation between immature language and immature theory of mind does not by itself tell us the nature of the dependence. There are three possibilities:

(1) Theory of mind is a necessary precursor to the syntax of attitude reports.
(2) Syntax of attitude reports is a necessary precursor to theory of mind.
(3) There is some third explanation, involving a common cause of both.

It is difficult to argue convincingly for one of these options over the others. But it is reasonable to favour the second: that grasp of the structure of attitude reports is a precursor to developing mature theory of mind. Common cause seems the least likely – what would the common cause be? Dependence of language on theory of mind looks unlikely, because there is no special reason why a grasp of the notion of false belief, or a fully representational theory of mind generally, should be required for these particular structural features of language. Consider, for example, the problem with 'When did the boy say how he hurt himself?' This certainly seems to be a syntactic phenomenon. It is hard to see why an immature theory of mind should lead to the child's answering the embedded interrogative form ('how he hurt himself'). And it is hard to see why an immature theory of mind should delay acquisition of the syntactic structure involved. Or, to put the point the other way around, it is hard to see why a representational theory of mind should be required for acquisition of the mature syntax of this linguistic construction. By contrast, the results would naturally be explained by a dependence of theory of mind on a grasp of the language.

Some corroboration of this analysis comes from study of deaf children whose language development is delayed. Gale *et al.* (1996) investigated the development of theory of mind in oral deaf children. These children were of average or high intelligence and normal social functioning. They were tested on a verbal theory of mind test that required them to answer questions involving attitude reports ('What did you think was in the box?'). They were also given one almost entirely non-verbal test, and one that did not involve any attitude reports. The former was a sticker finding game, (adapted from Povinelli and de Blois, 1992) testing for grasp of the relation between seeing and knowing. The latter involved a standard false belief scenario and the question 'Where will Johnny first look for his cake?'

It turned out that theory of mind as assessed by all three tests was severely delayed in these children; on average by about three years. This suggests that it is specifically a grasp of the language of attitude reports that is required for mature theory of mind. For if development of theory of mind were independent of the language of attitude reports, it is hard to see why these children should be delayed on the theory of mind tasks that do not require understanding of those constructions. Further, these children were also tested on a spontaneous explanation of action task, which tapped their tendency to use propositional attitude constructions. (They were shown a Tom and Jerry cartoon involving various actions on the parts of the characters, including deceptions etc., and asked to comment on what was going on.) It emerged that the children's spontaneous use of attitude reports correlated much more strongly with their performance on theory of mind tests than did their verbal mental age. This again points to a specific connection between the language of attitude reports and theory of mind.

It does seem, then, that maturation of the psychology faculty depends upon on maturation of grasp of attitude reports. This lends some support to my claim that the psychology faculty deploys the representations of total forms made available by the language faculty. The claim predicts the dependence. Of course, the argument is far from demonstrative, since there are other possible explanations of the dependence. But my account at least has the advantage of making the prediction directly. Accounts on which the representational resources of the two faculties are distinct do not by themselves predict the dependency, and will need to appeal to something adventitious. Their explanatory power will therefore be correspondingly less.

On the other hand, there is some evidence that seems, at first sight, to count directly against my shared resources theory.

4 Apparent counter-evidence

Rosemary Varley (this volume, chapter 6), reports the case of SA. SA is a fifty-year-old retired policeman with severe aphasia. As far as linguistic performance goes – in comprehension, speech and grammaticality judgements – SA does not manifest the capacity to grasp a linguistic structure of anything like the complexity of a total form. He does, however, do well at false belief tests. After a brief training period during which he was acquainted with the task, he was given eight trials and passed six of them. The two failures were apparently explicable in terms of problems of lexical retrieval rather than reasoning about the task. (This interpretation is confirmed by SA's success in Varley's follow-up study.)

The procedure for the tests was as follows. SA and an experimenter were seated at a table. A third person was also present, but unable to see events at the table. SA was presented with a familiar container, such as a pill bottle. The bottle contained something other than its normal contents (buttons rather than pills). SA was shown the contents. The contents were replaced in the bottle and the bottle was shown to the third person. SA was then asked two questions: a reality question (what is in the bottle?) and a false belief question about the third person (what does X think is in the bottle?). SA, however, lacks the linguistic capacity to understand questions like that posed in English. So the questions were accompanied by gestures, such as a pointing to the third person and a gesture for 'think'.

SA does present the appearance of someone who cannot construct representations of total forms and yet possesses a functioning mature psychology faculty. He appears therefore to be a counter-example to my account. But there are at least two ways explain away the data. The first alternative explanation is that SA has a bizarre performance deficit. The idea would be that he retains his unconscious knowledge of his language, cannot access this knowledge in linguistic tasks, but can do so in psychology tasks. Not likely perhaps, but just about possible.

The second alternative is more plausible. This is that the strategy he uses to pass the false-belief tests is not the normal one involving deployment of the full representational resources of the psychology faculty. There are two possibilities under this general heading.

The first possibility is that he doesn't really understand the task and is using some strategy that has little or nothing to do with theory of mind. He may not understand the false-belief question, and believe that the task is about, say, what is normally in a pill bottle. Remember the procedure for asking him the false-belief test. It is not at all obvious that he interprets the experimenter's gesturing performance in the intended way. Recall also that he did receive some training on the task. So he may simply have learned to respond to the enquiry that is posed by the gesturing by conveying what is normally in the bottle. I admit that this is not a particularly natural interpretation of the data. But it does appear to be compatible with it. And it is important to bear in mind how little SA himself has to go on in figuring out what he is being asked.

The second possibility is that he does understand the task, and gives the right answers for the right reasons. However, he arrives at the answers using, as it were, non-standard theory of mind. Recall that SA is an intelligent fifty-year-old man with considerable experience of police work. He may well remember a great deal about what people would normally believe in certain kinds of contexts, and be able to represent this knowledge without constructing total forms.

Further research would certainly help resolve these matters. Until then, open-mindedness appears to be a good policy.

I am indebted to Simon Baron-Cohen, Jill Boucher, Peter Carruthers, Noam Chomsky, Alison Gopnik, Josef Perner, Jill de Villiers, Helen Tager-Flusberg, Rosemary Varley, David Papineau, Keith Hossack, Mike Martin and Scott Sturgeon for helpful comments, criticisms and discussion.

8 Magic words: how language augments human computation

Andy Clark

1 Word power

Of course, words aren't magic. Neither are sextants, compasses, maps, slide rules and all the other paraphernalia which have accreted around the basic biological brains of *Homo sapiens*. In the case of these other tools and props, however, it is transparently clear that they function so as either to carry out or to facilitate computational operations important to various human projects. The slide rule transforms complex mathematical problems (ones that would baffle or tax the unaided subject) into simple tasks of perceptual recognition. The map provides geographical information in a format well suited to aid complex planning and strategic military operations. The compass gathers and displays a kind of information that (most) unaided human subjects do not seem to command. These various tools and props thus act to generate information, or to store it, or to transform it, or some combination of the three. In so doing, they impact on our individual and collective problem-solving capacities in much the same dramatic ways as various software packages impact the performance of a simple PC.

Public language, I shall argue, is just such a tool – it is a species of external artefact whose current adaptive value is partially constituted by its role in re-shaping the kinds of computational space that our biological brains must negotiate in order to solve certain types of problems, or to carry out certain complex projects. This computational role of language has been somewhat neglected (not un-noticed, but not rigorously pursued either) in recent cognitive science, due perhaps to a (quite proper) fascination with and concentration upon, that other obvious dimension: the role of language as an instrument of interpersonal communication. Work on sentence parsing, language use and story understanding has thus concentrated on the role of language in processes of information transfer between agents and on information retrieval from texts. But it has had little to say about the computational role of the linguistic formulations themselves, or about the special properties of the external media that support linguistic encodings.

In this chapter, I hope to display the broad shape of such an alternative interest. I begin by discussing the views of some recent (and not-so-recent) authors who recognise, in various ways, the potential role of language and text in transforming, reshaping and simplifying the computational tasks that confront the biological brain. Sections 3 and 4 pursue this broad vision across a variety of cases involving planning, co-ordination, learning and the construction of complex thoughts and arguments. The fifth section extends these last considerations to encompass the rather special class of *meta-cognitive* operations and tries to implicate language as an essential part of the process of thinking about our own thoughts and cognitive profiles. The final section suggests some broader implications and raises some questions concerning the boundary between the intelligent agent and the world.

2 Supra-communicative views of language

The idea that language may do far more than merely serve as a vehicle for communication is not new. It is clearly present in the work of developmentalists such as Vygotsky (1934), and more recently that of Laura Berk and others (see e.g. essays in Diaz and Berk, 1992). It figures in the philosophical conjectures and arguments of e.g. Peter Carruthers (1996a) and Ray Jackendoff (to appear). And it surfaces in the more cognitive science oriented speculations of Daniel Dennett (1991). It will be helpful to begin by rehearsing some of the central ideas in this literature, before pursuing our own version – *viz*. the idea of language as a computational transformer which allows pattern-completing brains to tackle otherwise intractable classes of cognitive problems.

Lev Vygotsky, a Soviet psychologist of the 1930s, pioneered the idea that the use of public language had profound effects on cognitive development. He posited powerful links between speech, social experience and learning. Two especially pertinent Vygotskian ideas, for present purposes, concern the role of private speech, and of scaffolded action (action within the so-called zone of proximal development – see Vygotsky, trans., 1962). We may call an action 'scaffolded' to the extent that it relies on some kind of external support. Such support could come from the use of tools, or the knowledge and skills of others; that is to say, scaffolding (as I shall use the term) denotes a broad class of physical, cognitive and social augmentations – augmentations which allow us to achieve some goal which would otherwise be beyond us. Simple examples include the use of a compass and pencil to draw a perfect circle, the role of other crew members in enabling a ship's pilot to steer a course, and the infant's ability to take its first steps only while suspended in the enabling grip of its parents. Vygotsky's focus on what was termed the zone of proximal development was concerned with this latter type of case, in which a child is temporarily able to succeed at designated tasks only by courtesy of the guidance or help provided by another human being (usually, a parent or teacher). This idea dovetails with Vygotsky's interest in private speech in the following way. When the child, confronted by a tricky challenge, is 'talked through' the problem by a more experienced agent, the child can often succeed at tasks which would otherwise prove impossible (think of learning to tie your shoelaces).[1] Later on, when the adult is absent, the child can conduct a similar dialogue, but this time with herself. But even in this latter case, it is argued, the speech (be it vocal or 'internalised') functions so as to guide behaviour, to focus attention, and to guard against common errors. In such cases, the role of language is to guide and shape our own behaviour – it is a tool for structuring and controlling action and not merely a medium of information transfer between agents.

This Vygotskian image is supported by more recent bodies of developmental research, such as that carried out by Laura Berk and Ruth Garvin. Berk and Garvin (1984) observed and recorded the ongoing speech of a group of 5–10-year-olds in Kentucky. They found that most of the children's private speech (speech not addressed to some other listener) seemed keyed to the direction and control of the child's own actions. They found that the incidence of such speech increased when the child was alone and engaged in trying to perform some difficult task. In subsequent studies (Bivens and Berk, 1990; Berk, 1994) it was found that the children who made the most self-directed comments were the ones who subsequently mastered the tasks best. Berk's conclusions, from these and other studies, was that self-directed speech (be it vocal or silent inner rehearsal) is a crucial cognitive tool that allows us to highlight the most puzzling features of new situations, and to direct and control our own problem-solving actions.

The theme of language as a tool has also been developed by the philosopher Christopher Gauker. Gauker's concern, however, is to re-think the intra-individual role of language in terms of (what he calls) a 'cause–effect analysis'. The idea here is to depict public language 'not as a tool for representing the world or expressing one's thoughts but a tool for effecting changes in one's environment' (Gauker, 1990, p. 31). To get the flavour, consider the use of a symbol, by a chimpanzee, to request a banana. The chimp touches a specific key on a key-pad (the precise physical location of the key can be varied between trials) and learns that making *that* symbol light tends to promote the arrival of bananas. The chimp's quasi-linguistic understanding is explicable, Gauker suggests, in terms of the chimp's apprecia-

[1] The point here is not that without linguistic instruction such learning is impossible. That, as a referee usefully pointed out, is very implausible. Rather, it is that a child whose own observations and practice leave her currently unable to perform the task may often succeed with the benefit of a few well-chosen words of advice from an adult. The child may later rehearse the adult's words as a guide so as to succeed on her own.

tion of a cause–effect relationship between the symbol production and changes in its local environment. Gauker looks at a variety of symbol-using behaviours and concludes that they all succumb to this kind of analysis. This leads him to hypothesise that, although clearly more complex, human beings' linguistic understanding likewise 'consists in a grasp of the causal relations into which linguistic signs may enter' (Gauker, 1990, p. 44).

Gauker tends to see the role of language as, if you like, directly causal: as a way of getting things done, much like reaching out your hand and grabbing a cake. However, the idea that we learn, by experience, of the peculiar causal potencies of specific signs and symbols is in principle much broader. We might even, as in the Vygotskian examples and as argued in Dennett (1991), discover that the self-directed utterance of words and phrases has certain effects on our own behaviour! We might also learn to exploit language as a tool in a variety of even less direct ways, as a means of altering the shape of computational problem spaces (see section 3 following).

One obvious question which the putative role of language as a self-directed tool raises is 'how does it work?' What is it about self-directed speech, for example, which fits it to play a guiding role? After all, it is not at all clear how we can tell ourselves anything we don't already know! Surely, all that public language can ever be is a medium for expressing ideas which are already formulated and understood in some other, more basic, inner code? It is precisely this view which a supra-communicative account of language has ultimately to reject.

One way to do so is to depict public language as itself the medium of a special kind of thought.[2] Another (not altogether distinct) way is to depict linguaform inputs as having distinctive *effects* on some inner computational device. Peter Carruthers[3] (1996a) champions the first of these, while Daniel Dennett (1991) offers a version of the second. Thus Carruthers argues that, in this case at least, we should take very seriously the evidence of our own introspection. It certainly often seems as if our very thoughts

[2] This talk of language as a medium (or sometimes as a vehicle) of thought is meant to capture the distinction between the proposition, content, or message expressed and the code, or type of code, used to express it. On some views, there is a kind of intermingling of code and message such that it is false to imagine that we might first entertain the thought and only subsequently render it 'in' the code. On other views the required independence exists even if the actual properties of the code, or type of code, then make a large difference to the ways in which the content can be manipulated and exploited. Both options allow a 'supra-communicative' dimension to linguistic ability. But they conceive the content/vehicle relation in different ways. (Thanks to an anonymous referee for pointing out the need for further clarification at this point.)

[3] A major focus of both Carruthers' and Dennett's treatments is the relation between language and consciousness. I will not discuss these issues here, save to say that my sympathies lie more with Churchland (1995, chapter 10), who depicts basic consciousness as the common property of humans and many non-linguistic animals. Language fantastically augments the power of human cognition. But it does not, I believe, bring into being the basic apprehensions of pleasure, pain and the sensory world in which the true mystery of consciousness inheres.

are composed of the words and sentences of public language. And the reason we have this impression, Carruthers argues, is because it is true: inner thinking is literally done in inner speech (see Carruthers, 1996a, chs. 2 and 8 for an extensive discussion). By extension, Carruthers is able to view many intra-personal uses of language as less a matter of simple communication than of (what he nicely terms) *public thinking*. This perspective fits satisfyingly with the Vygotskian view championed by Berk, and is also applicable to the interesting case of writing down our ideas. Here Carruthers suggests 'one does not *first* entertain a private thought and *then* write it down: rather, the thinking *is* the writing' (Carruthers, 1996a, p. 52). I shall return to this point later (see section 3), since I believe that what Carruthers says is *almost* right, but that we can better understand the kind of case he has in mind by treating the writing as an environmental manipulation which transforms the problem space for human brains.

Carruthers, in depicting language as itself the vehicle of (certain types of) thought, is nonetheless careful to reject what he calls the 'Whorfian Relativism of the Standard Social Science Model' (1996a, p. 278). The reference here is to the idea, promoted by Benjamin Whorf (1956), that human minds are profoundly shaped and altered by the *particular* public languages we come to speak. Carruthers view is *not* that specific languages somehow deeply alter or re-programme the brain, but rather[4] that certain kinds of human thinking are actually constituted by sequences of public language symbols (written down, spoken, or internally imagined). Such a hypothesis, Carruthers argues, can help account for a wide range of both introspective and experimental and pathological data.[5]

An alternative way to unpack a supra-communicative view of language, we noted, is to suppose that the linguistic inputs actually re-programme or otherwise alter the high-level computational structure of the brain itself. The exegesis is delicate (and therefore tentative), but something akin to this view seems to be held by Daniel Dennett when he suggests that 'conscious human minds are more-or-less serial virtual machines implemented – inefficiently – on the parallel hardware that evolution has provided for us' (Dennett, 1991, p. 278). In this and other passages, the idea seems to be that the bombardment of (something like) parallel processing, connectionist, pattern-completing brains by (amongst other things) public language texts and sentences (reminders, plans, exhortations, questions, etc.), results in a kind of cognitive re-organisation akin to that which occurs when one com-

[4] Carruthers' position, unlike Whorf's, is thus compatible with both a realist conception of the mental and a fair degree of linguistic nativism.

[5] A quick sampling of this data includes: the developmental lock-step of cognitive and linguistic abilities, the difficulties which language-deficient humans have with certain kinds of temporal discourse and the deficits of abstract thought found in global aphasics. See Carruthers (1996a), esp. pp. 267–8.

puter system *simulates* another. In such cases, the installation of a new programme allows the user to treat e.g. a serial LISP machine as if it was a massively parallel connectionist device. What Dennett is proposing is, he tells us (1991, p. 218) the same trick in reverse – *viz*. the simulation of something like a serial logic engine using the altogether different resources of the massively parallel neural networks which biological evolution rightly favours for real-world, real-time survival and action.

Strikingly, Dennett suggests that it is this subtle re-programming of the brain by (primarily) linguistic bombardment which yields the phenomena of human consciousness (our sense of self) and enables us to far surpass the behavioural and cognitive achievements of most other animals (see e.g. Dennett, 1995, pp. 370–3). Dennett thus depicts our advanced cognitive skills as in large part a result not of our innate hardware (which may differ only in small, though important, ways from that of other animals) but of the special way that various plastic (programmable) features of the brain are modified by the effects of culture and language. As Dennett puts it, the serial machine is installed courtesy of 'myriad microsettings in the plasticity of the brain' (Dennett, 1991, p. 219). Of course, mere exposure to culture and language is not sufficient to ensure human-like cognition. You can expose a cockroach to all the language you like and get no trace of the cognitive transformations which Dennett sees in us. Dennett's claim is not that there are *no* initial hardware level differences. Rather it is that some relatively small hardware differences (e.g. between us and a chimpanzee) allow us to both create and benefit from public language and other cultural developments in ways which lead to a great snowball of cognitive change and augmentation, including, crucially, the literal installation of a new kind of computational device inside the brain.

Dennett's vision is complex, and not altogether unambiguous. The view I want to develop is clearly deeply related, but differs (I think) in one crucial respect. Where Dennett sees public language as effecting a profound but subtle re-organisation of the brain itself, I am inclined to see it as in essence an external resource which complements – but does not profoundly alter – the brain's own basic modes of representation and computation. That is to say, I see the changes as relatively superficial ones, geared to allowing us to use and exploit various *external* resources to the full. The positions are not, of course, wholly distinct.[6] The mere fact that we often mentally rehearse

[6] Indeed, Dennett suggests (personal communication) that his view is rather that exposure to language leads to a variety of relatively superficial changes at the neural/computational level, but that these changes nonetheless amount to something close to the inner implementation of a system of moveable symbols. The sense in which we may come to implement a classical virtual machine is thus stronger than any mere input–output level similarity, yet weaker than the kind of fine-grained simulation of an alternative computational architecture found in, e.g., Touretsky's connectionist implementation of a production system.

sentences in our head and use them to guide and alter our behaviour means that one cannot (and should not) treat language and culture as wholly external resources. Nonetheless, it remains possible that such rehearsal neither requires nor results in the installation of any fundamentally different kind of computational device in the brain, but rather involves the use of the same old (essentially pattern-completing) resources to model the special kinds of behaviour observed in the public linguistic world. And as Paul Churchland (1995, pp. 264–9) points out, there is indeed a class of connectionist networks ('recurrent networks' – see Elman, 1993, and further discussion in Clark, 1993) which do seem well-suited to modelling such behaviour.

This view of inner rehearsal is nicely developed by the connectionists Rumelhart, Smolensky, McClelland, and Hinton (1986) who argue that the general strategy of 'mentally modelling' the behaviour of selected aspects of our environment is especially important insofar as it allows us to imagine external resources with which we have previously physically interacted, and to replay the dynamics of such interactions in our heads. Thus experience with drawing and using Venn diagrams allows us to train a neural network which subsequently allows us to manipulate *imagined* Venn diagrams in our heads. Such imaginative manipulations require a specially trained neural resource to be sure. But there is no reason to suppose that such training results in the installation of a different *kind* of computational device. It is the same old process of pattern completion in high dimensional representational spaces, but applied to the special domain of a specific kind of *external* representation. The link to a Vygotskian image is clear and remarked upon by the authors who the summarise their view saying:

> We can be instructed to behave in a particular way. Responding to instructions in this way can be viewed simply as responding to some environmental event. We can also remember such an instruction and 'tell ourselves' what to do. We have, in this way, internalised the instruction. We believe that the process of following instructions is essentially the same whether we have told ourselves or have been told what to do. Thus even here we have a kind of internalisation of an external representational format. (Rumelhart *et al.*, 1986, p. 47.)

The larger passage (pp. 44–8) from which the above is extracted is, in fact, remarkably rich and touches on several of our major themes. The authors note that such external formalisms are especially hard to invent and slow to develop, and are themselves the kinds of product which (in an innocently bootstrapping kind of way) can evolve only thanks to the linguistically mediated processes of cultural storage and gradual refinement over many lifetimes. They also note that by using real external representations we put ourselves in a position to use our basic perceptual/motor skills to separate problems into parts and to attend to a series of sub-problems, storing intermediate results along the way.

The Rumelhart *et al.* vision thus depicts language as a key element in a variety of environmentally extended computational processes. This notion of computational processes inhering in larger systems (ones that may incorporate the activities of many individual biological brains) is further developed and defended in Hutchins (1995). Hutchins offers a beautiful and detailed treatment that highlights the ways representation may flow and be transformed within larger, socially and technologically extended systems. Hutchins' main example involves the way maps, instruments, texts and vocalisations all contribute to the complex process of ship navigation: a process that is best analysed as an extended sequence of computational transitions, many of whose roles is to transform problems into formats better situated to the perceptual and pattern-completing capacities of biological brains. The environmental operations thus *complement* the activities of the biological brains.

The tack I am about to pursue likewise depicts language as an external artefact designed to complement, rather than recapitulate or transfigure, the basic processing profile we share with other animals. It does not depict experience with language as a source of profound inner re-programming (*pace* Dennett). Whether it depicts inner linguistic rehearsal as literally constitutive of specific human cognizings (as Carruthers claims) is moot. Certainly, inner rehearsals, when they occur, are quite literally models of linguistic productions. But what is most important, I believe, is not to try to answer the question, 'do we actually think *in* words' (to which the answer is 'in a way yes, in a way no'!) but to try to see what computational benefits accrue to biological pattern-completing brains in virtue of their ability to manipulate and sometimes model external representational artefacts.

3 Language and computation: the six ways

Here, then, are six broad ways in which linguistic artefacts can complement the activity of the pattern-completing brain.

3.1 Memory augmentation

This is, of course, the most obvious and oft-remarked case. Here we simply use the artefactual world of texts, diaries, notebooks and the like as a means of systematically storing large and often complex bodies of data. We may also use simple external manipulations (such as leaving a note on the mirror) to prompt the recall, from on-board biological memory, of appropriate information and intentions at the right time. Here, the use of linguistic artefacts is perfectly continuous with a variety of other, simpler, environmental manipulations, such as leaving the empty olive oil bottle by the door so that you cannot help but run across it (and hence recall the need for olive oil) as you set out for the shops.

3.2 Environmental simplification

This has both an obvious and a not-so-obvious aspect. The obvious (but still important) aspect concerns the use of labels to provide perceptually simple clues to help us negotiate complex environments. Signs for the cloakrooms, for nightclubs, and for city centres all fulfil this role. They allow a little learning to go a very long way, helping you find your targets in new cities without knowing in advance what, in detail, to seek or even where exactly to seek it. McClamrock (1995, p. 88) describes this strategy as one in which we 'enforce on the environment certain kinds of stable properties that will lessen our computational burdens and the demands on us for inference'.

Closely related, but much less obvious, is the provision, by the use of linguistic labels, of a greatly simplified *learning* environment. It can be shown, for example, that the provision of linguistic labels for classes of perceptually presented objects can speed category learning in artificial neural networks. This is because the presentation of the same label accompanying a series of slightly different perceptual inputs (e.g., different views of dogs) gives the network a heavy hint. It flags the presence of some further underlying structure and thus invites the network to seek the perceptual commonality (for a detailed discussion see Schyns, 1991; Clark, 1993, chapter 5). It also seems likely (though no formal demonstration exists) that for certain very abstract concepts, the *only* route to successful learning may go via the provision of linguistic glosses. Concepts such as charity, extortion and black hole seem pitched too far from perceptual facts to be learnable without exposure to linguistically formulated theories. Language may thus enable us to comprehend equivalence classes that would otherwise lie forever outside our intellectual horizons.

3.3 Co-ordination and the reduction of on-line deliberation

Human beings often make explicit plans. We say to others that we will be at such and such a place at such and such a time. We even play this game with ourselves, perhaps by writing down a list of what we will do on what days and so on. Superficially, the role of such explicit planning is to allow the *co-ordination* of actions. Thus, if the other person knows you have said you'll be at the station at 9.00 a.m., they can time their taxi accordingly. Or, in the solo case, if you have to buy the paint before touching up the car, and if you have to go to the shops to buy other items anyway, you can minimise your efforts and enforce proper sequencing by following a plan. As the space of demands and opportunities grows, it often becomes necessary to use pencil and paper to organise and to re-organise the options, and then to preserve the result as a kind of external control structure available to guide your subsequent actions.

Closely related to such co-ordinative functions is the function of oiling the wheels of collaborative problem-solving. Collaborative problem solving (see e.g., Tomasello *et al.*, 1993) involves much more than the mere exchange of information and orchestration of activity. It involves actively prompting the other to work harder at certain aspects of a problem, and allowing the other to focus your own attention in places you might otherwise ignore. Here, then, the co-ordinative function of linguistic exchange phases into the further one of manipulating attention and controlling resource allocation (see 3.5 below).

Such broadly co-ordinative functions, though important, do not exhaust the benefits of explicit (usually language-based) planning. As Michael Bratman has recently pointed out, the creation of explicit plans may play a special role in reducing the on-line cognitive load on resource-limited agents like ourselves. The idea here is that our plans have a kind of stability which pays dividends by reducing the amount of deliberation in which we engage as we go about much of our daily business. Of course, new information can, and often does, cause us to revise our plans. But we do not let every slight change prompt a re-assessment of our plans and intentions, even when, other things being equal, we might now choose slightly differently. Human plans and intentions, Bratman suggests, play the role of blocking a wasteful process of continual re-assessment and choice, except in cases where there is some quite major pay-off for the disruption. (See Bratman, 1987, for a full discussion.)

Linguistic exchange and formulation thus plays a key role in co-ordinating activities (both at an inter- and intra-personal level) *and* in reducing the amount of daily on-line deliberation in which we engage.

3.4 Taming path-dependent learning

Human learning, like learning in Artificial Neural Networks, looks hostage to at least some degree of path dependency. Certain ideas can be understood only once others are in place. The training received by one mind fits it to grasp and expand upon ideas which gain no foothold of comprehension in another. The processes of formal education, indeed, are geared to take young (and not so young) minds along a genuine intellectual journey, which may involve beginning with ideas now known to be incorrect, but which alone seem able to prime the system to later appreciate a finer grained truth. Such mundane facts are a reflection of cognitive path dependence – you can't get everywhere from anywhere; where you are now strongly constrains your future intellectual trajectory. Moreover, such path dependency is nicely explained (see e.g., Elman, 1993) by treating intellectual progress as involving something like a process of computational search in a large and complex space. Previous learning inclines the system to try out certain locations in the space and not others. When the prior learning is appropriate, the job of learning some new regularity is made tractable: the prior learning acts as a filter on the space of options to be explored. Artificial Neural Networks which employ gradient descent learning methods are highly constrained insofar as the learning routine forces the network always to explore at the edges of its current weight assignments. Since these constitute its current knowledge, it means that such networks cannot 'jump around' in hypothesis space. The network's current location in weight space (its current knowledge) is thus a major constraint on what new 'ideas' it can next explore (see Elman, 1993, p. 94).

When confronting devices which exhibit some degree of path dependency, the mundane observation that language allows ideas to be preserved and to migrate between individuals takes on a new force. For we can now appreciate how such migrations may allow the communal construction of extremely delicate and difficult intellectual trajectories and progressions. An idea which only Joe's prior experience could make available, but which can flourish only in the intellectual niche currently provided by the brain of Mary, can now realise its full potential by journeying between agents as and when required. Moreover, the sheer number of intellectual niches available within a linguistically linked community provides a stunning matrix of possible inter-agent trajectories. The observation that public language allows human cognition to be collective (e.g. Churchland, 1995, p. 270) takes on new depth once we recognise the role of such collective endeavour in transcending the path-dependent nature of individual human cognition.

3.5 *Attention and resource allocation*

Ron McClamrock reports a nice case from Marr[7] in which we see a control loop which runs outside the head and into the local environment, In McClamrock's words:

> Flies, it turns out, don't quite know that to fly they should flap their wings. They don't take off by sending some signal from the brain to the wings. Rather, there is a direct control link from the fly's *feet* to its wings, such that when the feet cease to be

[7] Marr (1982), pp.32–3.

in contact with a surface, the fly's wings begin to flap. To take off, the fly simply jumps and then lets the signal from the feet trigger the wings. (McClamrock, 1995, p. 85; emphasis in original)

Notice, then, how written and spoken language at times serves a similar goal. We write down a note to do such and such, thus creating an externalised control loop for our own future behaviour. We follow someone's vocal instructions as we learn to windsurf. Or we mentally rehearse such instruction as we practise on our own. Such phenomena reveal linguistic formulations as somehow helping to focus, monitor and control behaviour. I do not think we yet understand exactly how language (especially mental rehearsal of instructions) interacts with more basic on-line resources so as to yield these benefits. But that it does indeed play some such role seems clear.

3.6 Data manipulation and representation

This final benefit accrues most directly to the use of actual text. As I construct this chapter, for example, I am continually creating, putting aside, and re-organising chunks of text. I have a file which contains all kinds of hints and fragments, stored up over a long period of time, which may be germane to the discussion. I have source texts and papers full of notes and annotations. As I (literally, physically) move these things about, interacting first with one, then another, making new notes, annotations and plans, so the intellectual shape of the chapter grows and solidifies. It is a shape which does not spring fully developed from inner cogitations. Instead, it is the product of a sustained and iterated sequence of *interactions* between my brain and a variety of external props. In these cases, I am willing to say, a good deal of actual thinking involves loops and circuits which run outside the head and through the local environment. Extended intellectual arguments and theses are almost always the product of brains acting in concert with multiple external resources. These resources enable us to pursue manipulations and juxtapositions of ideas and data which would quickly baffle the un-augmented brain. (The simple case of physically manipulating Scrabble tiles to present new potential word-fragments to a pattern-completing brain – see Kirsh, to appear – is a micro-version of the same strategy). In all such cases, the real environment of printed words and symbols allows us to search, store, sequence and re-organise data in ways alien to the on-board repertoire of the biological brain.

The moral of the six ways is thus clear. The role of public language and text in human cognition is not limited to the preservation and communication of ideas. Instead, these external resources make available concepts, strategies and learning trajectories which are simply not available to individual, un-augmented brains. Much of the true power of language lies in its underappreciated capacity to re-shape the computational spaces which confront intelligent agents.

4 Words as filters

The 'six ways' pursued in the previous section revolve around two broad, and rather distinct, themes. One is the use of text and/or speech as forms of external memory and workspace. The other is the (putative) role of words and sentences (preserved and transmitted through the medium of public language) to act as transformers of the very shape of the cognitive and computational spaces we inhabit. This second theme, it seems to me, is the more generally neglected of the two, and so it may be worth expanding on it a little further.

Consider the idea of words as filters on the search space for a biological learning device. The idea here (a kind of corollary of some of Elman's ideas as rehearsed in the previous section) is that learning to associate concepts with discrete arbitrary labels (words) somehow makes it easier to use those concepts to constrain computational search and hence enables the acquisition of a cascade of more complex and increasingly abstract ideas. The claim (*see also* Clark and Thornton, 1997) is thus that associating a perceptually simple, stable, external item (such as a word) with an idea, concept or piece of knowledge effectively freezes the concept into a sort of cognitive building block – an item that can then be treated as a simple baseline feature for future episodes of thought, learning and search.

This broad conjecture (whose statistical and computational foundations are explored in the co-authored piece mentioned above) seems to be supported by some recent work on chimp cognition. Thompson *et al.*, (in press) is a study of problem solving in pan troglodytes and concerns the abilities of the chimps to solve puzzles that require matching relations-between-relations. Merely matching (first order) relations might involve e.g. training the chimps to match the identical items (such as two identical cups) in an array. Matching relations-between-relations, by contrast, involves e.g. getting the chimps to match pairs of identical items (e.g. two identical shoes) to other pairs of (different) identical items (such as two identical cups). And conversely, matching pairs of different items (e.g. a cup and a shoe) to other pairs of different items (e.g. a pen and a padlock). The higher-order task is thus not to match the items themselves but to match the relations that obtain between them – it is to match the pairs in terms of the relational properties they exhibit irrespective of the specific items involved.

What makes the higher-order task higher order, it should be clear, is that there is an additional step of reasoning involved. The chimps must first represent the two (within pair) items as being the same, and then match the pairs of pairs according to whether or not each member of the pair of pairs exhibits the same relational property (sameness or difference). Now it is well known (see e.g. the review in Thompson and Oden, 1996) that non-language trained infant chimps can perceptually detect the basic relations of similarity and difference, but that they cannot make the higher-order judgements pairing instantiations of the relations themselves. It is also well known (though highly illuminating) that language trained chimps *can* learn to perform this higher-order task. These are chimps who have learnt to use symbols for 'same' and 'different' and have, in addition, attained some degree of minimal syntactic competence such as the ability to compose proto-sentences (see e.g. Premack and Premack, 1983). What Thompson *et al.* nicely go on to demonstrate is that (*pace* Premack and Premack) what is responsible for this 'cognitive bonus' is not syntactic competence *per se* but simply the experience of associating abstract relations with arbitrary tokens. Thus chimps with no compositional linguistic training but with a history of rewards for associating e.g. a plastic heart token with the presentation of pairs exhibiting sameness and a diagonal token with the presentation of pairs exhibiting difference, are shown to learn the higher-order matching task as easily as the others. Chimps with no history of associating the relations with external tokens (predictably) fail to perform the higher-order task.

Naturally, such experiments involve in addition a whole host of careful controls and important experimental details. I here refer the reader to the detailed study in Thompson *et al.* (in press) and the background review in Thompson and Oden (1996). The authors' conclusions, however, bear repeating. They conclude that (in this case at least) it is the use of simple, arbitrary external tags for independently identifiable relational properties that opens up the more abstract space of knowledge about relations between relations. This fits perfectly with Dennett's (1994) suspicion that it is the practice of tagging and labelling itself, rather than full-blooded syntactic competence *per se*, that may have been the crucial innovation that opened up new cognitive horizons to proto-language using creatures. Learning such a set of tags and labels (which we all do when we learn a language) is, I would speculate, rather closely akin to acquiring a new perceptual modality. For, like a perceptual modality, it renders certain features of our world concrete and salient, and allows us to target our thoughts (and learning algorithms) on a new domain of basic objects. This new domain compresses what were previously complex and unruly sensory patterns into simple objects. These simple objects can then be attended to in ways that quickly reveal further (otherwise hidden) patterns, as in the case of relations-between-relations. And of course the whole process is deeply iterative – we coin new words and labels to concretise regularities that we could only originally conceptualise thanks to a backdrop of other words and labels. The most powerful and familiar incarnation of this iterative strategy is, perhaps, the edifice of human science.

5 Mangroves and meta-cognition.

If a tree is seen growing on an island, which do you suppose came first? It is natural (and usually correct) to assume that the island provided the fertile soil in which a lucky seed came to rest. Mangrove forests,[8] however, constitute a revealing exception to this general rule. The Mangrove grows from a floating seed which establishes itself in the water, rooting in shallow mud flats. The seedling sends complex vertical roots through the surface of the water, culminating in what looks to all intents and purposes like a small tree posing on stilts. The complex system of aerial roots, however, soon traps floating soil, weed and debris. After a time, the accumulation of trapped matter forms a small island. As more time passes, the island grows larger and larger. A growing mass of such islands can eventually merge, effectively extending the shoreline out to the trees! Throughout this process, and despite our prior intuitions, it is the land which is progressively built by the trees.

Something like the Mangrove effect, I suspect, is operative in some species of human thought. It is natural to suppose that words are always rooted in the fertile soil of pre-existing thoughts. But sometimes, at least, the influence seems to run in the other direction. A simple example is poetry. In constructing a poem, we do not simply use words to express thoughts. Rather, it is often the properties of the words (their structure and cadence) which determine the thoughts that the poem comes to express. A similar partial reversal can occur during the construction of complex texts and arguments. By writing down our ideas we generate a trace in a format which opens up a range of new possibilities. We can then inspect and re-inspect the same ideas, coming at them from many different angles and in many different frames of mind. We can hold the original ideas steady so that we may judge them, and safely experiment with subtle alterations. We can store them in ways which allow us to compare and combine them with other complexes of ideas in ways which would quickly defeat the un-augmented imagination. In these ways, and as remarked in the previous section, the real properties of physical text transform the space of possible thoughts.

[8] A particularly stunning example is the large Mangrove forest extending north from Key West, Florida to the Everglades region known as Ten Thousand Islands. The black Mangroves of this region can reach heights of 80 feet – see Landi (1982), pp.361–3.

Such observations lead me to the following conjecture. Perhaps it is public language which is responsible for a complex of rather distinctive features of human thought – *viz*, our ability to display *second-order cognitive dynamics*. By second-order cognitive dynamics I mean a cluster of powerful capacities involving self-evaluation, self-criticism and finely honed remedial responses.[9] Examples would include: recognising a flaw in our own plan or argument, and dedicating further cognitive efforts to fixing it; reflecting on the unreliability of our own initial judgements in certain types of situations and proceeding with special caution as a result; coming to see why we reached a particular conclusion by appreciating the logical transitions in our own thought; thinking about the conditions under which we think best and trying to bring them about. The list could be continued, but the pattern should be clear. In all these cases, we are effectively thinking about our own cognitive profiles or about specific thoughts. This 'thinking about thinking', is a good candidate for a distinctively human capacity – one not evidently shared by the other, non-language-using animals who share our planet. As such, it is natural to wonder whether this might be an entire species of thought in which language plays the generative role – a species of thought which is not just reflected in, or extended by, our use of words but is directly dependent upon language for its very existence. Public language and the inner rehearsal of sentences would, on this model, act like the aerial roots of the Mangrove tree – the words would serve as fixed points capable of attracting and positioning additional intellectual matter, creating the islands of second-order thought so characteristic of the cognitive landscape of *Homo sapiens*.

It is easy to see, in broad outline, how this might come about. For as soon as we formulate a thought in words (or on paper), it becomes an object for both ourselves and for others. As an object, it is the kind of thing we can have thoughts about. In creating the object, we need have no thoughts about thoughts – but once it is there, the opportunity immediately exists to attend to it as an object in its own right. The process of linguistic formulation thus creates the stable structure to which subsequent thinkings attach.

Just such a twist on potential role of the inner rehearsal of sentences has been suggested by the linguist Ray Jackendoff. Jackendoff (1996) suggests that the mental rehearsal of sentences may be the primary means by which our own thoughts are able to become objects of further attention and reflection. The key claim is that linguistic formulation makes complex thoughts

[9] Two very recent treatments which emphasise these themes have been brought to my attention. Jean-Pierre Changeux (a neuroscientist and molecular biologist) and Alain Connes (a mathematician) suggest that self-evaluation is the mark of true intelligence – see Changeux and Connes (1995). Derek Bickerton (a linguist) celebrates 'off-line thinking' and notes that no other species seems to isolate problems in their own performance and take pointed action to rectify them – see Bickerton (1995).

available to processes of mental attention, and that this, in turn open them up to a range of further mental operations. It enables us, for example, to pick out different elements of complex thoughts and to scrutinise each in turn. It enables us to 'stabilise' very abstract ideas in working memory. And it enables us to inspect and criticise our own reasoning in ways that no other representational modality allows.

What fits internal sentence-based rehearsal to play such an unusual role? The answer, I suggest, must lie in the more mundane (and temporally antecedent) role of language as an instrument of communication. For in order to function as an efficient instrument of communication, public language will have been moulded into a code well-suited to the kinds of interpersonal exchange in which ideas are presented, inspected and subsequently critiqued. And this, in turn involves the development of a type of code which minimises contextuality (most words retain more-or-less the same meaning in the different sentences in which they occur), is effectively modality-neutral (an idea may be prompted by visual, auditory or tactile input and yet be preserved using the same verbal formula), and allows easy rote memorisation of simple strings.[10] By 'freezing' our own thoughts in the memorable, context-resistant and modality-transcending format of a sentence we thus create a special kind of mental object – an object which is apt for scrutiny from multiple different cognitive angles, which is not doomed to alter or change every time we are exposed to new inputs or information, and which fixes the ideas at a fairly high level of abstraction from the idiosyncratic details of their proximal origins in sensory input. Such a mental object is, I suggest, ideally suited to figure in the evaluative, critical and tightly focused operations distinction of second-order cognition. It is an object fit for the close and repeated inspections highlighted by Jackendoff under the rubric of *attending* to our own thoughts. The coding system of public language is thus especially apt to be co-opted for more private purposes of inner display, self-inspection and self-criticism, exactly as predicted by the Vygotskian treatments mentioned in section 2 above. Language stands revealed as a key resource by which we effectively redescribe[11] our own thoughts in a format which makes them available for a variety of new operations and manipulations.

The emergence of such second-order cognitive dynamics is plausibly seen

[10] The modality neutral dimensions of public language are stressed by Karmiloff-Smith in her closely related work on representational re-description – see note 11 below. The relative context – independence of the signs and symbols of public language is discussed in Kirsh (1991) and Clark (1993), chapter 6.

[11] The idea that advanced cognition involves repeated processes in which achieved knowledge and representation is redescribed in new formats (which support new kinds of cognitive operation and access) is pursued in much more detail in Karmiloff-Smith 1992; Clark 1993; Clark and Karmiloff-Smith 1994; and Dennett 1994. The original hypothesis of representational redescription was developed by Karmiloff-Smith (1979, 1986).

as one root of the veritable explosion of types and varieties of external scaffolding structures in human cultural evolution. It is because we can think about our own thinking that we can actively structure our world in ways designed to promote, support and extend our own cognitive achievements. This process also feeds itself, as when the arrival of written text and notation allowed us to begin to fix ever more complex and extended sequences of thought and reason as objects for further scrutiny and attention.

To complete this picture, we should reflect that once the apparatus (internal and external) of sentential and text-based reflection is in place, we may expect the development of new types of non-linguistic thought and encoding – ones dedicated to the task of managing and interacting with the sentences and texts in more powerful and efficient ways.[12] The linguistic constructions, thus viewed, are a new class of objects which invite us to develop new (non-linguistically based) skills of use, recognition and manipulation. Sentential and non-sentential modes of thought this co-evolve so as to complement, but not replicate, each other's special cognitive virtues.

It is a failure to appreciate this deep complementarity that, I suspect, leads Paul Churchland (one of the best and most imaginative neuro-philosophers around) to dismiss linguaform expression as just a shallow reflection of our 'real' knowledge. Churchland fears that without such marginalization we might mistakenly depict all thought and cognition as involving the unconscious rehearsal of sentence-like symbol strings, and thus be blinded to the powerful, pattern-and-prototype-based encodings which look to be biologically and evolutionarily fundamental. But we have now scouted much fertile intermediate territory.[13] In combining an array of biologically basic pattern-recognition skills with the special 'cognitive fixatives' of word and text, we (like the Mangroves) create new landscapes, new fixed points in the sea of thought. Viewed as a complementary cognitive artefact, language can genuinely extend our cognitive horizons – and without the impossible burden of re-capitulating the detailed contents of non-linguistic thought.

6 Studying the extended mind

Speech and text, we have seen, greatly extend the problem-solving capacities of humankind. More profoundly, the practice of putting thoughts into words alters the nature of human experience. Our thoughts become deter-

[12] See e.g. Bechtel (1996) p.125–31; Clark (1996b), pp.120–5.

[13] Dennett (1991) explores just such a intermediate territory. I discuss Churchland's down-playing of language in detail in Clark (1996b). For examples of such downplaying see P. M. Churchland (1989) p.18; P. S. and P. M. Churchland (1996), pp. 265–70.

minate and public objects, apt for rational assessment and for all kinds of meta-cognitive scrutiny. In thus recognising public language as a powerful transformer of individual computational and experiential space, we invite reflection of a number of further topics. I will end by mentioning just two.

The first concerns the nature of the internal representations that guide human action. A popular image, often associated with Jerry Fodor's reflections on the need for a 'language of thought' (e.g., Fodor, 1975, 1987), depicts the internal representational arena as itself a locus of propositionally structured items – sentences in Mentalese. This image has lately been the subject of a damaging series of criticisms stemming from the successes of non-linguaform computational approaches – especially those of connectionist (or parallel distributed processing) models.[14] The perspective developed above might, I suspect, encourage us to approach some of these issues in a slightly different way. For the Fodorian view is at least intuitively linked to views of language as essentially a communicative tool. This is because the Fodorian sees linguistic formulations as reasonably faithful reflections of both the contents and the structural forms of internal representations. The view I have been developing is quite different insofar as it depicts the linguistic formulations as importing genuine novelties onto our cognitive horizons. The linguistic formulations are seen as novel both in content and in structure. There is content-novelty insofar as linguistic expression makes new thoughts available by effectively freezing other thoughts as types of static object[15] (images can do this too, but they are not so easily traded in public exchange). And there is structural novelty insofar as the value of the linguistic formulations (especially in written text) partly consists, we saw, in their amenability to a variety of operations and transformations that do not come naturally to the biological brain working in non-linguistic mode. Such novelties, I contend, are not at all predicted by the image of a pre-existing inner code whose basic features and properties are merely recapitulated in our public language formulations. By contrast, they are exactly what would be expected if the public code is not a handy recapitulation of our non-linguistic resources so much as a powerful complement to them.[16]

Such a view suggests a certain gloss on the history and origin of the Fodorian image itself. For perhaps one mistake of classical Artificial Intelligence (upon which the image purports to be based) lay in its mistaking the properties of the linguistically augmented and environmentally

[14] For a perfect introduction to the debate, see the various essays gathered in MacDonald and MacDonald (eds.) (1995).

[15] See also Dennett's discussion of belief versus opinion, in Dennett (1987).

[16] There is of course, a midway option: that public language later becomes a 'language of thought' and that Fodor's image is misguided only in its claim that all thoughts occur in Mentalese. For discussion, see Carruthers (1996a).

extended cognitive agent (the person plus a variety of external representations, especially texts) for the cognitive profile of the basic biological brain. Thus the neat classical separation of data and process, and of static symbol structures and CPU, may have reflected nothing so much as the gross separation between the biological agent and an external scaffolding of ideas persisting on paper, in filing cabinets and in electronic media.

This notion of the biological agent leads nicely to the second issue I wish to mention. It concerns the question of where the mind ends and the rest of the world begins. Otherwise put, the question concerns how to conceive and locate the boundary between an intelligent system and its world. For certain external (to the biological unit) props and aids may play such a deep role in determining the shape and flow of our thoughts as to invite depiction as part and parcel of the very mechanism of human reason. This depiction is most plausible in the case of the external props of written text and spoken words. For interactions with these external media are ubiquitous (in educated modern cultures), reliable and developmentally basic. Our biologic brains, after learning, expect the presence of text and speech as much as they expect to encounter weight, force, friction and gravity. Language for us is a constant, and as such can be safely relied upon as the backdrop against which on-line processes of neural computation take shape and develop. Just as a neural network controller for moving the arm to a target in space must define its commands to factor in the spring of muscles and the effects of gravity, so the processes of on-board reason may come to factor in the potential contributions of textual off-loading and re-organisation, and vocal exchange. The overall cognitive competencies which we identify as mind and intellect may thus be more like ship navigation than capacities of the bare biological brain. Ship navigation (see Hutchins, 1995) is a global emergent from the well-orchestrated adaptation of an extended complex system (comprising individuals, instruments, and practices). Much of what we uncritically identify as our mental capacities may likewise, I suspect, turn out to be properties of the wider, extended systems of which human brains are just one (important) part. In constructing an academic paper, for example, it is common practice to deploy multiple annotated texts, sets of notes and files, plans, lists and more. The writing process often depends heavily on manipulations of these props – new notes are created, old ones juxtaposed, source materials are wheeled on and off of work surfaces, etc. In giving credit for the final product, however, we often marginalise the special contributions of these external manipulations, and speak as if the biological brain did all the work. No parallel temptation afflicts the person who uses a crane to lift large weights, or a motorised digger to plough trenches! In these cases, it is clear that the person uses additional tools whose capacities extend and complement those of the unaided labourer. The relative invisibility of the special cognitive roles of text and words are a reflection, I think, of their ubiquity and ease of use: a reflection, indeed, of our tendency to think of these operations as proper to the biological agent rather than (like the crane) as technological additions. Perhaps the truth lies midway – the use of spoken words may be as biologically proper, to the human agent, as the use of webs is to the spider.[17] And the use of written text may thus straddle the intuitive divide between the web (biologically proper) and the crane (a true artefact).

The point, in any case, is that use of words and texts may usefully be seen as computationally complementary to the more primitive and biologically basic kinds of pattern-completing abilities that characterise natural cognition. These complementary operations essentially involve the creation of self-standing structures (short-term ones, like spoken sentences, or long-term ones, like text) that can perform a variety of useful functions such as the sequencing and control of behaviour and the freezing of thoughts and ideas into objects for further attention and analysis. The availability of these functions extends the bound of human cognition as surely as the provision of a new board extends the bounds of a personal computer. In particular, it is our capacity to create and operate upon external representations that allows us to use manipulations of the physical environment as integral parts of so many of our problem-solving routines. In thus reaching out to the world we blunt the dividing line between the intelligent system and the world. We create wider computational webs whose understanding and analysis may require us to apply the tools and concepts of cognitive science to larger, hybrid entities comprising brains, bodies and a variety of external structures, traces and processes.

To endorse a notion of computational processes as criss-crossing brain, body and world is not yet to endorse a parallel notion of cognitive or mental processes. Perhaps cognition is all in the head, but computation spreads liberally out into the world. My own inclinations are less conservative. I suspect that our intuitive notions of mind and cognition actually do pick out these larger extended systems and that as a result the biological brain is only one component of the intelligent system we call the mind.[18] But I will settle for a weaker conclusion – one that merely implicates our linguistic capacities in some highly productive transformations of our overall computational powers. This power of computational transformation constitutes a neglected virtue of linguistic practice. It reveals language as the ultimate upgrade: so ubiquitous it is almost invisible; so intimate, it is not clear whether it is a kind of tool or an added dimension

[17] See Dawkins' lovely (1982) book, *The Extended Phenotype* (Freeman) for an especially biologically astute treatment of this kind of case.

[18] See Clark (1996a, chapter 10); Clark and Chalmers (1995).

of the user. But whatever the boundaries, we confront a complex coalition in which the basic biological brain is fantastically empowered by some of its strangest and most recent creations: words in the air, symbols on the printed page.

Special thanks to Daniel Dennett, both for his great encouragement and for his own inspirational work on the theme of language as a cognition-enhancing tool. Thanks too to Jim Wertsch, Roger Thompson, Peter Carruthers, Keith Frankish, Barry Smith, Chris Thornton, and Charles Fernyhough for ideas, comments and criticisms. Finally, I would like to thank both Peter Carruthers and the Hang Seng Centre for Cognitive Science at the University of Sheffield for allowing me to participate in the wonderful and thought-provoking series of meetings that culminated in the 1996 conference on Language and Thought.

9 The mapping between the mental and the public lexicon

Dan Sperber and Deirdre Wilson

1 Introduction

There are words in the language we speak and concepts in our minds. For present purposes, we can use a relatively common-sense, unsophisticated notion of a linguistic word. A bit more needs to be said, now and later, about what we mean by a concept. We assume that mental representations have a structure not wholly unlike that of a sentence, and combine elements from a mental repertoire not wholly unlike a lexicon. These elements are mental concepts: so to speak, 'words of Mentalese'. Mental concepts are relatively stable and distinct structures in the mind, comparable to entries in an encyclopaedia or to permanent files in a data-base. Their occurrence in a mental representation may determine matching causal and formal (semantic or logical) relationships. On the one hand, there are relationships between the mind and the world. The activation of a concept may play a major role in causal interactions between the organism and external objects that fall under that concept. On the other hand, there are relationships among representations within the mind. The occurrence of a concept in a mental representation may play a causal role in the derivation of further representations, and may also contribute to the justification of this derivation.

2 Three types of mapping

What kind of mapping is there (if any) between mental concepts and public words? One extreme view is that natural languages such as English or Swahili are the sole medium of thought. In this case, obviously, there is a genuine one-to-one correspondence between public words and mental concepts. An opposite extreme view is that there are no such things as individual mental concepts at all, and therefore no conceptual counterparts to public words. We will ignore these extreme views. We assume that there are mental concepts, and that they are not just internalisations of public words, so that the kind and degree of correspondence between concepts and words is a genuine and interesting empirical issue.

In principle, the mapping between mental concepts and public words might be exhaustive (so that every concept corresponds to a word and conversely), or partial. If it is partial, this may be because some concepts lack a corresponding word, because some words lack a corresponding concept, or both. The mapping between words and concepts may be one-to-one, one-to-many, many-to-one, or a mixture of these. However, the idea that there is an exhaustive, one-to-one mapping between concepts and words is quite implausible.

Some words (for instance the third person pronoun 'it') are more like place-holders and do not encode concepts at all. Many words seem to encode not a full-fledged concept but what might be called a pro-concept (for example 'my', 'have', 'near', 'long' – while each of these examples may be contentious, the existence of the general category should not be). Unlike pronouns, these words have some conceptual content. As with pronouns, their semantic contribution *must* be contextually specified for the associated utterance to have a truth-value. For instance, 'this is my book' may be true if 'my book' is interpreted as meaning *the book I am thinking of*, and false if it means *the book I wrote* (and since there are indefinitely many possible interpretations, finding the right one involves more than merely disambiguation). Similarly, whether 'the school is near the house' is true or false depends on a contextually specified criterion or scale; and so on. We believe that pro-concepts are quite common, but the argument of this chapter does not depend on that assumption (or even on the existence of pro-concepts). What we will argue is that, quite commonly, all words behave *as if* they encoded pro-concepts: that is, whether or not a word encodes a full concept, the concept it is used to convey in a given utterance has to be contextually worked out.

Some concepts have no corresponding word, and can be encoded only by a phrase. For instance, it is arguable that most of us have a non-lexicalised concept of *uncle-or-aunt*. We have many beliefs and expectations about uncles-or-aunts (i.e. siblings of parents, and, by extension, their spouses). It makes sense to assume that these beliefs and expectations are mentally stored together in a non-lexicalised mental concept, which has the lexicalised concepts of *uncle* and *aunt* as sub-categories. Similarly, people who do not have the word 'sibling' in their public lexicon (or speakers of French, where no such word exists) may nonetheless have the concept of *sibling* characterised as *child of the same parents*, and object of many beliefs and expectations – a concept which has *brother* and *sister* as sub-categories. So it seems plausible that not all words map onto concepts, nor all concepts onto words.

The phenomenon of polysemy is worth considering here. Suppose Mary says to Peter:

(1) Open the bottle.

In most situations, she would be understood as asking him to uncork or uncap the bottle. One way of accounting for this would be to suggest that the general meaning of the verb 'open' gets specified by the properties of its direct object: thus, opening a corked bottle means uncorking it, and so on. However, this cannot be the whole story. Uncorking a bottle may be the standard way of opening it, but another way is to saw off the bottom, and on some occasion, this might be what Mary was asking Peter to do. Or suppose Mary says to Peter:

(2) Open the washing machine.

In most situations, she will probably be asking him to open the lid of the machine. However, if Peter is a plumber, she might be asking him to unscrew the back; in other situations, she might be asking him to blow the machine open, or whatever.

The general point of these examples is that a word like 'open' can be used to convey indefinitely many concepts. It is impossible for all of these to be listed in the lexicon. Nor can they be generated at a purely linguistic level by taking the linguistic context, and in particular the direct object, into account. It seems reasonable to conclude that a word like 'open' is often used to convey a concept that is encoded neither by the word itself nor by the verb phrase 'open X'. (For discussion of similar examples from alternative perspectives, see Caramazza and Grober 1976; Lyons, 1977; Searle, 1980, 1983; Lehrer, 1990; Pinkal, 1995; Pustejovsky, 1995; Fodor and Lepore, 1996; Pustejovsky and Boguraev, 1996.)

So far, we have argued that there are words which do not encode concepts and concepts which are not encoded by words. More trivially, the existence of synonyms (e.g. 'snake' and 'serpent') shows that several words may correspond to a single concept, and the existence of homonyms (e.g. 'cat' or 'bank') shows that several concepts may correspond to a single word. So the mapping between concepts and words is neither exhaustive nor one-to-one.

Although the mapping between words and concepts is imperfect, it is not haphazard. Here are three contrasting claims about what this imperfect mapping might be like:

(3) Nearly all individual concepts are lexicalised, but many words encode complex conceptual structures rather than individual concepts. So there are fewer concepts than words, and the mapping is partial mostly because many words do not map onto individual concepts.

(4) Genuine synonyms, genuine homonyms, non-lexicalised

concepts and words that do not encode concepts are all relatively rare, so there is roughly a one-to-one mapping between words and concepts.

(5) The mapping is partial, and the main reason for this is that only a fraction of the conceptual repertoire is lexicalised. Most mental concepts do not map onto words.

In *The Language of Thought* (1975), Jerry Fodor famously argued against (3) and in favour of (4). According to the version of claim (3) he criticised, words correspond in the mind to definitions couched in terms of a relatively compact repertoire of primitive concepts: for example, the word 'bachelor' might have as its conceptual counterpart the complex mental expression *unmarried man*; the word 'kill' might have as its conceptual counterpart the complex mental expression *cause to die*, and so on. Many words – perhaps most – would be abbreviations for complex conceptual expressions, rather than encoding individual concepts. Against this view, Fodor argued that most words have no plausible definitions and must therefore correspond to mental primitives. There are psycholinguistic reasons for thinking that even a word like 'bachelor', which seems to have a definition, is best treated as encoding a single concept *bachelor*, which would itself be a (mental rather than public) abbreviation for a complex mental expression (Fodor, 1975, p. 152).

As Fodor points out, verbal comprehension is fast, and unaffected by the alleged semantic complexity of lexical items. 'Kill' is no harder to process than 'die', and 'bachelor' is no harder than 'unmarried', even though it might be argued that the meaning of 'die' is included in the meaning of 'kill', and the meaning of 'unmarried' is included in the meaning of 'bachelor'. All this suggests to Fodor that the structure of mental messages is very close to that of the public sentences standardly used to communicate them. 'It may be that the resources of the inner code are rather directly represented in the resources we use for communication' (Fodor, 1975, p. 156).

Fodor's argument against (3), combined with a rather traditional view of linguistic communication, seems to weigh in favour of (4). Fodor does, as he says himself, view language 'the good old way':

> A speaker is, above all, someone with something he intends to communicate. For want of a better term, I shall call what he has in mind a message. If he is to communicate by using a language, his problem is to construct a wave form which is a token of the (or a) type standardly used for expressing that message in that language. (Fodor, 1975, p. 106.)

Here, Fodor is adopting an updated version of what we have called the code theory of verbal communication (Sperber and Wilson, 1986/1995). The classical code theory was based on the following assumptions:

(6) For every thought that can be linguistically communicated, there is a sentence identical to it in content.
(7) The communication of a thought is achieved by uttering a sentence identical to it in content.

Assumption (7) is clearly too strong. Sentences with pronouns are obvious counter-examples: they are used to communicate different thoughts on different occasions, and are not identical in content to any of these thoughts. The updated code theory accepts (6), but rejects (7) in favour of the weaker assumption (8):

(8) The communication of any thought *can be* achieved by uttering a sentence identical to it in content.

For the classical code theory, the only way to communicate thoughts is to encode them. For the updated code theory, this is still the basic way, but there are also inferential short-cuts. The updated theory admits that the basic coding-decoding process can be speeded up, supplemented, or even by-passed by use of contextually informed inferential routines. Though full encoding is possible, the theory goes, it is often unnecessary. By exploiting shared contextual information and inferential abilities, communication can succeed even when a name or description is replaced by a pronoun, a phrase is ellipsed, or a whole thought is indirectly suggested rather than directly encoded.

Still, on both classical and updated versions of the code theory, the semantic resources of a language must be rich enough to encode all communicable thoughts. Every concept that can be communicated must be linguistically encodable. There may be a few non-lexicalised concepts (e.g. *uncle-or-aunt*) which are encodable only by a phrase; but it is reasonable to think that, in general, the recurrent use of a concept in communication would favour the introduction and stabilisation of a corresponding word in the public language.

Because Fodor uncritically accepts the code theory of communication, and because he does not even consider claim (5), let alone argue against it, his excellent arguments against claim (3) do not unequivocally point to the conclusion in (4). Claim (5) might still be correct. We want to argue that it is, and hence that most mental concepts do not map onto words.

There are two interpretations of claim (5) on which it would be trivially true, or at least easily acceptable. First, it is clear that the number of perceptual stimuli that humans can discriminate is vastly greater than the number of words available to name them: for instance, it has been claimed that we can discriminate anything up to millions of colours, while English has a colour vocabulary of a few hundred non-synonymous terms, only a dozen of which are in frequent use (Hardin, 1988, pp. 182–3). If we have a concept for every colour that we can discriminate (or even for every colour that we have had the opportunity to discriminate), it is clear that we have many more concepts than words. However, a discrimination is not the same as a conceptualisation of the items discriminated. Someone may discriminate two shades of vermilion, and even think, *here are two shades of vermilion*, without forming a distinct mental structure, let alone a stable one, for each of these two shades.

A concept, as we understand the term, is an enduring elementary mental structure, which is capable of playing different discriminatory or inferential roles on different occasions in an individual's mental life. We are not considering ephemeral representations of particulars (e.g. an individual tree, an individual person, a particular taste), attended to for a brief moment and then forgotten. Nor are we considering complex conceptual structures, built from more elementary mental concepts, which correspond to phrases rather than words, and are not stored in long-term memory. Even so, it might be argued that people do form many idiosyncratic, non-lexicalised concepts on the basis of private and unshareable experience. For example, you may have a proper concept of a certain kind of pain, or a certain kind of smell, which allows you to recognise new occurrences, and draw inferences on the basis of this recognition, even though you cannot linguistically express this concept, or bring others to grasp and share it. More generally, it is arguable that each of us has ineffable concepts – perhaps a great many of them. This would again make claim (5) trivially true.

We will return to this point later, and argue that effability is a matter of degree. For the time being, we will restrict ourselves to effable concepts: concepts that can be part of the content of a communicable thought. We want to argue that, even on this interpretation, claim (5) is true: there are a great many *stable* and *effable* mental concepts that do not map onto words.

3 Inference and relevance

The alternative to a code theory of verbal communication is an inferential theory. The basic idea for this comes from the work of Paul Grice (1989); we have developed such a theory in detail in our book *Relevance: Communication and Cognition* (1986/1995). According to the inferential theory, all a communicator has to do in order to convey a thought is to give her audience appropriate evidence of her intention to convey it. More generally, a mental state may be revealed by a behaviour (or by the trace a behaviour leaves in the environment). Behaviour capable of revealing the content of a mental state may also succeed in *communicating* this content to an audience. For this to happen, it must be used ostensively: that is, it must be displayed so as to make manifest an intention to inform the audience of this content.

Peter asks Mary if she wants to go to the cinema. Mary half-closes her eyes and mimes a yawn. This is a piece of ostensive behaviour. Peter recognises it as such and infers, non-demonstratively, that Mary is tired, that she wants to rest, and that she therefore does not want to go to the cinema. Mary has communicated a refusal to go to the cinema, and a reason for this refusal, by giving Peter some evidence of her thoughts. The evidence was her mimed yawning, which she could expect to activate in Peter's mind the idea of her being tired. The ostensive nature of her behaviour could be expected to suggest to Peter that she *intended* to activate this idea in his mind. Mary thought that the idea activated, and the manifestly intentional nature of its activation, would act as the starting point for an inferential process that would lead to the discovery of her meaning. She might have achieved roughly the same effect by saying 'I'm tired'. This would also have automatically activated the idea of her being tired (this time by linguistic decoding). It would have done so in a manifestly intentional way, thus providing Peter with strong evidence of Mary's full meaning.

In general, inferential communication involves a communicator ostensively engaging in some behaviour (e.g. a piece of miming or the production of a coded signal) likely to activate in the addressee (via recognition or decoding) some specific conceptual structure or idea. The addressee takes this deliberately induced effect, together with contextual information, as the starting point for an inferential process which should lead to the discovery of the message (in the sense of proposition plus propositional attitude) that the communicator intended to convey.

The idea activated and the message inferred are normally very different. The idea is merely a trigger for discovery of the message. Often, the triggering idea is a fragment, or an incomplete schematic version, of the message to be communicated. The inferential process then consists in complementing or fleshing out the triggering idea.

It is possible, at least in principle, for the idea activated by the communicator's behaviour to consist of a proposition and a propositional attitude (i.e. a full thought) which is just the message she intended to convey. In this limiting case, the inferential process will simply amount to realising that this is all the communicator meant. The classical code theory treats this limiting case as the only one. Every act of communication is seen as involving the production of a coded signal (e.g. a token of a sentence) which encodes exactly the intended message. No inferential process is needed. The sentence meaning (or, more generally, the signal meaning) is supposed to be identical to the speaker's meaning. The updated code theory treats this limiting case as the basic and paradigmatic one. Hearers should assume by default that the sentence meaning is the speaker's message, but be prepared to revise this assumption on the basis of linguistic evidence (the sentence does not encode a full message) or contextual evidence (the speaker could not plausibly have meant what the sentence means).

Since the classical code theory is patently wrong, the updated code theory might seem more attractive. However, the classical theory had the advantage of offering a simple, powerful and self-contained account of how communication is possible at all. The updated theory loses this advantage by invoking an inferential mechanism to explain how more can be communicated than is actually encoded. The updated theory offers two distinct mechanisms – coding–decoding and inference – which may be singly or jointly invoked to explain how a given message is communicated. Why should the first of these be fundamental and necessary to human linguistic communication, while the second is peripheral and dispensable? The classical theory, which treats coding–decoding as the *only* explanation of communication, entails as a core theoretical claim that every communicable message is fully encodable. In the updated theory, this is a contingent empirical claim, with little empirical support and no explanatory purchase.

What is the role of inference in communication? Is it merely to provide short-cuts along the normal paths of coding–decoding (in which case any inferentially communicated message could have been fully encoded)? Or does inference open up new paths, to otherwise inaccessible end-points, making it possible to communicate meanings that were not linguistically encodable? (By 'not linguistically encodable' we mean not encodable in the public language actually being used, rather than not encodable in any possible language.) In the absence of any plausible account of the inferential processes involved in comprehension, the reasonable, conservative option might be to assume that inference does not enrich the repertoire of communicable meanings. For example, if all we had to go on was Grice's ground-breaking but very sketchy original account (in his 1967 William James lectures, reprinted in Grice, 1989), we would have very little idea of how inferential comprehension processes actually work, how powerful they are, and whether and how they might extend the range of communicable concepts.

Relevance theory (Sperber and Wilson, 1986/1995; see also references therein) offers a more explicit account of comprehension processes, which claims that what can be communicated goes well beyond what can be encoded. Here, we will give a brief, intuitive outline of relevant aspects of the theory.

The basic ideas of the theory are contained in a definition of relevance and two principles. Relevance is defined as a property of inputs to cognitive processes. The processing of an input (e.g. an utterance) may yield some cognitive effects (e.g. revisions of beliefs). Everything else being equal, the greater the effects, the greater the relevance of the input. The processing of the input (and the derivation of these effects) involves some cognitive effort. Everything else being equal, the greater the effort, the lower the relevance. On the basis of this definition, two principles are proposed:

(9) *Cognitive principle of relevance*: Human cognition tends to be geared to the maximisation of relevance.

(10) *Communicative principle of relevance*: Every act of ostensive communication communicates a presumption of its own relevance.

More specifically, we claim that the speaker, by the very act of addressing someone, communicates that her utterance is the most relevant one compatible with her abilities and preferences, and is at least relevant enough to be worth his processing effort.

As noted above, ostensive behaviour automatically activates in the addressee some conceptual structure or idea: for example, the automatic decoding of an utterance leads to the construction of a logical form. This initial step in the comprehension process involves some cognitive effort. According to the communicative principle of relevance, the effort required gives some indication of the effect to expect. The effect should be enough to justify the effort (or at least enough for it to have seemed to the speaker that it would seem to the hearer to justify the effort – but we will ignore this qualification, which plays a role only when the speaker deliberately or accidentally fails to provide the hearer with sufficiently relevant information; see Sperber, 1994).

4 Relevance and meaning

The communicative principle of relevance provides the motivation for the following comprehension procedure, which we claim is automatically applied to the on-line processing of attended verbal inputs. The hearer takes the conceptual structure constructed by linguistic decoding; following a path of least effort, he enriches this at the explicit level and complements it at the implicit level, until the resulting interpretation meets his expectations of relevance; at which point, he stops.

We will illustrate this procedure by considering the interpretation of Mary's utterance in (11):

(11) *Peter* Do you want to go to the cinema?
Mary I'm tired.

Let's assume (though we will soon qualify this) that Peter decodes Mary's utterance as asserting that Mary is tired. By itself, the information that

Mary is tired does not answer Peter's question. However, he is justified in trying to use it to draw inferences that would answer his question and thus satisfy his expectations of relevance. If the first assumption to occur to him is that Mary's being tired is a good enough reason for her not to want to go to the cinema, he will assume she meant him to use this assumption as an implicit premise and derive the implicit conclusion that she doesn't want to go to the cinema because she is tired. Peter's interpretation of Mary's utterance contains the following assumptions:

(12) (a) Mary is tired.
(b) Mary's being tired is a sufficient reason for her not to want to go to the cinema.
(c) Mary doesn't to want to go to the cinema because she is tired.

Mary could have answered Peter's question directly by telling him she didn't want to go to the cinema. Notice, though, that the extra (inferential) effort required by her indirect reply is offset by extra effect: she conveys not just a refusal to go, but a reason for this refusal. There may, of course, be many other conclusions that Peter could derive from her utterance, for example those in (13):

(13) (a) Mary had a busy day.
(b) Mary wouldn't want to do a series of press-ups.

But even if these conclusions were highly relevant to Peter, they would not help to satisfy the specific expectations of relevance created by Mary's utterance. The fact that she was replying to his question made it reasonable for him to expect the kind and degree of relevance that he himself had suggested he was looking for by asking this question, and no more.

However, there is a problem. How plausible is it that the fact that Mary is tired is a good enough reason for her not to want to go to the cinema? Why should Peter accept this as an implicit premise of her utterance? Does Mary never want to go to the cinema when she is tired, even if she is just a little tired, tired enough for it not to be false to say that she is strictly speaking tired? Surely, in these or other circumstances, Peter might have been aware that Mary was somewhat tired, without treating it as evidence that she didn't want to go to the cinema.

As noted above, a hearer using the relevance–theoretic comprehension procedure should follow a path of least effort, enriching and complementing the decoded conceptual structure until the resulting interpretation meets his expectations of relevance. We have shown how this procedure would apply to Mary's utterance in (11) to yield the implicatures (12b) and (12c). This is a case where the explicit content is complemented at the implicit level. However, for this complementation to make sense, some enrichment must also take place at the level of what is explicitly communicated.

If comprehension is to be treated as a properly inferential process, the inferences must be sound (in a sense that applies to non-demonstrative inference). From the mere fact that Mary is tired, Peter cannot soundly infer that she doesn't want to go to the cinema. For the implicatures (12b) and (12c) to be soundly derived, Mary must be understood as saying something stronger than that she is tired *tout court*: her meaning must be enriched to the point where it warrants the intended inferences. The process is one of parallel adjustment: expectations of relevance warrant the derivation of specific implicatures, for which the explicit content must be adequately enriched.

Mary is therefore conveying something more than simply the proposition that she is tired, which would be satisfied by whatever is the minimal degree of tiredness: she is conveying that she is tired enough not to want to go to the cinema. If she were 'technically' tired, but not tired enough for it to matter, her utterance would be misleading, not just by suggesting a wrong reason for her not wanting to go to the cinema, but also by giving a wrong indication of her degree of tiredness. Suppose Peter thought that she was being disingenuous in using her tiredness as an excuse for not going to the cinema. He might answer:

(14) Come on, you're not *that* tired!

He would not be denying that she is tired: merely that she is tired to the degree conveyed by her utterance.

How tired is that? Well, there is no absolute scale of tiredness (and if there were, no specific value would be indicated here). Mary is communicating that she is tired enough for it to be reasonable for her not to want to go to the cinema on that occasion. This is an *ad hoc*, circumstantial notion of tiredness. It is the degree of tiredness that has this consequence.

In saying (11), Mary thus communicates a notion more specific than the one encoded by the English word 'tired'. This notion is not lexicalised in English. It may be that Mary will never find another use for it, in which case it will not have the kind of stability in her mental life that we took to be a condition for mental concepthood. Alternatively, she may recognise this particular sort of tiredness, and have a permanent mental 'entry' or 'file' for it, in which case it is a proper concept. In the same way, Peter's grasp of the notion of tiredness Mary is invoking may be ephemeral, or he may recognise it as something that applies to Mary, and perhaps others, on different occasions, in which case he has the concept too.

It might be argued that the word 'tired' in Mary's utterance, when properly enriched, just means *too tired to want to go to the cinema*. This is a meaning which is perfectly encodable in English, even though it is not lexicalised. Suppose this were so, and that Mary has a stable concept of this kind of tiredness: her utterance would still illustrate our point that there may be many non-lexicalised mental concepts. The fact that this concept is encodable by a complex phrase would be no reason to think Mary does not have it as an elementary concept, any more than the fact that 'bachelor' can be defined is any reason to think we have no elementary mental concept of *bachelor*.

In any case, it is unlikely that Mary's answer in (11) is really synonymous with her answer in (15):

(15) *Peter* Do you want to go to the cinema?
Mary I'm too tired to want to go to the cinema.

Mary's answer in (11) has a degree of indeterminacy that is lost in (15). Quite apart from this, the apparent paraphrasability of her answer in (11) is linked to the fact that she is answering a yes–no question, which drastically narrows down the range of potential implicatures and the enrichment needed to warrant them. Yet the enrichment mechanism is itself quite general, and applies in contexts where the range of implicatures is much vaguer, as we will show with two further examples.

Imagine that Peter and Mary, on holiday in Italy, are visiting a museum. Mary says:

(16) I'm tired!

As before, if her utterance is to be relevant to Peter, she must mean more than just that she is strictly speaking tired. This time, though, the implications that might make her utterance relevant are only loosely suggested. They might include:

(17) (a) Mary's enjoyment of this visit is diminishing.
(b) Mary would like to cut short their visit to the museum.
(c) Mary is encouraging Peter to admit that he is also tired and wants to cut short the visit.
(d) Mary would like them to go back to their hotel after this visit to the museum, rather than visiting the Duomo, as they had planned.

If these and other such conclusions are implicatures of her utterance, they are only weak implicatures: implications that Peter is encouraged to derive and accept, but for which he has to take some of the responsibility himself (for the notion of 'weak implicature', see Sperber and Wilson, 1986/1995, chapter 4). Whatever implicatures he ends up treating as intended (or suggested) by Mary, he will have to adjust his understanding of her explicit meaning so as to warrant their derivation. Mary will be understood as having conveyed that she is tired to such a degree or in such a way as to warrant the derivation of these implicatures. This overall interpretation is itself justified by the expectation of relevance created by Mary's utterance (i.e. by this particular instantiation of the communicative principle of relevance).

That evening, at a trattoria, Mary says to Peter:

(18) I love Italian food!

She does not, of course, mean that she loves all Italian food, nor does she merely mean that there is some Italian food she loves. So what does she mean? It is often suggested that in a case like this, the expression 'Italian food' denotes a prototype, here *prototypical Italian food*. This presupposes that there is a readily available and relatively context-independent prototype. In the situation described above, it so happens that Mary is a vegetarian. Moreover, her understanding of Italian food is largely based on what she finds in an 'Italian' vegetarian restaurant in her own country where she sometimes goes with Peter, which serves several dishes such as 'tofu pizza' that are definitely not Italian. Mary's utterance achieves relevance for Peter by implicating that she is enjoying her food, and sees it as belonging to a distinct category which the expression 'Italian food' suggests but does not describe.

Even if Mary's use of the term 'Italian food' were less idiosyncratic, it would not follow that all Peter has to do to understand it is recover a prototype. Much recent research has cast doubt on the view that word meanings can be analysed in terms of context-independent prototypes, and suggests instead that *ad hoc* meanings are constructed in context (see e.g. Barsalou, 1987; Franks and Braisby, 1990; Franks, 1995; Butler, 1995). We would add that this contextual construction is a by-product of the relevance-guided comprehension process. The explicit content of an utterance, and in particular the meaning of specific expressions, is adjusted so as to warrant the derivation of implicatures which themselves justify the expectations of relevance created by the utterance act. These occasional meanings may stabilise into concepts, for the speaker, the hearer, or both.

These examples are designed to show how a word which encodes a given concept can be used to convey (as a component of a speaker's meaning) another concept that neither it nor any other expression in the language actually encodes. There is nothing exceptional about such uses: almost any word can be used in this way. Quite generally, the occurrence of a word in an utterance provides a piece of evidence, a pointer to a concept involved in the speaker's meaning. It may so happen that the intended concept is the very one encoded by the word, which is therefore used in its strictly literal sense. However, we would argue that this is no more than a possibility, not a preferred or default interpretation. Any interpretation, whether literal or not, results from mutual adjustment of the explicit and implicit content of the utterance. This adjustment process stabilises when the hypothesised implicit content is warranted by the hypothesised explicit content together with the context, and when the overall interpretation is warranted by (the particular instantiation of) the communicative principle of relevance.

This approach sheds some light on the phenomenon of polysemy illustrated by the example of 'open' above. A verb like 'open' acts as a pointer to indefinitely many notions or concepts. In some cases, the intended concept is jointly indicated by the verb and its direct object (as with the ordinary sense of 'open the washing machine'), so that the inferential route is short and obvious. There may be cases where such routinely reachable senses become lexicalised. In general, though, polysemy is the outcome of a pragmatic process whereby intended senses are inferred on the basis of encoded concepts and contextual information. These inferred senses may be ephemeral notions or stable concepts; they may be shared by few or many speakers, or by whole communities; the inference pattern may be a first-time affair or a routine pattern – and it may be a first-time affair for one interlocutor and a routine affair for another, who, despite these differences, manage to communicate successfully. (For relevance–theoretic accounts of polysemy, see Carston, 1996, in preparation; Deane, 1988; Groefsema, 1995; Papafragou, in preparation; Wilson and Sperber, in press.)

5 Implications

Our argument so far has been that, given the inferential nature of comprehension, the words in a language can be used to convey not only the concepts they encode, but also indefinitely many other related concepts to which they might point in a given context. We see this not as a mere theoretical possibility, but as a universal practice, suggesting that there are many times more concepts in our minds than words in our language.

Despite their different theoretical perspectives, many other researchers in philosophy, psychology and linguistics have converged on the idea that new senses are constantly being constructed in context (e.g. Franks and Braisby, 1990; Goshke and Koppelberg, 1992; Barsalou, 1987; Gibbs, 1994; Franks, 1995; Recanati, 1995; Nunberg, 1996; Carston, 1996, in preparation). However, it is possible to believe that new senses can be contextually constructed, without accepting that there are more mental concepts than public words.

Someone might argue, for example, that the only stable concepts are linguistically encodable ones. Unless a new sense constructed in context is linguistically encodable, it cannot be a stable concept of the speaker's, and will never stabilise as a mental concept in the hearer. When Mary says at the museum that she is tired, the understanding that she and Peter have of her kind and degree of tiredness cannot be divorced from their understanding of the whole situation. They do not construct or use an *ad hoc* concept of tiredness. Rather, they have a global representation of the situation, which gives its particular contextual import to the ordinary concept of tiredness.

We would reply as follows. We do not deny – indeed, we insist – that most occasional representations of a property (or an object, event or state) do not stabilise into a concept. Most contextually represented properties are not recognised as having been previously encountered, and are not remembered when the situation in which they were represented is itself forgotten. However, some properties are recognised and/or remembered even when many or all of the contextual elements of their initial identification are lost. For example, you look at your friend and recognise the symptoms of a mood for which you have no word, which you might be unable to describe exactly, and whose previous occurrences you only dimly remember; but you know that mood, and you know how it is likely to affect her and you. Similarly, you look at the landscape and the sky, and you recognise the weather, you know how it will feel, but you have no word for it. Or you feel a pain, you recognise it and know what to expect, but have no word for it; and so on. You are capable not just of recognising these phenomena but also of anticipating them, imagining them, regretting or rejoicing that they are not actual. You can communicate thoughts about them to interlocutors who are capable of recognising them, if not spontaneously, at least with the help of your communication. Your ability to recognise and think about the mood, the weather, the pain, is evidence that you have a corresponding stable mental file or entry, i.e. a mental concept. The evidence is not, of course, conclusive, and there could be a better hypothesis. However the suggestion that what has been contextually grasped can only be remembered with all the relevant particulars of the initial context is not that better hypothesis.

There is a more general reason for believing that we have many more concepts than words. The stabilisation of a word in a language is a social and historical affair. It is a slow and relatively rare process, involving co-ordination among many individuals over time. A plausible guess is that, in most relatively homogenous speech communities in human history, less than a dozen new words (including homonyms of older words and excluding proper names) would stabilise in a year. On the other hand, the addition of new concepts to an individual's mind is comparatively unconstrained. It is not a matter of co-ordinating with others, but of internal memory management. There is no question that we are capable of acquiring a huge amount of new information every day. Do we store it all in pre-existing files, or do we sometimes – perhaps a few times a day – open a new file, i.e. stabilise a new concept? Notice that this would not involve adding extra information to long-term memory but merely organising information that we are going to add anyhow in a different, and arguably more efficient way.

Information filed together tends to be accessed together, and efficient memory management involves not only filing together what is generally best accessed together, but also filing separately what is generally best accessed separately. Thus, you may be able to recognise a certain type of food (which the public linguistic expression 'Italian food' may hint at in an appropriate context but does not describe), and this ability may play a role in your mental life: say in deciding what to eat or cook on a given occasion. Where is information about this kind of food stored in your memory? Does it have its own address, or does it have to be reassembled from information filed elsewhere every time it is used?

How and how often we open new files, and thus stabilise new mental concepts, is an empirical question, to be investigated with the methods of psychology. However, the hypothesis that we can open a new file only when we have a public word that corresponds to it is a costly one, with no obvious merit. It amounts to imposing an arbitrary and counter-productive constraint on memory management. (This is not, of course, to deny the converse point that on encountering a new word you may stabilise a new concept, and that many of our concepts originate partly or wholly from linguistic communication – a point for which there is much evidence, in particular developmental, e.g. Gelman and Markman, 1986.)

While the kind of collective co-ordination needed to stabilise a word in a speech community is an elaborate affair, the typically pairwise co-ordination involved in any given communicative act is a relatively simpler achievement – the kind of achievement that a pragmatic theory such as relevance theory aims to explain. This co-ordination may be somewhat loose. When Mary says at the museum that she is tired, her utterance gets its explicit meaning through adjustment to a set of weak implicatures: that is, implicatures whose exact content is not wholly determined by the utterance. The *ad hoc* concept of tiredness that Peter constructs (i.e. the concept of tiredness which warrants the derivation of these weak implicatures) is unlikely to be exactly the same as the one Mary had in mind (since she did not foresee or intend exactly these implicatures). This is not a failure of communication. It is an illusion of the code theory that communication aims at duplication of meanings. Sometimes it does, but quite ordinarily a looser kind of understanding is intended and achieved. The type of co-ordination aimed at in most verbal exchanges is best compared to the co-ordination between people taking a stroll together rather than to that between people marching in step.

Returning to the question of effability, we would maintain that this is a matter of degree. Some concepts are properly shared, and can be unequivocally expressed: a mathematical discussion would provide good examples. Other concepts are idiosyncratic, but as a result of common experience or communication, are close enough to the idiosyncratic concepts of others to play a role in the co-ordination of behaviour. Still other concepts may be too idiosyncratic to be even loosely communicated. The fact that a public word exists, and is successfully used in communication, does not make it safe to assume that it encodes the same concept for all successful users; and in any case, the concept communicated will only occasionally be the same as the one encoded. Communication can succeed, despite possible semantic discrepancies, as long as the word used in a given situation points the hearer in the direction intended by the speaker. Thus, Peter and Mary might differ as to the exact extension of 'tired': Peter might regard as genuine though minimal tiredness a state that Mary would not regard as tiredness at all. Mary's successful use of the term in no way depends on their meaning exactly the same thing by it. Similarly, their concepts of Italy might pick out different entities in space or time (for example, is Ancient Roman History part of Italian History? That depends on what you mean by 'Italy'). Mary's successful use of the term 'Italian' should be unaffected by these discrepancies.

More generally, it does not much matter whether or not a word linguistically encodes a full-fledged concept, and, if so, whether it encodes the same concept for both speaker and hearer. Even if it does, comprehension is not guaranteed. Even if it does not, comprehension need not be impaired. Whether they encode concepts or pro-concepts, words are used as pointers to contextually intended senses. Utterances are merely pieces of evidence of the speaker's intention, and this has far-reaching implications, a few of which we have tried to outline here.

We would like to thank François Recanati, Robyn Carston, Eric Lormand, Peter Carruthers, Gloria Origgi, Anna Papafragou and Richard Breheny for discussions on the topic of this paper and comments on earlier versions.

10 Convention-based semantics and the development of language

Stephen Laurence

1 Introduction

A natural and historically popular view of the relation between meaning in public natural languages and thought is that thought is metaphysically prior, that natural language meaning depends on the meaning or content of mental states of one sort or another. Today this view is most closely associated with the work of Paul Grice and various philosophers broadly inspired by Grice's original work. This work (which I shall refer to collectively as 'Convention-Based Semantics') ultimately seeks to ground natural language meaning in a complex web of beliefs and intentions of language users. Many versions of Convention-Based Semantics have been put forward and, in spite of the numerous objections and purported counterexamples which have been raised against various versions of the theory, it remains the dominant view about the nature of natural language semantic properties amongst philosophers.

While I am sympathetic with these philosophers in their attempt to ground language in thought, I think that Convention-Based Semantics is wrong, not just in detail, but fundamentally. One basic way in which Convention-Based Semantics seems to me to go wrong is in assimilating natural language linguistic meaning to communicative phenomena generally. In my view it is a mistake to try to find a common reductive analysis that will ground natural language meaning and the meanings variously associated with pantomime gestures, with lighthouse beacon patterns, with hand gestures to help a friend back her car into a tight spot and any of a variety of other forms of meaningful communication. I think there exists substantial evidence for the special purpose nature of the language processor (see, for example, Bellugi *et al.*, 1993; Curtiss, 1988; Gopnik and Crago, 1991; Pinker, 1994; and Smith and Tsimpli, 1995), and the connection between natural language utterances and their semantic properties is likely to reflect the distinctive nature of this processor. Accordingly, the alternative general strategy I advocate attempts to ground natural language linguistic meaning in facts about principles and representations intimately associated with the language processor (in the spirit of Noam Chomsky's accounts of the nature of natural language syntactic properties).

I believe that my alternative 'Chomskian' account is superior to Convention-Based accounts of natural language meaning in a number of ways. I think my alternative is simpler and independently well motivated, whereas I think the Convention-Based account faces substantial empirical and methodological difficulties (not just a few relatively technical counter-examples). Achieving a proper evaluation of Convention-Based Semantics is not an easy matter, however. There are a number of different versions of Convention-Based Semantics, and theorists disagree rather substantially over the proper interpretation of the theory and its guiding motivations. In an earlier paper (Laurence, 1996) I took the Convention-Based theorist to be largely concerned with how the connections between meanings and particular utterance types are sustained. A common response to my argument there has been that there needn't be any conflict between my Chomskian account and Convention-Based accounts; perhaps, for example, we should see the Convention-Based theorist as principally interested in how the connections between meanings and particular utterance types get *established*, rather than how these connections are *sustained*. This was an issue that I didn't have room to address in the earlier paper, and it is worth exploring since at least some Convention-Based theorists seem to be motivated by such considerations. Accordingly, in this chapter, my discussion will centre around the claim that considerations pertaining to the development of natural language (in language acquisition, or in the history of the species) provide some reason for adopting Convention-Based semantics.

The structure of my discussion will be as follows. First, in section 2, I will give a broad outline of the form Convention-Based accounts typically take, followed by some brief discussion of some philosophical motivations for pursuing the theory, in section 3. In section 4, I will argue that developmental considerations do not support Convention-Based accounts and that, in fact, quite the contrary is true: a variety of developmental considerations actually provide a relatively compelling argument *against* such accounts. In section 5, I present my alternative to Convention-Based Semantics, arguing that this account is fully consistent with the data discussed in section 4. In this chapter, as in the earlier paper I mentioned, some of the arguments I give are strongly based on empirical considerations. And I think many philosophers who advocate Convention-Based Semantics think that these kind of empirical arguments are largely beside the point for one reason or another. This seems to be the sort of view that Grice himself held (see Grice, 1976/80 and below). Though this sort of view is not uncommon, it is not exactly clear to me how or why philosophical theories of meaning or other phenomena should escape empirical constraint. In any case, in the final section I discuss some philosophical strategies for evading such constraints which some might find appealing, and I argue for the minimal sort of empirical constraint on philosophical theories about meaning that they should at least be compatible with our best empirical theories of natural language and its processing, development and evolution.

Though I am mainly concerned in this chapter with the nature of natural language semantic properties, a related issue concerns the role of internal representations of natural language linguistic properties in cognition. Are such representations strictly limited to use in language processing, or do they play a wider role in our cognitive lives? In Peter Carruthers' (1996a) terms, this is the question of whether the communicative conception or the cognitive conception of language is correct. While Convention-Based Semantics seems committed to the communicative conception wherein natural language is basically limited to its role in communication (though see Devitt and Sterelny, 1987), my alternative position is compatible with either the cognitive or the communicative conception depending on the role in thought which the underlying representations posited by the account play. The arguments here may, however, undermine the motivations of those who accept the communicative view of natural language because they endorse the Convention-Based Semantics programme.

2 Speaker meaning, conventional meaning and Convention-Based Semantics

Following Grice, Convention-Based theorists typically distinguish two sorts of meaning, often called 'speaker meaning' and 'conventional meaning'. Speaker meaning is characterised as *what a given speaker means by uttering a given utterance*. 'Speaker' and 'utterance' here are to be read very liberally, so that speakers include also writers and signers and indeed any agent producing any actions which might be said to have meaning. So, if I mean something by waving a flag at you in a distinctive manner, then I am thereby to be counted as a 'speaker'. 'Utterance' is to be interpreted similarly, so that my flag-waving action counts as an utterance. Speaker meaning attaches to individual acts of utterance, and so on different occasions two acts of the same type might very well have different speaker meanings. Conventional meaning, in the case of language, is the literal linguistic meaning which attaches to expression types.

Convention-Based theories typically seek to reduce conventional meaning to beliefs and intentions of speakers and hearers by first reducing conventional meaning to speaker meaning, and then reducing speaker meaning to patterns of beliefs and intentions. We can also think of this in terms of construction rather than reduction if we like. So Convention-

Based theorists could equally be thought of as trying to construct conventional meaning out of speaker meaning and speaker meaning out of beliefs and intentions of speakers and hearers.

The first stage in the Convention-Based Semantics construction of meaning involves the construction of speaker meanings out of particular sorts of beliefs and intentions of speakers and hearers. The following account of speaker meaning is representative of the sort of account given at this stage:

> *Speaker meaning*
> For any speaker, S, audience, A, utterance, x, and meaning, p, S's uttering x has speaker meaning p just in case S uttered x intending,
> (1) A to come to believe p
> (2) A to recognise that S intends (1)
> (3) A to fulfil (1) partly on the basis of his fulfilment of (2).

So, for example, my uttering 'Cats have whiskers' has the speaker meaning that *Cats have whiskers* just in case:

> (1) I uttered 'Cats have whiskers' intending for you to come to believe that *Cats have whiskers*, and
> (2) I intended for you to recognise that I intended for you to come to believe that *Cats have whiskers*, and also
> (3) I intended for you to come to believe that *Cats have whiskers* partly on the basis of recognising that I intended for you to come to believe that *Cats have whiskers*.

The link between speaker meaning and conventional meaning at the second stage in the project is often given in terms of the existence of conventions, where these are understood roughly in terms of David Lewis' account (Lewis, 1969, 1983). According to Lewis, a regularity, R (among a population) counts as a convention when the following conditions hold:

> *Lewis' general account of conventions*
> (1) Everyone conforms to *R*.
> (2) Everyone believes that the others conform to *R*.
> (3) This belief that the others conform to *R* gives everyone a good and decisive reason to conform to *R* himself.
> (4) There is a general preference for general conformity to *R* rather than slightly-less-than-general conformity – in particular, rather than conformity by all but any one.
> (5) *R* is not the only possible regularity meeting the last two conditions.

(6) Finally, the various facts listed in conditions 1 to 5 are matters of *common* (or *mutual*) *knowledge*: they are known to everyone, it is known to everyone that they are known to everyone, and so on.
(1983, pp. 164–6.)

Some specific convention instantiating this general schema for conventions is then used to link conventional meaning to speaker meaning. The following example is representative of the sort of convention appealed to here.

Conventional meaning
A sentence, x, has the conventional meaning that p (among some population) just in case there is a convention to use x to speaker-mean p (see Davies 1996, p. 120).

This account of conventional meaning should be read with Lewis' general account of conventions in mind, so that we have, for example that everyone uses x to speaker-mean that p, and everyone believes that others use x to speaker-mean that p, and so on. Taking our earlier example, this means that everyone uses 'cats have whiskers' to speaker-mean that *cats have whiskers*, and everyone believes that others use 'cats have whiskers' to speaker-mean that *cats have whiskers*, and so on.

The full Convention-Based account is a rather complicated story. For example, if we spell out just the second clause of the convention here with reference to the account of speaker meaning given earlier, we find that, among other things, in order for 'cats have whiskers' to mean what it does we apparently need a fifth order attitude. You need to *believe* that I *intend* for you to *recognise* that I *intend* for you to *believe* that cats have whiskers. Of course the fact that the theory is complicated is in itself no objection to the theory. I don't see any reason why we should expect an account of the nature of meaning to be wholly uncomplicated when it is spelled out in full detail. But this range of empirical consequences will be relevant in determining whether developmental considerations argue for the theory.

3 The alleged priority of 'speaker meaning'

Michael Devitt and Kim Sterelny are among the philosophers who take developmental considerations to offer some support to Convention-Based Semantics. In their philosophy of language text *Language and Reality*, they argue that we should take conventional meanings to be built out of speaker meanings partly because we can have speaker meaning without conventional meaning but not vice versa. And they offer developmental considerations, among others, in support of this.

Devitt and Sterelny here seem to motivate their programme of analysing 'conventional meaning' in terms of 'speaker meaning' (and speaker meaning in terms of beliefs and intentions) by first noting that these two different sorts of meaning exist, and then asking which of the two we should take to be more primary. They write:

> We shall suppose then that the distinction [between speaker meaning and conventional meaning] is real. Which sort of meaning is more basic or prior? (1987, p. 121)

They then argue that conventional meaning cannot be taken as more basic since there are cases where we have speaker meaning but no conventional meaning, which suggests to them that it is speaker meaning which is primary. Devitt and Sterelny cite a variety of different sorts of cases here, including:

(1) Cases involving a slip of the tongue which produce nonsense strings like 'Can I morrow your dotes?' (for 'Can I borrow your notes?').[1]
(2) Cases involving communication through gestures and mime in the absence of a common language.
(3) Considerations involving 'the original development of language' (1987, p. 120)

Devitt and Sterelny's strategy here, though perhaps not uncommon, strikes me as rather strange. The assumption that if there are two types of meaning, speaker meaning and conventional meaning, one should reduce to the other seems unjustified to me. Consider the case of sense and reference, two types of meaning which play a role in a variety of semantical theories. Gottlob Frege, who introduced the distinction between sense and reference in his paper 'On Sense and Reference', used the example of the expressions 'the morning star' and 'the evening star'. Frege noted that there was a sense in which these expressions had the same meaning, in that they both referred to the same object (which, as it turns out, is the planet Venus). On the other hand, there is another sense in which they have different meanings, in that they have different 'cognitive contents' for us, and in particular, while it is trivial to say that 'the morning star is the morning star' it is not at all trivial to say that 'the morning star is the evening star'. The senses associated with these expressions correspond to the different ways in which we are conceiving of what turns out to be one and the same object (Venus) – the first presenting Venus as the last 'star' visible in morning sky, the second presenting Venus as the first 'star' visible in the night sky. Having distinguished these two types of meaning, though, we are not necessarily tempted to suppose that one of them (sense or reference) must be more basic and the

[1] Example from Fromkin, 1982, p.6.

other analysed in terms of it. And certainly the fact that there can be sense without reference (e.g., for the expression 'the present King of France') doesn't provide us with a compelling reason to suppose that reference reduces to sense. We can, if we like, just recognise the existence of two different sorts of meaning, neither of which reduces to the other (though they are related to one another in various ways). Why shouldn't we be able to say the same of 'speaker meaning' and 'conventional meaning'?

Though the general principle that if there are two types of meaning and one can exist in the absence of the other, the second reduces to the first does not seem to be a valid principle, it might be that there is something about the particular case of speaker meaning and conventional meaning that makes this principle applicable. So we should look more closely at the cases of dissociation that Devitt and Sterelny cite. Unfortunately, their remarks are fairly brief, but about the development of language they say the following.

> Consider the original development of language. Presumably this development was replete with examples of noises and gestures being used with communicative intent – with speaker meaning – before there existed a settled system of conventions for so using them. Communicative effort that was at least partly successful must have been a precondition for the development of linguistic conventions. The conventions came from regularities in speaker meanings. (1987, p. 120)

This passage is not easy to interpret, but Devitt and Sterelny seem to be claiming here that speaker meaning in some sense *had* to precede conventional meaning. We might try to reconstruct the argument here along something like the following lines. Conventional meaning is the shared meaning that expression types have amongst the members of a given community. But *shared* meanings could not exist until individual acts of meaning existed – indeed until a *number of individuals* meant the same thing by uttering tokens of a given expression type. Similarly, conventional meaning is by its very nature a meaning that is underwritten by the existence of a *practice* of meaning something by a given expression type. But *practices* require, by their very nature, more than one instance to become established. Much the same sort of argument might be made in the case of neologisms, and again perhaps in the case of language acquisition.

I don't know if this is the sort of argument Devitt and Sterelny have in mind or not. But I don't think it's a good argument. The argument is certainly encouraged by the fact that Devitt and Sterelny use the terms 'standard', 'literal' and 'conventional' interchangeably in connection with this type of meaning. This conflation, however, begs some important questions, not the least of which is whether there is some interesting sense in which literal linguistic meaning is *conventional*. Certainly there could be no such a thing as shared meaning unless there were several individuals who meant the same thing by their respective utterances of a given expression type. But shared meaning could as easily arise from the coincidence in *literal idiolect meaning* amongst several individuals as from speaker meanings. Similarly, though a practice of using a given expression may require more than one instance to become established, the instances on which the practice is based could well be instances of the literal use of a given expression type. So, since original meaning might just as well have been literal idiolect meaning, the argument does not show that speaker meaning must precede literal meaning.

Devitt and Sterelny's general argumentative strategy seems flawed in several ways, then. The existence of two types of meaning doesn't require one to be reduced to the other, so even if we could show that speaker meaning could exist without conventional meaning, but that the reverse was not true, this would not show that conventional meaning reduced to speaker meaning. And, moreover, it's not clear that the alleged asymmetry between speaker meaning and conventional meaning in fact exists.

4 Do developmental considerations argue for Convention-Based Semantics?

I want now to look more directly at some developmental considerations to consider their bearing on the plausibility of Convention-Based Semantics. Obviously I cannot undertake anything like a thorough review of language development as it might bear on Convention-Based Semantics. What I will do is briefly consider some relevant aspects of development and show that these aspects of development lend no obvious support to Convention-Based Semantics, and that some general features of the developmental problems in fact suggest the opposite conclusion.

4.1 The development of language in the individual

One place to look for developmental support for the Convention-Based account would be in language acquisition, and more particularly, in lexical acquisition. Perhaps the process of lexical acquisition crucially involves the patterns of mental states and processes the Convention-Based theorist posits (or provides more indirect support for these posits). Though the issue is extremely complex, not least because we are only just beginning to understand the processes involved in lexical acquisition, I will suggest two general sorts of considerations that argue against this hypothesis.

The first point is that the sorts of lexical acquisition principles currently under discussion in psychology do not seem to require any appeal to meta-beliefs. Psychologists studying lexical acquisition have posited the existence of a number of general principles children employ in determining the meanings of new words. For example, Ellen Markman (1989) has proposed that children hypothesise word meanings which group objects taxonomically, as opposed to thematically, despite the fact that young children show a preference for thematic groupings of objects in non-linguistic sorting tasks. Lila Gleitman (1990) has proposed a rather different sort of constraint. She posits the existence of a syntax–semantics mapping, and suggests that children's hypotheses about word meanings are constrained to respect the range of sub-categorisation frames associated with a given word. The syntax–semantics mapping determines a class of possible meanings for a word given the set of sub-categorisation frames associated with the word. Barbara Landau and her colleagues (Landau *et al.* 1988) have proposed that children hypothesise word meanings for count nouns that group objects according to shape. Applying principles like these, however, doesn't seem to require any appeal to meta-beliefs at all. It is not obvious that the application of such principles even requires any awareness that other languages are spoken, or even possible. For all these principles seem to care, children could take themselves to be discovering non-conventional facts about a wholly invariant system used for communication. So the process of lexical acquisition, as governed by these principles, looks unlikely to support the Convention-Based account. Of course these principles don't provide a full account of lexical acquisition, but they do underwrite a central aspect of meaning assignment where one might naturally expect the machinery in the Convention-Based account to show up if it was in fact essential to lexical acquisition.

The second point concerns the apparent dissociability of the aquirability of linguistic meaning from so-called 'theory of mind' abilities (our general capacity for reasoning about the mental states of others in terms of, for example, intentions, beliefs and desires). Evidence from recent studies of individuals with autism suggests that a central component of autism is the lack of a theory of mind (for a review of some of this literature, see Happé 1994). And, although most people with autism have poor or non-existent linguistic abilities and very low IQs, some 'high functioning' individuals have normal IQs and, despite some rather serious communicative abnormalities (being withdrawn, or overly inquisitive, or otherwise socially inappropriate), they can also have quite significant linguistic abilities. Of particular relevance here, however, is the fact that people with autism seem to assign normal linguistic meanings to a range of lexical items. Helen Tager-Flusberg compared the extensions assigned to a class of concrete nouns by subjects with autism and those of normal subjects and mentally retarded subjects (all of the same mental age). She found no significant difference in results among the subjects in these different groups.

Autistic children at the same general level of vocabulary as control children do not acquire idiosyncratic word meanings. Rather, they show the same patterns of generalisation of meaning as evidenced by their overextension and under-extension errors. And indeed the patterns reflect adult judgements of these stimuli too. (1985, p. 1175)

Subjects with autism do differ from normal subjects regarding some lexical items – for example, words referring to mental states (as one would expect given their apparent deficit in understanding the nature of the states these terms refer to). But it is significant that they seem to be capable of assigning normal linguistic meanings to a relatively large class of terms (just how far Tager-Flusberg's results generalise is not clear). It is extremely puzzling, though, how someone lacking a theory of mind could assign normal linguistic meanings to terms (or use words meaningfully at all) if the Convention-Based theorist is right about the nature of meaning, given the numerous attitudes concerning the propositional attitudes of others that the theory posits. As we saw above, even for the simplest cases of literal meaning we would need as many as five orders of attitudes![2]

Non-literal meaning may well require higher-order attitudes, as many pragmaticians have suggested. And interestingly, subjects with autism do selectively have difficulties with such meanings. Indeed people with autism may provide an important source of evidence for testing theories in pragmatics, given their apparent theory of mind deficits. Francesca Happé (1993) has recently exploited just this property to provide an extremely interesting source of confirming evidence for Dan Sperber and Dierdre Wilson's (1986/95) Relevance Theory. The same sort of reasoning, however, suggests that lexical acquisition does not involve the patterns of attitudes which Convention-Based Semantics is committed to for ordinary literal linguistic meanings. (For some further discussion *see also* Hobson, 1993; Baron-Cohen, 1988).

In principle, people with autism could be considered exceptions to the generalisations in the Convention-Based account. However, this move strikes me as somewhat ad hoc. Certainly we should expect there to be exceptions to the generalisations here, but presumably they should be local and otherwise explicable – like slips of the tongue, for example. They shouldn't involve entire classes of individuals who clearly and systematically fail to satisfy the account for all uses of language. Indeed, it is not clear why, on a Convention-Based account, such individuals should be considered to be members of the linguistic community at all.

[2] Much the same point could be made using young children, since children do not employ propositional attitude concepts in an adult-like manner until the age of four (see Carruthers, 1996a, pp. 78–9). But presumably we do not want to deny that children before the age of four mean things by their utterances!

4.2 The development of language in the species

Let's turn now briefly to the historical development of language in the species. Devitt and Sterelny describe a process of very slow development of language 'in humanoid society' by a process of 'lifting ourselves up by our own semantic bootstraps'. They suggest that at some point, early humans began to make noises with speaker meanings. When these 'caught on', conventional meanings were born. These became part of the culture, and were much easier to learn than they were originally to create. So energy could be focused on creation of further speaker meanings, which later would be conventionalised, and so on. For Devitt and Sterelny, it seems, natural languages are more or less the product of our general intellectual capacities applied to the linguistic domain. Their account of the development of language is not really an evolutionary account; language is a cultural artefact which required no language specific evolutionary adaptation to be produced.

Contrary to what this picture suggests, however, there seems to be good evidence that language *isn't* just a cultural artefact or human 'invention'. For example, there is no known correlation between the existence or complexity of language with cultural development, though we would expect there would be if language were a cultural artefact (Pinker, 1995). Further, language and general intelligence are dissociable. There are cases of normally intelligent people with extremely impoverished linguistic abilities, and there are cases of people with normal, even extraordinary, linguistic abilities despite severe general intellectual handicaps. The former sort of case is illustrated by the cases of Genie and Chelsea, neither of whom were exposed to a natural language until after the critical period, and whose linguistic abilities are severely impoverished (see Curtiss, 1988; Pinker, 1994). The latter sort of case is illustrated by the case of Christopher, studied by Smith and Tsimpli (1995). Christopher, despite having a non-verbal IQ of between 60 and 70 has normal English linguistic abilities, and moreover, has very impressive abilities in fifteen or sixteen other languages. Finally, languages that *are* the product of human invention are rejected in significant part by children learning language. Children exposed to pidgins – makeshift amalgams of several natural languages that are used for communication among a group of speakers with no single dominant language – reject them in favour of new languages of their own creation that are far richer than the pidgins they are exposed to (see Pinker, 1994). Similarly, deaf children studied by Susan Goldin-Meadow and her colleagues who were not exposed to a natural sign language, rejected the artificial manual communication system of their parents, in large part, substantially enriching and systematising it. So it looks like language is not a cultural artefact.

But if the Convention-Based theorist views language as a product of evolution and nevertheless looks to the evolutionary development of language for support for the Convention-Based account, then presumably the Convention-Based account would be about the development of language through precursors to language. It is certainly possible that some of the elements employed in the Convention-Based account (such as theory of mind abilities) formed a part of a precursor to language. But this is not the same as saying that the Convention-Based account itself was satisfied by some precursor to language. And, moreover, a precursor to language is not language itself – it is just a precursor (see Gómez, this volume). And we wouldn't say that because proto-vision (or proto-visual content) had such and such properties, vision (or visual content) must *reduce* to these properties. So it is not clear why we should say this in the case of language, even if the Convention-Based account were satisfied by some precursor to language.

5 A Chomskian account of natural language linguistic meaning

If Convention-Based Semantics isn't the right account of natural language linguistic meaning, what alternative account could be? The account that I favour is based on Noam Chomsky's general views on the nature of linguistic theory.[3] Chomsky claims that linguistics studies our knowledge of natural language, this knowledge forming a central and essential part of our capacities to acquire and process natural language. As with Convention-Based Semantics, there will naturally be a variety of different accounts in keeping with this general perspective on the nature of language. Focusing on linguistic meaning, we might provide something like the following sort of account, as a first pass.

> *Chomskian account of natural language linguistic meaning*
> A sentence in my idiolect means what it does because it is assigned that meaning by the grammar that I have internalised.

Filling this out a bit, we might say that the linguistic meaning of a natural language utterance is given by the meanings associated (in the lexicon) with the words it is composed of (where these words are typed non-semantically – and presumably in virtue of analogous Chomskian account of phonological, morphological and syntactic properties[4]) and combined according to

[3] I call the account 'Chomskian' because I take it to be broadly within the spirit of Chomsky's views on linguistics, though Chomsky himself may well not endorse such a view. (For further discussion, see Laurence, 1996. However, I take the account here to be preferable to the more performance based account used there for expository purposes).

[4] It is worth noting here that, though these other features of utterances are equally conventional (in the pre-theoretic sense), no one believes that people have the requisite beliefs and intentions a Convention-Based account of these properties would require. One of the virtues of the Chomskian account proposed here is that it provides parallel accounts of all these linguistic properties. (For elaboration of this point see Laurence, 1996).

the syntax of the sentence and the principles of compositional semantics embodied in the system. So 'Cats have whiskers' means that *Cats have whiskers* in my idiolect because the grammar I have internalised assigns that meaning to this sentence. My internalised grammar assigns this sentence that meaning because it pairs a particular logical form with the phonetic form corresponding to 'Cats have whiskers', and the principles of compositional semantics governing my idiolect together with the semantic properties my lexicon assigns to lexical items associated with the logical form ('cats' 'have' and 'whiskers') yield the meaning *Cats have whiskers*.

This account is perfectly compatible with the various developmental considerations we've just been looking at. The sorts of principles governing lexical acquisition posited by Markman and others do not conflict with the account in any way. Indeed the process of acquisition such principles feed into just is a process which sets up the correlations between public language utterances and mental representations, in the lexicon and mentally represented grammar, which the Chomskian account appeals to. The account has no difficulties with the fact that some people with autism can acquire language and use it meaningfully, since the account does not appeal to sophisticated knowledge concerning the propositional attitudes of language users which people with autism seem to lack. And the various facts pertaining to the historical development of language in the species are perfectly compatible with the account as well. In fact, many of the considerations that were raised there are points among those typically cited in support of the general Chomskian model that I am appealing to. Finally, it is also worth noting that the machinery appealed to in the account is independently well motivated. We have strong independent reasons to posit the existence of a lexicon and to suppose that the lexical items associated with logical forms are governed by a compositional semantics.

This account has a number of other interesting features that I take to be advantages of the theory, which I would like to at least briefly mention. One advantage is that this account is idiolect-based. This allows for the fine grainedness of differences amongst idiolects, while still accommodating public language generality (as some function of idiolects). Since the account makes available a notion of literal meaning that is independent of public natural language meaning, such meanings can be constructed from the prior idiolect-based linguistic meaning (as other public language linguistic properties can be constructed from prior idiolect-based linguistic properties generally). At the same time, the community can enter the account of idiolect meaning via the meanings of the mental representations which fix idiolect meaning, if this is desirable (via deference to experts, for example). There are many interesting questions that arise in connection with these issues, which I do not have space here to pursue – about the relations between public languages and idiolects, for example, or the 'normativity' of meaning and language. These issues will have to await a future paper, however.

6 Deflationary interpretations of Convention-Based Semantics

Though Convention-Based theorists do often suggest arguments based on developmental considerations in favour of their accounts, they typically do not present the developmental considerations as offering direct empirical support for their views. Some Convention-Based theorists even seem to hold that empirical considerations, such as those pertaining to the development of language (in the species or the individual) are wholly irrelevant to the evaluation to their accounts. I find this sort of claim somewhat puzzling. I suppose there might be some construal of 'conceptual analysis' under which the theorist is simply interested in analysing our pretheoretic conception of 'language' or 'meaning' and so needn't look any further than our pretheoretic intuitions about how these concepts should be applied in constructing theories. But this seems to be a deeply uninteresting exercise. After all, for the most part conceptual analysis is interesting to the extent that it illuminates not merely our concepts but also the phenomena they pertain to. So, at the very least, the conceptual analyst's theories mustn't conflict with well-established empirical results.

There may be ways of interpreting Convention-Based theories that substantially reduce their empirical commitments, though. And I want to end by briefly discussing how Convention-Based theorists might try to do this. A number of theorists suggest, for example, that they are engaged in a project of 'rational reconstruction', and that such projects do not have the empirical commitments of, for example, reductive accounts of kinds in special sciences like biology. They do not often provide any clear account of what rational reconstruction involves, though, or why one would want to give a rational reconstruction, or when one is licensed. Dorit Bar-On's brief discussion of these issues in a recent paper (Bar-On, 1995) is perhaps the fullest discussion available. Bar-On argues for a 'genetic' interpretation of Convention-Based Semantics. Regarding the apparent empirical consequences of her view she says:

> Now, of course, we are not to take this story as attempting to uncover actual historical conditions. It is not, for example, advanced as an empirical hypothesis of evolutionary biology. And the story would not be vitiated if it were somehow discovered that the actual facts did not bear it out. So what precisely is its status? My suggestion is that it should be seen as *a rational reconstruction of the condition under which language could emerge*. (1995, p. 97)

Bar-On distinguishes two kinds of 'rational reconstruction'. The first sort of rational reconstruction we might call 'Quasi-Empirical Rational

Reconstruction'. It attempts to provide a 'plausible' account of how a phenomena might come to be. Bar-On says of the Convention-Based account that while it doesn't purport to

> track down actual historical conditions, [it] may still be taken to have quasi-empirical ambitions. By this I mean that it is possible (and even natural) to read the genetic story as a reconstruction of a path languageless creatures (like our distant ancestors) might plausibly take to get to language.

As Bar-On makes clear in a footnote, however, the accuracy of the account to any real process is not essential. Citing some potential counterevidence, she suggests that,

> even in the face of such evidence, there is still room for a *plausible but false* story of the kind we have been telling here. Such a story might even be in some ways *better* – e.g., philosophically more interesting, illuminating, etc. – than a true empirical account according to which linguistic meaning emerged through evolutionary accident. (1995, p. 114)

Unfortunately, this is all that Bar-On says in clarification of this first variety of rational reconstruction. And it is clearly not enough. It isn't at all clear why a plausible but false story should be more illuminating or philosophically interesting than a true one (plausible or not). If the philosopher of language is trying to provide an account of linguistic meaning, and linguistic meaning is a natural kind studied in the special science of linguistics, it would be natural to suppose that accounts of the nature of this kind should be held to the same sorts of standards as accounts of the nature of other special science kinds. And presumably in providing accounts of the nature of biological, or geological, or economic kinds, plausible but false accounts are not worth much. At the very least, if linguistic theories and philosophical theories are both talking about the same subject matter – language – then philosophical theories should not conflict with well-established facts in linguistics (and related disciplines), just as philosophical theories in the philosophy of physics or biology should not conflict with well-established facts in those disciplines. The Quasi-Empirical variety of rational reconstruction doesn't seem particularly promising.

The other sort of rational reconstruction we might call 'Justificatory Myth Rational Reconstruction'. The idea here is to read the Convention-Based account as describing a mythical scenario for the development of language and to understand the role of the myth here as analogous to the role of the social contract myth in justifying political norms. The social contract myth describes a hypothetical state of nature and reconstructs the emergence of political norms in terms of people forming a social contract in the state of nature. For example, in John Rawls's extremely influential discussion, the 'original position' functions as the state of nature where people make decisions about society from behind a 'veil of ignorance' (that is, without knowing what their place in the society will be). Here we can see the claim that some *actual* society is just (or not) as the claim that it is (or isn't) the same sort of society as would be chosen in the original position. We are not committed to the historical accuracy of this process.

This, then, looks like it might be a promising way for the Convention-Based Semanticist to go. Unfortunately, it doesn't succeed. To see why we need to look a bit more carefully at how the account is supposed to work for the social contract case. Here, an actual society is counted as just (or not) depending on whether a society of that sort would be chosen in the original position. How, though, do we determine whether two societies are relevantly of the same sort? If we say that they are alike in justice, this seems to presuppose that facts about justice are settled independently of this procedure. So presumably we choose other sorts of properties, properties such as distribution of material wealth, access to food, shelter and so on. When societies share properties of these sorts, then they are also alike in terms of justice, and so if a real society is like a mythical one in these respects, and the mythical one would be chosen in the original position, then the real one is just as well.

Turning now to the case of semantics, the problem is that there are no properties which can play the role that the properties of distribution of material wealth, access to food, shelter and so on play in the social contract case. The properties in question can't just be non-semantic properties of utterances like shape or sound, for example, because something can share these properties with meaningful utterances and yet mean something completely different or nothing at all. Indeed this seems to follow directly from the very conventionality of language – the fact that our utterances in other circumstances might mean something entirely different or nothing at all. So, if a monolingual German produced a phonologically indistinguishable utterance to my utterance of 'Susan leaped' ('Susan liebt'), their utterance would not thereby mean the same as mine. And, similarly, if my cat produced the sound 'dog', it presumably wouldn't thereby mean *dog*. So sharing properties of sound or shape isn't sufficient for meaning. And, of course, we cannot appeal to shared beliefs and intentions, because we are appealing to the Justificatory Myth precisely in order to avoid empirical disconfirmation. If we weren't worried about all the relevant attitudes showing up in the actual account, there'd be no need to appeal to the Myth. So the Justificatory Myth version of Rational Reconstruction doesn't seem to help the Convention-Based theorist either. It looks like rational reconstruction is not a promising strategy for reducing the empirical commitments of the Convention-Based account.

7 Conclusion

In this chapter we explored the possibility that developmental considerations pertaining to language acquisition in the individual or the historical development of language in the species provided support of some sort to Convention-Based accounts of natural language semantic properties. We found that in both cases, the developmental facts not only tended not to provide positive support for Convention-Based accounts, but actually provided evidence against such accounts. On the other hand, it was argued that the alternative Chomskian account advocated here is fully consistent with such facts. Faced with the threat these empirical results posed for the theory, Convention-Based theorists attempted to find a plausible deflationary interpretation of the theory. The ad hoc nature of the Quasi-Empirical version of rational reconstruction drove us to the Justificatory Myth version. But this last resort for the Convention-Based account was found not to work. The myth couldn't be connected up with the reality. Fortunately, a better alternative can be found. We can use the Chomskian account I've outlined above, and let natural language linguistic properties, including linguistic meaning, be inherited from properties of representations connected with the internalised grammar. And then we won't need the myth.

Thanks to Graham Bird, Peter Carruthers, Ted Elkington, Eric Margolis, Bernard Molyneux, Murali Ramachandran, Gabriel Segal and Dan Sperber for helpful comments or discussion of this material.

Part III

Language and conscious reasoning

Introduction to part III

Peter Carruthers and Jill Boucher

The chapters in Part III all relate, more or less closely, to the distinction between conscious and non-conscious reasoning. As before, we say a few words of general introduction, before briefly commenting on each of the essays in this part of the book.

As we noted in chapter 1, one way of weakening the cognitive conception of language is by restricting its claims along a vertical (as opposed to horizontal, domain-specific) dimension – claiming that it is only *conscious* thought which crucially implicates language, and allowing that non-conscious thoughts may be carried by, for example, sentences of Mentalese or patterns of activation in a connectionist network. None of the chapters in Part III take quite this straightforward line (but see Carruthers, 1996a). Yet all pay attention to distinctions between kinds, or levels, of thinking – including the distinction between conscious and non-conscious thinking. (Note that the papers by Carruthers, chapter 5, and Clark, chapter 8, could also have been positioned in Part III, since much of their focus is on the role of language in conscious thought.) And all give at least some weight to the introspective datum that for much of the time our waking lives are occupied by a stream of 'inner speech', in which natural language words and sentences are imaged. This is certainly one of the battle-grounds on which the debate between cognitive and communicative conceptions of language needs to be played out, in our view. If the cognitive role of inner speech is like that of *thinking*, then a form of cognitive conception will be vindicated; whereas if it is more like the cognitive role of *conversation* (with *oneself* in this case, of course), then the communicative conception will, to that extent at least, be supported.

Chapter 11: Davies

The focus of Martin Davies' chapter is on the Language of Thought (LOT) hypothesis, according to which propositional thoughts are carried by structured, sentence-like, entities in the mind/brain. In previous publications (1991, 1992) Davies had put forward an argument of a relatively non-empirical kind (in contrast to the empirical arguments of Fodor, 1975), for a minimal version of the LOT hypothesis. More accurately, his claim was that a version of the LOT hypothesis could be derived from our best available *philosophical* theory of what it is to be a thinking being. This was 'Aunty's own argument for the language of thought'. ('Aunty' is Fodor's irreverent term for philosophers of orthodox *a prioristic* persuasion). Roughly, the argument proceeds by way of two claims. The first is that our concepts of *thought* and *thinking* commit us to the belief that thoughts are *causally systematic* – that is, that thoughts will lead to other thoughts in ways which reflect their composition out of component concepts. Then the second claim (again arrived at by *a priori* reflection) is that the inputs to any process which is causally systematic must be syntactically structured. From these two claims we may derive the conclusion that thoughts themselves are syntactically structured – that is to say, there is a language of thought (LOT).

In the present chapter, Davies returns to this argument, discussing a variety of worries which people have had about it. The first is that if the argument is sound, but it should turn out (as it may do) that the LOT hypothesis is false, then we would be faced with *eliminativism* about the mind. The second is that if the argument is sound, then we would appear, puzzlingly, to have a *non*-empirical route to substantive *empirical* claims about the kinds of information processing which take place in the mind/brain. And the third worry is that the argument involves a transition between *levels* – namely, between the personal level and the sub-personal level – in a way which is not obviously legitimate.

In the latter part of his chapter, Davies discusses the relationship between Aunty's own argument and some or other version of the cognitive conception of language – for example, that thoughts might be carried by sentences of what Chomsky calls 'logical form', or LF (see Carruthers, this volume chapter 5); or that conscious propositional thoughts might be carried by imaged natural language sentences (see Carruthers, 1996a). He concludes that thinking in LF could just as well serve the purposes of Aunty's argument as would thinking in Mentalese. But he also argues that having structured vehicles before the mind (imaged natural language sentences) is *not* enough, by itself, to serve the purposes of Aunty's argument – more would have to be said, at least, before Aunty could rest content.

Chapter 12: Frankish

In this chapter Keith Frankish sketches and defends a two-level theory of cognition, according to which we not only have *passively formed* beliefs and desires, but are also sometimes *active* in creating our own mental states – as when we make up, or change, our minds about some matter. Passively formed beliefs and desires we share with animals, and these have nothing much to do with language. But actively formed states are unique to humans, are characteristically conscious, and are – so Frankish argues – generally language-involving. At the heart of his account of actively formed states are policies of *premising*. To make up one's mind that *P*, on this view, is to decide to take *P* as a premise in one's future reasoning – resolving to think and act as one believes that a *P*-believer would. The way in which language then enters the picture, is that the simplest, most basic, way of formulating, referring to, and keeping track of one's premising commitments, is to express them in natural language sentences – sometimes aloud, but more usually in inner speech.

There are connections, here, with the arguments of Davies' chapter, since Frankish claims that his premising account can preserve – in robustly realist spirit – the systematicity of (actively formed) beliefs and desires, but without having to make any claims about the nature of sub-personal processing. There are also connections with the views of Perner and Dennett – see below. But Frankish differs from Dennett, at least, in thinking that the formation and execution of premising-policies is under personal control. So although language is constitutive of a certain level of cognition, language has its effects, not mechanistically, or by brute association, but in virtue of our intentions to use it and act on it as we do. We *decide* to take *P* as a premise in the light of our passively formed beliefs and goals; and we then have to *remember* and *act on* that commitment in the future, on this account.

Chapter 13: Perner

The focus of Josef Perner's paper is on the range of cognitive activities identified by psychologists as requiring 'executive function'. These include: planning and decision-making; trouble shooting (identifying sources of failure); learning of novel action sequences; dangerous or technically difficult actions; and overcoming strong habitual response-tendencies or temptations. Perner argues that all these activities crucially require meta-representational thinking (as when one thinks *about* one's own thoughts or goals) – which is why these activities are always conscious, given the correctness of a Higher-Order Thought (HOT) theory of consciousness (e.g. Carruthers, 1996a); and which is also why these activities seem always to be verbalisable and to implicate language, given that whatever system is responsible for HOTs also has access to the language system.

On Perner's account, then, the problems of executive function which are visible in childhood, in autism, and in schizophrenia are to be explained by the absence of, or damage to, a developed capacity for HOTs – that is to say, by the absence of, or damage to, the person's theory of mind (TOM) faculty. Perner adduces some empirical support for this hypothesis, and against the conflicting hypothesis that the difficulties these groups of people experience with theory-of-mind tasks is rather to be explained by a damaged (and independently characterisable) executive-function system.

Chapter 14: Dennett

Daniel Dennett was originally invited to provide the concluding address to the Sheffield conference from which the papers in this volume were drawn and developed. He did an exemplary job of weaving together some of the themes which had arisen, with explicit comment on many of the other papers. The general form and tone of that talk are replicated in the present chapter, which is included both for its intrinsic merits, and because Dennett defends a form of cognitive conception of language more extreme and ambitious than is endorsed by any of the other contributors to the volume – a position which, we felt, it was important to see represented.

In Dennett (1991), language is accorded a dual foundational role in human cognition. It is, on the one hand, what re-programmes the connectionist architectures of the brain into a serial processor; and it is also, on the other hand, what gives rise to and sustains our distinctive form of consciousness. According to Dennett, the human brain becomes rapidly colonised by *memes* during development (that is: ideas, or concepts – the notion of a 'meme' as a self-replicating mental item is borrowed from Dawkins, 1976, 1982). These memes are mostly carried by natural language phrases and lexical items, and are acquired from other people and the culture around us. They are supposed to transform the habits of thought and inferential dispositions of our brains, making possible whole new orders of complexity and abstractness. But these memes are also the source of our consciousness, since their tokening in inner speech forms the primary object of our introspective awareness, and since it is dispositions to report verbally on our mental states which is the most basic way for them to become conscious. So without language, we would have hardly any thoughts to think; and without language, what thoughts we did have would not be conscious ones.

In the present chapter both of the above themes recur, and are re-united with another idea from Dennett's 1991 – the attack on 'Cartesian Theatre' models of consciousness, together with the associated philosophical idea of a 'Central Executive'. The notion of a Cartesian Theatre is the idea of somewhere in the brain where 'everything comes together' and is displayed for the benefit of the audience – the self, or *res cogitans*. As Dennett rightly observes, there can be no such place; and the very idea borders on incoherence (is there then to be *another* Cartesian Theatre within the self itself, to explain how *its* activities get to be conscious?). It is to be replaced by a whole host of mindless mechanisms – 'contention scheduling all the way up' – whose activities and interactions collectively constitute the conscious subject. And, crucially in the present context, many of these mechanisms are held to operate on linguistic symbols. This is the idea of 'active symbols' which interact with one another in and of themselves, without the need for a 'meaner' – that is, a conscious agent who manipulates and transforms them. On Dennett's view, then, it is perhaps not too much of an exaggeration to say that *language maketh mankind.*

11 Language, thought and the language of thought (Aunty's own argument revisited)

Martin Davies

1 Introduction

In this chapter, I shall be examining an argument for the language of thought hypothesis – an argument which, in earlier work (Davies, 1992; *see also* 1991), I have called 'Aunty's own argument for the language of thought'. That will be the business of sections 2–5. In the final section, I shall briefly mention some points of contact between this argument for the language of thought (LOT) hypothesis and the hypothesis that is the topic of Peter Carruthers' (1996a) book, which I shall call the 'thinking in natural language' (TNL) hypothesis. Before beginning on Aunty's own argument, however, I shall briefly present a framework for organising questions about the relative priority of thought and language.

1.1 Orders of priority

Should questions in the theory of thought – questions about intentionality, beliefs and concept possession, for example – be approached directly or, instead, indirectly via questions about language? Suppose that Kylie believes that kangaroos seldom kick, and expresses this thought in the English sentence: 'Kangaroos seldom kick.' Which takes priority, the meaning of the English sentence or the content of Kylie's thought?

A claim of priority is the converse of a claim of one-way dependence: X enjoys priority over Y if Y depends on X but X does not depend on Y. So, any question of the relative priority of X and Y has four possible answers: (i) X has priority; (ii) Y has priority; (iii) X and Y are mutually dependent (inter-dependent); (iv) X and Y are independent. But the question of the relative priority of thought and language is unclear until the relevant kind of priority has been specified. I suggest that it is useful to distinguish three kinds of priority question: *ontological*, *epistemological*, and *analytical* (see Avramides, 1989, for a similar distinction).

To say that thought enjoys *ontological priority* over language is to say that language is ontologically dependent on thought, while thought is not so dependent on language. That is, there cannot be language without thought, but there can be thought without language. To say that thought enjoys *epistemological priority* over language is to say that the route to knowledge about language (specifically, about linguistic meaning) goes via knowledge about thought (specifically, about the contents of thought), while knowledge about thought can be had without going via knowledge about language.

Donald Davidson, for example, is a philosopher who would deny both these priority claims. As for ontological priority, he argues (Davidson, 1975) that there cannot be thought without language: in order to have thoughts (specifically, beliefs), a creature must be a member of a language community, and an interpreter of the speech of others. As for epistemological priority, he argues (Davidson, 1974) that it is not possible to find out in detail what a person believes without interpreting that person's speech.

Our third kind of priority, *analytical priority*, is priority in the order of philosophical analysis or elucidation. To say that X is analytically prior to Y is to say that key notions in the study of Y can be analysed or elucidated in terms of key notions in the study of X, while the analysis or elucidation of the X notions does not have to advert to the Y notions. If we fix on the notion of thought content, or intentionality, as a key notion in the study of thought, and the notion of linguistic meaning as a key notion in the study of language, then the four possible positions on the relative analytical priority of thought and language can be sketched as follows.

(i) *Priority for thought*: This is the view that a philosophical account of the content of thoughts can be given without essential appeal to language, and that the notion of linguistic meaning can then be analysed or elucidated in terms of the thoughts that language is used to express. Paul Grice's programme in the philosophy of language (Grice, 1989; Schiffer, 1972) was aimed, not merely at elucidation, but, more boldly, at an analysis of public language meaning in terms of the beliefs and intentions of language users. Grice did not, himself, offer any elucidatory account of the intentionality of mental states. But recent work in the philosophy of mind has brought forward several proposals for explaining the intentionality of mental states without appeal to linguistic meaning, including accounts in terms of causal co-variation, of teleology, and of functional role. So, we could imagine an elucidatory programme coupling one of these accounts of thought content with a Gricean analysis of linguistic meaning in terms of mental notions. In fact, it is now widely agreed that the Gricean analytical programme cannot be carried through (Schiffer, 1987). But, even if this is right, it need not rule out the possibility that thought enjoys analytical priority over language, provided that there is some other way of elucidating (if not analysing) the notion of linguistic meaning in terms of thought content.

Such an elucidation might follow the Gricean model by adverting very directly to the communicative use of language. But, in principle, it might equally proceed in two stages, first introducing a notion of idiolect meaning, and then explaining the idea of a public communicative practice in terms of shared, or overlapping, idiolects (see Laurence, this volume chapter 10).

(ii) *Priority for language*: On this, opposite, view, an account of linguistic meaning can be given without bringing in the intentionality of thoughts, and what a person's thoughts are about can then be analysed in terms of the use of language. This view can be found in Michael Dummett's work (Dummett, 1973, 1991, 1993). If a theorist attempts to give a substantive account of linguistic meaning in accordance with this view then the resources that can be invoked are seriously limited, since the account cannot presume upon everyday psychological notions such as belief and intention. Because of this, it would not be surprising to find hints of behaviourism in work that is influenced by this view.

(iii) *No priority (inter-dependence)*: This – the first of two possible 'no priority' positions – is the view that there is no way of giving an account of either intentionality or linguistic meaning without bringing in the other member of the pair. The two notions have to be explained together. This is the view of Davidson (1984), who thus maintains a combined ontological, epistemological and analytical no-priority position. These three no-priority claims go together quite naturally, but it is important to note that they are separable, and presumably logically independent, claims. The analytical no-priority claim is not entailed by the ontological no-priority claim, nor by the epistemological no-priority claim, nor by the two together.

(iv) *No priority (independence)*: This is the view that the notions of thought content and of linguistic meaning are unrelated. This position might be defended if a language is considered as an abstract entity, composed of a set of expressions together with a function that assigns a value to each expression (a proposition to each sentence, for example). On such a conception, meaning is a purely formal notion. But for the notion of linguistic meaning as it applies to a natural language in use, this fourth view is implausible.

The point – mentioned in (iii) – that ontological, epistemological, and analytic priority claims are independent of each other is a quite general one. It would be consistent to maintain, for example, that thought enjoys ontological priority over language (that there can be thought without language, but not language without thought), while denying that thought comes before language in the order of philosophical elucidation. Equally, it would be consistent to deny that thought enjoys ontological priority over language – insisting, instead, that there can be no thought without language

– while yet maintaining that thought comes first in the order of philosophical elucidation.

Indeed, it seems that these combinations remain consistent even if we consider ontological priority, or no-priority, claims that are supposed to be established by more or less purely philosophical arguments. Thus, for example, it would seem to be consistent to combine the claim that it is a conceptual truth that there can be thought without language (conceptually based ontological priority claim) with the claim that thought does not come first in the order of philosophical elucidation (analytical no-priority claim). Similarly, it would seem to be consistent to say both that it is a conceptual truth that there cannot be thought without language (conceptually based ontological no-priority claim) and that thought comes first in the order of philosophical elucidation (analytical priority claim). Such combinations of views may, though, be unattractive and difficult to motivate. Suppose, for example, that someone proposes a specifically Gricean version of the analytical priority of thought over language, according to which linguistic meaning involves a complex structure of beliefs and intentions in a population of language users. Then, an argument for the ontological no-priority claim (in particular, for the claim that there could not be thought without language) would have to show that there could not be any beliefs or intentions at all unless there was this complex structure of beliefs about beliefs about intentions; and it is far from easy to see how that could be shown.

The argument for the language of thought, to which we now turn, makes use of ideas that emerge within a framework that accords analytical priority to thought over language (Evans, 1982; Peacocke, 1992). While those ideas do not involve any specifically Gricean commitments, it would be fair to say that an assumption of ontological priority of thought over language is also in the background.

2 Aunty's own argument revisited

Jerry Fodor's Aunty 'speaks with the voice of the Establishment' (Fodor, 1987, p. 135) and is represented by Fodor as someone who resists the LOT hypothesis, preferring, perhaps, a connectionist picture of the mind's operations (*ibid.* p. 139). Aunty, as I imagine her to be, is a neo-Fregean who also maintains a proper regard for the work of Wittgenstein. The neo-Fregean framework provides – ironically enough, given Fodor's own presentation of Aunty – the resources for a relatively non-empirical argument for the LOT hypothesis. Thus, Aunty's own argument shows that the LOT hypothesis is derivable from what might be the best available philosophical account of what it is to be a thinking being. On the other hand, Aunty's residual

Wittgensteinian tendencies oblige her to check possible reasons for being sceptical about the very idea of a language of thought.

2.1 *Two possible reasons for scepticism*

One thought that would lead to scepticism is that the LOT hypothesis is bound to be regressive, involving either a regress of languages or a regress of interpreters (cf. Wittgenstein, *Blue Book* (1969), p. 3). It is, by now, a familiar point that the LOT hypothesis does not involve any such regress because sentences of the LOT are not presented to the thinking subject, nor to an inner homunculus, as syntactic objects standing in need of interpretation. But perhaps we can add one remark.

When I hear a sentence in a language that I understand, I do not hear the sentence as a phonological object standing in need of interpretation; rather, I hear the sentence as having a meaning. We might say that I hear the meaning clothed in phonology. So, now someone might suggest something similar in the case of the LOT. The suggestion would be that, while LOT sentences are not presented to the thinker as syntactic vehicles to which a meaning has to be assigned, still, in conscious thought at least, LOT sentences are presented to the thinking subject, but presented as interpreted. Thus, the non-semantic properties of LOT sentences can provide a phenomenal clothing for the contents of conscious thoughts. While it may be possible to make something of this suggestion, it is no part of the LOT hypothesis as I am conceiving it here. The LOT hypothesis as it figures in Aunty's own argument is a hypothesis about cognitive processing machinery; it is pitched at the sub-personal, rather than the personal, level. For that reason, it makes no contribution to the vitally important topic of conscious thought.

A second thought that might lead to scepticism about the very idea of a language of thought would be inspired by a familiar passage from Wittgenstein's *Zettel* (1981, p. 106): 'But why should the *system* continue further in the direction of the centre? Why should this order not proceed, so to speak, out of chaos?' We should not simply slide from the fact that psychological descriptions have a certain structure – an articulation into specific belief attributions, intention attributions, and so on – to the assumption that there is a matching articulation in the physiological structure of the brain. But there are two things to be said here. One is that the LOT hypothesis, while it is not pitched at the personal level of description, is not pitched at the physiological or neuro-anatomical level either. It is a hypothesis within information-processing psychology, constrained by the physiological facts, but nevertheless at some degree of abstraction from them. The second thing to be said is that Aunty's own argument is an argument. There may, of course, be something wrong with the argument. But what Aunty proposes is not simply to project the structure of common-sense (folk) psychological descriptions onto the sub-personal level information-processing substrate.

2.2 *The first step in Aunty's own argument: systematicity and syntax*

Aunty's own argument makes use of the notion of a tacitly known (or implicit) rule, where that notion is cashed out in terms of a certain kind of systematicity of causal processes. (See Davies, 1987, for some details omitted here; and Davies, 1995, for the notion of implicit rule applied to connectionist networks.) This notion of systematicity of process can be shown to require a certain structure in the inputs to the process, a structure that turns out to meet the minimal conditions for being syntactic structure. The first step in the argument is thus to establish a connection between implicit rules and syntactically structured representations. The notions that are involved in this first step – notions of causally systematic process, tacitly known rule, and syntactically structured input state – can be explained quite independently of any consideration of the LOT hypothesis.

The causal processes that are considered are transitions between representations. Thus the inputs to, and outputs from, the processes are physical configurations that have semantic properties. For example, the input configurations might represent letter strings, and the output configurations might represent pronunciations. Given such a process, there may be a pattern in the input-output relation when the inputs and outputs are described semantically. Thus, for example, it might be that whenever the input configuration represents a letter string beginning with 'b' the output configuration represents a pronunciation beginning with /B/. In such a case, we can say that the input-output transitions *conform* to a rule about the task domain; in the example, this would be the rule that letter strings beginning with 'b' have pronunciations beginning with /B/. But, for the sense of tacitly known, or implicit, rule that is in play here, to say that the transitions conform to the rule is not yet to say that the mechanism that mediates those transitions embodies tacit knowledge of that rule. Nor is it sufficient that this conformity to the rule should be non-accidental, holding good in nearby counterfactual situations as well as in the actual situation.

What is required for tacit knowledge of the 'b'–to–/B/ rule is that the transitions that conform to the rule should have a *common causal explanation*. This condition is met if there is, within the overall transition mediating mechanism, a component processor or module that operates as a *causal common factor* to mediate all the transitions that instantiate the 'b'–to–/B/ pattern.

Suppose that our transition mediating mechanism meets this condition, and so embodies tacit knowledge of this spelling-sound rule. Then the various input configurations that represent letter strings beginning with 'b' need to share some physical property that will engage or activate the 'b'–to–/B/ component processor. This will be (i) a physical property that (ii) is correlated with the semantic property that these input representations share (that they all represent letter strings beginning with 'b') and (iii) is a determinant of the input configuration's causal consequences. In short, this property will meet the minimal conditions for being a syntactic property (Fodor, 1987, pp. 16–21). Thus, quite independently of any consideration of the LOT hypothesis, we have the result that where transition mediating mechanisms embody tacit knowledge of rules there we find syntactically structured input representations.

2.3 *The second step in Aunty's own argument: inferences and their forms*

Aunty's own argument also makes use of a certain notion of inferential transitions between thoughts. (In earlier work, Davies, 1991, 1992, I developed this step of the argument in two slightly different ways, drawing in turn on Evans, 1982, and on Peacocke, 1992. Here I follow the version that uses the notion of possession conditions in Peacocke, 1992, chapter 1. One of Peacocke's proposals is that concepts can actually be individuated by their possession conditions, where those conditions are specified in terms of something like a functional (inferential) role. We should note, however, that Peacocke has subsequently changed his views somewhat; see his 1998a.) The key idea is that being able to think particular types of thought (that is, possessing particular concepts) involves a thinker in commitments to particular forms of inference. According to this idea, what is required of a subject is not just commitment to each of a number of inferences that happen to instantiate a particular form. Rather, the commitment is to accept (indeed, to perform) these inferences *in virtue of their form* (Peacocke, 1992, p. 6). The form of the inferences should figure in the causal explanation of the thinker's performing those inferences. One way to cash this out, without requiring the thinking subject to be able to specify the form of the inferences, nor to be able to offer an explicit account of the form as part of his or her reason for making the inferential transitions (*ibid.* p. 135), would be to require that the thinker meet the conditions for tacit knowledge of the inferential rule.

In order to see the consequences of this proposed way of cashing out the requirement, suppose that an occurrent thought involves the tokening of a specific physical configuration. (We assume, that is, intentional realism; see

Fodor, 1987, p. 135. See also the discussion of propositional modularity in Ramsey *et al.*, 1990.) If we apply the idea of a tacitly known rule to the case of causal transitions between these physical configurations, then we shall arrive at the conclusion that the physical configuration whose tokening is the information processing level correlate of a person's thinking a particular thought is syntactically structured. In short, we shall arrive at a version of the LOT hypothesis.

We should note two points about this second step in Aunty's own argument. One point is that it only takes us from intentional realism or propositional modularity to the LOT hypothesis. Properly speaking, Aunty needs to offer an argument to support the assumption of intentional realism. The second point is that Aunty's own argument involves a transition from the personal level to the sub-personal level of cognitive machinery – from a thinking person finding inferences compelling in virtue of their form to a requirement on causal mechanisms in the cognitive machinery, a requirement of causal systematicity of transitions that leads to a requirement of syntactic structure in representations.

In the next three sections, we address three problems for Aunty's own argument. First, the argument seems to present an invitation to eliminativism (section 3). Second, the argument seems to offer a non-empirical route to substantive knowledge about the world inside our skulls (section 4). Third, the argument may seem to be undermined by the very fact that it moves from the personal to the sub-personal level (section 5).

3 Eliminativism and conceptual negotiation

Aunty's own argument uncovers a necessary condition for a physical being to be a thinking person, and the necessary condition concerns internal cognitive architecture: a thinking being must be an LOT being. This cognitive architectural condition evidently goes beyond facts about behaviour. Thus, given any physical being whose behaviour *prima facie* warrants the attribution to it of beliefs and other attitudes, in accordance with the intentional stance (Dennett, 1987), it is an epistemic possibility that the being does not meet the condition on internal cognitive architecture. So, Aunty's own argument appears to present an invitation to eliminativism. If we turn out not to be LOT beings, then we also turn out not to be thinking persons.

3.1 Theoretical options in a disobliging world

In order to see what is at issue here, suppose, for a moment, that developments in the scientific investigation of the mind – whether in cognitive psychology or in neuroscience – were to show that the cognitive architectural condition was not, in fact, met; in short, that we are not LOT beings. Then there would be a number of theoretical options available. One option would be to conclude that some of the pieces of philosophical theory drawn on in Aunty's own argument are wrong. Another option – the opposite extreme – would be to abandon wholesale our folk psychological practice of describing, interpreting, and explaining what people do as acting for reasons that are based on beliefs, wants, hopes, fears, and the rest.

If we consider only these two theoretical options, then the thought that the second option is not genuinely available to us – that our engagement in ordinary folk psychological practice is philosophically non-negotiable – may seem to constitute a powerful objection to Aunty's own argument. If that objection is a good one, then it does not apply to Aunty's own argument alone. Rather, it would apply equally to any philosophical argument that appears to uncover substantive cognitive architectural necessary conditions for being a thinking person. So, the question that we need to ask is whether one can argue from the non-negotiability of our engagement in folk psychological practice to the incorrectness of all such *architecturalist* arguments.

One problem with this putative line of argument is that it depends on overlooking a third theoretical option, namely, that we might maintain our folk psychological practice even though many of the claims made in folk psychological descriptions, interpretations, and explanations were false. But even setting that problem aside, there is a worry about the idea of a blanket rejection of all architecturalist arguments. For the competing piece of conceptual analysis that would be suggested by that rejection is itself arguably out of line with our intuitive judgements about which physical beings are thinking persons.

What the blanket rejection of all arguments that uncover cognitive architectural commitments suggests is that an analysis of the concept of a thinking person should impose no necessary conditions at all on internal cognitive architecture and, indeed, no necessary conditions that go beyond behaviour. This entails that if two physical beings are behavioural (or, perhaps better: trajectorial) duplicates in actual, and nearby counterfactual, situations, then either both are thinking persons or neither is. But that doctrine is revealed as being out of line with our intuitions when we consider imaginary examples of physical beings that produce the right behaviour by way of unusual internal architectures, such as the string-searching machine of Block (1981) or the Martian marionette of Peacocke (1983). The string-searching machine, which stores a finite but massive collection of interpretable sequences of behaviour, can *ex hypothesi* meet any behavioural requirements for being a thinking person. But, as Block remarks (1990, p. 252), 'it has the intelligence of a jukebox'.

The two options of, on the one hand, rejecting all architecturalist arguments and, on the other hand, abandoning our folk psychological practice if things turn out badly, do not exhaust the options. In between, there lies the possibility of conceptual negotiation. In order to see how this possibility would work, suppose that the pieces of philosophical theory that are drawn on in Aunty's own argument do correctly elaborate and precisify our current conception of a thinking person and that the argument correctly uncovers the commitments of that conception. Then imagine that things turn out badly – that we turn out not to be LOT beings. Evidently, in those circumstances, we ourselves would not fall under (the best elaboration and precisification of) our current conception of a thinking person. But we might still be able rationally to sustain the greater part of our folk psychological practice if we could negotiate our way to a new, revised, conception of what it is to be a thinking person. The details of the negotiations would depend on the particular ways in which things turned out badly. They would also depend on the philosophical theories connecting those empirical discoveries with our current conceptions of folk psychological phenomena.

3.2 The appeal to consciousness

The upshot of our discussion so far in this section is intended to be that it is no objection to an architecturalist argument, such as Aunty's own argument, that it presents the possibility of an eliminativist *modus tollens*. But it might be said that there is something unsatisfactory about the way that we have dealt with the presumed non-negotiability of folk psychological practice. Our strategy (two paragraphs back) was to suggest that, if what is wanted is a guarantee that those who engage in the practice really are thinking persons, then the price to be paid is commitment to a counter-intuitive doctrine about trajectorial duplicates. In response to this strategy, it might be said that there is something that can be known about persons, at least in the case of the first person singular, which goes beyond behaviour yet has nothing to do with internal cognitive architecture. So, it may be said, it is possible to reject all architecturalist arguments without paying the price of commitment to the counter-intuitive doctrine about trajectorial duplicates. For it is open to someone to maintain that an account of thinking persons should impose no necessary conditions that go beyond behaviour *plus consciousness*.

There is more than one way to develop this suggestion, and some of the ways do not seem satisfactory at all. Thus suppose, for example, that we focus on the notion of consciousness that applies to itches, pains and tickles. Though the issues are complex, it is difficult to be convinced that we move closer to a thinking person by adding bare sensations to a string-searching machine or a Martian marionette. But suppose that we consider, not sensations, but conscious thought. Then the suggestion may be that, by introspection, I can know that I think many things, and more generally can know that I am a thinking being. So, an account of thinking persons may go beyond behaviour by adverting to what can be known by introspection, yet without taking on any cognitive architectural commitments.

There are two points to note about this suggestion. One point is that it cannot really underwrite the non-negotiability of folk psychological practice, since it is restricted to the first person singular. The second point is that, in the face of an architecturalist argument, such as Aunty's own argument, the suggestion is apt to seem question-begging. It may be true that thinking persons can know by introspection that they think many things, and can know that they are indeed thinking beings. But, according to Aunty's own argument, if we turn out not to be LOT beings then we shall not be thinking beings. In those circumstances, we should not be able to know, whether by introspection or any other way, that we are beings who think.

The suggestion emerging from the appeal to consciousness seems to be question-begging. But, in fact, the idea of first personal introspective knowledge of our thoughts leads to a serious problem for Aunty's own argument, and the solution to the problem involves a further concession to the intuition of non-negotiability. This is the topic for the next section.

4 The problem of armchair knowledge

The problem to be considered in this section arises when we consider arguments of the following general form (MC):

(1) I have mental property M.
(2) If I have mental property M then I meet condition C.
Therefore:
(3) I meet condition C.

in cases where premise (2) is justified by an architecturalist argument, such as Aunty's own argument. Specifically, the problematic argument is LOT(MC):

LOT(1) I am a thinking being.
LOT(2) If I am a thinking being then I am an LOT being.
Therefore:
LOT(3) I am an LOT being.

Let us say that a thesis of *first-person authority* about a mental property, M, is a thesis to the effect that we have a distinctively first personal and specially authoritative way of knowing that we ourselves have property M, when we do have it, without needing to conduct any detailed empirical investigation of the world outside or within. If we assume a thesis of first-person authority about the property of being a thinking being – in line with the suggestion at the end of section 3 – then the problem is clear.

I do not need to engage in any detailed empirical investigation of my internal cognitive architecture to know premise LOT(1); I know with first-person authority that I think many things. Nor, do I need to engage in empirical research in order to know premise LOT(2); it is underwritten by a philosophical argument. It is obvious that the conclusion LOT(3) follows from these two premises. Yet, even supposing that the conclusion is true, it is massively implausible that its truth can be known from the armchair. Questions about internal cognitive architecture – about whether we are LOT beings, for example – cannot be settled without major programmes of empirical research. This is the problem of armchair knowledge. Aunty's own argument, in combination with a thesis of first-person authority, seems to offer us an unacceptably non-empirical route to knowledge of substantive empirical facts about cognitive architecture.

4.1 Limiting knowledge by inference

In recent work (Davies, 1998), I have suggested that the way to deal with this problem is to impose limitations on knowledge by inference. As a first attempt, I proposed two limitation principles:

First Limitation Principle
Epistemic warrant cannot be transferred from A to B, even given an *a priori* known entailment from A to B, if the truth of B is a precondition of our warrant for A counting as a warrant.

Second Limitation Principle
Epistemic warrant cannot be transferred from A to B, even given an *a priori* known entailment from A to B, if the truth of B is a precondition of the knower even being able to believe the proposition A.

It is the second of these that was supposed to deal with the problem of armchair knowledge posed by the LOT(MC) argument.

The principle works by blocking the transfer of epistemic warrant from premises to conclusion in that argument. Even though I can know LOT(1) and LOT(2) without rising from my armchair, I cannot, according to the Second Limitation Principle, thereby come to know LOT(3), even though it plainly follows from those premises.

According to Aunty's own argument, if I am a thinking being, then I am an LOT being. If that argument is correct then, even in order to believe that I am a thinking being, I need to be an LOT being. Aunty's own argument might be wrong, of course. But if it is right then it triggers application of the Second Limitation Principle, and epistemic warrant cannot be transferred from LOT(1) to LOT(3), even given the *a priori* known entailment in LOT(2). Given the Second Limitation Principle, the very argument that gives rise to the problem of armchair knowledge also provides for its solution. So, given that principle, it would be wrong to press that problem as an objection against Aunty's own argument.

The Second Limitation Principle allows us to block the unacceptably non-empirical route to knowledge of substantive empirical facts. But I provided little enough motivation for the principle, and it seems very plausible that the principle is open to counter-examples. What I propose to do here is to provide some motivation for (modified versions of) the limitation principles.

4.2 Improving the principles

The intuitive idea behind both limitation principles is something like this. In any given epistemic project, some propositions will have a presuppositional status. Suppose that the focus of the project P is the proposition A, and that the investigation is carried out using method N. Then within project P it is presupposed, for example, that A is a hypothesis that can be coherently entertained (can be believed, doubted, confirmed, disconfirmed); and it is also presupposed that N is a method that can yield knowledge, at least with respect to A. Suppose that B is some proposition that has this presuppositional status in project P. Then P cannot itself yield knowledge that B; nor can P play an essential role in yielding knowledge that B.

The First Limitation Principle can be regarded as an attempt at codifying this intuitive idea as it relates to the presupposition about the method: as the principle is formulated, *our warrant for A counting as a warrant* stands in for the investigative method being such as to yield knowledge. The Second Limitation Principle likewise attempts to codify the idea as it relates to the presupposition about the hypothesis: as the principle is formulated, *the knower being able to believe the proposition A* stands in for the hypothesis being such as can be coherently entertained.

It is easy to construct counter-examples to the limitation principles as they were originally formulated. Consider, for example, the simple inference from the premise:

I believe that water is wet

to the conclusion:

Someone is able to believe something

It is not obvious that we should want to block the possibility of knowledge by inference here. But, the truth of the conclusion is a necessary condition for my being able to believe the premise; so application of the Second Limitation Principle would be triggered.

We need to tighten up the Second Limitation Principle (and the First Limitation Principle, too). To that end, let us suppose for the moment that the two basic presuppositions in an epistemic project P using method N and with target hypothesis A are:

(i) the proposition that method N is knowledge yielding (at least with respect to A); and
(ii) the proposition that there is such a proposition as the proposition A for the putative knower to entertain (that the conceptual practices on which A draws are not internally incoherent, for example).

Suppose too that other propositions become derived presuppositions in project P by being shown to follow from propositions that are already presuppositions in P by way of some circumscribed set of resources that are already in use in P. Then we might be led to an improved version of the Second Limitation Principle as follows:

Second Limitation Principle (revised version)
Epistemic warrant cannot be transferred from A to B, even given an *a priori* known entailment from A to B, if the truth of B can be shown *by resources that are used in the epistemic project* [e.g. the resources used to derive B from A] to be a precondition of *there being any such proposition for the knower to entertain or believe as the proposition A*.

(I shall not pause over revisions to the First Limitation Principle, since it is not directly relevant to the problem that concerns us.) But the difficulty that we now face is that the improved version of the Second Limitation Principle is no longer adequate to deal with the problem of armchair knowledge posed by Aunty's own argument.

Aunty's own argument would indeed have the consequence that if a putative knower is not an LOT being then that putative knower would not even be able to think the thought:

LOT(1) I am a thinking being.

But Aunty's own argument, which uncovers necessary conditions for being a thinking being, does not have the consequence that if the putative knower does not meet the cognitive architectural condition then there is no such proposition as the proposition LOT(1). Aunty's own argument does not reveal any internal incoherence in the very notion of a thinking being in the disobliging circumstance that the cognitive architectural necessary condition is not met.

4.3 Modifying the solution

Under what circumstances would the failure of a being X to meet a necessary condition for falling under a concept C reveal an internal incoherence within the C-conception, rather than merely revealing that X is a non-C? One circumstance would be that there are sufficient conditions for falling under the concept C, and X does meet those conditions.

More generally, a conception may involve a sufficient conditions component and a necessary conditions component. It may be – familiarly – that some objects do not meet the sufficient conditions but do meet the necessary conditions. On such objects, the conception does not pronounce one way or the other on the question, 'Is it a C?'. The possibility that I am now raising is that an object might meet the sufficient conditions but not meet the necessary conditions. On such objects, the conception produces a contradictory pronouncement; the conception is – perhaps thanks to a disobliging world – internally incoherent. Conceptual revision and negotiation are required.

One way in which this possibility could come about would involve a sufficient conditions component based on paradigm exemplars that turn out not to meet the necessary conditions component. So, suppose that the conception of a thinking being involves not only an architecturalist necessary conditions component but also an exemplar-based sufficient conditions component: you and I are to count as thinking beings. Then our meeting the architecturalist requirement for thought really would be a precondition of the internal coherence of the concept of a thinking being, of there being any such proposition as: X is a thinking being.

The upshot of this would be that, in any epistemic project in which the conception of a thinking being figures, it is a presupposition that the paradigm exemplars meet whatever necessary conditions may be built into that conception. Aunty's own argument raises the specific proposition that the paradigm exemplars are LOT beings to presuppositional status and in doing so disqualifies any proposition to the effect that some paradigm exemplar (like me) is a LOT being from being a potential recipient of epistemic warrant in a project using that argument. Thus, we may be able to solve the problem of armchair knowledge that is posed by Aunty's own argument; but the solution involves more of a concession to the non-negotiability of folk psychological practice than we envisaged in section 3. What we are conceding here is not that those who engage in folk psychological practice are guaranteed to be thinking persons. But we are accepting that our current conception of thinking persons has no coherent use unless it applies to those – like you and me – who engage in that practice.

5 Moving from the personal to the sub-personal level

The problem of armchair knowledge, and the solution that we have proposed in section 4, have a somewhat technical character. The worry to be addressed in this section is a more fundamental one; namely, that Aunty's own argument is undermined by the very fact that it moves from the personal to the sub-personal level. According to this worry, a philosophical account of what it is to be a thinking being should not directly invoke any sub-personal level notions, and should not support any substantive entailments between the personal and sub-personal levels either.

My preferred conception of the inter-level relation is as *interaction without reduction*. According to that conception, what we typically find are downward entailments from the personal to the sub-personal level, but explanatory gaps when we try to reconstruct personal level notions out of sub-personal level resources. In slightly more detail, at the personal level of description we find many notions – subjective, normative – that have no place in science, and we find a distinctive kind of intelligibility. But these personal level descriptions also make use of causal notions, and the correctness of these descriptions is not indifferent to issues about sub-personal level information processing machinery (interaction – downward entailments). On the other hand, an account in information processing terms of the system that constitutes (is in the same place as) a thinking person is not adequate to supplant the original personal level description (without reduction – upward explanatory gaps).

This is not the place to give an extended defence of that conception. What I propose to do is to return to the topic of inferences that are performed in virtue of their form (section 2.3) and elaborate the description of those inferential transitions in terms that belong very clearly to the personal level. Then I shall consider an objection to Aunty's own argument that is based on that description, and suggest that the objection depends on the idea that claims about causation at the personal level are utterly indifferent to facts about information processing machinery – a claim that we have no reason to accept.

5.1 *Reasoning as a conscious, rational, knowledge-yielding activity*

Suppose that Bruce believes that *A or B* and also believes that *not-A*. Then it is likely that Bruce will also believe that *B*, or will come to believe it if the question whether *B* arises. Bruce's little piece of reasoning is liable to be a conscious activity, and the transition in thought that he makes is a rational one; it is the kind of transition that could (despite the limitation principles discussed in section 4) yield Bruce knowledge that *B* if he started out from knowledge that *A or B* and that *not-A*. What are the conditions under which we are able to regard a personal level causal transition such as this as rational and potentially knowledge-yielding?

One condition, surely, is that Bruce's first two beliefs should actually constitute a reason for believing the third thing. We would show that this condition is met by pointing out that the first two believed propositions entail the third. The argument with the first two beliefs as premises and the third belief as conclusion, instantiates a valid form. The general point here is that, in order to show how Bruce's transition at least could be a rational one, we need to conduct an investigation with an abstract subject matter: we plot the contours of the abstract space of reasons.

Our investigation of the abstract space of reasons reveals that, if Bruce believes that *A or B* and that *not-A*, then the right thing for Bruce to think in addition is that *B*. Those first two things that Bruce thinks are a reason for someone to think that *B*. But if they are to be Bruce's reason, then something more must be true: Bruce's believing, or coming to believe, the first two things must cause him to believe the third thing.

However, this is not yet sufficient for Bruce's transition to be a rational one. The problem is to connect the reason condition and the causal condition in the right way, so that it is because believing that *A or B* and that *not-A* is a reason to believe that *B* that Bruce's believing those two things causes him to believe the third thing (see e.g. Antony, 1989, 1991; Brewer, 1995). This problem is not going to be solved here, but there are two suggestions that it would be natural to make.

The first suggestion is one that has already been mentioned (section 2.3); namely, that Bruce should perform the transition in thought because it is of that valid form. As we have already said, this is not to require that Bruce can conceptualise or spell out what that form is; and still less is it to require that Bruce should use as an extra premise a belief that *((A or B) and not-A) entails B*. The second suggestion is that, although he need not conceptualise the form, still, in some way, Bruce should be aware of his beliefs, and the transition between them, as instantiating that form. (This second suggestion is intended to be in the spirit of Brewer, 1995.)

5.2 *An objection to Aunty's own argument, and a response*

Someone might now say that Aunty's own argument is undermined by our imposing these conditions at the personal level – in particular, the condition that Bruce should be aware of the form of the inference. For, if the form of the inference is already transparent to the thinker, why does it need, in addition, to be encoded in sub-personal level physical configurations?

Expressed like this, the objection misses its mark. Aunty's own argument makes use of the idea of an inferential transition being performed because it is of a certain form (where this is not to be cashed out in terms of a statement of the validity of the form being added as an extra premise to the inference). We have just suggested that, if the transition is to be rational, then the thinker should be aware of the form of the inference. But clearly, a thinker's being aware of the form of an inference is not sufficient for the form's figuring in the explanation of the thinker's performing the inference. So this recently suggested personal level condition is not one that figures directly in Aunty's own argument. Similarly, at the sub-personal level, it is not syntactic structure in physical configurations, but tacit knowledge of the rule of inference, that is supposed to cash out the requirement that the inference should be performed in virtue of its form. Syntactic structure in physical encodings is a necessary, but not a sufficient, condition for the presence of tacit knowledge.

The real question, then, is not whether Bruce's being aware of the form of his inference renders the language of thought hypothesis redundant. Rather, the question is whether the personal level requirement that Bruce should perform the transition in thought because it is of that form removes the motivation for the requirement that the cognitive machinery underpinning Bruce's inferential transitions should embody tacit knowledge of the rule of inference. It is difficult to see how the motivation for the condition on cognitive machinery would be removed by our imposing the personal level requirement, unless we could rely on a general principle to the effect that the truth of personal level claims about causal relations and the structure of causal explanations is indifferent to facts about cognitive machinery. But we have no reason to accept that general principle. (See Stone and Davies, 1993, for an example of the way in which a personal level claim about the causal order could be threatened by an empirical claim about the structure of an information processing system.)

We have been considering three problems for Aunty's own argument. The argument seems to offer an invitation to eliminativism; but in a disobliging world one option is conceptual negotiation (section 3). The argument seems to offer a non-empirical route to substantive empirical knowledge;

but that route can be blocked by limitation principles on knowledge by inference (section 4). The argument may seem to be undermined by the very fact that it moves from the personal to the sub-personal level; but this would be so only if causal claims at the personal level were indifferent to the causal order at the level of information processing machinery (section 5). We turn now – finally and briefly – to the idea of thinking in natural language.

6 Thinking in natural language

There are several points of contact between Aunty's own argument for the LOT hypothesis and the thinking in natural language (TNL) hypothesis that is developed and defended by Peter Carruthers (1996a, this volume chapter 5). Carruthers sets up an opposition between the *communicative conception* and the *cognitive conception* of language, and then argues for the cognitive conception. According to the communicative conception, 'the function and purpose of natural language is to facilitate communication and *not* . . . to facilitate thinking' (1996a, p. 1). According to the cognitive conception, in contrast, 'we often think *in* language, and the trains of reasoning which lead up to many of our decisions and actions will consist in sequences of natural-language sentences' (1996a, p. 2).

Carruthers starts out by accepting broadly Fodorian considerations in favour of a language of thought. But Fodor's language of thought is an innate and universal language – Mentalese – whereas Carruthers defends the thesis that at least some thinking involves the thinker's natural language; in particular, that some conscious thoughts (namely, conscious propositional thoughts) are constituted by tokenings of natural language sentences. Thus, as between Fodor's LOT hypothesis and Carruthers' TNL hypothesis, 'The main focus for debate will concern *which* sentences are constitutive of our (conscious propositional) thoughts – those of Mentalese, or those of natural language' (1996a, p. 39).

6.1 Imagined speech and LF representations

It is not obvious whether it is right to equate conscious propositional thoughts with thoughts that are clothed in natural language sentences. Ray Jackendoff, for example, argues that, although we 'very often experience our thought as "talking to ourselves"', still thought and language are very different phenomena (1997, p. 183). Indeed, he goes so far as to suggest that 'thought per se is *never* conscious' (*ibid.* p. 187). Many other people report that the sentences that go through their minds when they are thinking carefully and attentively seem to constitute a kind of commentary on their thinking, rather than expressing the contents of their first-order thoughts. (*See also* Peacocke, 1998b, for an account of conscious thinking that draws on the notion of attention, but not verbalisation.) But, whether or not it is right to make this equation, there surely is such a thing as thinking by imagining speaking. According to the TNL hypothesis, such thinking involves the activation of a PF (Phonetic Form) representation. But a PF representation is not enough to account for the fact that the imagined sentence is understood; for that, we need an LF (Logical Form) representation as well. For, while a PF representation is 'interpreted' at the 'articulatory-perceptual interface', an LF representation is 'interpreted' at the 'conceptual-intentional interface' (Chomsky, 1995b, p. 219). This is to say that it is only in virtue of its relation to an LF representation that a PF representation comes to have a meaning.

The LOT hypothesis is intended to be compatible with the evident fact that people speak as well as think, that people hear meaning in natural language sentences (see section 2.1 above), and that people can engage in imagined speech. Presumably, the LOT story about imagined speech will be somewhat similar to the TNL story, though it must be part of the LOT story that, in addition to the activation of an LF representation, there will also be activation of an LOT sentence lying, as it were, just on the other side of the conceptual–intentional interface.

It seems plausible that a decision between these competing accounts of imagined speech will rest on detailed matters, many of which will be highly theory internal. It would be relevant to consider, for example, whether the language module was to be regarded in Fodor's way (1983) – where modules are contrasted with the central system – or in Chomsky's way (1986, p. 14) – where linguistic knowledge is embodied in a central system which nevertheless has some of the properties of Fodorian modules, 'a fact that brings the entire picture into question'. It would also be relevant to consider, in detail, the nature of the supposed conceptual–intentional interface as that figures in Chomsky's account and, more generally, the nature of the relationship between LF representations and LOT sentences. In respect of this latter, it would be important to have a detailed account of the way that semantically non-specific LF representations map to semantically specific LOT sentences (Sperber and Wilson, 1986, this volume chapter 9) – an account that could then be compared, in explanatory potential, with the TNL account of the semantic non-specificity of natural language sentences.

What Aunty's own argument requires is that the physical configurations whose tokenings are the information processing level correlates of a person's acts of (propositional) thinking should be syntactically structured. There is nothing in that argument to rule out the possibility that those physical configurations should turn out to be tokenings of LF representations.

To that extent, Aunty's own argument, although it is presented as an argument for the LOT hypothesis, does not really differentiate between the LOT hypothesis and a version of the TNL hypothesis; namely, the hypothesis that LF representations are the sub-personal level correlates of thoughts.

On the other hand, there is a way of understanding the idea of thinking in natural language – focusing on the personal, rather than the sub-personal, level – according to which the TNL hypothesis might not measure up to the requirements imposed by Aunty's own argument.

6.2 Imagined speech and awareness of structure

Carruthers' argument for the TNL hypothesis is complex, drawing on nothing less than a theory of consciousness. But his starting point – evidence that is supposed, at least, to count as a plausibility consideration in favour of the TNL hypothesis – is furnished by introspection. Often, when we think, we find ourselves imagining, or imaging, sentences of our natural language. What this introspected evidence suggests is that, 'It is images of natural language sentences which are the primary vehicles of conscious thoughts' (1996a, p. 51).

The TNL hypothesis says that conscious propositional thinking is constituted by imagings of natural language sentences rather than by tokenings of sentences in Fodor's Mentalese. As we have been understanding it (section 2.1), Fodor's LOT hypothesis concerns the sub-personal level of cognitive machinery. In contrast, the TNL hypothesis – at least when it is conceived as a claim that can be supported by introspection – is pitched at the personal level. So, it may seem that the TNL hypothesis can offer a way of meeting the requirements of Aunty's own argument without descending to the sub-personal level of cognitive machinery. What section 5.2 should already suggest, however, is that this idea is not right.

What Aunty's own argument requires is that the sub-personal vehicles of thought – and so, *inter alia*, of conscious thought – should be syntactically structured. It is not enough that a thinker should hear or imagine *as structured* natural language sentences. To say this is not to deny the importance of the fact that someone who understands a sentence hears, or imagines, it in such a way as to be aware of the way that it is built up from familiar words and constructions. Arguably, this is vital to an epistemology of understanding. (Again, this is intended to be in the spirit of Brewer, 1995.) But from the fact that Bruce imagines the sentences '*A or B*' and '*not-A*' as structured and moves in imagination to the sentence '*B*', it does not follow that he performs that transition in virtue of its form.

To make this point clearer, let us set aside, for a moment, the idea of conscious awareness of structure, and simply consider the transition from

'*A or B*' and '*not-A*' to '*B*'. Then it is clear (from section 2.2) that the fact that the transition instantiates a form is not sufficient for the form to figure in the causal explanation of the transition. Nor is it enough that Bruce does, in the actual situation, and would, in nearby counterfactual situations, perform other transitions that instantiate the same form. Conformity to a rule – even non-accidental conformity – is not sufficient for tacit knowledge of the rule. The point in the previous paragraph is that adding in the further condition that Bruce is aware of the structure of these sentences, and of the transition between them, still does not guarantee that the form figures in the causal explanation of the transition that Bruce performs. Even if thoughts are clothed in imagined sentences, still the requirements of Aunty's own argument have to be met at the sub-personal level.

There are thus two aspects of the TNL hypothesis to be considered. One is that LF representations might serve as the sub-personal level vehicles of thought instead of sentences of Mentalese. The other is that personal level imaginings of natural language sentences might constitute conscious thoughts. From the point of view of the friend of Aunty's own argument, the second of these aspects is more problematic than the first.

Early versions of some sections of this chapter have been included in talks given at the University of Michigan and the University of Tasmania, at a workshop on the personal/sub-personal distinction held at the University of Stirling, and at a conference of the European Society for Philosophy and Psychology held in Barcelona. I am grateful to the audiences in all these places, and to Peter Carruthers for several very helpful comments on later versions.

12 Natural language and virtual belief

Keith Frankish

1 Introduction

It is sometimes claimed that we can think *in* natural language – that natural language sentences can act as vehicles of thought and that we can think by tokening them – usually in the form of silent auditory or articulatory images (see, for example, Bickerton, 1995; Carruthers, 1996a; Harman, 1973.) There is some introspective evidence for this view (which is sometimes called the *cognitive conception* of language), and, given a certain view of what it is for thought to be conscious, a powerful argument can be run to the conclusion that conscious propositional thinking occurs in natural language (see Carruthers, 1996a).

Now, defence of the cognitive conception usually proceeds in two stages. First, it is argued that thought-processes are computational in character, the computations in question being understood as occurring at a subpersonal level. It is then argued that, in some thought-episodes at least, the *medium* of computation is natural language. In this chapter I shall outline an alternative way of arguing for the cognitive conception. The argument will not require a defence of computationalism, but will start with the claim that some intentional states are *actively formed.*

The chapter falls into two halves. The first aims to show that some beliefs, or belief-like states, are actively formed. I begin by describing two psychological phenomena which seem to have an active dimension. Then, following a suggestion by Daniel Dennett, I go on to develop a unified account of these phenomena, based around the idea that there exists a class of *virtual beliefs*, formed by actively adopting policies of *premising*. The second half of the chapter aims to show that virtual belief formation will typically involve natural language. I argue that, although there is no *conceptual* link between premising and natural language, there are grounds for thinking that premising – and hence virtual belief formation – will in fact usually take a linguistic form. Some uses of language, I conclude, have a cognitive role in the formation and manipulation of virtual beliefs. A final section briefly compares this defence of the cognitive conception with the more standard one, and suggests that it is to be preferred.

2 Virtual belief

2.1 Change of mind

In this section I want to tease out a relatively neglected strand of our common-sense psychological discourse – our talking of *making up* and *changing* our minds. We frequently refer to such events, and tend to speak of them as free, intentional actions (we urge the indecisive to *make up* their minds and blame the irresolute for *changing* them). Changes and makings up of mind have, however, received little philosophical attention – perhaps because it has been assumed that they can be identified with the formation and revision of intentions to action.[1] It is, of course, true that many changes and makings up of mind occur in practical reasoning. So, for example, I might *make up* my mind to go to Italy this year, or *change my mind* about which political party to vote for. And such cases do seem to involve simply the formation or revision of action-plans. It would be hasty, however, to assume that all changes and makings up of mind are such. We can make up our minds about what to *think*, as well as about what to *do*. Thus I can *change my mind* about the truth of a theory, or *make up my mind* that a certain politician is untrustworthy.[2]

If this is right, then some changes of mind are changes in belief, or in something very like belief. But the converse does not hold. As Annette Baier emphasises, in one of the few philosophical analyses of the subject, one does not make up, or change, one's mind whenever one acquires new beliefs or revises old ones (Baier, 1979). Baier lists several distinguishing features of changes of mind. First, they typically occur in *anticipation* of experience, rather than in reaction to it. A person who mistakenly thinks the ice will support them and ends up sinking can be said to have *learned better*, but not to have *changed his or her mind* (Baier's example). To be able to change your mind is, in part, to be able to anticipate experience and to alter erroneous beliefs before the world changes them for you. Secondly, changes of mind are *reflective* rather than routine. Suppose I misread the map, and you correct me (again, the example is Baier's). We would not say that, in accepting the correction, I had *changed my mind* about the route. Part of the reason for this, Baier suggests, is that I never needed to *make up* my mind about it. Where we defer to an authority or trust to a routine

[1] There has, in fact, been a good deal of discussion of the conditions under which deliberate belief revision would be *rational* – particularly in the literature on *acceptance* (see below). But there has been little attempt to explain exactly *how* such revisions can be carried out, or how they are related to other cognitive states and processes.

[2] Interestingly, this extends to desires, as well. We can make up and change our minds about what we *want*, as well as about what we *think*; and we often tell people – children especially – to do just that.

calculation, there is no call for us to make up our minds. Similarly, in practical reasoning, changes of plan that are dictated by circumstances or by longer-term plans do not count as changes of mind (taking a different route to avoid a traffic jam, say, or giving up one's job if one wins the lottery). Thirdly, changes of belief that result from large-scale cognitive or emotional upheaval are not changes of mind (Saul did not *change his mind* on the road to Damascus). Fourthly, Baier suggests, change of mind involves a kind of *commitment* – as to a rule, convention, or plan. In cases involving practical reasoning this is easy to see: the commitment in question will be to a plan of action. Baier does not explain, however, what sort of commitment is involved in *theoretical* changes of mind – cases in which one decides, not what to do, but what to think.

A distinctive feature of the various cognitive revisions excluded from the class of changes of mind, Baier suggests, is that they are *passively* undergone or assented to: the changes involved are too unreflective, too routine or too overwhelming for active deliberation to be needed. A change of mind, on the other hand, follows upon a revaluation of one's options, and involves a kind of free, creative judgement.

If Baier's analysis is on the right lines, then, it seems, we exhibit two rather different kinds of cognitive state, not clearly distinguished in everyday psychological discourse: passive belief, formed in an automatic and unreflective way, and another kind of cognitive state, formed by freely making up or changing one's mind, and involving a kind of commitment.[3]

2.2 *Acceptance*

The second strand of thought I want to introduce is the philosophical – and, more specifically, epistemological – literature on *acceptance*. 'Acceptance' here is a technical term for a kind of propositional attitude allied to, but distinct from, belief. There is no universal agreement about the properties of acceptance, but certain claims recur.

First, acceptance is qualitative, not quantitative. When we think about the role of belief in guiding action and decision-making, it is very tempting to suppose that belief is a matter of *degree*, with individual beliefs reflecting subjective probabilities of the sort assigned by Bayesian decision theory. (A probabilistic view of this kind also seems to be required if we are to resolve certain paradoxes of belief – in particular those of the lottery and the preface.) On the other hand, common-sense epistemology seems to treat belief as a qualitative, ungraded state. Unqualified belief is, for example, often assumed to be a necessary condition for knowledge. (It would seem

[3] Note that the distinction between these two kinds of state is drawn in terms of *form*, not *content*. I shall assume, for simplicity's sake, that the same range of contents can be entertained both passively and actively.

odd to say that one *knows* that *p*, but does not *fully* believe it.) And we tend to think of our sincere assertions as claims to *truth*, rather than as expressions of subjective probability. Many epistemologists think that the way to reconcile these intuitions is to suppose that everyday belief-talk fails to distinguish two distinct kinds of cognitive state – *belief* and *acceptance* – one of which is quantitative, the other qualitative (see, in particular, Levi, 1967; de Sousa, 1971; Kaplan, 1981).

Secondly, states of acceptance, unlike beliefs, are often supposed to be *actively formed* (de Sousa, 1971; Bratman, 1992). The idea is that, whereas belief is generated by automatic subpersonal processes, acceptance results from the act of deliberately *endorsing* or *assenting to* a proposition. This would explain why acceptance is qualitative (for any given proposition, one either has, or has not, actively accepted it).

Thirdly, acceptance is often characterised as a *behavioural* state (de Sousa, 1971; Kaplan, 1981). It is easy to show that, if acceptance were both a qualitative state *and* a state of confidence of any degree lower than certainty, then a rational agent would be required to accept contradictory propositions (the paradoxes of the lottery and the preface again; see Kaplan, 1981). One way to avoid this conclusion is to suppose that acceptance, unlike belief, is not a state of *confidence* at all, but a *behavioural* state. It has been suggested, for example, that accepting a proposition involves being disposed to bet on its truth (de Sousa), or to defend it for epistemic purposes (Kaplan), or to use it as a premise in one's reasoning (Cohen).

The view that acceptances are behavioural states harmonises nicely with the view that they are actively formed. That we can actively choose to display certain patterns of behaviour is uncontroversial. That we can choose to have a certain degree of confidence in a proposition is, on the other hand, dubious, if not downright incoherent.

2.3 *Virtual belief*

We have, then, two strands of thought, one implicit in common-sense psychological discourse, the other arising from reflection on the nature of belief, each of which posits the existence of a distinct kind of actively formed cognitive state. And the states they posit have much in common. As well as being actively formed, both are qualitative (making up one's mind, like acceptance, seems to be all-or-nothing), both require a degree of cognitive sophistication, and both involve a kind of behavioural commitment. It is very tempting, then, to identify them. (The suggestion is first made, I believe, in Dennett, 1978, chapter 16, though it may be implicit in some earlier work on acceptance, particularly de Sousa, 1971.) We could then appeal to acceptance-theory to provide an account of the commitment involved in theoretical change of mind. Dennett takes this line, suggesting that we complement Baier's account of change of mind with de Sousa's account of acceptance as a *bet on the truth of a sentence*. The states that result from such bets he calls *opinions*.

This suggestion is, I think, on the right lines. However, truth-betting (or 'sentence-collecting' as Dennett sometimes puts it) seems inadequate as a model for change and making up of mind.[4] There must, for example, be more to making up one's mind than simply betting on a *sentence*. A monoglot English speaker cannot make up his or her mind by betting on a suitably vouched-for *Russian* sentence. In any case, it would be a tactical mistake for me to begin by identifying makings up and changes of mind with attitudes to linguistic items. For I want to *argue* that language does *in fact* play a constitutive role in these processes. (This conclusion really does have to be argued for – Baier, for example, rejects it; 1979, pp. 166–7.) It would be unpersuasive, then, simply to *define* them as linguistic – unless, of course, it could be shown that no other characterisation was available.

And, in fact, alternative characterisations are ready-to-hand. In particular, I want to make use of Cohen's (1992) account of acceptance as *premising*. States of acceptance, Cohen argues, are not only actively initiated, but involve an extended 'pattern, system, or policy' of mental action (Cohen 1992, p. 12). To accept a proposition, Cohen explains, is to commit oneself to taking it as a premise or inference-licence in one's conscious deliberations. Such deliberations, he writes, will be:

> guided, implicitly or explicitly, by the premises or inference-rules that you have accepted previously. So in such cases you will be deliberately schooling your present thoughts to fit such premises or rules, and you will evaluate your hypotheses as correct or incorrect, probable or improbable, in accordance with those criteria. (1992, p. 23)

For Cohen, then, accepting a proposition involves committing oneself to a series of further personal actions – to deliberately regulating or 'schooling' one's thoughts in order to keep them in line with the premise. Presumably, this means calculating what conclusions the premise entails or excludes and then making appropriate further acts of acceptance and intention-formation. In due course we will need to consider just how these calculations might be made. (Cohen suggests that it involves applying learned inference-rules, though, as we shall see, this view is too restrictive.) But for the moment this rough characterisation will suffice.

I want to suggest, then, that making up one's mind about a matter of fact, *p*, involves accepting that *p* in Cohen's sense – that is, forming the intention to take *p* as a premise in one's conscious reasoning. This suggestion harmonises well with Baier's analysis of a change of mind as a kind of

[4] For an analysis of Dennett's views on opinion, see my 1996.

commitment. Deciding to take *p* as a premise means choosing to impose certain normative constraints upon one's future deliberations. The proposal also nicely integrates our accounts of change of mind in practical and theoretical reasoning: both involve committing oneself to a plan of some kind – in one case to a plan of action, in the other to a strategy of reasoning. (Indeed, since deciding to adopt a reasoning strategy is just forming a certain kind of intention to action, the one is a species of the other.)

It may be objected that I have ignored one feature of acceptance that is often stressed by writers on the subject, and by Cohen in particular. This is its *context relativity* (Bratman, 1992; Cohen, 1992, pp. 12–13). A person may decide to accept a proposition in one context (because their job requires them to treat it as true, say), but not in another (for example, where their aim is to ascertain the truth). And this fact seems to rule out a straightforward identification of acceptance with making up of mind. (The lawyer who decides, for professional reasons, to adopt the premise that a client is innocent, does not thereby *make up* his or her mind that the individual in question is innocent.) This objection is not fatal, however. It does not show that makings up of mind are not acceptances – only that not all acceptances are makings up of mind. We can still think of makings up of mind as a *subset* of acceptances – those, perhaps, that are motivated in a suitable way. For people have general epistemic ends, as well as short-term pragmatic ones. They desire to possess truths (or, perhaps, if they are epistemologists, to maximise *cognitive utility*). And it is such general ends that motivate them when they make up their minds or decide what to think about something. So I suggest that we identify makings up of mind with the class of acceptances that are motivated in this way by general epistemic ends.[5]

Suppose, then, that acts of change of mind, making up of mind and suitably motivated acceptance all introduce essentially the same kind of state – a behavioural state involving commitment to a policy of premising. I suggested that folk psychology does not explicitly distinguish this state from passively formed (or, as I shall sometimes put it, 'low-level') belief. So what exactly is the relation between the two states? Well, from a behavioural point of view, they will be almost indistinguishable. (This would explain, of course, why they are often conflated.) A person who premises that *p* will make much the same inferences and perform much the same actions as one who has the low-level belief that *p*. The principal difference between them will be that the premiser deliberately *guides* their inferential processes in

[5] I think this deliberately conservative policy on the role of pragmatic factors in making up of mind best captures our ordinary way of speaking; but the formulation can easily be revised so as to allow pragmatic factors a more substantial role. (In fact, all I need to claim is that makings up of mind are a *subset* of acceptances; discerning the exact boundaries of this subset is a matter for another time.)

order to keep them in line with the premise, whereas the ordinary believer leaves them to subpersonal control. Borrowing a term from computer science, we might say that the premiser intentionally *emulates* the inferential processes of a low-level believer. Or, to use another computing term, we might say they have a *virtual* belief.[6]

The term is quite appropriate. A virtual machine is one, in Daniel Dennett's phrase, 'made of rules rather than wires' – that is to say, formed by programming a flexible low-level physical system so as to cause it to display high-level functional states characteristic of a different type of machine (that is, to *emulate* that machine). Thus by executing an appropriate programme, a personal computer can mimic the behaviour of a card-index, a typewriter, or even another computer. Similarly, by executing an appropriate reasoning strategy, a person can mimic the inferential behaviour of someone with a certain belief. Just as a computer simulation is driven by the system's low-level programming instructions, so premising behaviour is driven by the premiser's low-level beliefs and desires. Thus, having decided to adopt a certain premise, the premiser *wants* to stick to this policy, *believes* that doing so requires accepting certain conclusions and rejecting others, and acts accordingly. Note that I am not suggesting that premisers will entertain these beliefs and desires *at a conscious level.* Typically, they will not. When one makes up one's mind about the truth or falsity of a proposition, all one consciously thinks about is the proposition and the evidence for and against it. I do claim, however, that making up one's mind involves manipulating premises (or representations of them) in ways which can best be explained by reference to one's low-level beliefs and desires about those premises.

I suggest then, that premising behaviour creates a kind of *virtual inference engine* which processes virtual beliefs. Note that a machine may be 'virtual' in this sense without lacking any essential properties of the real thing. To say that a machine is *virtual* is not to say that it is not *real*, only that it does not have a dedicated physical architecture. Thus in saying that virtual believers *emulate* or *mimic* belief, I do not mean to suggest that they do not really *have* the emulated beliefs. Rather, I want to suggest that emulating a certain belief is a distinct way of having that belief.[7]

[6] I owe the term *virtual belief* to Chris Hookway.

[7] The distinction between belief and virtual belief has some affinities with Dan Sperber's distinction between *intuitive* and *non-intuitive* beliefs (Sperber, 1997). Intuitive beliefs, Sperber argues, are those generated by spontaneous and unreflective processes – those acquired through perception, or the verbal communication of information which could have been presented perceptually, or by means of unconscious inferential processes. Non-intuitive beliefs, by contrast, are those that are acquired by conscious and deliberate inference or through the communication of ideas which could not have been presented perceptually. (Complex theoretical propositions are typical examples.) Non-intuitive beliefs are thus formed by the sort of deliberate premising that is involved in virtual belief formation.

Now it may seem that I am begging an important question here. For since premising is under voluntary control, it follows that, in suggesting that some premisings constitute a kind of *belief*, I am endorsing a form of *voluntarism* about belief. And there is a large philosophical literature devoted to showing that voluntarism is false, even incoherent. (For some anti-voluntarist arguments, see Williams, 1973; Winters, 1979; Pojman, 1985; and Bennett, 1990.) For example, voluntarism is often taken to involve the claim that we can induce beliefs in ourselves for purely practical reasons and regardless of the evidence for their truth. And this claim does, indeed, look very implausible. (It is hard to see how one could consistently think of a state induced in this way *as* a belief; see Williams, 1973 and Pojman, 1985). But nothing in my account commits me to the claim that virtual beliefs can be induced without regard to the evidence. I identified virtual belief formation with acts of acceptance that are motivated by general epistemic ends. And for an act of acceptance to be motivated in this way is just for it to be motivated *by* the evidence. (I cannot believe that I will advance my general epistemic ends by accepting that *p*, unless I believe that there is reasonably good evidence for the truth of *p*.) So while I accept that some kinds of belief formation are active, I deny that they are unconstrained by evidence. I am thus committed only to a *weak* form of voluntarism.[8]

2.4 Levels of mind

In this section I want to draw out one consequence of my story for theories of mind and mental processing. The consequence is salutary and constitutes, I think, another consideration in favour of the account.

If there are two distinct levels of mentality, then there may be distinct kinds of *processing* underlying them. Cohen suggests that this is indeed the case. The distinction between acceptance and belief, he claims, corresponds neatly to that between *digital* and *connectionist* processing. Because acceptance is a discrete, sequential, rule-governed process, it can be adequately modelled by digital computer programs. Belief states, on the other hand, being graded and overlapping, are better modelled by connectionist systems (Cohen, 1992, p. 56).

[8] Another objection centres on the voluntarist claim that beliefs can be induced *directly*, simply by *willing* to acquire them. Acquiring a belief, the objector points out, typically seems to be something that *happens to* one, rather than something one *does*. This is especially true of beliefs arising from perception, memory and certain basic inferential processes (see, for example, Pojman, 1985). Again, I can concede the point. I contend only that *some* types of belief can be induced voluntarily – the kind of reflective or theoretical beliefs that result from changing or making up one's mind. Nor do I claim that we can form virtual beliefs *simply* by willing to do so. Virtual belief formation is, we may say, *intentionally indirect*. That is to say, one forms a virtual belief *by* doing something else – by intentionally committing oneself to a policy of premising.

Cohen does not develop the suggestion, and, indeed, a lot of work would be required to turn it into a serious proposal. (In particular, it would be important to think hard about the relation between the two processing levels.) But I think that it points in the right direction, and that, properly construed, a two-level theory offers the best tactic for reconciling a connectionist cognitive science with a common-sense view of the mind. Let me explain briefly.

Many cognitive scientists believe that connectionist systems of some variety will eventually afford our best models of the human mind. Certainly, they seem to be the most neurologically plausible. But there is a persisting difficulty in seeing how connectionist systems can exhibit the sort of psychological states and processes which we ordinarily attribute to each other. The problem is that common-sense psychology seems to be strongly *realist*. It supposes that beliefs and other psychological states are real, functionally discrete, internal states, which can be individually formed, activated and erased. One of the key pieces of evidence for this claim is the fact that we often pick out individual beliefs and desires as causally responsible for particular actions, even when we know that the agent possessed other beliefs and desires which would equally have justified the action. For example, I may have several long-standing beliefs, each of which would independently justify my going into town (I need to buy food, want to go to the bank, and have a message to deliver), yet only one of these reasons (the need to buy food, say) may be *the* causally effective reason for my actually going into town this afternoon. But if beliefs can be individually effective in this way, then they are functionally discrete; and if they are functionally discrete, then, it seems, they must have discrete *internal* representations (see Ramsey *et al.*, 1991).

Many of the most effective connectionist systems, however, appear to lack discrete internal states of this kind. These systems store information in a distributed, heavily overlapping way, which seems to preclude the selective activation of individual items of knowledge. Thus there is an apparent tension between connectionism and common sense – a tension which both sides have an interest in diffusing. Realists about folk psychology would welcome the news that connectionism poses no threat to them, while connectionists for their part would be reassured to know that they are not going to have to deny that people really do have beliefs and other folk psychological states.

There are two popular strategies for diffusing the tension. One is to argue that connectionist systems do, in fact, despite appearances, possess functionally discrete internal representations, at least of *occurrent* thoughts (see Botterill, 1994; Clark, 1990; O'Brien, 1991). The second, more radical, response, is to adopt a weak, quasi-behaviouristic, reading of folk psychological talk (see, for example, Clark, 1993). Neither strategy, I think, is wholly satisfactory. (The first offers, at best, a partial solution, while the second requires us to accept a significant weakening of our common-sense intuitions.)

But if our realist intuitions relate principally to *virtual belief*, rather than to its low-level counterpart, then we have, I think, another option. Since virtual beliefs are policy adoptions, their processing takes place entirely at a *personal* level. It involves a person *doing* various things: *endorsing* a premise, *keeping track* of it, *working out* what conclusions it entails, and so on. So virtual beliefs are, in a sense, *behavioural* states (stretching the term 'behaviour' a little to include certain kinds of mental behaviour such as silent acceptance and conscious deliberation). Now the existence of various kinds of human *behaviour* is not an issue between the folk psychological realist and the connectionist. The debate between them is over the nature of the processing required to support that behaviour. In so far as realists are concerned only with virtual belief, then, they can have no quarrel with connectionists.

Moreover, virtual beliefs will be functionally discrete in the way that realists suppose beliefs to be. Premising policies can be selectively adopted, executed and abandoned. Consider, for example, the role of virtual belief in guiding action. A particular premise will get to influence behaviour only if the premiser deliberately employs it in their practical reasoning. (At least, that is the only way it will get to influence behaviour *as a premise*; it may have unintended side-effects.) And it will be deliberately used in reasoning only if it is consciously *recalled* at appropriate moments. But relevant premises will not always be recalled at such moments. Suppose, for example, that I have separately endorsed the premises *I need to buy food* and *I need to go to the bank*, each of which would independently warrant my going into town this afternoon. And suppose, too, that right now I recollect just one of these premises – the need to buy food, say. (I need not explicitly think of it *as* a premise; it is enough that I recollect it with an appropriate degree of commitment and am disposed to use it in inference.) I recognise that this requires me to go into town, and decide to go. Here we can say that, although I had endorsed both premises, and would, if prompted, have acknowledged that I was committed to both of them, nevertheless I *acted upon* only one of them. So, we can say that on this occasion only one of my two virtual beliefs was causally active. Moreover, we can say all of this without saying anything about my subpersonal neural states. (Thus we can explain my failure to act upon my belief about the bank as due to the fact that *I* temporarily *lost track* of the relevant premise, failing to recollect it and use it in inference.) So we can explain how virtual beliefs can have a selective causal influence on behaviour without having to suppose that it involves the selective activation of discrete neural subcomponents.

Of course, the proposed strategy for reconciling connectionism and common sense will work only if our common-sense commitment to realism does not extend to low-level belief.[9] And it is not clear that this is so. For the story requires us to suppose that the personal-level actions and events involved in the processing of virtual beliefs have fairly determinate psychological characterisations – that they can properly be described as acts of *deciding to adopt a premise* p, *recalling that one has accepted* p, *working out that* p *entails* q, and so on. Only if this is so will we be able to speak of a subject selectively recollecting and employing in inference one of a number of semantically relevant premises. And the worry, of course, is that the characterisations just given are in terms of the agent's *low-level* psychological states. So it might seem that we will, after all, have to buy into a fairly strong form of realism about low-level belief.

I think this worry is misplaced, however. For although the story requires us to ascribe certain low-level beliefs to virtual believers, it does not require us to give semantic characterisations to neural components or subpersonal processes. In fact, it requires only two assumptions: (1) that premising policies, like other policies, can be individually formed, recalled and executed, and (2) that the actions involved in forming and executing a premising policy can be given fairly determinate semantic characterisations – sufficient, at least, to individuate the policies concerned. It is possible to accept both of these assumptions without endorsing a strong form of realism about low-level belief. (Note that if we typically give our premises linguistic form, as I shall argue we do, then condition (2) above will be relatively uncontroversial: premising policies will be adequately individuated by their associated linguistic representations.)[10]

[9] The strategy does not, of course, assume the *falsity* of realism about low-level belief; but it does assume the absence of any common-sense commitment to its *truth*.

[10] The reader may ask why, given the two assumptions just mentioned, single-level theorists cannot say everything I say about the functional discreteness of beliefs. They can say, of the case mentioned in the text, that I recalled that I needed to buy food (a personal episode with a determinate semantic characterisation), and that this recollection caused me to go to the grocery. I failed to recall that I needed to go to the bank, and hence was not impelled to go there. This position is, in effect, that adopted by advocates of the first conciliatory strategy mentioned in the text. My reasons for rejecting it are two-fold. First, although it accounts for the functional discreteness of *occurrent* thoughts, it does not do the same for *standing-state* beliefs. In particular, I suspect that it cannot give a satisfactory account of the status of the temporarily dormant beliefs, such as my belief about the bank. Secondly, it is not clear from this story why a belief should have to be *explicitly recalled* in order for it to influence behaviour (indeed, it would be very odd to say that it has). At any rate, the story is incomplete until supplemented with an account of the cognitive role of explicitly recalled beliefs. This, I suggest, is just what virtual belief theory provides.

3 Natural language

3.1 Premising and language

I avoided characterising virtual belief as an essentially linguistic state, preferring a more neutral characterisation in terms of premising. Of course, this leaves open the possibility that premising is *itself* a language-dependent activity. Cohen takes this view, and I am going to argue for a slightly weaker version of the same claim. Premising, I shall argue, does not *have* to involve language, but will in fact typically do so. Given that premising is constitutive of virtual belief formation, this conclusion will give us our limited vindication of the cognitive conception of language.

Note that this defence will extend only to *virtual* belief. For simplicity's sake I shall assume that low-level belief does *not* constitutively involve natural language. I shall assume also that there is no limit to the range of contents that can be entertained as objects of low-level belief. To deny either of these assumptions would be to embark on a much wider defence of the cognitive conception.

Given these assumptions, however, it looks as if it will be difficult to show that premising is linguistic. If one can *entertain* the content *p* without putting it into words, then there is no obvious reason why one could not decide to take *p* as a *premise* without putting it into words. One might weigh up the various bits of evidence one has for *p*, think about how it coheres with one's other premises and beliefs, and finally decide to accept it as a premise in one's reasoning. Of course, adopting any sort of premising policy would probably require a degree of conceptual sophistication not to be found in creatures without language. But even so, this would not establish the conclusion we want. To say that premising would be beyond the reach of languageless creatures is not to say that it is *itself* a linguistic activity.

It would be rash, however, to conclude from this that language is inessential to premising. For even if there is no need to give a proposition linguistic form in order to decide to *adopt* the policy of treating it as a premise, it might still be necessary to do so in order to *execute* that policy. We will have to look more closely at just what premising involves.

Premising that *p* means taking *p* as a given in one's conscious explicit reasoning – *schooling one's thoughts* to fit *p*, as Cohen puts it. This, I suggested, involves calculating what conclusions *p* entails and excludes and then making appropriate further acts of acceptance and intention-formation.[11]

[11] Unless, of course, these conclusions are so unpalatable as to induce one to repudiate the original premise.

Premisers, then, will need some way of making these calculations – some way of *evaluating* their premising commitments. (They would also need to make such evaluations in the course of deciding whether or not to accept, or continue to accept, a premise – since it would be important to know exactly what a positive decision would commit them to.) Of course, if they *believed* their premises (believed them, that is, in a passive, low-level way), then such conclusions might occur to them spontaneously. The required inferential operations would be performed by automatic subpersonal mechanisms. But premisers undertake intentionally to *emulate* the operation of those mechanisms. They need not, of course, employ the very same algorithms as those employed at a subpersonal level, though they will need to use ones that generate the same results.[12] And for this they must have *personal* mastery of some technique, or set of techniques, for deriving normatively warranted conclusions from their premises. Of course, premisers need not work out *all* the entailments of their premises (a tedious task, given that there will be an infinite number of them). Rather, they will need to employ techniques which reliably generate some of their more useful and informative entailments (working out that from *p* and *q* one can infer *p&q* might be useful; working out that one can infer $r \rightarrow p$, $s \rightarrow p$, $t \rightarrow p$ . . . probably would not).

The obvious strategy here would be to apply learned rules of inference. This is what Cohen envisages. Acceptance, he says, is 'consciously guided by voluntarily accepted rules' (1992, p. 56). And these rules, he argues, together with the premises upon which they operate, will necessarily be linguistic:

> Premises and rules of inference have to be conceived in linguistic terms . . . That is how logic can get to grips with inference and formulate its principles as rules for linguistic transformation (1992, p. 12).

Thus, there is, he claims, an 'a priori conceptual requirement' that the objects of acceptance must be linguistically expressed – though not necessarily overtly vocalised.

One can see why Cohen thinks this. Inference-rules will need to have a degree of generality (rules for making *individual*, content-specific, inferences would be of little use). That is to say, they will have to specify *formal* operations. So, for example, one useful inference-rule might be *modus ponens*, which tells us that a pair of premises of the form 'If *p* then *q*' and '*p*', entail a conclusion of the form '*q*'. Another useful rule might be one to the effect that premises of the form '*x* is a dog' normatively warrant conclusions of the form '*x* is an animal'. (Although this reflects a semantical prin-

[12] Or, at any rate, which they *take* to generate the same results; some people may, after all, be rather bad at emulating belief.

ciple rather than a logical one, it is still specified in formal terms.) But if premising involves applying rules which, like these, specify formal operations, then it does seem to follow that premises must be linguistically expressed. For to apply formal inference-rules, one would need to have access to the *form* of one's premises. And this means that those premises must be represented in a medium to whose formal properties one has access. The obvious candidate for such a medium is natural language.

This is too swift, however. It is true that useful inference-rules must specify formal operations, and true, too, that we do not have direct *perceptual* access to the formal properties of our non-linguistic thoughts. But we might nonetheless have a kind of *reflective* access to them. For example, if I know that I accept the premise, *If the butler did not murder the colonel, then the rector's wife must have done so*, then I can tell that I accept a conditional (assuming I have the concept *conditional*, of course). And if I also know that I accept the premise, *The butler did not murder the colonel*, then I can tell that I accept the antecedent of this same conditional. And if I am familiar with *modus ponens*, then I can go ahead and apply it to these premises. If I can entertain all of these thoughts non-linguistically, then I can apply formal inference-rules non-linguistically too.

Cohen is wrong, then, to say that there is an *a priori conceptual* requirement for inference-rules to be linguistically expressed. Nevertheless, it seems likely that they will *in practice* be so. Semantical principles, in particular (that is, information about the inferential roles of particular concepts) will almost certainly be derived from reflection on our linguistic practices. It is just this sort of information that is codified in dictionaries. Logical principles, too, are usually acquired and applied as rules for performing linguistic transformations.

Besides, there may be another, more direct, argument for the involvement of language in premising. Most people are able to construct and evaluate arguments without applying explicit rules of inference. Instead, they make use of *practical* inferential skills, which can be thought of as embedding implicit or procedural knowledge of such rules. These skills are typically acquired in the course of linguistic interaction, and consist in being able to spot certain formal patterns in people's utterances, and to impose similar patterns upon one's own. Learning them is, in effect, learning how to engage in reasoned argument.

Now people with these skills could easily employ them to evaluate their premising commitments. Suppose, for example, that I have learned to spot patterns of inference which instantiate *modus ponens* and to classify them as valid. This skill could be entirely procedural; I do not need to be able to articulate *modus ponens*, but simply to recognise inferences of *that*, demonstratively identified, form as valid. Suppose, too, that I have learnt to regulate my own argumentative utterances in accordance with *modus ponens* – again without articulating the rule. So if I have asserted sentences of the form 'If *p* then *q*' and '*p*', I regard myself as licensed to assert a sentence of the form '*q*', too, and as obliged to refrain from asserting any sentence incompatible with one of that form. Then, if I were to *accept* sentences of those forms as premises, it would be natural for me to regard myself as committed to accepting the corresponding conclusion as a further premise, and to rejecting any premises that conflict with it. (Just *saying* the premises over to myself might prompt me to supply the dictated conclusion.) In this way it would be possible for me to execute a premising strategy without drawing on explicit theory at all, but relying entirely on my pre-theoretical argumentative skills.

Moreover, these skills will, I think, be essentially linguistic. It is very hard to think of any non-linguistic (or at any rate non-symbolic) personal routines which could embed implicit inference-rules. We have no perceptual access to the form of our thoughts, and cannot directly manipulate propositions in the way that we can manipulate their representations. And although we can have reflective knowledge of the formal properties of our thoughts, such knowledge would be useless accompanied by an equally reflective grasp of inferential rules. (For example, the knowledge that I accept a conditional and its antecedent will be of little use to me, unless I can remember what I am licensed to infer from such a conjunction.) Of course, we can think of our *subpersonal* processes of belief formation and revision as embedding implicit rules of inference. But these processes cannot be directly controlled and exploited by the premiser as part of a deliberate reasoning strategy (though, as we shall see, they can be *indirectly* exploited).

I think we can conclude, then, that premising strategies which exploit procedural knowledge of inferential rules will be language-based. Moreover, such strategies are likely to be rather more widespread than ones exploiting explicit knowledge. People tend to acquire skills procedurally before they begin to theorise them. Certainly, many people can classify certain patterns of inference as good or bad without being able to say precisely what their goodness or badness consists in. Cohen seems to overlook this, supposing that inference-rules will always be acquired explicitly in the first place, even if they subsequently become second-nature (1992, pp. 12, 23, 56). Nothing hinges on this claim, however, and dropping it would only strengthen his case for the linguistic dependency of premising.

3.2 *Simulation routines*

It looks, then, as if language-based forms of premising will be both simpler and easier to acquire than non-linguistic ones. We must not be too hasty, however. For there is another kind of inferential technique which seems to be both powerful and yet not essentially linguistic. This is *simulation*. Many philosophers, and some psychologists, believe that our skill in ascribing psychological states to other people depends on our ability to run cognitive simulations (see, for example, Goldman, 1989, 1992; Gordon, 1986; Heal, 1986, 1995; Harris, 1989, 1992). The idea is this. In order to work out what another person is likely to think or do, one pretends to share their beliefs, lets one's inferential system run 'off-line' (so that its outputs are not passed to memory or motor control), and waits to see what conclusions one comes to. One then ascribes belief in these conclusions to the other person. What I want to suggest here is that one could also run *self-simulations* in order to evaluate one's premising commitments. That is to say, one could pretend that one *believes* one's premises, run an off-line simulation, see what conclusions one comes to, and then accept these conclusions as new premises.

For example, suppose that Miss Marple accepts the premise, *The butler was at the public house all evening*. She runs an off-line simulation upon this premise and finds that the proposition, *The butler did not murder the colonel* is generated as output. (This reflects her belief that the colonel was murdered at home, shortly after dinner.) Miss Marple now knows that if she *believed* the premise, then she would infer that the butler did not murder the colonel. Since she is committed to making just those inferences that she would make if she believed her premises, she concludes that she is committed to accepting that the butler did not murder the colonel.

Assuming it can be done at will, simulation seems to offer a powerful tool for evaluating premising commitments. Indeed, it would facilitate certain sorts of inference which the other procedures we have considered do not encompass. For example, there are no simple rules or procedures for deriving sound abductive inferences (that is, for working out which of various possible hypotheses is the *best explanation* of a set of data). Making such inferences involves testing candidate hypotheses for coherence with one's network of background beliefs. Simulation, being an holistic process, would facilitate this. For the same reason, it would afford an excellent means of assessing candidate premises for acceptability prior to formal acceptance. Conscientious premisers would doubtless make full use of it. But there seems to be no crucial role here for language. If one can entertain a thought non-linguistically, then there is no obvious reason why one could not run a simulation from it non-linguistically, too.

There are some problems with simulation, however. First, premising policies guided by simulation will be rather more extensive than those guided by explicit rules or localised inferential procedures. In the latter cases, when one adopts a premise, *p*, one commits oneself to accepting whatever conclusions one can derive from *p* by applying appropriate rules or procedures. In simulation-based premising, by contrast, one commits oneself to accepting *whatever* conclusions one would draw if one *believed* that *p*. And this is a much wider commitment. For the outcome of simulation routines will be determined, not only by one's explicitly accepted premises, but also by all of one's background beliefs. (Simulating the belief that *p* does not involve pretending that one believes *only* that *p*, but that one believes that *p in addition to* all one's other beliefs.) For example, suppose that when Miss Marple runs a simulation on the premise, *The butler was at the public house all evening*, she derives the simulated conclusion, *The butler is morally depraved*. (Suppose she tacitly believes that all people who frequent public houses are morally depraved.) And suppose, too, that she wishes to reject this conclusion. (She also thinks the butler is a cat-lover and believes that no cat-lover is morally depraved.) Now if a premising policy just *is* a policy of accepting the results of simulation, then a refusal to accept one of these results will mark an *abandonment* of the policy – and thus, given our identification of premising with making up of mind – a change of mind. But it would be absurd to say that in refusing to accept that the butler was morally depraved Miss Marple thereby *changed her mind* about his being at the public house.

So if making up one's mind involves committing oneself to a policy of reasoning, then this policy cannot be one of accepting without exception all the results of simulation. Nor is it clear how simulation could be restricted in scope so as to exclude background beliefs irrelevant to the premising process. Simulation, then, on its own, would not offer a satisfactory means of evaluating one's premising commitments. It would have to be *supplemented* with rules or procedures for assessing simulated conclusions for normative warrant, relative to one's current premises. And, as we have seen, such rules and procedures will generally be linguistic.

A second problem for simulation arises from the fact that premisers may know they have instinctive inferential *defects*. For example, I may know that I have a deep-rooted tendency to make certain mistakes in reasoning with conditionals, or to be influenced by wishful thinking on certain topics. Now simulation-based premising would reflect these tendencies. (Simulation, remember, involves feeding a premise to your instinctive inferential processes.) But it would be odd to suppose that in committing myself to a premising policy, I commit myself to replicating my known inferential defects. If anything, one would think, I commit myself to trying to *rectify* them. But simulation will offer no guidance as to how to do this. It will tell me what I *would* infer if I believed that *p*, not what I *should* infer. Again, it seems, simulation will have to be supplemented by more specific inferential procedures or principles. And, again, these will generally be language-based. It appears, then, that premisers will inevitably have to draw at some point on specific inferential principles, either explicitly represented or embedded in practical inferential skills.

It may be objected that to suppose that we adhere to principles of inference is to suppose that some inferential transitions are non-negotiable (analytic) and thus that there are canonical procedures for revising and updating one's belief system in the light of conflicts with new evidence. (If it is a semantical rule that all bachelors are unmarried men, then the inference 'Fred is bachelor → Fred is an unmarried man' is non-negotiable: were I to uncover evidence that Fred is not an unmarried man, then I would have to repudiate belief in his bachelorhood.) But, as Quine famously argued, there are no non-negotiable inferential transitions. Any inference may be revised, provided one makes sufficiently drastic changes to other elements of one's belief system. And in updating our beliefs, what matters is not that we respect local semantical rules, but that we maintain the most stable global configuration in our belief system.

Now this may be true enough of low-level belief. But if the above argument is sound, it is not true of virtual belief. Forming a virtual belief involves adopting inferential strategies that are relatively *insulated* from one's background beliefs. We should not, I think, find this conclusion surprising, given what we know about virtual belief. Forming a virtual belief involves deliberately schooling one's thoughts. And it will be easier to do this by applying discrete local principles than by making assessments of global coherence. This conclusion also reflects what we know about the function of virtual belief formation. To make up one's mind about a matter is, in effect, to *foreclose* on deliberation about it – to give it, as it were, the status of cognitive *trumps*. And it would make sense to keep items with this status relatively insulated from mundane changes in one's background beliefs.

3.3 Some conclusions

Let me sum up the state of play. Cohen is wrong to suppose that premising *must* be linguistic. In theory, it could exploit explicit inference-rules that are not formulated in language. In practice, however, such rules will generally be linguistically formulated, coming to us via dictionaries and logic primers. Moreover, the simplest and most easily acquired forms of premising (ones employing practical inferential skills, rather than explicit theory) will be language-based. Simulation, too, although apparently not requiring language, would have to be supplemented either by explicit theory or by practical skills. Given this, I think it is safe to conclude that non-linguistic premising, if it occurs at all, will be a late and sophisticated development – probably involving *suppression* of a linguistic component – rather like the ability to read in silence.

We can now fit this conclusion into the wider argument of this chapter. So far, our defence of the cognitive conception of language has followed something of a self-denying ordinance, ignoring the introspective evidence for the role of language in thought, and concentrating instead on relatively a prioristic considerations. Thus, I have suggested that we can actively form some of our mental states (that we can *accept* propositions, and *make up* and *change* our minds) and have argued that we do so by engaging in policies of premising. And I have outlined some reasons for thinking that premising will generally take a linguistic form. On this basis, one could predict that, whenever we find creatures who make up and change their minds, we will find them talking and reasoning with themselves, either silently or out loud. And this of course is just what we *do* find in our own case.

We talk to ourselves a lot, and it seems that when we do so we are not just idling, but engaging in genuine ratiocination. This intuitive view, however, cries out for theoretical underpinning – for an explanation of how it is possible for language to have a cognitive role. And this is just what our story about virtual belief has provided. Sometimes, when we speak to ourselves, what we are doing is silently articulating premises for adoption or manipulation, thus forming and processing virtual beliefs. (This may not, of course, be quite how we *think* of our activity at such moments; but, if I am right, it is the best way of characterising it.) It is important to note that this view assumes that inner speech is entertained as *interpreted speech*. That is to say, our inner verbalisations present themselves to us as expressions of various *propositional contents* which are available for acceptance or rejection. So in claiming that we think in language, I am *not* claiming that we think by manipulating *uninterpreted* natural language symbols. (That view would be rather unattractive, given that such symbols will often be ambiguous in a way that thought is not.) Indeed, it might be better to say that we think *with* language, rather than *in* it; language provides a kind of *scaffolding* for our premising activities.

Of course, as I noted earlier, there are other, and more widely accepted, explanations of how language can have a cognitive role. In the final section of this chapter I shall briefly compare these accounts with the one outlined here.

3.4 A comparison

All defenders of the cognitive conception of language agree that we can think by tokening[13] natural language sentences. And all agree that what

[13] Either by overtly uttering them, or, more often, by forming auditory or articulatory *images* of them (see Carruthers, 1996a).

makes a tokened sentence a judgement, rather than a fantasy, say, or idle speculation, is, in a broad sense, its causal role: beliefs have certain systematic effects on subsequent reasoning and behaviour that fantasies and idle speculations do not. The theories differ, however, in the accounts they give of the *determinants* of causal role.

According to what I shall call the *standard* version of the cognitive conception, the determining factors are subpersonal. What makes a sentence-token a judgement rather than a fantasy is the fact that it has a certain computational role – that it would causally interact in a certain characteristic way with various other token states, linguistic and non-linguistic. These relational facts, the story goes, supervene upon intrinsic properties of the token state and the local environment in which it is tokened. There are various ways of developing this view. According to one, there exists a specialised cognitive processor dedicated to the manipulation of natural language sentences. Advocates of such a view include Carruthers (1996a) and, possibly, Bickerton (1995). A weaker version of the standard view holds that the causal role of sentence-tokens is determined by associative mechanisms: activating a representation of a natural language sentence tends to lead to the activation of other, semantically related, sentences. This view is advocated by Smolensky (1988), and, in a more guarded form, by Dennett (1991).

According to the version of the cognitive conception defended here, by contrast, the determinants of causal role are certain *intentional actions*. One can *decide* whether a sentence is going to function as a judgement by deciding whether or not to endorse it as a premise. If one does choose to endorse it, then the sentence will acquire the causal role of a belief in virtue of subsequent *personal* events – remembering that one is committed to taking it as a premise, working out that it mandates certain further acts of acceptance, determining to honour one's premising commitments by performing these acts, and so on. Call this view the *intentionalist* version of the cognitive conception.

I think this view has some distinct advantages over its rivals. First, it does not require there to be a dedicated hardwired cognitive processor for natural language sentences. The processing of virtual beliefs is done by a kind of *virtual* processor, which is realised in the subject's low-level psychological processes. This is a consequence of the fact that the formation and processing of virtual beliefs is under intentional control. People accept the consequences of their premises, not because they are wired up to do so, but because they *believe* the consequences are warranted and *want* to honour their premising commitments. (Let me emphasise again that these beliefs and desires will not, as a rule, be *consciously* entertained.) Evolutionary considerations, I think, favour this story over its rival. For virtual processors will be much easier and cheaper to install than hardwired ones; existing cognitive systems would not have to be rewired or reduplicated, simply *reprogrammed.* Indeed, given the apparent recency of language on the evolutionary time-scale, it is not clear that there would have been time for the necessary rewiring to occur.

The intentionalist story also has advantages over the weaker, associationist, version of the standard defence. For associationism seems to offer no scope for active, one-off, making up of mind. Associationist processes are not under intentional control. One cannot *decide* that a certain sentence will have the sort of cognitive associations that a belief ought to have: one can only *hope* that it will do so. The intentionalist story, by contrast, is much more flexible. One can decide that a certain sentence will function as a premise by deciding to *treat* it as one, employing it in appropriate inferential strategies.

Why, then, is the intentionalist account not widely accepted? One reason may be that it seems to imply that inner speech is under *personal control.* And this looks wrong: words can just pop into our heads, as unbidden as the thoughts they carry. This objection, however, misrepresents the intentionalist position. The intentionalist need not claim that the *production* of sentence tokens is always under personal control – only that the act of *endorsing* them is. Note, too, that in saying that the cognitive mode of inner speech is under personal control, the intentionalist is *not* committed to claiming that there is a central executive which decides how sentence-tokens are to function. Nor is the intentionalist committed to denying that personal actions may issue from low-level *pandemonium* processes of the sort Marvin Minsky has described (processes, that is to say, of evolutionary competition among unintelligent neural subsystems or 'demons'; see Minsky, 1985). The distinction between centralised and pandemonium accounts of the genesis of intentional action is *orthogonal* to the distinction between subpersonal and intentionalist versions of the cognitive conception. Advocates of pandemonium models are not committed to denying that there *is* a personal/subpersonal distinction, at least of a rough-and-ready kind; they merely seek to reject one account of what the distinction consists in. And this is all that the intentionalist defender of the cognitive conception needs. The intentionalist's thesis is simply that there is a distinction, at least of degree, between those events and processes that are under personal control and those that are not, and that the events which determine the cognitive role of natural language sentence-tokens often fall into the former class.

The bulk of this chapter, linking change of mind with premising and premising with language, has been devoted to outlining one line of argument for this conclusion. But I think that everyday experience also confirms it. It is wrong to suppose that inner speech always comes to us with its psychological mode (speech act, judgement, whimsy, whatever) pre-determined. Suppose I am listening to a speaker delivering a long and rather dense paper. As I struggle to make sense of his words, the sentence 'He's talking nonsense' suddenly pops into my head. Do these words constitute a serious thought or just a display of idle pique? Consider what may happen next. I may think about the words, decide, after brief reflection, that they cannot be justified, and put them down to irritation at the speaker's prolixity. Alternatively, the words may alert me to the fact that the paper really is very bad. In this case, I will endorse the sentence and start to reason with it as a premise. (I will begin to wonder why the speaker was invited, what I ought to say if he asks my opinion of his paper, and so on.)

Scenarios such as this suggest that it will not do to say that the cognitive role of sentence tokens is determined wholly by subpersonal processes occurring upstream of their tokening. Equally important are subsequent personal decisions to employ a sentence in one role or another. This is not to deny, of course, that some verbalisations spontaneously assume a certain role for us, without our needing to make any decision at all. Such cases need not cause a problem for the intentionalist. For omissions as well as actions can be intentional. The intentionalist can allow that premises may be endorsed *by default* – by failing to reject them – as well as by datable acts of endorsement.

The intentionalist may also, I think, be able to motivate a rather stronger claim. For in some cases it does seem possible to control the direction of one's inner speech, much as one can control the direction of a conversation. Think of a case in which one is deliberately trying to reason one's way to the solution of some problem. It is not implausible to suggest that in such cases our long-term argumentative goals can influence the direction and content of our silent soliloquising. If so, then our personal control of inner speech may sometimes extend upstream as well as down.

I am grateful to Jill Boucher, Peter Carruthers, Jonathan Cohen, Gloria Origgi, Dan Sperber, Yorick Wilks and three anonymous referees for comments on earlier drafts of this paper, and to all the participants in the Hang Seng conference on Language and Thought for some stimulating discussions. Thanks, too, to Gavin Boyce, Tom Dickins, Ewan McEachran and Jenny Saul.

13 The meta-intentional nature of executive functions and theory of mind

Josef Perner

1 Introduction

There is a strong intuition that what we express linguistically we are (on the whole) conscious of, and Dennett (1978) has seen the essence of conscious thought in the availability of its contents to verbal report. On intuitive grounds a similarly close relationship exists between consciousness and voluntary control. In fact, Jacoby's (1991) famous 'process dissociation procedure' for determining the relative contributions of implicit/unconscious and explicit/conscious information to performance in memory or subliminal perception tasks (Debner and Jacoby, 1994) presupposes that conscious information consists of those contents of memory over which one can exert voluntary control. And naturally, voluntary control in these experiments consists in the ability to implement the verbal instructions, to either include or exclude specified events of the past in one's test answers.

I now want to analyse the representational pre-requisites for controlled action at some length in order to show that it requires a meta-intentional representation of one's own intentions. This requirement then provides the basis for explaining its kinship with language and conscious thought.

The close link between conscious processing of verbal information and (executive) control is also emphasised in the more standard model of working memory. I chose the term *Executive Function* (e.g., Ozonoff *et al.* 1991) as a generic term for those functions that are allegedly served by, e.g., the *Central Executive* within working memory (Baddeley and Hitch, 1974) or the *Supervisory Attentional System* (SAS) of Norman and Shallice (1980/1986), which all bear a close family resemblance to each other (Shallice and Burgess, 1993, p. 173). With the term 'executive function' I want to dispel any commitment to the idea that these functions have to be served by some 'central' agent (homunculus) or have to take place within some central space (Cartesian Theatre, Dennett, 1991). The notion that there is a central executive or supervisor involved comes from the phenomenal experience that it is 'us' who are in charge of our intentional behaviour. And these actions for which we feel fully responsible share a cluster of phenomenal properties:

(1) we are *in charge and responsible* for these actions (it incorporates our sense of 'self');
(2) we are *conscious* of these actions;
(3) we can *talk about and justify* our actions;
(4) we can follow *verbal instructions*;
(5) we have *limited capacity* for carrying out these actions simultaneously.

To explain these features by reference to a central executive has superficial appeal but little deeper explanatory value, since its theoretical specification amounts to little more than the positing of a homunculus (Baddeley, 1996). The appeal stems from the fact that a central executive re-describes the phenomenal experience of intentional action as actions of a person. What is needed is some explanation of why we have these phenomenal experiences.

My main focus is on the empirical content that the central executive has been given in its incarnation as SAS (supervisory attentional system), which is deemed necessary for a cluster of tasks (Norman and Shallice, 1980/6, pp. 2–3) characterised by the unifying feature of involving the prefrontal cortex. I try to argue that, instead of positing a central agency, the phenomenal and empirical facts clustering around executive functions are to be explained by the ability to take a stance towards ones own volition (i.e., represent one's own acts of wanting or entertaining certain goals). This argument starts with a representational analysis of intentional action.

2 Intentional action as meta-intentional

To see why intentional action involves meta-intentional representations it is best to contrast it with other behaviour and action that is not intentional. All behaviour is activity in the service of achieving some goal. However, for achieving a goal, the goal itself need not be represented by the organism. McFarland (1989a) speaks of *goal-seeking* or *goal-achieving* systems, and animal psychologists (e.g., Heyes and Dickinson, 1993) speak of responses to stimuli. Here, the organism is seen as having a tendency to behave in a certain way in response to a particular stimulus. This behaviour, though, is goal seeking in the sense that, due to the existing contingencies in the world, it brings the organism closer to the goal that satisfies its motivational state. The behaviour is, however, not primarily under the control of the organism but under that of the stimulus.

Action, in contrast to responses, requires the organism to represent its desired goal and to represent which action leads to that (desired) state (e.g., Heyes and Dickinson, 1993). In this case the behaviour is directed by the goal (McFarland, 1989a) and by knowledge of worldly contingencies. Yet, it is still not fully under the organism's control, as the organism remains the slave to its desires (Frankfurt, 1971).

Of fully controlled action we can only speak if the organism represents the determinants of its actions (i.e., its desires and knowledge of contingencies) and can thus have the potential for deliberating changes in its desires and knowledge. For instance, what would be required is knowledge of the fact that the goal is what one *wants* and knowledge of the fact that one acts because one knows that this action leads to what one wants. McFarland (1989b) captured this by saying that the organism needs a declarative representation of what it believes its behaviour to be about (see Appendix for the distinction between declarative and procedural representations in this context).

That some such higher-order knowledge is involved in intentional action – action which is fully under our control and for which we, therefore, are held responsible – is plausible from the following thought experiment. Assume we did an implicit memory experiment on people who desperately hate their uncles. Half of the group is subliminally made to believe that the combination of two individually beneficial substances form a hitherto unknown poisonous mixture (experimental condition). Indeed, a substantial proportion of them add this mixture to their uncle's medicine. In contrast, none of the control subjects do so, who also hate their uncle but have not been exposed to this subliminal information. This shows that our experimental subjects believed that the combination is poisonous. Yet, when asked, none of them (genuinely) reports having received this information or knowing this novel fact. It would be hard to accuse them of intentionally trying to kill their uncle, wouldn't it?

Searle (1983) argued that for intentional action for which we bear responsibility it is not enough that our intentions cause the action, but that they have to be causally self-referential in the sense that our intentions specify that they are intended to cause our action. His case rests on examples like that of the young man (one of the participants in the above thought experiment) who intends to kill his uncle. This intention causes him to overlook a pedestrian, resulting in a fatal accident for the pedestrian who happens to be his uncle. Even though the intention was causally responsible for the death of the uncle, the young man could not be accused of murder because, so Searle claims, the young man's intention did not causally self-referentially specify that the particular lethal action be caused by it.

To my mind these analyses and thought experiments demonstrate that higher-order meta-volitions play a necessary role in the origins of intentional action. However, one should not conclude that their role is as immediate triggers of such action, i.e., it may not be necessary for intentional action that an occurrent thought 'I intend my intention to be the cause of this action', or 'I know that this action leads to the result I desire' be part of the internal trigger of the action. It may be sufficient that these higher-order volitions and thoughts only play a role in *installing* representationally less complex S–R schemata which are sufficient on their own for triggering intentional action at the precise instant. In other words, the higher-order volitions are not unmediated internal causes of action (Goschke, 1996, pp. 601–11) but are causally one step removed as modulators of the direct causes of action (S–R schemata). This idea is also compatible with the SAS model of action control put forward by Norman and Shallice. I will now look whether meta-intentions are necessary for those tasks for which the SAS is supposed to be required.

3 The meta-intentional nature of the SAS

Norman and Shallice's (1980/6) model is a particularly useful one since it gives a fairly detailed account of how automatic action is controlled and provides an empirical specification for when 'supervisory' control (the SAS) is required. Two dimensions of control structure are postulated: the *horizontal* strands, responsible for automatic, well established action sequences, and the *vertical* strand involving the SAS, as shown in Figure 13.1.

The lowest level consists of particular modular processing structures for producing action. They are controlled by the middle layer of action (and thought) schemata, akin to productions in a production system (Shallice, 1994). This layer of control constitutes the *horizontal strands*, which are basically complex versions of the behaviourists' responses. They consist of schemata that are triggered by appropriate environmental and internal stimuli (e.g., in Anderson's, 1983, ACT model productions fire when their triggering conditions match external conditions and the contents of the goal box[1]). Any conflict between these schemata is resolved by a mutually inhibitory process called *contention scheduling*.

The top layer consists of the Supervisory Attentional System (SAS) that exerts control *vertically* onto the schemata of the horizontal strands. According to Norman and Shallice (1980, p. 14) this vertical strand of control has access to, among other things: past and present states of the

[1] It is important to note that the representation of the goal (desire) box in these productions is only procedural, not declarative (see Appendix).

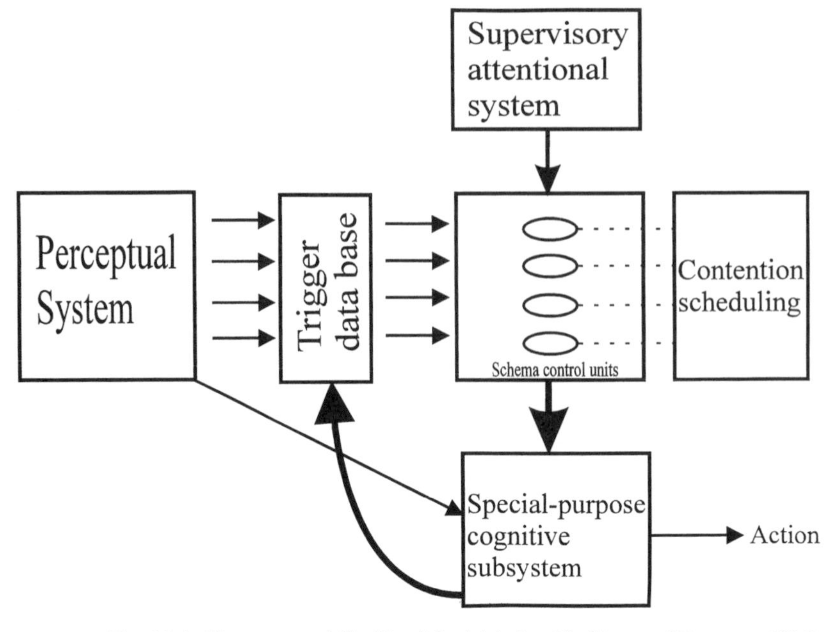

Fig. 13.1. Norman and Shallice Model (after Shallice and Burgess, 1993)

environment, goals, intentions, the schemata (of the horizontal strands) and aspects of the operation of those schemata. Vertical control is not routinely required, but only on occasion. Norman and Shallice (1986, pp. 2–3) provide the following list of *'SAS-tasks'*:

(1) planning/decision-making;
(2) trouble shooting;
(3) novel/ill-learned action sequences;
(4) dangerous or technically difficult actions;
(5) overcoming strong habitual response tendencies or temptation (e.g., Stroop).

My aim is now to show that all these tasks require a facility (my interpretation of the SAS) that has access to *declarative* representations of ones goals. To develop my argument let me first focus on how novel schemata are formed (case 3). The horizontal control strands involve established schemata that sort out their priorities automatically by a conflict resolution algorithm which is well established in itself (contention scheduling). How can new schemata be instantiated? There are three main ways: learning through trial and error, verbal instructions, and planning.

In trial-and-error learning an S–R association (schema, production, connection) is activated (initially by sheer accident or through shaping by a trainer). Positive feedback then strengthens this association until it becomes the predominant response to the particular stimulus conditions, i.e., a novel schema has been established. The critical point here is that the feedback mechanism adjusts the association strength of whichever schema has been activated without representing that schema or its representational (intentional) content. Learning through feedback is, therefore, wholly within the pail of contention scheduling. The vertical strands of the SAS are not needed. And indeed, what Norman and Shallice have in mind is not learning through trial and error but the ability of frontal lobe patients to follow verbal instructions or to engage in planning (case 1).

The ability to follow *verbal instructions* or engage in *planning* may establish a novel schema by the same means as learning through feedback as envisaged in the SAS model: it strengthens the relevant association between stimulus and response. The difference is that the relevant schema cannot be selected on the basis of current activation, since no schema has been activated. The control mechanism responsible for strengthening the relevant schema must, therefore, address the schema by its content, e.g., if the instructions or the result of the planning are 'if S1 then do A1' then the link between S1 and A1 has to be strengthened – under content descriptions S1 and A1 and not under the description of being an active link.

So, for this to work one has to first know what the verbal instructions or the results of the planning are. This knowledge must consist of a declarative representation marked as representing something desired (rather than as facts), i.e., as something the speaker wants me to do or as something that is best for me that I should do.

Knowing what the speaker wants me to do, and even knowing what I should do (due to my own deliberations), does not necessarily make me intend to do it. I still need to appropriate his desire or my insight in what is best for me as my desire, and turn it into an actual response tendency. The first step in this appropriation is to make a decision to do this. What does this act of deciding consist in? One plausible interpretation is that it consists in the initiation of a higher-order schema which installs lower-order schemata, i.e., an actual procedure (action tendency), so that I will indeed do A1 when S1 arises. For this we must be equipped with a sort of higher-order action schema, that given the desire to do A1 when S1 occurs strengthens the association between S1 and A1:

> Higher-order schema: 'I should [do a1 when s1 occurs] $\rightarrow$ "s1 $\rightarrow$ a1"'[2]

[2] With 's1 $\rightarrow$ a1' I denote the mental implementation of the action tendency (schema S1 $\Rightarrow$ A1) to do action A1 in stimulus situation S1. Accordingly, 's1' denotes the procedural representation (see Appendix) of S1, 'a1' of A1, and '$\rightarrow$' denotes the causal link between the occurrence of 's1' leading to an occurrence of 'a1' which procedurally represents the sequential link '$\Rightarrow$' between stimulus and response.

Importantly, this higher-order schema is itself just an action tendency (i.e., a mechanism that reacts to my higher-order intentions by installing/modulating the appropriate first-order action tendency). It is not a declarative representation of that mechanism. In that sense it is not different from contention scheduling where one schema influences the activation of other schemata through mutual inhibition or excitation. What makes it different from contention scheduling is that one part of it is not an action schema but a meta-intentional state with a declarative representation of what I want.

This is the appropriate point to hark back to the issue of intentional action being meta-intentional and causally self-referential (Searle, 1983). As a rough definition we could say that an intentional action is one that is due to an action schema which has been established by such a higher-order schema (and has not been overlooked for revision by a new higher-order schema that should have deactivated it). Even though there is no declarative representation of causal self-referentiality involved in this process of establishing an action schema, it can explain why Searle's young man cannot be accused of murdering his uncle. The killing was unintentional, since despite the clear deliberation of killing his uncle the actual fatal act was not due to an action schema of the form, 'when my uncle is in front of the car – run him over' that was installed (made dominant) by the explicit deliberations (planning).

This need not mean that Searle's criterion of causal self-reference is completely beside the point. Even though there need be no declarative representation of intending one's intention to be causally responsible for one's action, the higher-order schema could be said to 'procedurally' represent such causal self-reference since it has the function to implement action schemata as causes of actions in accordance with one's intentions.

Back to the main topic. I have shown that the installing of novel action schemata by verbal instructions or through planning (case 1) requires access to declarative representations of one's desires, so that the correct novel action schema can be boosted. The same holds for the further strengthening of novel and ill-learned action sequences (case 3) and the strengthening of dangerous and difficult actions in order to ensure careful execution (case 4).

In sum, cases (1, 3, and 4) require representation of a certain course of action as the desired one (meta-intentional representation) in order to implement a new action schema. I call the required representations 'meta-intentional' because one has to be in a higher-order intentional state of knowing, wanting or deciding that has as its content another intentional state. For this, I need *not* represent that there is some physical carrier (representational vehicle) representing these propositions (representational content) (see Perner, 1991, 1995). For that reason I refer to these higher-order mental states as 'meta-intentional' and not as 'meta-representational'. For cases (2 and 5) in Norman and Shallice's list, metarepresentation might be required.

4 Meta-representational requirements

In contrast to tasks 1, 3, and 4 which concern novel or difficult action schemata, tasks 2 and 5 concern the interference from or malfunctioning of particular well-established schemata. One way of controlling an interfering schema (Case 5) is by representing the action sequence that is generated by this schema as *undesirable*. In analogy to the representation of *desired* sequences boosting the corresponding schemata implanting these sequences, the representation of undesirable sequences could inhibit the corresponding schemata.

The problem is that infinitely many action sequences are undesirable. Why pick on that particular one? The reason is that it is one that is implemented in my schemata. Hence to know which action sequences to watch out for I have to conceptualise them as action tendencies that I have. In other words, I (my SAS) needs to concern myself with the meta-representational issue of a causal reason for why I act a certain way.

Although Norman and Shallice only mention habits and temptations as examples of Case 5, the above reasoning also applies to the case of a new schema 's1 → a2' competing against an old (even though not very powerful) schema with the same external trigger: 's1 → a1' . The only factor favouring the new over the old is the verbal instructions. In this case too, it might be necessary for the SAS to not just boost the new schema with its intentional content, but meta-represent the existence of the undesirable competitor in order to suppress it.

The meta-representational aspect is perhaps most clearly required for Case 4 (trouble shooting). Here too, the fault lies not with undesirable action sequences, but with the schemata implementing them, i.e., the vehicle implementing (and procedurally representing) undesirable action sequences.

The above distinction between tasks (1, 3, and 4) that need meta-intentional representations and tasks (2 and 5) that require meta-representational control, I want to claim, is also reflected in the development of self-control in step with children's growing theory of mind.

5 Executive function and theory of mind

Since executive functions are characterised by formulation of higher-order intentions and representations, they need the conceptual repertoire for expressing these higher-order states, i.e., a theory of mind. So one would expect people with a deficient theory of mind to have executive function problems. Wimmer (1989; Perner, 1991, chapter 9) made this suggestion for normal development, namely that children's self-control increases as their theory of mind improves. Frith (1992) made this connection for schizophrenia and autism.

Russell *et al.* (1991; 1994) produced data showing that executive problems (the inability to overcome the natural tendency of pointing where an object is rather than pointing to the empty box) are overcome at the age of about four years when children start to understand false belief. Similarly, Frye *et al.* (1995) found that understanding false belief (and related abilities, e.g., distinguishing appearance from reality) correlates with strategy change tasks. For instance, after a few trials where cards had to be sorted by colour such that the *red* car (S1) has to go to the red-flower location (R1) and the *yellow* flower (S2) has to go to the yellow-car location (R2), the sorting criterion changed so that the stimulus–response contingencies reversed: S1 – R2, and S2 – R1. Zelazo *et al.*, (1996) reported that the young children are able to state the new sorting criterion (cars go to the car-location, flowers to the flower-location), but when handed a stimulus card they sort it the old way.

Also older children with autism who fail false belief tests have similar executive problems as three year olds (Russell *et al.*, 1991). These data can be interpreted in two ways (Bishop, 1993): either they show that theory of mind tests rely on executive function abilities (e.g., Russell, 1996, p. 165, section 3.4), or executive function requires theory of mind (Perner, 1993). Ozonoff *et al.* (1991) reported that children with autism had a more severe impairment of executive function (Wisconsin Card Sorting) than theory of mind. Although the authors' conclusion was that, therefore, executive function deficits are more central to autism, this evidence is also compatible with the position that a theory of mind deficit is primary and the executive function depends on theory of mind. For, in that case a partial impairment in theory of mind should result in a more severe impairment on executive function tasks since the SAS's dependence on theory of mind magnifies the theory of mind impairment.

There is some evidence in the theory of mind literature that makes it implausible that young children's failure on the false belief test reflects an executive function problem. The typical ploy is to argue that children have a dominant strategy to predict that a person will go to get a desired object where the object really is (the typical error in the false belief task). The central executive is required (Russell, 1996, p. 223) to prop up the weakly established rule (take into consideration what the person thinks, i.e., an instance of case 1 of Norman and Shallice) and to suppress the dominant reality-oriented prediction strategy (an instance of case 5). Independently of any executive function problems, the 'pull of reality' has been seen by many as a central difficulty of the young with the false-belief task (e.g., Fodor, 1992; Mitchell, 1994; Zaitchik, 1991). Although there is some evidence for this position, the empirical evidence at large speaks against it (see Perner, 1995 for a lengthy discussion and counter-evidence, and also Russell, 1996, for a very cautious stance in favour of executive function problems).

Additional evidence against executive function problems in the false belief task is provided by the finding that children show awareness of the false belief by *looking at* the correct location where the protagonist thinks the object is, before they can answer explicitly with the correct location (Clements and Perner, 1994). Furthermore, if children have to act, e.g., to move a mat to catch the protagonist, children tend to move it to the correct location (as many as look to it) provided they move it spontaneously (Clements, 1995). Of those children who need prompting only a few move the mat to the correct location (as few as give correct verbal answers). If answering the false belief question were an executive problem of overcoming the pull of reality then one would expect that that pull would be first overcome in the hesitant, reflected action or verbal answers and not – as the data show – in (unconscious) looking or spontaneous, unreflected action. If anything, it should be spontaneous action that is governed by the horizontal strands of control escaping the control of the executive and not verbal responses.

If performance on false belief tests cannot be explained by executive demands of the test then we need another explanation of the developmental and psycho-pathological correlations between performance on the false-belief test and the executive-function test. The only other game in town is that the conceptual advances assessed by the false-belief test are required for certain executive functions, in particular those that I have identified above as requiring meta-representational concerns (above and beyond the meta-intentional concerns that are defining of executive function). It is clear that not all tasks for which the SAS is deemed necessary pose a problem for three-year old children – for instance, establishing a novel action sequence through verbal instruction (Case 3). To illustrate, Frye *et al.* (1995) instructed even their youngest children successfully and without much difficulty to sort cards according to one criterion (novel action sequence).[3] These children's problems only started when the now-existing action sequence had to be replaced upon new instructions with an incompatible one.

[3] Novel action schemata of this complexity do pose a problem for children below the age of three years (Zelazo and Reznick, 1991).

In my analysis of the SAS above I argued that implementing a new action sequence requires the meta-intentional capacity of declaratively representing the content of the verbal instructions as something desired. An existing higher-order action schema can then implement the desired S–R sequence as a first level procedure. Representation of the instructions' intentional content is necessary so that the higher-order procedure strengthens the connection between the correct stimulus-response pair. No representation of the existence of any particular first-level procedure is needed. However, when the new schema has to be implemented in opposition to an existing schema one has to make the existence of a particular action schema of undesirable properties a theme, i.e., one has to *represent* the existence of the *representational* vehicle implementing the undesirable action sequence in order to influence (suppress) that particular schema. In other words, the task that children have difficulty with is one that requires meta-representational abilities.

That this ability should develop in parallel with children's understanding of false belief makes good sense on my theory (Perner, 1991, 1995) that the specific difficulty in the false-belief test is the need to understand that the holder of the belief conceives of something (reality) as being different. Since this distinction is essentially the same as that required for understanding representations as entities that represent something as being a certain way, my suggestion is that understanding of false belief develops within the context of the theoretically related concept of representation in general. Recently we have started to obtain suggestive evidence for this position. Parkin (1994) found that the ability to describe the intentional content of misleading direction signs (that unlike pictures require understanding of the fact that they misrepresent reality as being different) correlates highly with understanding false belief. Doherty (1995) investigated children's understanding of synonyms as being different representational vehicles with the same meaning and found high correlations with understanding false belief after partialling out mental age.

6 Rounding off: conscious thought and language

I have argued that an interface with declarative representation of meta-intentions is a necessary and uniting feature of all intentional and controlled action (executive function) as assessed by the 'SAS tasks'. These tasks include planning, following of verbal instructions, and the suppression of predominant action tendencies. Interestingly, these activities also share the feature that they are carried out consciously. The intuition that this connection is more than a coincidence has led Jacoby (1991) in his process dissociation technique to use escape from voluntary control as a measure of implicitness/unconsciousness. The question now is how the connection between volition, planning, language use and consciousness can be integrated into my argument.

My analysis can be extended in that direction with the help of the Higher-Order Thought Theory of consciousness. Alternative versions of this theory differ as to the nature of the second-order state required. For instance, Armstrong (1980) sees it as a perceptual state, Rosenthal (1986) as a more cognitive state (higher-order, non-dispositional, assertoric), and Carruthers (1996a) sees it as a potential for being recursively embedded in higher-order states. According to Carruthers a content is conscious if it is held in a C store (C for *c*onscious) whose function it is to make contents recursively accessible to other thoughts. Carruthers uses the notion of a central C store only exemplarily as a convenient example of how recursive accessibility could be implemented. He emphasises (p. 218) that there need be no physiologically identifiable central store. It can be functionally distributed. In fact, instead of 'being in the C-store' it could be any other feature of a representation that makes it recursively accessible to higher-order thoughts. If we now assume that whichever feature makes a representation recursively accessible to higher-order thoughts also makes it accessible to other propositional attitudes and vice versa then we can explain why volition, planning and linguistic acts tend to be conscious.

Intentional and controlled action (SAS tasks) are conscious because, according to my argument, these actions depend on declarative meta-intentional representations of the situation-action-goal sequence. Hence, these sequences must be represented in such a way that they are recursively accessible to higher-order states, which is the hallmark of consciousness. Moreover, as Carruthers has pointed out for consciousness, the fact that higher-order thoughts contain a proposition about ourselves as holders of the first order attitude explains why intentional action (and consciousness) involves a sense of 'self', an agent who is in charge of such action.

The content of planning (and of other acts of hypothetical thinking) is conscious because thoughts about hypothetical action sequences must mark these sequences as 'merely existing in thought' (as opposed to being real). Hence the *knowledge* that these sequences are merely *thought* about constitutes a higher-order thought which, by the theory, makes its content conscious.

To bring language into this picture we need to admit the intentional relationship between the linguistic vehicle and its content (meaning) on a par with the mental attitudes and their intentional content. Normal language production and comprehension co-ordinates the linguistic vehicle with its intentional content. Hence, the mental processes of language production and comprehension are meta-intentional states since their contents concern the intentional relationship between linguistic vehicle and its content. By hypothesis, the contents of our linguistic exchanges are represented in such a way that they are recursively accessible to higher-order intentional states, which makes them conscious.

This fits our intuition that we cannot steer successfully through a meaningful linguistic exchange like an absent minded driver can steer her car through the vicissitudes of rush hour traffic. There are exceptions – e.g., when I sing the daily lullaby to my children I can steer the right course through long stretches of the song and then suddenly realise that my mind had been wandering without any awareness left of what I had been singing. But there is no contradiction since the right sequence of words in a well practised song can be produced without any concern for their meaning. In other words, that kind of linguistic production is not a meta-intentional act. On the comprehension side we also find the confirmatory intuition that, although we can 'listen' to someone's instructions without paying attention, such 'listening' will not enable us to follow those instructions successfully. It may be the key to hypnosis that the natural link between language, volition and consciousness becomes severed.

In sum, my analysis proceeded from showing that our common-sense notion of intentional action and the empirical test for controlled action (SAS tasks) presuppose declarative representation of one's volitions. This requirement provides a theoretical basis for relating the acquisition of self-control to advances in theory of mind and explains why volition together with language-use tend to be conscious. It also makes it unnecessary to delegate these 'executive functions' to a central agency within us, a homunculus that has little explanatory value (Baddeley, 1996). This gives me leave to agree with Dennett's (conference discussion) dictum: 'It's contention scheduling all the way up' – it's only that some contentions are more equal than others.

Appendix

Procedural and declarative knowledge

Although the distinction between procedural and declarative representations (knowledge) is often appealed to, it is hardly ever spelled out clearly what precisely it amounts to. So, I will try to spell it out in the context of how action schemata (S–R associations) can be said to represent. Schemata are procedures that make the organism do something under certain conditions. Such procedures are often said to incorporate procedural knowledge, e.g., that the animal knows how to get food. That suggests that it represents the contingencies that response R1 in situation S1 leads to reward. So what precisely is 'procedural' as opposed to 'declarative' about this representation?

On the surface the distinction is, of course, that procedural knowledge is active and effects behaviour, while declarative knowledge is mere passive contemplation. I want to argue that underneath this surface difference lies a deeper representational distinction that has to do with declarative knowledge representing *that* something is the case.

To see what the difference is let me point out what is amiss in the schema 's1 → r1' as procedural representation of the regularity that S1 is followed by R1, i.e.: S1 ⇒ R1. In particular what does the schema represent about S1? This representation is dormant most of the time. It is a tacit thought or belief about S1. When it gets activated by S1 because the appropriate stimulus impinges on the organism's sensory system, we can say that the organism has an occurrent thought about S1, *or* that it knows (believes) that S1 is the case. But those are two different things: the *occurrence of the thought about S1* and the *occurrence of S1*. The point is that in the case of the procedural representation they cannot be separated. This is fine for the purpose of procedures but not for declarative representations, because I could not think about S1 in the absence of S1 without being deluded about the presence of S1.

What is needed for declarative representations to make the necessary distinction is to separately represent particular situations, their type and their occurrence. This allows predication of occurrence (at a particular time) and type – like in language where I can refer to a particular situation as the one that is the case now and as being of a certain kind: 'What is happening *now* is that I (the rat) am in the room with the lever to press.' We have been using the term predication–explicit (Dienes and Perner, 1996; Perner, 1996) for representations that offer that facility. In the case of the procedural representation one can say that the predication of type of situation and its occurrence are implicit in the occurrence of the thought about the situation.

Without predication these representations would not be fit as propositional contents that stipulate satisfaction conditions. For, to know [s1] or to want [s1] it is important to distinguish whether S1 is or is not the case because to know is to know that S1 is the case and to want is to desire that S1 materialise.

I would like to express my gratitude to Peter Carruthers who helped shape the idea to this chapter and for his extensive comments on an earlier draft; to Dan Dennett, Stevan Harnad, Barry Lee, Gabriel Segal, Barry Smith, and Andrew Woodfield for their insightful comments and helpful references to relevant literature after my conference presentation.

14 Reflections on language and mind

Daniel C. Dennett

1 A seductive bad idea: central processing

A theme that emerged at the Sheffield Conference with particular force, to my way of thinking, was a new way of recognising, and then avoiding, a seductive bad idea. One of its many guises is what I have called the Cartesian Theatre, but it also appears in the roles of Central Processing, or Central Executive, or Norman and Shallice's SAS, or Fodor's non-modular central arena of belief fixation. What is wrong with this idea is not (just) that it (apparently) postulates an *anatomically* discernible central region of the brain – maximally non-peripheral, one might say – but that it supposes that there is a functionally identifiable *subsystem* (however located or even distributed in the brain) that has some all too remarkable competencies achieved by some all too remarkable means. There are many routes to it. Here is one that starts off in an excellent direction but then veers off. The mistaken fork is not explicitly endorsed by anybody that I can think of, but I daresay it has covertly influenced a lot of thinking on the topic.

(a) One of the things we human beings do is talk to others.

(b) Another is that we talk to ourselves – out loud.

(c) A refinement of (b) is to talk silently to oneself, but still in the words of a natural language, often with tone of voice and timing still intact. (One can often answer such questions as this: 'Are you thinking in English or French as you work on this problem?')

So far, so good, but watch out for the next step:

(d) A further refinement of (c) is to drop the auditory/phonemic features (indeed all the features that would tie one's act to a specific natural language) and just think to oneself in *bare propositions*.

Introspection declares that something like this does indeed occur, but we must be circumspect in how we describe this phenomenon, since the temptation is to use it to anchor a remarkable set of dubious implications, to wit:

(e) Since propositions, like numbers, are abstract objects, they would need some vehicles of embodiment in the brain. Moreover, when one thinks in bare propositions, one's thoughts still have one feature of sentences:

logical form. (They must have logical form if we are going to explain the phenomenon of reliable deductive inference as the manipulation of these items.) So there must be a medium of representation distinct from any natural language (call it the Language of Thought, or LOT) that has this feature.

And finally:

(f) This activity of manipulating formulae of LOT is the fundamental variety of thinking – 'thinking proper' or 'real thinking' or even (as somebody said in discussion at Sheffield) 'where the understanding happens.'

When someone, for instance Peter Carruthers, speaks of 'the use of peripheral modules in central processing,' this *suggests* (without quite assuming or implying) that there is a LOT-wielding central processing system surrounding itself with a set of tools that can be put to use, on occasion, to augment the fundamental thinking powers of the LOT system. The central processing unit (CPU) of a von Neumann machine, with its requirement that all instructions be in its proprietary machine language – the only language it 'understands' – is perhaps the chief inspiration for this image.

But there are other ways of imagining the phenomenon of wordless thought. It can be seen as a rather exotic specimen instead of the foundation of all cognition, a type of mental event that rather rarely occurs, and depends, when it does, on the preparation of the thinker's mind for this sort of feat by years of practice with more explicit, word-clothed or image-supported varieties of self-stimulation. Contrast the all too inviting image of a systematic central clearing-house conducting all its affairs in its inborn *lingua franca* with the image of an anarchic, *competitive* arena in which many different sorts of things happen – Grand Central Station, in which groups of visitors speaking many tongues try to find like-minded cohorts by calling out to each other, sweeping across the floor in growing crowds, waving their hands, pushing and shoving and gesturing. In this vision, most successful activities depend on enlisting large multi-modal coalitions, involving the excitation of several largish areas simultaneously, but occasionally swifter, more efficient contacts co-ordinate activity with hardly any commotion at all. These rare, hyper-sophisticated transitions occur when very sketchy images of linguistic representations serve as mnemonic triggers for 'inferential' processes that generate further sketchy images of linguistic representations and so forth.

It may not be words that we learn how to leave out when we engage in such wordless thought. This sort of short-cut transition can take place in any modality, any system of associations. For a trained musician, the circle of fifths imposes itself automatically and involuntarily on a fragment of heard or imagined music, just the way *modus ponens* intrudes on the perceptions of a trained logician, or the offside line does on a trained soccer player. This way of trying to imagine word-free 'logical inference' makes it look rather like barefoot water-skiing – a stunt that professionals can make look easy, hardly the basic building block of successful transportation or cognition in the everyday concrete world. It is just an impressionistic image, so far, but without such images-in-advance-of-models, we tend to get sucked back into the image of the LOT-wielding CPU, as if it were the only possible way our minds could work.

We do introspect ourselves thinking, and sometimes it does seem that our thinking is wordless but 'propositional.' This is an indisputable (hetero) phenomenological fact.[1] It is bolstered by such widely acknowledged experiences as the tip-of-the-tongue phenomenon, in which we surely do have a particular content 'in mind' and are frustrated in our attempts to find the word that normally clothes it or accompanies it. Publishers have brought out humorous dictionaries of neologisms to fill in the gaps in English: 'sniglets' is proposed, I seem to recall, as a word for those handy little metal sleeves on the ends of shoelaces, and 'yinks' would name the pathetic strands of hair that some men drape carefully but ineffectively over their bald spots. We have all thought of (noticed, reflected upon) these items before – that's why these books are able to strike a humorous chord in us – so obviously we can have bare or wordless concepts in our consciousness. And so, it seems, we can think bare propositions composed of them.

This kind of thinking is a personal level activity, an intentional activity, something we *do*. (Think of the sign that admonishes 'THINK!') It is not just something that happens in our bodies. When we think thoughts of this sort, we do, it seems, *manipulate* our thoughts, and it can be difficult or easy work. The undeniable existence of this important variety of phenomena obliged Gilbert Ryle to include in *The Concept of Mind* (1949) his notoriously unsuccessful late chapter on 'The Intellect,' but also impelled him, for the rest of his career (see Ryle, 1979), to grapple with a tantalising question about *Le Penseur*, Rodin's famous chin-in-fist concentrator: What is he *doing*?

These phenomena are part of the hetero-phenomenology of consciousness, and hence form part of the explicandum of any theory. But it is *not* given to introspection, nor does it follow from any well-considered theoretical considerations, that the cognitive transitions in us that are not personal actions but do just happen in our bodies, occur in a 'propositional' medium involving the transformation or manipulation of formulae of LOT.

[1] Hetero-phenomenology is phenomenology from the third-person point of view, or in other words, the empirical, scientific study of the way it seems to individual subjects of experience. The methods and assumptions of hetero-phenomenology are explained and defended in Dennett, 1982 and 1991.

Even if the (d) phenomenon occurs quite frequently *in people like us*, professional thinkers, (e) and (f) do not follow, and there are good reasons to resist them. Here is one of the most important. If we view LOT or Mentalese as the *lingua franca* of all cognition, and view it as 'automatically understood', this apparently secures a 'solution' to the problem of understanding. But in spite of declarations by Fodor and others that LOT does not itself require interpretation by the brain that speaks it, this solution-by-fiat is both unsupported and costly: it creates an artifactual problem about the 'access' of consciousness.

How? If Mentalese is the *lingua franca* of all cognition, it must be the *lingua franca* of all the *unconscious* cognition in addition to the conscious thinking. Unconscious cognitive processes are granted on all sides, and if it is conducted in Mentalese (as is commonly asserted or assumed by theorists of the LOT persuasion), getting some content translated into Mentalese cannot be sufficient for getting it into consciousness, even if it is sufficient for getting it understood. There must then be some further translation or transduction, into an even more central arena than Central Processing, into some extra system – for instance, Ned Block's (1991) postulated consciousness module. Beyond understanding lies conscious appreciation, according to this image, and it needs a place to happen in.[2] This is what I have called the Myth of Double Transduction, and I have criticised it elsewhere (Dennett, 1996a), and will not pursue it further here.

2 A better idea: contention scheduling all the way up

The person – the star of the personal level – who does the thinking is not and cannot be a central subsystem. The person must be the supersystem composed of the subsystems, but it is hard to understand how this could be so.

If 'Central Processing' were understood to be just the name of a centralish arena in which competitions are held, with no knowing supervisor, it would not be an objectionable term. If there is no central agent doing things – and hence no problem of *this agent's* 'access' to anything, then the only access that needs accounting for is the access that one subsystem or another has to the fruits of another subsystem. (We could acquiesce in the jargon and call these modules or quasi-modules, but unlike Fodorian modules, they do not pour their output into Central Processing, there to be 'accessed' by . . . *Moi*.) We have to get rid of the Central Understander, the Central

[2] If we follow Jackendoff's idea (1987), this would not be the *central* summit but a sort of ring surrounding that summit – a tempting idea, but not, I think, one to run with. (I'd rather get the benefits of Jackendoff's vision by other routes, other images, but that's a topic for another occasion.)

Meaner, the Central Thinker. And to accomplish this, the thoughts are going to have to think themselves somehow.

How? By 'contention scheduling' all the way up. (I am particularly grateful to Josef Perner for re-introducing Norman and Shallice's model into the discussion at Sheffield.) Norman and Shallice (1980) contrasted 'automatic' contention scheduling – an unsupervised competition between independent modules that handles the routine bulk of unconscious conflict resolutions – with the labours of the Supervisory Attentional System (SAS), an ominously wise overseer-homunculus who handles the hard cases in the workshop of consciousness.

Shallice's 1988 book has some valuable insights on how to soften this contrast, but I propose to reject it altogether. How could the Supervisory Attentional System do its work? To the Norman and Shallice model of low-level contention scheduling we have to add layers (layers upon layers) of *further* contention scheduling, with suppression, coalition, subversion, and so forth of higher-level contestants.

How could the SAS suppress the habits determined by lower-level contention scheduling? A homunculus with big strong arms? No. These habits have to be resisted by counter-habits, things of basically the same sort: further contestants, in other words. What are these contestants? We might as well call them 'thoughts' made out of 'concepts,' but we mustn't understand these in the traditional way. You don't move your thoughts around; your thoughts move you around. You don't make your thoughts; your thoughts make you.

Several participants at Sheffield expressed the basic idea: 'cognition is deeply involved in dialogical activity', 'cognitive and communicative factors merge'. How could thinking be anything other than communicating? The bad idea supposes that propositions get 'grasped' by the mind (as Frege said) when they get expressed in Mentalese. But how could a brain's central system merely writing Mentalese in itself count as thinking? How could that do any work, how could that guarantee understanding? Only by enabling something. What? Enabling the multitudinous items of information that are variously distributed and embedded around in the brain to influence each other, and ongoing processes, so that new, better informational structures get *built* (usually temporarily) and then further manipulated. But the manipulanda have to manipulate themselves.

For many years, Douglas Hofstadter has spoken of 'active symbols', an epithet which surely points in the right direction, since it moves us away from the idea of inert, passive symbols that just lie there until manipulated by some knowing symbol-user. The germ of truth in the idea of using the von Neumann machine CPU as our model of Central Processing is the fact that each member of the CPU's instruction set is a sort – a rigid sort – of active symbol. Whenever it appears in the instruction register, its mere tokening there makes something happen; it triggers a specific activity – adding or multiplying or checking the sign of the number in the accumulator, or whatever – because its defining shape *turns on* a particular bit of special-purpose circuitry. These symbols are all imperatives, the 'understanding' of which consists in automatic obedience. There may be hundreds of specialised circuits or just a few (as in the recent return to Reduced Instruction Set Computers); in either case the vocabulary is in tight correspondence to the hardware (or micro-code). Unless Mentalese is considered to be restricted to such imperatives of internal operation (and I have never encountered so much as a hint of this in philosophers' discussions of it), there is simply no analogy at all between Mentalese and machine language. So the promise of 'automatic understanding' of Mentalese or LOT is an empty one.

3 Making tools to think with

Now we need to work out how active symbols might come into existence. Andy Clark and Annette Karmiloff-Smith (1994) contrast embedded concepts with those that are disembedded via re-representation, and Josef Perner (this volume, chapter 13) speaks of explicit concepts. How does this re-representation or explicitation multiply the powers of a concept? Part of the answer may come from reconsidering Köhler's classic set of experiments with problem-solving apes (1925).

Contrary to popular misunderstanding, Köhler's apes did not just sit and think up the solutions. They had to have many hours of exposure to the relevant props – the boxes and sticks, for instance – and they engaged in much manipulation of these items. Those apes that discovered the solutions – some never did – accomplished it with the aid of many hours of trial and error manipulating. Now were they thinking when they were fussing about in their cages? What were they manipulating? Boxes and sticks. It is all too tempting to suppose that their external, visible manipulations were accompanied by, and driven by, internal, covert manipulations – but succumbing to this temptation is losing the main chance. What they were attending to, manipulating and turning over and rearranging were boxes and sticks, not thoughts.

We *Homo sapiens* engage in much similar behaviour, moving things around in the world. For instance, most Scrabble players would be seriously handicapped if they were prevented from sliding the little tiles around on their little shelf. We write words on index cards and slips of paper, doodle and diagram and sketch. These concrete activities are crutches for thinking, and once we get practised at these activities, we can internalise these manipulations.

Can you alphabetise the words in this sentence in your head?

Yes, probably, but what you do is not easy. It is not easy because, as Keith Frankish stressed in Sheffield, you have to *keep track of* things. To perform this stunt, you need to use visual imagery and auditory rehearsal. You work to make each component as vivid as possible, to help you do the required tracking. If we were to expand the task just a little bit by making the words hard to distinguish visually, or by lengthening the sentence, you would find it impossible to alphabetise in your head – and this very sentence is such an instance. Try it.

As Barry Smith noted at Sheffield, the metaphysical claim that thought depends on language can be traded in for something much more interesting: the scientific hypothesis that there is a deep natural necessity for thought – our kind of thought – to involve language. As he pointed out, 'Thoughts are not the sort of thing you can grasp like an apple (*pace* Frege)' – but words and sentences *are* things you can grasp like an apple. They are *manipulanda*, like Köhler's boxes and Scrabble tiles.

For the moment, set grammar (and logical form) aside and think of words just as isolated objects – images or labels, not parts of sentences obeying the relevant rules. This is not a natural act for a philosopher of language, so impressed have we all been with the combinatorial and analytic power of syntax. But you don't have to tie the good idea of inference to logical form. Some of us do on occasion think whole arguments in our heads – because we've taken and passed logic class. But it is obviously true that most people never engage in *explicit* non-enthymematic formal reasoning; whether people covertly or unconsciously do their thinking by symbol manipulation ought to be a matter of controversy at best. Johnson-Laird and others have urged us not to take this as our model for rational, useful thought. What other models do we have? Johnson-Laird's account of mental models (1983) is one, but I'll mention another: Hofstadter's model of analogical thinking (Mitchell, 1993; Hofstadter, 1995; French, 1995).

In Hofstadter and Mitchell's Copycat programme, a simple analogy-finding game is played, using the alphabet as the toy world in which all perception and action happens. Suppose it is my turn: I make a move by altering some alphabetic string. You must respond by altering your string (which is given in advance) 'in the same way'. Thus if my move is to turn 'abc' into 'abd' it is pretty obvious that your response should be to turn 'pqr' into 'pqs' (advancing the last or rightmost symbol in an alphabetic sequence by one). But what if your sequence was not 'pqr' but 'bbccdd'? Change it to 'bbccee' probably, treating the repetition of the letters as creating twin-elements to be treated as one. The 'probably' in the previous sentence is key. There are no correct or incorrect answers in Copycat, only better or worse, more or less satisfying or elegant or deep responses.

Consider if my move is to change 'fgh' to 'ffggghhhh'. What is your best move if your initial string is 'cba'? It might be 'ccbbbaaaa' or you might think that alphabetical order is more important than left-right order, and go instead with 'ccccbbbaa'. The Copycat programme plays this game. You give it your move (and its initial string) and it figures out a response. In the course of its deliberations, different 'concepts' are *built*, out of the existing resources. They are built on the fly, and allowed to evaporate when no longer needed. (A point also made by Sperber and Wilson, this volume, chapter 9.)

The Copycat programme does well on many Copycat problems, but there are classes of Copycat problems we human beings find relatively easy that are beyond it. Consider, for instance, your best response in the following case. I change 'abcdjf' to 'abcdef', and your string is 'pwppp'. Isn't it obvious that to do the same thing to your string you should turn it into 'ppppp'? We English speakers have a word (and concept) for this move: 'repair'. I fixed my defective alphabetic string, so you must fix your defective five-of-a-kind string. The concept of *repair* is a tool in your kit, but it simply cannot be built from the existing resources (to date) in Copycat. Similarly, as Andy Clark (this volume, chapter 8) demonstrates in his discussion of Thompson *et al.* (forthcoming), chimps can have their repertoire of *usable* concepts enlarged by adding a symbol for 'sameness'. This discrimination becomes available or usable by the chimps only when they are given a crutch: a token or symbol that they can lean on to help them track the pattern. The thought processes exhibited here (by Copycat, by the chimps) are familiar human thought processes, and they are not logical arguments; they are (roughly) processes of competitive concept-building. In order to engage in these processes, however, one must be able to keep track of the building blocks, and tracking and recognition are not for free. Our concepts are clothed in re-identifiable words for the same reason the players on a sports team are clothed in uniforms of the same *familiar* colour: so that they can keep track of each other better (so that they can find each other readily in the Grand Central Station of the brain).

4 What we can do with these tools that no other animals can do

If we are enabled to know things other animals don't know about their own minds, this has to have some payoff. There must be things we can do that they can't do. There are: lots. As Carruthers (this volume, chapter 5) says, the point of human consciousness is to make various mental contents recursively available for further processing. Consciousness enables us to *say* (to others) what we're doing. Less trivially, it enables us to say *to ourselves* what we're doing. And when we do this, we find we can (often) understand what we're saying! We can then use this little bit of extra leverage, leverage provided by our new recursive tool, to learn how to do things better. As Barry Smith noted at Sheffield, knowing you have a belief gains you leverage you don't have by just having that belief.

Consider a familiar human activity that we rely on in many problem-solving circumstances: we 'query the belief box', as somebody put it in Sheffield. We ask ourselves explicit questions. This practice has no readily imaginable counterpart in non-linguistic animals, but what does it gain us, if anything? I think the answer can be seen in Plato's analogy, in the *Theaetetus*, between human memory and an aviary:

> SOCRATES Now consider whether knowledge is a thing you can possess in that way without having it about you, like a man who has caught some wild birds – pigeons or what not – and keeps them in an aviary for them at home. In a sense, of course, we might say that he 'has' them all the time inasmuch as he possesses them, mightn't we?
>
> THEAETETUS Yes.
>
> SOCRATES But in another sense he 'has' none of them, though he has got control of them, now that he has made them captive in an enclosure of his own; he can take and have hold of them whenever he likes by catching any bird he chooses, and let them go again; and it is open to him to do that as often as he pleases.

Possession is good, but not much use unless you have the ability to get the right bird to come when you need it. How do we do it? By means of technology. We build elaborate systems of mnemonic association – pointers, labels, chutes and ladders, hooks and chains. We refine our resources by incessant rehearsal and tinkering, turning our brains (and all the associated peripheral gear we acquire) into a huge structured network of competencies. In our own case, the principle components of this technology for brain-manipulation are words, and no evidence yet unearthed shows that any other animal is capable of doing anything like what we do with our words.

Have you ever danced with a movie star? Do you know where to buy live eels? Could you climb five flights of stairs carrying a bicycle and a cello? These are questions the answers to which were probably not already formulated and handily stored in your brain, and yet they are readily answered reliably by most people. How do we do it? By engaging in relatively effortless and automatic 'reasoning'. (See Powers, 1987 for valuable reflections on these processes.) In the first case, if no recollection of the presumably memorable event is provoked by considering the question, you conclude that the answer is No. The second question initiates a swift survey (pet stores? fancy restaurants? fish markets or live bait dealers?), and the third provokes some mental imagery which 'automatically' poses the relevant further questions, which, when posed to the 'belief box', yield their answers. That is how we get the right birds to come – by asking ourselves questions (as Socrates noted) and discovering that we know the answers.

5 Consciousness: 'access' for whom?

Perner suggested at Sheffield that 'predicative representation is necessary for consciousness' a theme also expressed with variations by Carruthers and Smith. I suggest that such explicit predicative representation is typically sufficient for consciousness, but not necessary. What *is* necessary? Just the sort of cerebral dominance I have analogised to *fame*: Consciousness is more like fame than television (1996b). Contents 'enter consciousness' (a very misleading way of speaking) by being temporary winners of the competitions, persisting in the cerebral arena, and hence having more and more influence, more and more staying power (in memory – which is not a separate system or box). As Michael Holderness has aptly observed, the winners get to write history – indeed, that's what winning is, in the brain. One very good way of achieving cerebral celebrity is to form lots of coalitions with words and other labels. All this has to *happen* in the central arena, in 'central processing', but not under the direction of anything like a subsystem. The person is the Virtual Governor, not a real governor; the person is the *effect* of all the processes, not their cause.

A common reaction to this suggestion about human consciousness is frank bewilderment, expressed more or less as follows: 'Suppose all these strange competitive processes are going on in my brain, and suppose that, as you say, the conscious processes are simply those that win the competitions. How does *that* make them conscious? What happens next to them that makes it true that *I* know about them? For after all, it is *my* consciousness, as I know it from the first-person point of view, that needs explaining!' Such questions betray a deep confusion, for they presuppose that what *you* are is something *else*, some Cartesian *res cogitans* in addition to all this brain-and-body activity. What you are, however, just *is* this organisation of all the competitive activity between a host of competencies that your body has developed. You 'automatically' know about these things going on in your body, because if you didn't, it wouldn't be your body![3]

[3] Barry Smith noted at Sheffield that 'there is a way our minds are known to us that is not available to animal minds'. I agree, but I am inclined to disagree with his softening of this striking claim: 'There is no reason to deny them an inner life.' There is indeed a reason: They aren't *first persons* in the way we are. They don't have to be, so anything they have in the way of an inner life must be so dimensionally thin, so impoverished to the vanishing point as hardly to count as an inner life at all.

The acts and events you can tell us about, and the reasons for them, are yours because you made them – and because they made you. What you are is that agent whose life you can tell about. You can tell us, and you can tell yourself. The process of self-description begins in earliest childhood, and includes a good deal of fantasy from the outset. (Think of Snoopy in the *Peanuts* cartoon, sitting on his doghouse and thinking 'Here's the World War I ace, flying into battle. . .') It continues through life. (Think of the café waiter in Jean Paul Sartre's discussion of 'bad faith' in *Being and Nothingness* (1943), who is all wrapped up in learning how to live up to his self-description as a waiter.) It is what *we* do. It is what *we* are.[4]

Several speakers in Sheffield drew attention to cognitive abilities that are particularly human, and that thus raise the question of whether they can be shared even in rudimentary form by animals without language. Perner, for instance, drew attention to Norman and Shallice's list of the five specialities of the SAS: planning, troubleshooting, dealing with novelty, dealing with danger, and overcoming habits. There are plenty of familiar anecdotes proclaiming that birds and mammals – at least – exhibit these talents on occasion, but the very fact that these anecdotes get retold shows that they recount remarkable and impressive cases. Just how good are chimpanzees, really, at these five accomplishments, for instance? In addition to the anecdotes of glory, there is evidence, both experimental and anecdotal, of their widespread failure to rise to challenges of this sort. It is not easy to design experiments that test in both language-free and unequivocal fashion for such skills as troubleshooting or dealing with novelty, but the design project promises to repay us for our efforts in two ways. First, even when we are thwarted in our attempt to design a suitable experiment, the obstacles encountered may illuminate the role that language plays in our own case, and second, when we succeed, our experiments promise to clarify further the limits of non-linguistic thinking by other species.

[4] Parts of the preceding paragraphs are drawn, with slight revisions, from Dennett (1996a).

References

Acredolo, L. P. and Goodwyn, S. W. (1988). Symbolic gesturing in normal infants. *Child Development*, 59, 450–66.

(1990). The spontaneous development of symbolic gestures. In V. Volterra and C. Erting (eds.), *From Language to Gesture in Hearing and Deaf Children*. New York: Springer-Verlag, pp. 68–78.

Allen, C. and Bekoff, M. (1997). *Species of Mind: The Philosophy and Biology of Cognitive Ethology*. Cambridge, MA: MIT Press.

Anderson, J. R. (1983). *The Architecture of Cognition*. Cambridge, Mass: Harvard University Press.

Anderson, M. (1992). *Intelligence and Development: A Cognitive Theory*. Oxford: Blackwell.

Andrews, J., Livingston, K. and Harnad, S. (submitted). Categorical perception effects induced by category learning.

Antony, L. (1989). Anomalous monism and the problem of explanatory force. *Philosophical Review*, 98, 153–87.

(1991). The causal relevance of the mental. *Mind and Language*, 6, 295–327.

Armstrong, D. (1980). *The Nature of Mind and other Essays*. Ithaca: Cornell University Press.

Atran, S. (1990). *Cognitive Foundations of Natural History*. Cambridge: Cambridge University Press.

Atkinson, R. L., Atkinson, R. C., Smith, E., Bem, D, and Hilgard, E. (1990). *Introduction to Psychology*. San Diego: Harcourt Brace Jovanovich.

Avramides, A. (1989). *Meaning and Mind: An Examination of a Gricean Account of Language*. Cambridge Mass.: MIT Press.

Baddeley, A. (1986). *Working Memory*. Oxford: Oxford University Press.

(1988). *Human Memory*. Hillsdale, NJ: Lawrence Erlbaum.

(1996). Exploring the central executive. *The Quarterly Journal of Experimental Psychology*, 49A (1), 5–28.

Baddeley, A. and Hitch, G. J. (1974). Working memory. In G. Bower (ed.), *The Psychology of Learning and Motivation*, vol. 8, pp. 47–90. New York: Academic Press.

Baier, A. (1979). Mind and change of mind. *Midwest Studies in Philosophy*, 4, 157–76.

Barkow, J., Cosmides, L. and Tooby, J. (eds.), (1992). *The Adapted Mind*. Oxford: Oxford University Press.

Bar-On, D. (1995). 'Meaning' Reconstructed: Grice and the naturalizing of semantics. *Pacific Philosophical Quarterly*, 76, 83–116.

Baron-Cohen, S. (1988). Social and pragmatic deficits in autism: Cognitive or affective? *Journal of Autism and Developmental Disorders*, 18.3, 379–402.

(1994). How to build a baby that can read minds: cognitive mechanisms in mind-reading. *Current Psychology of Cognition*, 13(5), 513–52.

(1995). *Mindblindness: An Essay on Autism and Theory of Mind.* Cambridge, Mass.: MIT Press.

Baron-Cohen, S., Cox, A., Baird, G., Swettenham, J., Drew, A., Nightingale, N., Morgan, K. and Charman, T. (1996). Psychological markers of autism at eighteen months of age in a large population. *British Journal of Psychiatry*, vol. 168, 158–63.

Barsalou, L. (1987). The instability of graded structure: implications for the nature of concepts. In U. Neisser (ed.), *Concepts and Conceptual Development: Ecological and Intellectual Factors in Categorisation*, pp. 101–40. Cambridge: Cambridge University Press.

Bates, E., Bretherton, I. and Snyder, L. (1988). *From First Words to Grammar*. Cambridge: Cambridge University Press.

Bates, E. and MacWhinney, B. (1987). Competition, variation, and language learning. In B. MacWhinney (ed.), *Mechanisms of Language Acquisition.* Hillsdale, NJ: Lawrence Erlbaum, pp. 157–94.

Bates, E., Thal, D. and Marchman, V. (1991). Symbols and syntax: a Darwinian approach to language development. In N. Krasnegor, D. Rumbaugh, R. Schiefelbusch, and M. Studdert-Kennedy (eds.), *Biological and Behavioural Determinants of Language Development*. Hillsdale, NJ: Lawrence Erlbaum, pp. 29–66.

Bechtel, B. (1996). What should a connectionist philosophy of science look like? In R. McCauley (ed.), *The Churchlands and their Critics*, pp. 121–44. Oxford: Blackwell.

Bekken, K. (1989). Is there 'Motherese' in gesture? Unpublished doctoral dissertation, University of Chicago.

Bellugi, U., Marks, S., Bihrle, A. and Sabo, H. (1993). Dissociation between language and cognitive functions in Williams Syndrome. In Bishop and Mogford (eds.), *Language Development in Exceptional Circumstances*, pp. 177–89. Hillsdale, NJ: Lawrence Erlbaum.

Bennett, J. (1990). Why is belief involuntary? *Analysis*, 50, 87–107.

Benton, A. (1977). The amusias. In M. Critchley and R. Henson (eds.), *Music and the Brain*, pp. 378–97. London: Heinemann.

Berk, L. (1994). Why children talk to themselves. *Scientific American,* November, 78–83.

Berk, L. and R. Garvin. (1984). Development of private speech among low-income Appalachian children. *Developmental Psychology*, 20(2), 271–86.

Berman, R. A. and Slobin, D. I. (1994). *Relating Events in Narrative: A Crosslinguistic Developmental Study*. Hillsdale, NJ: Lawrence Erlbaum.

Bickerton, D. (1984). The language bioprogramme hypothesis. *The Behavioural and Brain Sciences*, 7, 173–88; 212–18.

(1990). *Language and Species.* Chicago: University of Chicago Press.

(1995). *Language and Human Behaviour*. Seattle: University of Washington Press, London: UCL Press.

Bishop, D. V. M. (1992). The underlying nature of specific language impairment. *Journal of Child Psychology and Psychiatry*, 33, 3–66.

(1993). Annotation: Autism, executive functions and theory of mind: A neuropsychological perspective. *Journal of Child Psychology and Psychiatry*, 34(3), 279–93.

Bivens, J. and Berk, L. (1990). A longitutional study of development of elementary school children's private speech. *Merril-Palmer Quarterly*, 36, 443–63.

Block, N. (1981). Psychologism and behaviorism. *Philosophical Review*, 90, 5–43.

(1990). The computer model of the mind. In D. N. Osherson and E. E. Smith (eds.), *An Invitation to Cognitive Science, Volume 3: Thinking*. Cambridge, Mass.: MIT Press, 247–89.

(1992). Begging the question against phenomenal consciousness (commentary on Kinsbourne and Dennett). *Behavioural and Brain Sciences*, 15, 205–6.

Bloom, L. (1970). *Language Development: Form and function in emerging grammars*. Cambridge, Mass.: MIT Press.

Bloom, L., Miller, P. and Hood, L. (1975). Variation and reduction as aspects of competence in language development. In A. Pick (ed.), *Minnesota Symposium on Child Psychology*, vol. 19, pp. 3–55. Minneapolis, University of Minnesota Press.

Bloom, P. (1990). Subjectless sentences in child language. *Linguistic Inquiry*, 21, 491–504.

Blumstein, S., Milberg, W. and Shrier, R. (1982). Semantic processing in aphasia: evidence from an auditory lexical decision task. *Brain and Language*, 17, 301–15.

Botterill, G. (1994). Beliefs, functionally discrete states, and connectionist networks: a comment on Ramsey, Stich and Garon. *British Journal for the Philosophy of Science*, 45, 899–906.

Bowerman, M. (1982). Reorganizational processes in lexical and syntactic development. In E. Wanner and L. R. Gleitman (eds.), *Language Acquisition: The State of the Art*, pp. 319–46. New York: Cambridge University Press.

Bratman, M. (1987). *Intentions, Plans and Practical Reason*. Cambridge, Mass.: Harvard University Press.

(1992). Practical reasoning and acceptance in a context. *Mind*, 101, 1–15.

Brewer, B. (1995). Compulsion by reason. *Proceedings of the Aristotelian Society, Supplementary Volume* 64, 237–53.

Broca, P. (1861). Remarques sur le siege de la faculte de la parole articulee, suivies d'une observation d'aphemie (perte de parole). *Bulletin de la Societe d'Anatomie* (Paris), 36, 330–57.

Brothers, L. (1990). The social brain: a project for integrating primate behaviour and neurophysiology in a new domain. *Concepts in Neuroscience*, 1, 27–51.

Brown, G. D. A., Preece, T. and Hulme, C. (In press). Oscillator-based memory for serial order. *Psychological Review*.

Brust, J. (1980). Music and language: musical alexia and agraphia. *Brain*, 103, 367–92.

Burgess, N. and Hitch, G. J. (1994). A connectionist model of STM for serial order. In S. E. Gathercole (ed.), *Models of Short-Term Memory*, pp. 51–72. Hove, England: Psychology Press.

Butcher, C. Mylander, C. and Goldin-Meadow, S. (1991). Displaced communication in a self-styled gesture system: Pointing at the non-present. *Cognitive Development*, 6, 315–42.

Butler, K. (1995). Content, context and compositionality. *Mind and Language* 10, 3–24.

Byrne, R. (1995). *The Thinking Ape.* Oxford: Oxford University Press.

Byrne, R. and Whiten, A. (eds.), (1988). *Machiavellian Intelligence*. Oxford: Oxford University Press.

Caramazza, A., Berndt, R. and Brownell, H. (1982). The semantic deficit hypothesis: perceptual parsing and object classification by aphasic patients. *Brain and Language*, 15, 161–89.

Caramazza, A. and. Grober, E. (1976). Polysemy and the structure of the subjective lexicon. In C. Rameh (ed.), *Semantics: Theory and Application,* pp. 181–206, Georgetown University Round Table on Language and Linguistics. Washington DC, Georgetown University Press.

Carey, S. (1985). *Conceptual Change in Childhood.* Cambridge, Mass.: MIT Press.

Carruthers, P. (1996a). *Language, Thought and Consciousness: An Essay in Philosophical Psychology*. Cambridge: Cambridge University Press.

(1996b). Simulation and self-knowledge: a defence of theory-theory. In P. Carruthers and P. K. Smith (eds.), 1996, 22–38.

(1996c). Autism as mind-blindness: an elaboration and partial defence. In P. Carruthers and P. K. Smith (eds.), 1996, 257–76.

Carruthers, P. and Smith, P. K. (eds.), (1996). *Theories of Theories of Mind.* Cambridge: Cambridge University Press.

Carston, R. (1996). Enrichment and loosening: Complementary processes in deriving the proposition expressed? *University College London Working Papers in Linguistics*, 8.

Carston, R. (in preparation). *Pragmatics and the Explicit–Implicit Distinction.* University of London PhD thesis.

Changeux, J-P. and Connes, A. (1995). *Conversations on Mind, Matter and Mathematics*. Princeton, NJ: Princeton University Press.

Chater, N. and Conkey, P. (1994). Sequence processing with recurrent neural networks. In M. Oaksford and G. D. A. Brown (eds.), *Neurodynamics and Psychology.* London: Academic Press, pp. 269–94.

Cheney, D. L. and Seyfarth, R. M. (1990). *How Monkeys See the World.* Chicago: Chicago University Press.

Choi, S. and Bowerman, M. (1991). Learning to express motion events in English and Korean: The influence of language-specific lexicalization patterns. *Cognition*, 43, 83–121.

Chomsky, N. (1957). *Syntactic Structures.* The Hague: Mouton.

(1980). *Rules and Representations.* New York: Columbia University Press.

(1986). *Knowledge of Language: Its Nature, Origins and Use*. New York: Praeger.

(1988). *Language and Problems of Knowledge.* Cambridge, Mass.: MIT Press.

(1995a). Language and Nature. *Mind,* 104, 1–61.

(1995b). *The Minimalist Program*. Cambridge, Mass.: MIT Press.

Churchland, P. M. (1981). Eliminative materialism and propositional attitudes. *Journal of Philosophy*, vol. 78, 67–90.

(1989). *The Neurocomputational Perspective*. Cambridge, Mass.: MIT/Bradford Books.

(1995). *The Engine of Reason, the Seat of the Soul.* Cambridge, Mass.: MIT Press.

Churchland, P. S. and P. M. (1996). Replies. In R. McCauley (ed.) *The Churchlands and their Critics*. Oxford: Blackwell.

Clark, A. (1989). *Microcognition: Philosophy, Cognitive Science and Parallel Distributed Processing*. Cambridge, Mass.: MIT Press.

(1990). Connectionist minds. *Proceedings of the Aristotelian Society*, 90, 83–102.

(1993). *Associative Engines: Connectionism, Concepts and Representational Change*. Cambridge, Mass.: MIT Press.

(1996a). *Being There: Putting Brain, Body and World Together Again*. Cambridge, Mass.: MIT Press.

(1996b). Connectionism, moral cognition and collaborative problem solving. In L. May, M. Friedman, and A. Clark (eds.), *Mind and Morals,* pp. 109–28. Cambridge, Mass.: MIT Press.

Clark, A. and Chalmers, D. (1995). *The Extended Mind.* Philosophy/Neuroscience/Psychology Research Report. Washington University, St. Louis.

Clark, A. and Karmiloff-Smith, A. (1994). The cognizer's innards: A psychological and philosophical perspective on the development of thought. *Mind and Language*, 8, 487–519.

Clark, A. and Thornton, C. (1997). Trading spaces: Computation, representation, and the limits of uninformed learning. *Behavioural and Brain Sciences*, 20, 57–66.

Clark, E. V. and Carpenter, K. L. (1989). The notion of source in language acquisition. *Language*, 65, 1–30.

Clements, W. A. (1995). *Implicit Theories of Mind.* Unpublished doctoral dissertation, University of Sussex.

Clements, W. and Perner, J. (1994). Implicit understanding of belief. *Cognitive Development*, 9, 377–97.

Cohen, L. J. (1992). *An Essay on Belief and Acceptance.* Oxford: Oxford University Press.

Cohen, R., Kelter, S. and Woll, G. (1979). Conceptual impairment in aphasia. In R. Bauerle, U. Egli, and A. von Stechow (eds.), *Semantics from Different Points of View*, pp. 353–63. Berlin: Springer Verlag.

Conrad, R. (1971). The chronology of the development of covert speech in children. *Developmental Psychology*, 5, 398–405.

(1979). *The Deaf Child.* London: Harper and Row.

Cosmides, L. and Tooby, J. (1992). Cognitive adaptations for social exchange. In J. Barkow, L. Cosmides and J. Tooby (eds.), *The Adapted Mind,* pp. 163–228. Oxford: Oxford University Press.

Crary, M. (1993). *Developmental Motor Speech Disorders.* London: Whurr Press.

Cromer, R. (1994). A case study of dissociations between language and cognition. In H. Tager-Flusberg (ed.), *Constraints on Language Acquistion: Studies of Atypical Children.* Hillsdale NJ: Lawrence Erlbaum, pp. 141–54.

Curtiss, S. (1977). *Genie: A Psycholinguistic Study of a Modern-Day 'Wild Child'*. New York: Academic Press.

(1988). Abnormal language acquisition and the modularity of language. In Newmeyer (ed.), *Linguistics: The Cambridge Survey, vol. 2*, pp. 96–116. Cambridge: Cambridge University Press.

Curtiss, S. and Yamada, J. (1981). Selectively intact grammatical development in a retarded child. *UCLA Working Papers in Cognitive Linguistics*, 3, 61–91.

Davidson, D. (1974). Belief and the basis of meaning. *Synthèse*, 27, 309–23. Reprinted in Davidson (1984).

(1975). Thought and talk. In S. Guttenplan (ed.), *Mind and Language,* pp. 7–23. Oxford: Oxford University Press. Reprinted in Davidson (1984).

(1982). Rational Animals. In E. Lepore and B. McLaughlin (eds.), (1986), *Actions and Events*, Oxford: Blackwell.

(1984). *Inquiries into Truth and Interpretation*. Oxford: Oxford University Press.

Davies, M. (1987). Tacit knowledge and semantic theory: Can a five per cent difference matter? *Mind*, 96, 441–62.

(1991). Concepts, connectionism, and the language of thought. In W. Ramsey, S. Stich and D. Rumelhart (eds.), *Philosophy and Connectionist Theory*, pp. 229–57. Hillsdale, NJ: Lawrence Erlbaum.

(1992). Aunty's own argument for the language of thought. In J. Ezquerro and J. Larrazabel (eds.), *Cognition, Semantics and Philosophy,* pp. 235–71. Dordrecht: Kluwer Academic press.

(1995). Two notions of implicit rules. In J. Tomberlin (ed.), *Philosophical Perspectives, 9: AI, Connectionism, and Philosophical Psychology*, pp. 153–83. Atascadero, CA: Ridgeview Publishing Company.

(1996). Philosophy of language. In Bunnin and Tsui-James (eds.), *Blackwell's Companion to Philosophy*, pp. 90–139. Oxford: Blackwell.

(1998). Externalism, architecturalism, and epistemic warrant. In C. Wright, B. C. Smith and C. Macdonald (eds.), *Knowing Our Own Minds*. Oxford: Oxford University Press.

Dawkins, R. (1976). *The Selfish Gene.* Oxford: Oxford University Press.

(1982). *The Extended Phenotype*. Oxford, Oxford University Press.

Deane, P. (1988). Polysemy and cognition. *Lingua,* 75, 325–61.

Debner, J. A. and Jacoby, L. L. (1994). Unconscious perception: Attention, awareness, and control. *Journal of Experimental Psychology: Learning, Memory, and Cognition*, 20, 304–17.

Dennett, D. C. (1978). *Brainstorms: Philosophical essays on mind and psychology*. Montgomery, VT: Bradford Books (UK edition, Sussex: Harvester).

(1982). How to study consciousness empirically: or nothing comes to mind. *Synthese*, 53, 159–80.

(1987). *The Intentional Stance*. Cambridge, Mass.: MIT Press.

(1991). *Consciousness Explained.* New York: Little Brown and Co. (UK: Allen Lane: Penguin).

(1994). Labelling and learning. (Commentary on Clark and Karmiloff-Smith 1994.) *Mind and Language, 8*, 54–48.

(1995). *Darwin's Dangerous Idea*. New York: Simon and Schuster.

(1996a). *Kinds of Minds*, New York: Basic Books. UK: Weidenfeld and Nicolson.

(1996b). "Bewusstsein hat mehr mit Ruhm als mit Fernsehen zu tun," in Christa Maar, Ernst Pöppel, and Thomas Christaller, (eds.), *Die Technik auf dem Weg zur Seele*, pp. 147–68. Munich: Rowohlt.

de Sousa, R. (1971). How to give a piece of your mind: or, the logic of belief and assent. *Review of Metaphysics,* 25(1), 52–79.

de Villiers, J. (1995). Steps in the mastery of sentence complements. Paper delivered at the Symposium on Language and Theory of Mind, Society for Research in Child Development, Indianapolis, IN.

de Villiers, J. and Desjarlais, P. (1997). How preschool children report what was said: truth, lies and mistakes. Manuscript.

de Villiers, J., Roeper, T. and Vainikka, A. (1990). The acquisition of long distance rules. In Lyn Frazier and Jill de Villiers (eds.), *Language Processing and Acquisition.* Dordrecht: Kluwer, pp. 257–97.

Devitt, M. and Sterelny, K. (1987). *Language and Reality*. Cambridge, Mass.: MIT Press.

Diaz, R. and Berk, L. (eds.), (1992). *Private Speech: From Social Interaction to Self-Regulation*. Hillsdale, NJ: Lawrence Erlbaum.

Dienes, Z., and Perner, J. (1996). Implicit knowledge in people and connectionist networks. In G. Underwood (ed.), *Implicit Cognition,* pp. 227–55. Oxford: Oxford University Press.

Dixon, R. M. W. (1979). Ergativity. *Language*, 55, 59–138.

Doherty, M. J. (1995). *Metalinguistic understanding and theory of mind.* Unpublished doctoral dissertation, University of Sussex.

Dowker, A., Hermelin, B. and Pring, L. (1996). A savant poet. *Psychological Medicine*, 26, 913–24.

Dummett, M. (1973). *Frege: Philosophy of Language*. London: Duckworth.

(1981). *The Interpretation of Frege's Philosophy.* London: Duckworth.

(1991). *Frege and Other Philosophers*. Oxford: Oxford University Press.

(1993). *The Seas of Language*. Oxford: Oxford University Press.

Dunbar, R. (1993). Coevolution of neocortical size, group size and language in humans. *Behavioural and Brain Sciences*, 16, 681–94.

(1996). *Grooming, Gossip and the Evolution of Language*. London: Faber and Faber.

Elman, J. L. (1991). Incremental learning, or the importance of starting small. *CRL Technical Report 9101.* San Diego: University of California.

(1993). Learning and development in neural networks: the importance of starting small. *Cognition,* 48: 71–99.

Elman, J., Bates, E., Johnson, M., Karmiloff-Smith, A., Parisi, D. and Plunkett, K. (1996). *Rethinking Innateness: A Connectionist Perspective on Development*. Cambridge, Mass.: MIT Press.

Evans, C. S. and Marler, P. (1995). Language and animal communication: parallels and contrasts. In H. L. Roitblat and J-A. Meyer (eds.), *Comparative Approaches to Cognitive Science*, pp. 341–82. Cambridge, Mass.: MIT Press.

Evans, G. (1982). *The Varieties of Reference*. Oxford: Oxford University Press.

Fant, L. J. (1972). *Ameslan: An Introduction to American Sign Language.* Silver Springs, Md.: National Association of the Deaf.

Fein, D., Dunn, M., Allen, D., Aram, D., Hall, N. and Wilson, B. (1996). Language and neuropsychological findings. In I. Rapin (ed.), *Preschool Children with Inadequate Communication.* Cambridge: Cambridge University Press for Mac Keith Press, pp. 123–54.

Feldman, H., Goldin-Meadow, S. and Gleitman, L. (1978). Beyond Herodotus: The creation of language by linguistically deprived deaf children. In A. Lock (ed.), *Action, Symbol, and Gesture: The Emergence of Language*, pp. 351–414. New York: Academic Press.

Flavell, J. (1985). *Cognitive Development*. Second Edition. New York: Prentice Hall.

Fletcher, P. (1990). Speech and language defects. *Nature*, 346, 226.

Fodor, J. (1975). *The Language of Thought*. New York: Crowell. UK: Hassocks: Harvester Press.

(1978). 'Propositional attitudes'. Reprinted in J. Fodor (1981), *RePresentations.* Hassocks: Harvester Press.

(1983). *The Modularity of Mind.* Cambridge, Mass.: MIT Press.

(1987). *Psychosemantics: The Problem of Meaning in the Philosophy of Mind.* Cambridge, Mass.: MIT Press.

(1992). A theory of the child's theory of mind. *Cognition* 44, 283–96.

Fodor, J. and Lepore, E. (1996). *The Emptiness of the Lexicon: Critical Reflections on J. Pustejovsky's The Generative Lexicon.* RuCCS, Rutgers University, Technical report, 27.

Franks, B. (1995). Sense generation: a 'quasi-classical' approach to concepts and concept combination. *Cognitive Science,* 19, 441–505.

Franks, B. and Braisby, N. (1990). Sense generation or how to make a mental lexicon flexible. In *Proceedings of the 12th Annual Conference of the Cognitive Science Society* (July). Cambridge, Mass.: MIT Press.

Frankfurt, H. (1971). Freedom of the will and the concept of a person. *Journal of Philosophy,* 68, 5–20.

Frankish, K. (1996). Dennett's opinions. Unpublished typescript: University of Sheffield.

French, R. (1995). *The Subtlety of Sameness.* Cambridge, Mass: MIT Press.

Frith, C. D. (1992). *The Cognitive Neuropsychology of Schizophrenia.* Hillsdale, NJ: Lawrence Erlbaum Associates.

Fromkin, V. (1982). Introduction in Fromkin (ed.), *Errors in Linguistic Performance: Slips of the Tongue, Ear, Pen and Hand,* pp. 1–12. New York: Academic Press.

Frye, D., Zelazo, P. D. and Palfai, T. (1995). Theory of mind and rule-based reasoning. *Cognitive Development,* 10, 483–527.

Gale, E., de Villiers, P., de Villiers, J. and Pyers, J. (1996). Language and theory of mind in oral deaf children. *Proceedings of the 20th Annual Boston University Conference on Language Development.* Somerville, Mass.: Cascadilla Press.

García-Albea, J. E. (1993). *Mente y conducta.* Madrid: Trotta.

Gardner, H. (1983). *Frames of Mind: the theory of multiple intelligences.* London: Heinemann.

Gardner, R. A. and Gardner, B. T. (1969). Teaching sign language to a chimpanzee. *Science, 165,* 3894: 664–72.

Garrett, M. (1982). Production of speech: observations from normal and pathological language use. In A. Ellis (ed.), *Normality and Pathology in Cognitive Functions,* pp. 19–76. London: Academic Press.

Gathercole, S. E. and Baddeley, A. (1989). The role of phonological memory in normal and disordered language development. In C. von Euler, I. Lundberg and G. Lennestrand (eds.), *Brain and Reading.* London: Macmillan Press.

(1993). *Working Memory and Language.* New York: Lawrence Erlbaum.

Gauker, C. (1990). How to learn a language like a chimpanzee. *Philosophical Psychology,* 3(1): 31–53.

Gelman, S. and Markman, E. (1986). Categories and induction in young children. *Cognition,* 23, 183–209.

Gentner, D. and Boroditsky, L. (1997). Individuation, linguistic relativity and early word learning. In M. Bowerman and S. Levinson (eds.), *Language Acquisition and Conceptual Development* (in press). Cambridge: Cambridge University Press.

Gerken, L. A. (1991). The metrical basis for children's subjectless sentences. *Journal of Memory and Language*, 30, 431–51.

Gibbs, R. (1994). *The Poetics of Mind.* Cambridge: Cambridge University Press.

Giere, R. (1988). *Explaining Science: A Cognitive Approach.* Chicago: Chicago University Press.

Gleitman, L. (1990). Structural sources of word meaning. *Language Acquisition*, 1, 3–55.

Goldin-Meadow, S. (1982). The resilience of recursion: A study of a communication system developed without a conventional language model. In E. Wanner and L. R. Gleitman (eds.), *Language Acquisition: The State of the Art*. New York: Cambridge University Press.

(1985). Language development under atypical learning conditions: Replication and implications of a study of deaf children of hearing parents. In K. Nelson (ed.), *Children's Language.* vol. 5, pp. 197–245. Hillsdale, NJ: Lawrence Erlbaum.

(1993). When does gesture become language? A study of gesture used as a primary communication system by deaf children of hearing parents. In K. R. Gibson and T. Ingold (eds.), *Tools, Language and Cognition in Human Evolution*, pp. 63–85. New York: Cambridge University Press.

(1997). The resilience of language in humans. In C. T. Snowdon and M. Hausberger (eds.), *Social Influences on Vocal Development* (in press). New York: Cambridge University Press.

Goldin-Meadow, S., Butcher, C., Mylander, C. and Dodge, M. (1994). Nouns and verbs in a self-styled gesture system: What's in a name? *Cognitive Psychology*, 27, 259–319.

Goldin-Meadow, S. and Feldman, H. (1977). The development of language-like communication without a language model. *Science*, 197, 401–3.

Goldin-Meadow, S., McNeill, D. and Singleton, J. (1996). Silence is liberating: Removing the handcuffs on grammatical expression in the manual modality. *Psychological Review*, 103, 34–55.

Goldin-Meadow, S. and Morford, M. (1985) Gesture in early child language: studies of deaf and hearing children. *Merrill-Palmer Quarterly*, 31, 145–76.

Goldin-Meadow, S., and Mylander, C. (1983). Gestural communication in deaf children: The non-effects of parental input on language development. *Science*, 221, 372–4.

(1984). Gestural communication in deaf children: The effects and non-effects of parental input on early language development. *Monographs of the Society for Research in Child Development*, 49, 1–121.

(1990). Beyond the input given: The child's role in the acquisition of language. *Language*, 66(2), 323–55.

Goldin-Meadow, S., Mylander, C. and Butcher, C. (1995). The resilience of combinatorial structure at the word level: Morphology in self-styled gesture systems. *Cognition*, 56, 195–262.

Goldman, A. (1989). Interpretation psychologized. *Mind and Language*, 4, 161–85.

(1992). In defence of the simulation theory. *Mind and Language*, 7, 104–19.

Goldstein, K. (1948). *Language and Language Disturbances*. New York: Grune and Stratton.

Goldstone, R. (1994). Influences of categorisation on perceptual discrimination. *Journal of Experimental Psychology: General*, vol. 123, 178–200.

Gómez, J. C. (1990). The emergence of intentional communication as a problem-solving strategy in the gorilla. In S. Parker and K. Gibson (eds.), *'Language' and Intelligence in Monkeys and Apes: Comparative Developmental Perspectives*, pp. 333–55. Cambridge, Mass.: Cambridge University Press.

(1991). Visual behaviour as a window for reading the minds of others in primates. In A. Whiten (ed.), *Natural Theories of Mind: Evolution, Development and Simulation of Everyday Mind-Reading,* pp. 195–207. Oxford: Blackwell.

(1992). *El Desarrollo de la Comunicación Intencional en el Gorila.* PhD Dissertation, Universidad Autónoma de Madrid.

(1994). Mutual awareness in primate communication: a Gricean approach. In S. Parker, M. Boccia., and R. Mittchel (eds.), *Self-Recognition and Awareness in Apes, Monkeys and Children*, pp. 61–80. Cambridge, Mass.: Cambridge University Press.

(1996a). Non-human primate theories of (non-human primate) minds: some issues concerning the origins of mind-reading. In P. Carruthers and P. K. Smith (eds.), 1996, pp. 330–43.

(1996b). Ostensive behaviour in the great apes: the role of eye contact. In A. Russon, S., Parker., and K. Bard. (eds.), *Reaching into Thought*, pp. 131–51. Cambridge, Mass.: Cambridge University Press.

Gómez, J. C., Sarriá, E. and Tamarit, J. (1993). The comparative study of early communication and theories of mind: ontogeny, phylogeny and pathology. In S. Baron-Cohen., H. Tager-Flusberg., and D. Cohen (eds.), *Understanding Other Minds: Perspectives from Autism*, pp. 397–426. Oxford: Oxford University Press.

Goodall, J. V. L. (1968). The behaviour of free-living chimpanzees in the Gombe Stream area. *Animal Behaviour Monographs*, 1, 161–311.

Goodglass, H., Denes, G. and Calderon, M. (1974). The absence of covert verbal mediation in aphasia. *Cortex*, 10, 264–9.

Gopnik, A. (1988). Conceptual and semantic development and theory change. *Mind and Language,* 3, 197–217.

(1996). Theories and modules: creation myths, developmental realities, and Neurath's boat. In P. Carruthers and P. K. Smith (eds.), 1996, pp. 169–83.

Gopnik, A. and Wellman, H. (1992). Why the child's theory of mind really is a theory. *Mind and Language,* 7, 145–71.

Gopnik, M. and Crago, M. (1991). Familial aggregation of a developmental language disorder. *Cognition*, 39, 1–50.

Gordon, R. M. (1986). Folk psychology as simulation. *Mind and Language*, 1(2), 158–71.

Goschke, T. (1996). Wille und Kognition: Zur funktionalen Architektur der intentionalen Handlungssteuerung: *Enzyklopädie der Psychologie: Motivation, Volition und Handlung*, Bd. 4 (hrsg. v. J. Kuhl and H. Heckhausen, S. pp. 583–663). Göttingen: Hogrefe.

Goshke, T. and Koppelberg, D. (1992). The concept of representation and the representation of concepts in connectionist models. In W. Ramsey, S. Stich and D. Rumelhart (eds.), *Philosophy and Connectionist Theory*. Hillsdale, NJ: Laurence Erlbaum.

Gouzoules, H., Gouzoules, S. and Ashley, J. (1995). Representational signalling in non-human primate vocal communication. In E. Zimmermann, J. D. Newman and U. Jürgens (eds.), *Current Topics in Primate Vocal Communication*, pp. 235–52. New York: Plenum.

Greenfield, P. M. (1991). Language, tools and brain: the ontogeny and phylogeny of hierarchically organized sequential behaviour. *Behavioural and Brain Sciences*, 14(4), 531–51.

Grice, H. P. (1957). Meaning. *Philosophical Review*, 66, 377–88. Reprinted in Grice (1989), pp. 213–23.

(1969). Utterer's meaning and intention. *Philosophical Review*, 78.

(1976/80). Meaning revisited. Reprinted in Grice (1989), pp. 283–303.

(1989). *Studies in the Way of Words.* Cambridge, Mass.: Harvard University Press.

Griffin, D. (1984). *Animal Thinking*. Cambridge, Mass.: Harvard University Press.

Groefsema, M. (1995). 'Can', 'may', 'must' and 'should': A relevance-theoretic approach. *Journal of Linguistics*, 31, 53–79.

Happé, F. (1991). *Theory of Mind and Communication in Autism*. Unpublished PhD Thesis. University of London

(1993). Communicative competence and theory of mind in autism: a test of relevance theory. *Cognition*, 48, 101–19.

(1994). *Autism: An Introduction to Psychological Theory*. London: UCL Press. (Cambridge: Cambridge University Press).

Hardin, C. (1988). *Color for Philosophers.* New York: Hackett.

Harman, G. (1973). *Thought*. Princeton, New Jersey: Princeton University Press.

Harris, P. (1989). *Children and Emotion: The Development of Psychological Understanding*. Oxford: Blackwell.

(1992). From simulation to folk psychology: the case for development. *Mind and Language*, 7, 120–44.

(1996). Desires, beliefs, and language. In P. Carruthers and P. K. Smith (eds.), 1996, pp. 200–20.

Hatfield, F. and Zangwill, O. (1974). Ideation in aphasia: the picture-story method. *Neuropsychologia* 12, 389–93.

Hauser, M. D. (1996). *The Evolution of Communication*. Cambridge, Mass.: MIT Press

Head, H. (1926). *Aphasia and Kindred Disorders of Speech*. Cambridge: Cambridge University Press.

Heal, J. (1986). Replication and functionalism. In J. Butterfield (ed.), *Language, Mind and Logic*, pp. 135–50. Cambridge: Cambridge University Press.

(1995). How to think about thinking. In M. Davies and T. Stone (eds.), *Mental Simulation: Philosophical and Psychological Studies*, pp. 33–52. Oxford: Blackwell.

Heyes, C. and Dickinson, A. (1993). The intentionality of animal action. In M. Davies and G. W. Humphreys (eds.), *Consciousness*, pp. 105–20. Oxford: Blackwell.

Higginbotham, J. (1986). Linguistic theory and Davidson's programme in semantics. In E. LePore (ed.), *Truth and Interpretation: Perspectives on the Philosophy of Donald Davidson*, pp. 29–48, Oxford: Basil Blackwell.

Hobson, P. (1993). *Autism and the Development of Mind*. Hillsdale, NJ: LEA.

Hoffmeister, R. and Wilbur, R. (1980). Developmental: The acquisition of sign language. In H. Lane and F. Grosjean (eds.), *Recent Perspectives on American Sign Language*, pp. 61–78. Hillsdale, NJ: Lawrence Erlbaum.

Hofstadter, D. (1995). *Fluid Concepts and Creative Analogies*. Basic Books.

Hughlings Jackson, J. (1866). Notes on the physiology and pathology of language. Reprinted in *Selected Writings of John Hughlings Jackson,* (1958), yol. 2, pp. 121–8. London: Staples Press.

Humphrey, N. (1986). *The Inner Eye*. London: Faber and Faber.

Hurlburt, R. (1990). *Sampling Normal and Schizophrenic Inner Experience*. New York: Plenum Press.

Hutchins, E. (1995). *Cognition in the Wild*. Cambridge, Mass.: MIT Press.

Imai, M. (1995). Development of a bias toward language-specific categorization. Paper presented at the Biannual Meeting for the International Cognitive Linguistic Association, Albuquerque, New Mexico.

Imai, M. and Gentner, D. (1997). A crosslinguistic study of early word meaning: Linguistic input and universal ontology. *Cognition* (in press).

Jackendoff, R. (1987). *Consciousness and the Computational Mind*. Cambridge, Mass: MIT Press.

(1990). *Semantics and Cognition*. Cambridge, Mass: MIT Press.

(1996). How language helps us think. *Pragmatics and Cognition,* 4:1, 1–34.

(1997). *The Architecture of the Language Faculty*. Cambridge, Mass.: MIT Press.

Jackendoff, R. and Landau, B. (1991). Spatial language and spatial cognition. In D. J. Napoli and J. Kegl (eds.), *Bridges between Psychology and Linguistics: A Swarthmore Festschrift for Lila Gleitman*. Hillsdale, NJ: Lawrence Erlbaum.

Jacoby, L. L. (1991). A process dissociation framework: Separating automatic from intentional uses of memory. *Journal of Memory and Language*, 30, 513–41.

Jarrold, C., Carruthers, P., Smith, P. K. and Boucher, J. (1994). Pretend play: is it meta-representational? *Mind and Language*, 9, 445–68.

Johnson-Laird (1983). *Mental Models*. Cambridge: Cambridge University Press.

Johnston, J. and Ellis Weismer, S. (1983). Mental rotation abilities in language-disordered children. *Journal of Speech and Hearing Research*, 32, 33–8.

Kaplan, M. (1981). Rational acceptance. *Philosophical Studies*, 40, 129–45.

Karmiloff-Smith, A. (1979). *A Functional Approach to Child Language*. Cambridge: Cambridge University Press.

(1986). From meta-process to conscious access. *Cognition*, 23, 95–147.

(1992). *Beyond Modularity: A Developmental Perspective on Cognitive Science*. Cambridge, Mass.: MIT Press/Bradford Books.

Karmiloff-Smith, A., Klima, E., Bellugi, U., Grant, J. and Baron-Cohen, S. (1995). Is there a social module? Language, face processing, and theory of mind in individuals with Williams syndrome. *Journal of Cognitive Neuorscience*, 7, 196–208.

Kay, J., Lesser, R. and Coltheart, M. (1992). *Psycholinguistic Assessment of Language Processing in Aphasia*. Hove: Lawrence Erlbaum.

Kelter, S., Cohen, R., Engel, D., List, G. and Strohner, H. (1977). Verbal coding and visual memory in aphasics. *Neuropsychologia*, 15, 51–60.

Kertesz, A. (1988). Cognitive function in severe aphasia. In L. Weiskrantz (ed.), 1988, pp. 451–63.

Kertesz, A., Lesk, D. and McCabe, P. (1977). Isotope localisation of infarcts in aphasia. *Archives of Neurology*, 34, 540–601.

Kirsh, D. (1991). When is information explicitly represented? In P. Hanson (ed.), *Information, Language and Cognition: Vancouver Studies in Cognitive Science 1*, pp. 340–65. Vancouver, BC: University of British Columbia Press.

(1995). The intelligent use of space. *Artificial Intelligence*, 72, 1–52

Kirsh, D. and Maglio, P. (1992). *Reaction and Reflection in Tetris*. Artificial Intelligence Planning Systems: Proceedings of the First Annual International Conference AIPS 92, San Mateo, CA: Morgan Kaufman.

Köhler, W. (1921). *Intelligenzprüfungen an Menschenaffen*. Berlín: Springer. English translations: (1925). *The Mentality of Apes*. New York: Harcourt Brace and World. (1927). *The Mentality of Apes*. New York: Vintage.

Kosslyn, S. (1994). *Image and Brain*. Cambridge, Mass.: MIT Press.

Kracke, I. (1975). Perception of rhythmic sequences by receptive aphasic and deaf children. *British Journal of Communication Disorders*, 10, 43–51.

Landau, B., Smith, L. and Jones, S. (1988). The importance of shape in early lexical learning. *Cognitive Development*, 3, 299–321.

Landi, V. (1982). *The Great American Countryside*. London: Collier MacMillan.

Larson, R., and Ludlow, P., (1993). Interpreted logical forms. *Synthese* 95:305–55.

Larson, R. and Segal, G. (1995). *Knowledge of Meaning: An Introduction to Semantic Theory*. Cambridge, Mass.: MIT Press.

Lashley, K. (1950). In search of the engram. *In Symposia for the Society for Experimental Biology*, no. 4. Cambridge: Cambridge University Press.

Laurence, S. (1996). A Chomskian alternative to convention-based semantics. *Mind*, 105, 269–301.

Lehrer, A. (1990). Polysemy, conventionality and the structure of the lexicon. *Cognitive Linguistics*, 1–2, 207–46.

Leibniz, G. (1704). *New Essays on the Understanding*.

Lenneberg, E. H. (1964). Capacity for language acquisition. In J. A. Fodor and J. J. Katz (eds.), *The Structure of Language: Readings in the Philosophy of Language*, pp. 579–603. NJ: Prentice-Hall.

(1967). *Biological Foundations of Language*. New York: John Wiley and Sons.

Leonard, L. B., Sabbadini, L., Leonard, J. S. and Volterra, V. (1987). Specific language impairment in children: a cross-linguistic study. *Brain and Language*, 32, 233–52.

Leonard, L. B., Sabbadini, L., Volterra., V. and Leonard, J. S. (1988). Some influences on the grammar of English- and Italian- speaking children with specific language impairment. *Applied Psycholinguistics*, 9, 39–57.

Leslie, A. (1987). Pretence and representation: the origins of 'theory of mind'. *Psychological Review*, 94, 412–26.

(1994). Pretending and believing: Issues in the theory of ToMM. *Cognition*, 50, 211–38.

Leslie, A. M. and Roth, D. (1993). What autism teaches us about metarepresentation. In S. Baron-Cohen, H. Tager-Flusberg, and D. Cohen (eds.), *Understanding other Minds: Perspectives from Autism*, pp. 83–111. Oxford: Oxford University Press.

Lesser, R. (1989). *Linguistic Investigations of Aphasia*. London: Whurr.

Levelt, W. (1989). *Speaking: From Intention to Articulation*. Cambridge, Mass.: MIT.

Levi, I. (1967). *Gambling with Truth*. London: Routledge and Kegan Paul.

Levin, B. and Rappaport Hovav, M. (1991). The lexical semantics of verbs of motion: the perspective from unaccusativity. In I. Roca (ed.), *Thematic Structure: Its Role in Grammar*. Berlin: Walter de Gruyter.

Lewis, D. (1966). An argument for the identity theory. *Journal of Philosophy*, vol. 63, 17–25.

(1969). *Convention*. Oxford: Blackwell.

(1983). Language and languages. In his *Philosophical Papers*, vol. 1, pp. 163–88. Oxford: Oxford University Press.

Linebarger, M., Schwartz, M. and Saffran, E. (1983). Sensitivity to grammatical structure in so-called agrammatic aphasics. *Cognition,* 13, 361–92.

Locke, J. (1690). *An Essay Concerning Human Understanding*.

Locke, J. L. (1993). *The Child's Path to Spoken Language.* Cambridge, Mass.: Harvard University Press.

(1994). Are developmental language disorders primarily grammatical? Speculations from an evolutionary model. In R. Paul (ed.), *The Speech/Language Connection.* Baltimore, MD: Paul H. Brookes.

Lucy, J. A. (1992a). *Grammatical Categories and Cognition: A Case Study of the Linguistic Relativity Hypothesis*. New York: Cambridge University Press.

(1992b). *Language Diversity and Thought: A Reformulation of the Linguistic Relativity Hypothesis*. New York: Cambridge University Press.

(1993). Reflexive language and the human disciplines. In J. A. Lucy (ed.), *Reflexive Language: Reported Speech and Metapragmatics*, pp. 9–32. New York: Cambridge University Press.

(1996). The scope of linguistic relativity: An analysis and review of empirical research. In J. Gumperz and S. Levinson (eds.), *Rethinking Linguistic Relativity.* New York: Cambridge University Press.

Luria, A. (1959). The directive function of speech in development and dissolution. *Word*, 15, 341–52.

Luria, A., Tsvetkova, L. and Futer, D. (1965). Aphasia in a composer. *Journal of the Neurological Sciences* 2, 288–92.

Luria, A. and Yudovich, F. (1956). *Speech and the Development of Mental Processes in the Child.* Translation by. Kovasc and Simon (1959). London: Penguin Books.

Lyons, J. (1977). *Semantics*. Cambridge, Cambridge University Press.

MacDonald, C., and MacDonald, G. (eds.), (1995). *Connectionism: Debates on Psychological Explanation*. Oxford: Blackwell.

Macedonia, J. M., and Evans, C. S. (1993). Variation among mammalian alarm call systems and the problem of meaning in animal signals. *Journal of Ethology*, 93(3), 177–97.

Malotki, E. (1983). *Hopi Time*. Berlin: Mouton.

Marchman, V. A., and Bates, E. (1994). Continuity in lexical and morphological development: a test of the critical mass hypothesis. *Journal of Child Language*, 21, 339–66.

Marie, P. (1906). The third left frontal convolution plays no special role in the function of language. Reprinted in M. F. Cole (1971), *Pierre Marie's Papers on Speech Disorders*. New York: Academic.

Markman, E. (1989). *Categorization and Naming in Children: Problems of Induction*. Cambridge, Mass.: MIT Press.

Marr, D. (1982). *Vision*. San Francisco, CA: Freeman.

Marshall, J., Pring, T. and Chiat, S. (1993). Sentence processing therapy: working at the level of the event. *Aphasiology,* 7, 177–99.

Mayberry, R. I. (1992). The cognitive development of deaf children: Recent insights. In S. Segalowitz and I. Rapin (eds.), *Child Neuropsychology, Volume 7, Handbook of Neuropsychology*, pp. 51–68. F. Boller and J. Graffman (series eds.). Amsterdam: Elsevier.

McClamrock, R. (1995). *Existential Cognition.* Chicago: University of Chicago Press.

McDowell, J. (1994). *Mind and World.* Cambridge, Mass.: Harvard University Press.

McFarland, D. (1989a). Goals, no-goals and own goals. In A. Montefiori and D. Noble (eds.), *Goals, No-goals and Own goals: A Debate on Goal-Directed and Intentional Behaviour*, pp. 39–57. London: Unwin Hyman.

(1989b). Swan song of a phoenix. In A. Montefiori and D. Noble (eds.), *Goals, No-Goals and Own Goals: A Debate on Goal-Directed and Intentional Behaviour*, pp. 283–94. London: Unwin Hyman.

McNeill, D. and Duncan, S. D. (1997). The growth point. In A. Kendon, D. McNeill, and S. Wilcox (eds.), *Gesture: An Emerging Field of Study* (in press).

Meadow, K. (1968). Early manual communication in relation to the deaf child's intellectual, social, and communicative functioning. *American Annals of the Deaf,* 113, 29–41.

Menzel, E. W. (1973). Leadership and communication in young chimpanzees. In E. W. Menzel (ed.), *Precultural Primate Behaviour,* pp. 192–225. Basel: Karger.

Milberg, W. and Blumstein. S. (1981). Lexical decision and aphasia: evidence for semantic processing. *Brain and Language,* 14, 371–85.

Miller, G. (1996). Sexual selection in human evolution. In C. Crawford and D. Krebs (eds.), *Evolution and Human Behaviour*. Hove: Lawrence Erlbaum.

Minsky, M. (1985). *The Society of Mind.* New York: Simon and Schuster.

Mitchell, M. (1993). *Analogy-Making as Perception*, Cambridge, Mass.: MIT Press.

Mitchell, P. (1994). Realism and early conception of mind: A synthesis of phylogenetic and ontogenetic issues. In C. Lewis and P. Mitchell (eds.), *Children's Early Understanding of Mind: Origins and development,* pp. 261–86. Hove: Lawrence Erlbaum.

Mithen, S. (1996). *The Prehistory of the Mind.* London: Thames and Hudson.

Moores, D. F. (1974). Nonvocal systems of verbal behavior. In R. L. Schiefelbusch and L. L. Lloyd (eds.), *Language Perspectives: Acquisition, Retardation, and Intervention*, pp. 377–418. Baltimore: University Park Press.

Morford, M. and Goldin-Meadow, S. (1992). Comprehension and production of gesture in combination with speech in one-word speakers. *Journal of Child Language*, 9, 559–80.

Morford, J. P., Singleton, J. L. and Goldin-Meadow, S. (1995). From homesign to ASL: Identifying the influences of a self-generated childhood gesture system upon language proficiency in adulthood. In D. MacLaughlin and S. McEwen (eds.), *Proceedings of the 19th Annual Boston University Conference on Language Development, Volume 2,* pp. 403–14. Somerville, Mass.: Cascadilla Press.

Newport, E. L. and Meier, R. P. (1985). The acquisition of American Sign

Language. In D. I. Slobin (ed.), *The Cross-Linguistic Study of Language Acquisition, Volume 1: The Data*, pp. 881–938. Hillsdale, NJ: Lawrence Erlbaum.

Noble, W. and Davidson, I. (1996). *Human Evolution, Language and Mind.* Cambridge: Cambridge University Press.

Norman, D. A. and Shallice, T. (1980). Attention to action: Willed and automatic control of behaviour. Center for Human Information Processing Technical Report No. 99. Reprinted in revised form in R. J. Davidson, G. E. Schwartz and D. Shapiro (eds.), *Consciousness and Self Regulation*, Vol. 4, (1986), pp. 1–18. New York: Plenum.

Nunberg, G. (1996). Transfers of meaning. In J. Pustejovsky, and B. Boguraev (eds.), *Lexical Semantics: The Problem of Polysemy*, pp. 109–32. Oxford: Clarendon Press.

O'Brien, G. (1991). Is connectionism common-sense? *Philosophical Psychology*, 4, (2), 165–78.

Ozonoff, S., Pennington, B. F. and Rogers, S. J. (1991). Executive function deficits in high-functioning autistic individuals: Relationship to theory of mind. *Journal of Child Psychology and Psychiatry*, 32, 1081–105.

Paivio, A. (1971). *Imagery and Verbal Processes.* New York: Holt, Rinehart and Winston.

Papafragou, A. (in preparation). *Modality and the Semantics-Pragmatics Interface.* University of London PhD thesis.

Parkin, L. J. (1994). *Normal and Autistic Children's Theory of Representation.* Unpublished doctoral dissertation, University of Sussex.

Peacocke, C. (1983). *Sense and Content*. Oxford: Oxford University Press.

(1992). *A Study of Concepts*. Cambridge, Mass.: MIT Press.

(1998a). Implicit conceptions, understanding and rationality. In E. Villanueva (ed.), *Philosophical Issues*, 9. Atascadero, CA: Ridgeview Publishing Company.

(1998b). Conscious attitudes, attention and self-knowledge. In C. Wright, B. C. Smith and C. Macdonald (eds.), *Knowing Our Own Minds*. Oxford: Oxford University Press.

Perner, J. (1991). *Understanding the Representational Mind.* Cambridge, Mass.: The MIT Press.

(1993). The theory of mind deficit in autism: Rethinking the metarepresentation theory. In S. Baron-Cohen, H. Tager-Flusberg, D. Cohen and F. Volkmar (eds.), *Understanding Other Minds: Perspectives from Autism,* pp. 112–37. Oxford: Oxford University Press.

(1995). The many faces of belief: Reflections on Fodor's and the child's theory of mind. *Cognition,* 57, 241–69.

(1996). Simulation as explicitation of predication-implicit knowledge about the mind: Arguments for a simulation-theory mix. In P. Carruthers and P. K. Smith (eds.) 1996, pp. 90–104.

Piaget, J. (1932). *The Language and Thought of the Child.* London: Routledge and Kegan Paul.

Pinkal, M. (1995). *Logic and Lexicon*. Dordrecht: Kluwer.

Pinker, S. (1994). *The Language Instinct*. London: Penguin Books. US: New York: William Morrow.

(1995). Facts about human language relevant to its evolution. In Changeux and Chavaillon (eds.), *Origins of the Human Brain*, pp. 262–83. Oxford: Clarendon Press.

Pinker, S. and Bloom, P. (1990). Natural language and natural selection. *Behavioural and Brain Sciences,* 13, 707–27.

Premack, D. (1983). The codes of man and beasts. *Behavioural and Brain Sciences,* 6, 125–67.

(1988). Minds with and without Language. In L. Weiskrantz (ed.), 1988, pp. 46–65.

Premack, D. and Premack, A. (1983) *The Mind of an Ape*. New York: Norton and Co.

Pojman, L. P. (1985). Believing and willing. *Canadian Journal of Philosophy*, 15(1), 37–55.

Povinelli, D. J. and de Blois, S. (1992) Young children's (Homo Sapiens) understanding of knowledge formation in themselves and others. *Journal of Comparative Psychology* 104: 203–10.

Povinelli, D. J. and Eddy, T. J. (1996). What young chimpanzees know about seeing. *Monographs of the Society for Research in Child Development*, 61(3), 1–190.

Powers, L. (1987). Knowledge by deduction. *Philosophical Review*, 87, 337–71.

Pullum, G. (1991). *The Great Eskimo Language Hoax*. Chicago: University of Chicago Press.

Pustejovsky, J. (1995). *The Generative Lexicon*. Cambridge, Mass., MIT Press.

Pustejovsky, J. and Boguraev, B. (eds.), (1996). *Lexical Semantics: The problem of polysemy*. Oxford: Clarendon Press.

Ramsey, W., Stich, S. and Garon, J. (1990). Connectionism, eliminativism and the future of folk psychology. In J. Tomberlin (ed.), *Philosophical Perspectives 4: Action Theory and Philosophy of Mind*, pp. 499–533. Atascadero, CA: Ridgeview Publishing Company.

(1991). Connectionism, eliminativism and the future of folk psychology. In. J. D. Greenwood (ed.), *The Future of Folk Psychology,* pp. 93–119. Cambridge: Cambridge University Press.

Rapin, I. (1996). Developmental language disorders: a clinical update. *Journal of Child Psychology and Psychiatry*, 37, 643–56.

Raven, J. C. (1965). *Guide to Using the Coloured Progressive Matrices*. London: H. K. Lewis.

Rawls, J. (1971). *A Theory of Justice*. Cambridge, Mass.: Harvard University Press.

Recanati, F. (1995). The alleged priority of literal interpretation. *Cognitive Science,* 19, 207–32.

Reed, H. (1918). Associative aids. *Psychological Review*, 25, 128–401.

Roeper, T. and de Villiers, J. (1994). Lexical links in the WH chain. In B. Lust, G. Hermon, and J. Kornflit (eds.), *Syntactic Theory and First Language Acquisition: Cross Linguistic Perspectives, Vol. II: Binding, Dependence and Learnability*. Hillsdale, NJ: Lawrence Erlbaum.

Rondal, J. (1994). Language development and mental retardation. In H. Tager-Flusberg (ed.), *Constraints on Language Acquisition: Studies of Atypical Children.* Hillsdale NJ: Lawrence Erlbaum.

Rosenthal, D. M. (1986). Two concepts of consciousness. *Philosophical Studies*, 49, 329–59.

Rumelhart, D. and McClelland, J. (1986). On learning the past tenses of English verbs. In D. Rumelhart *et al.*, *Parallel Distributed Processing: Explorations in the Microstructure of Cognition* (1986), 2: 216–71. Cambridge, Mass.: MIT Press.

Rumelhart, D., Smolensky, P., McClelland, J. and Hinton, G. (1986). *Parallel Distributed Processing: Explorations in the Microstructure of Cognition.* Cambridge, Mass.: MIT Press.

Russell, B. (1921). *The Analysis of Mind.* London: Allen and Unwin.

Russell, J. (1996). *Agency. Its Role in Mental Development.* Hove: Lawrence Erlbaum.

Russell, J., Mauthner, N., Sharpe, S., and Tidswell, T. (1991). The 'windows task' as a measure of strategic deception in preschoolers and autistic subjects. *British Journal of Developmental Psychology*, 9, 331–49.

Russell, J., Jarrold, C., and Potel, D. (1994). What makes strategic deception difficult for children – the deception or the strategy? *British Journal of Developmental Psychology*, 12, 301–14.

Ryle, G. (1949). *The Concept of Mind.* London: Hutchinson.

(1979). *On Thinking*. Totowa, NJ: Rowman and Littlefield.

Savage-Rumbaugh, E. S. (1991). Language learning in the bonobo: how and why they learn. In N. A. Krasnegor, D. M. Rumbaugh, R. L. Schiefelbusch, and M. Studdert-Kennedy (eds.), *Biological and Behavioural Determinants of Language Development,* pp. 209–33. Hillsdale, NJ: Lawrence Erlbaum.

Savage-Rumbaugh, E. S., Murphy, J., Sevcik, R. A., Brakke, K. E., Williams, S. L. and Rumbaugh, D. M. (1993). Language comprehension in ape and child. *Monographs of the Society for Research in Child Development*, 58, *3–4*.

Savage-Rumbaugh, E. S., Rumbaugh, D. M. and Boysen, S. (1980). Do apes use language? *American Scientist*, 68(1), 49–61.

Schacter, D., McAndrews, M. and Moscovitch, M. (1988). Access to consciousness: dissociations between implicit and explicit knowledge in neuropsychological syndromes. In L. Weiskrantz (ed.), 1988, pp. 242–78.

Schiffer, S. (1972). *Meaning*. Oxford: Oxford University Press (second edition, 1988).

(1987). *The Remnants of Meaning*. Cambridge Mass.: MIT Press.

Schyns, P. (1991). A modular neural network model for concept acquisition. *Cognitive Science*, 15, 401–508.

Searle, J. (1980). The background of meaning. In J. Searle and F. Kiefer (eds.), *Speech-Act Theory and Pragmatics,* pp. 221–32. Dordrecht: Reidel.

(1983). *Intentionality.* Cambridge: Cambridge University Press.

Sebeok, T. A., and Umiker-Sebeok, J. (eds.), (1980). *Speaking of Apes: A Critical Anthology*. New York: Plenum Press.

Segal, G. (forthcoming). Frege's Puzzle as some problems in science. *Rivista di Linguistica.*

Semenza, C., Denes, G., Lucchese, D. and Bisiacchi, P. (1980). Selective deficit of conceptual structures in aphasia: class versus thematic relations. *Brain and Language,* 10, 243–8.

Seyfarth, R. M. (1987). Vocal communication and its relation to language. In B. B. Smuts, D. L. Cheney, R. M. Seyfarth, R. W. Wrangham, and T. T.

Struhsaker (eds.), *Primate Societies*, pp. 440–51. Chicago: University of Chicago Press.
Shallice, T. (1988). *From Neuropsychology to Mental Structure*. Cambridge: Cambridge University Press.
(1994). Multiple levels of control processes. In C. Umiltà and M. Moscovitch (eds.), *Attention and Performance XV. Conscious and Nonconscious Information Processing,* pp. 395–420. Cambridge, Mass.: MIT Press, A Bradford Book.
Shallice, T. and Burgess, P. (1993). Supervisory control of action and thought selection. In A. Baddeley and L. Weiskrantz (eds.), *Attention. Selection, Awareness and Control. A Tribute to Donald Broadbent*, pp. 171–87. Oxford: Clarendon Press.
Shatz, M. (1982). On mechanisms of language acquisition: Can features of the communicative environment account for development? In E. Wanner and L. R. Gleitman (eds.), *Language Acquisition: The State of the Art*, pp. 102–27. New York: Cambridge University Press.
Shields, J., Varley, R., Broks, P.,and Simpson, A. (1996). Hemispheric function in developmental language disorders and high-level autism. *Developmental Medicine and Child Neurology*, 38, 473–86.
Silverstein, M. (1976). Hierarchy of features and ergativity. In R. M. W. Dixon (ed.), *Grammatical Categories in Australian Languages*, pp. 112–71. Canberra: Australian Institute of Aboriginal Studies.
Skinner, B. S. (1957). *Verbal Behaviour.* New York: Appleton-Century-Crofts.
Slobin, D. I. (1985). Crosslinguistic evidence for the language-making capacity. In D. I. Slobin (ed.), *The Crosslinguistic Study of Language Acquisition. Volume 2: Theoretical Issues*, pp. 1157–256. Hillsdale, NJ: Lawrence Erlbaum.
(1987). Thinking for speaking. *Proceedings of the Thirteenth Annual Meeting of the Berkeley Linguistic Society*, 13, 435–44.
(1996a). Two ways to travel: Verbs of motion in English and Spanish. In M. Shibatani and S. A. Thompson (eds.), *Grammatical Constructions: Their Form and Meaning,* pp. 195–219. Oxford: Oxford University Press.
(1996b). The origins of grammaticizable notions: Beyond the individual mind. To appear in D. I. Slobin (ed.), *The Crosslinguistic Study of Language Acquisition, Vol. 5, Expanding the Contexts*. Hillsdale, NJ: Lawrence Erlbaum.
Slobin, D. I. and Hoiting, N. (1994). Reference to movement in spoken and signed languages: Typological considerations. *Proceedings of the Twentieth Annual Berkeley Linguistic Society*, 20, 487–505.
Smith, P. K. (1982). Does play matter? Functional and evolutionary aspects of animal and human play. *Behavioural and Brain Sciences*, 5, 139–55.
Smith, N. and Tsimpli, I-M. (1995). *The Mind of a Savant: Language-Learning and Modularity*. Oxford: Blackwell.
Smolensky, P. (1988). On the proper treatment of connectionism. *Behavioural and Brain Sciences*, 11, 1–74.
Sokolov, A. (1972). *Inner Speech and Thought*. New York: Plenum Press.
Spearman, C. (1927). *The Abilities of Man*. London: Macmillan.
Spelke, E., Phillips, A. and Woodward, A. (1995). Infant's knowledge of object motion and human action. In D. Sperber, D. Premack and A. Premack (eds.), *Causal Cognition*, pp. 44–78. Oxford: Oxford University Press.

Sperber, D. (1990). The evolution of the language faculty: a paradox and its solution. *Behavioural and Brain Sciences*, 13(4), 756–8.

(1994). Understanding verbal understanding. In J. Khalfa (ed.), *What is Intelligence?* pp. 179–98. Cambridge: Cambridge University Press.

(1996). *Explaining Culture: A Naturalistic Approach*. Oxford: Blackwell.

(1997). Intuitive and reflective beliefs. *Mind and Language*, 12(1), 67–83.

Sperber, D., Premack, A. and Premack D. (eds.) (1995). *Causal Cognition*. Oxford: Oxford University Press.

Sperber, D. and Wilson, D. (1986). *Relevance: Communication and Cognition*. 2nd edition 1995. Oxford: Blackwell. US: Cambridge, Mass.: Harvard University Press.

Stackhouse, J. (1992). Developmental verbal dyspraxia: I. A review and critique. *European Journal of Disorders of Communication*, 27, 19–34.

Stone, T. and Davies, M. (1993). Cognitive neuropsychology and the philosophy of mind. *British Journal for the Philosophy of Science*, 44, 589–622.

Supalla, T. (1982). Structure and Acquisition of Verbs of Motion and Location in American Sign Language. Unpublished PhD dissertation, University of California, San Diego.

Swettenham, J., Gómez, J. C., Baron-Cohen, S. and Walsh, S. (1996). What's inside someone's head? Conceiving of the mind as a camera helps children with autism acquire an alternative to a theory of mind. *Cognitive Neuropsychiatry*, 1(1), 73–88.

Tager-Flusberg, H. (1995). The conceptual basis for referential word meaning in children with autism. *Child Development*, 56, 1167–78.

(forthcoming). Language acquisition and theory of mind: contributions from the study of autism. In L. B Adamson and M. A Romski, (eds.), *Research on Communication and Language Disorders: Contributions to Theories of Language Development*. Baltimore MD: Paul Brookes Publishing.

Tallal, P., Sainberg, R. and Jernigan, T. (1991). The neuropathology of developmental dysphasia: Behavioural, morphological and physiological evidence for a pervasive temporal processing disorder. *Reading and Writing*, 3, 363–77.

Tallal, P., Stark, R. and Mellits, D. (1985). Identification of language-impaired children on the basis of rapid perception and production skills. *Brain and Language*, 25, 314–22.

Talmy, L. (1985). Lexicalization patterns: Semantic structure in lexical forms. In T. Shopen (ed.), *Language Typology and Syntactic Description, Volume III: Grammatical Categories and the Lexicon*, pp. 57–149. New York: Cambridge University Press.

(1996). The windowing of attention in language. In M. Shibatani and S. Thompson (eds.), *Essays in Semantics* (in press). Oxford: Oxford University Press,.

Terrace, H. S., Petitto, L. A., Sanders, R. J. and Bever, T. G. (1979). Can an ape create a sentence? *Science*, 206, 891–902.

Tervoort, B. T. (1961). Esoteric symbolism in the communication behavior of young deaf children. *American Annals of the Deaf*, 106, 436–80.

Thompson, R., Oden, D. and Boyson, S. (In press). Language-naive chimpanzees (pan troglodytes) judge relations between relations in an abstract matching task. *Journal of Experimental Psychology: Animal Behaviour Processes*.

Thompson, R. and Oden, D. (1996). 'A profound disparity re-visited: Perception and judgement of abstract identity relations by chimpanzees, human infants and monkeys.' *Behavioural Processes* 35: 149–61.

Tomasello, K. *et al.* (1993). Cultural learning. *Behavioural and Brain Sciences 16*: 495–552.

Tooby, J., and Cosmides, L. (1992). The psychological foundations of culture. In J. Barkow, L. Cosmides, and J. Tooby (eds.), *The Adapted Mind,* pp. 19–136. Oxford: Oxford University Press.

Treisman, M., Cook, N., Naish, P. L. N. and MacCrone, J. K. (1994). The internal clock: Electroencephalographic evidence for oscillatory processes underlying time perception. *The Quarterly Journal of Experimental Psychology,* 47A, 241–89.

Tyler, L. (1992). *Spoken Language Comprehension.* Cambridge, Mass.: MIT Press:

Valian, V. (1991). Syntactic subjects in the early speech of American and Italian children. *Cognition*, 40, 21–81.

Valian, V., Hoeffner, J. and Aubry, S. (1996). Young children's imitation of sentence subjects: Evidence of processing limitations. *Developmental Psychology*, 32, 153–64.

van der Lely, H. (1996). Empirical evidence for the modularity of language from grammatical SLI children. In A. Stringfellow, D. Cahana-Amitay, E. Hughes and A. Zukowski, (eds.), *Proceedings of the 20th Annual Boston University Conference on Language Development, Vol. 2.* Somerville, MA: Cascadilla Press.

van Mourik, M., Verschaeve, M., Boon, P., Paquier, P. and van Harskamp, F. (1992). Cognition in global aphasia: indicators for therapy. *Aphasiology* 6, 491–9.

Vargha-Khadem, F., Watkins, K., Alcock, K., Fletcher., P. and Passingham, R. (1995). Praxic and non-verbal cognitive deficits in a large family with a genetically transmitted speech and language disorder. *Proceedings of the National Academy of Science, USA,* 92, 930–3.

Vygotsky, L. (1934). *Thought and Language*, translated by. Kozulin (1962). Reprinted (1986), Cambridge, Mass.: MIT Press.

Walker, J. (1983). *Animal Thought*. London: Routledge.

Wallman, J. (1992). *Aping Language*. Cambridge: Cambridge University Press.

Wang, X-l., Mylander, C. and Goldin-Meadow, S. (1993). Language and environment: A cross-cultural study of the gestural communication systems of Chinese and American deaf children. *Belgian Journal of Linguistics*, 8, 167–85.

Wayland. S. and Taplin, J. (1982). Nonverbal categorization in fluent and nonfluent anomic aphasics. *Brain and Language,* 16, 87–108.

Wechsler, D. (1981). *Wechsler Adult Intelligence Scale – Revised.* San Antonio: The Psychological Corporation.

Weiskrantz, L. (ed.), (1988). *Thought without Language.* Oxford: Oxford University Press.

Wellman, H. (1990). *The Child' s Theory of Mind.* Cambridge Mass.: MIT Press.

Wernicke. C. (1874). *The Aphasic Symptom Complex: A Psychological Study on a*

Neurological Basis. Breslau: Kohn and Weigert. Reprinted in G. H. Eggert, Wernicke's works on aphasia, pp. 91–145. The Hague: Mouton.

Whitehouse, P., Caramazza, A. and Zurif, E. (1978). Naming in aphasia: interacting effects of form and function. *Brain and Language*, 6, 63–74.

Whorf, B. L. (1956). *Language, Thought and Reality: Selected Writings of Benjamin Lee Whorf*. Cambridge, Mass.: MIT Press. US: New Jersey, Wiley.

Williams, B. (1973). Deciding to believe. In B. Williams *Problems of the Self*, pp. 136–51. Cambridge: Cambridge University Press.

Wilson, D. and Sperber, D. (in press). Pragmatics and time. To appear in R. Carston and S. Uchida (eds.), *Relevance Theory: Applications and Implications*. Amsterdam: Benjamins.

Wimmer, H. (1989). Common-sense mentalismus und emotion: Einige entwicklungspsycho-logische Implikationen. In E. Roth (ed.), *Denken und Fühlen*, pp. 56–66. Berlin: Springer Verlag.

Wimmer, H. and Perner, J. (1983). Beliefs about beliefs: Representation and constraining of wrong beliefs in young children's understanding of deception. *Cognition*, 13, 103–28.

Winters, B. (1979). Believing at will. *Journal of Philosophy*, 76, 243–56.

Wittgenstein, L. (1921). *Tractatus Logico-Philosophicus*. London: Routledge.

(1953). *Philosophical Investigations*. Oxford: Blackwell.

(1969). *The Blue and Brown Books*. Oxford: Blackwell.

(1981). *Zettel*. Oxford: Blackwell.

Wynn, T. (1993). Two developments in the mind of early Homo. *Journal of Anthropological Archaeology*, 12, 299–322.

Zaitchik, D. (1991). Is only seeing really believing?: Sources of the true belief in the false belief task. *Cognitive Development*, 6, 91–103.

Zangwill, O. (1964). Intelligence in aphasia. In A. de Reuck and M. O'Connor (eds.), *Disorders of Language*, pp. 261–74. London: Churchill.

Zelazo, P. D., Frye, D. and Rapus, T. (1996). An age-related dissociation between knowing rules and using them. *Cognitive Development*, 11, 37–63.

Zelazo, P. D. and Reznick, J. S. (1991). Response control and the execution of verbal rules. *Developmental Psychology*, 31, 508–17.

Author index

Subject index